Engendering The Development: Real or Rhetoric!

(With Specific Reference to Nepal's Water Sector 2000-2020)

Engendering The Development: Real or Rhetoric!

(With Specific Reference to Nepal's Water Sector 2000-2020)

Shibesh Chandra Regmi

ADROIT

Adroit Publishers

NEW DELHI • KATHMANDU

ISBN : 978-81-87393-93-1

2022

Published by
ADROIT PUBLISHERS 4675/21, Ganpati Bhawan, Ansari Road,
Daryaganj, New Delhi-110 002 Phone : 011-23266030
adroitpublishers@gmail.com

Typeset in Garamond Premier Pro by Arun, Akriti Graphic
Solution, Delhi-110081 E-mail: arun263923@gmail.com,
Ph: 9999414390

For my adorable father
Late Prof. Shree Satish Chandra Regmi

Contents

Abbreviations .... *ix*

Foreword .... *xv*

Acknowledgements .... *xix*

PART I: Setting the Context

1. Evolution of Gender in the Water Sector 3
2. Selecting An Appropriate Gender Lens 24

PART II: Gender Integration for Meeting Practical and Strategic Gender Needs

3. Study Contexts and Research Methods 45
4. Gender in International Water Policies Prior to 2000 66
5. Gender Focus in National Water Policies Prior to 2000 80
6. Gender Mainstreaming in Water Agencies Prior to 2000 98
7. Gender Mainstreaming in Water Projects Prior to 2000 132
8. Meeting Practical and Strategic Gender Needs 151

PART III: Gender Transformation in Water Policies, Conclusion and Policy Implications

9. Gender Transformation in International Water Policies Post-2000 183
10. Gender Integration in Nepal's Development Plans 231
11. Gender Integration in Nepal's Water Sector Post 2000 249
12. Conclusion and Policy Implications 288

Bibliography *307*

Abbreviations

ACORD	African Centre for the Constructive Resolution of Disputes
ADB	Asian Development Bank
ADRA	Adventist Development and Relief Agency
AusAID	Australian Agency for International Development
BASE	Backward Area Society Education
BRAC	Bangladesh Rural Advancement Committee
BS	Bikram Sambat
CAEP	Community Awareness and Education Programme
CBOs	Community Based Organisations
CBS	Central Bureau of Statistics
CESCR	Committee on Economic, Social and Cultural Rights
CHVs	Community Health Volunteers
CLTS	Community Led Total Sanitation
CMS	Consolidated Management Systems
CPMO	Central Project Management Office
CRSD	Centre of Rural Studies and Development
CWSS	Community Water Supply and Sanitation Scheme
DAC	Development Assistance Committee
DANIDA	Danish International Development Agency
DC	District Council
DDC	District Development Committee
DfID	Department for International Development
DMCs	Developing Member Countries
DPU	District Project Unit
DSU	District Support Unit

DWR	Drinking Water Rules
DWSMA	Drinking Water and Sanitation Management Act
DWSO	District Water Supply and Sanitation Office
DWSS	Department of Water Supply and Sewerage
DWSSM	Department of Water Supply and Sewerage Management
DWSSSPs	Drinking Water Supply and Sanitation Sector Projects
ESA	External Support Agencies
EU	European Union
FAO	Food and Agriculture Organisation
FASEB	Federation of American Societies for Experimental Biology
FHVs	Female Health Volunteers
FINNIDA	Finnish International Development Agency
FM	Finnish Mark
FRWSSSP	Fourth Rural Water Supply and Sanitation Sector Project
GAD	Gender and Development
GAM	Gender Analysis Matrix
GAP	Gender and Poverty
GATS	General Agreement on Trade in Services
GBV	Gender Based Violence
GDP	Gross Domestic Product
GEI	Gender Empowerment Index
GESI	Gender Equality and Social Inclusion
GLASS	Global Analysis and Assessment of Sanitation and Drinking Water
GoN	Government of Nepal
GSS	Gramin Sewa Sangh
GWA	Gender and Water Alliance
GWSP	Global Water Security and Sanitation Partnership
HDI	Human Development Index
HMG	His Majesty's Government
HRBA	Human Rights Based Approach
HRC	Human Rights Council
HRM	Harinas Rural Municipality

HRW	Human Rights Watch
HRWS	Human Right to Water and Sanitation
ICESCR	International Covenant on Economic, Social and Cultural Rights
ICIMOD	International Centre for Integrated Mountain Development
IDA	International Development Association
IDRC	International Development Research Centre
IDS	Institute of Development Studies
IDWSSD	International Drinking Water Supply and Sanitation Decade
IFRC	International Federation of Red Cross
IIED	International Institute for Environment and Development
IISD	International Institute for Sustainable Development
ILO	International Labour Organisation
INGO	International Non-Governmental Organisation
INSTRAW	International Research and Training Institute for the Advancement of Women
IOM	International Organisation for Migration
IRC	International Centre for Water and Sanitation
IWA	International Water Association
IWRM	International Water Resources Management
JICA	Japan International Cooperation Agency
JVS	Jalshrot Vikas Sanstha
KBC	Kenya Broadcasting Corporation
LDC	Least Developed Country
LDD	Local Development Department
LSG	Local Self-Governance
LTSS	Long-Term Sustainability Study
MDGs	Millennium Development Goals
MHM	Menstrual Hygiene Management
MHPP	Ministry of Housing and Physical Planning
MLD	Ministry of Local Development
MoFAoF	Ministry of Foreign Affairs of Finland
MoH	Ministry of Health
MoHP	Ministry of Health and Population

MPLD	Ministry of Panchayat and Local Development
MPS	Mahila Punarutthan Samuha
NDHS	Nepal Demographic Health Survey
NEWAH	Nepal Water for Health
NGO	Non-Governmental Organisation
NLSS	Nepal Living Standard Survey
NMIP	National Management Information Project
NPC	National Planning Commission
NPR	National Public Radio
NRCS	Nepal Red Cross Society
NSAC	Nepal South Asia Centre
NSHMP	National Sanitation and Hygiene Master Plan
NWC	National Women's Commission
NWP	National Water Plan
NWSC	Nepal Water Supply Corporation
NWSSP	National Water Supply Sector Policy
NWSSSP	National Water Supply and Sanitation Sector Policy
NWSSTC	National Water Supply and Sanitation Training Centre
ODA	Overseas Development Administration
ODF	Open Defecation Free
ORT	Oral Rehydration Therapy
PAR	Participatory Action Research
PCI	Per Capita Income
PCRW	Production Credit for Rural Women
PIMS	Project Information and Management System
PMC	Project Management Committee
PPTA	Project Preparation Technical Assistance
PRA	Participatory Rural Appraisal
PROWWESS	Promotion of the Role of Women in Water and Environmental Sanitation Services
PSU	Project Support Unit
RAP	Rapid Assessment Procedure
RCS	Red Crescent Societies

RPMOs	Regional Project Management Offices
RRN	Rural Reconstruction Nepal
RVWRMP	Rural Village Water Resource Management Project
RWSSFB	Rural Water Supply and Sanitation Fund Board
RWSSNP	Rural Water Supply and Sanitation National Policy
RWSSNS	Rural Water Supply and Sanitation National Strategy
RWSSP	Rural Water Supply and Sanitation Project
SACOSAN	South Asian Conference on Sanitation
SDGs	Sustainable Development Goals
SFDP	Small Farmers Development Programme
SIDA	Swedish International Development Agency
SLC	School Leaving Certificate Examination
SMT	Senior Management Team
SSNCC	Social Service National Coordination Council
SuWASH	Sustainable Water, Sanitation and Hygiene
SWC	Social Welfare Council
THT	The Himalayan Times
TNCs	Trans-National Corporations
TSTWSSSP	Third Small Town Water Supply and Sanitation Sector Project
UDHR	Universal Declaration of Human Rights
UN	United Nations
UNCED	United National Conference on the Environment and Development
UNDESA	United Nations Department of Economic and Social Affairs
UNDP	United National Development Programme
UNESCO	United National Educational, Scientific and Cultural Organisation
UNFPA	United National Population Fund
UNGA	United Nations General Assembly
UNHRC	United Nations Human Rights Council
UNICEF	United Nations Children's Fund
UNWC	United Nations Water-Courses Convention
US/ USA	United States/ United States of America

USD	United States Dollar
UWSSSP	Urban Water Supply and Sanitation Sector Policy
VAW	Violence Against Women
VC	Village Council
VDC	Village Development Committee
VHLs	Village Health Leaders
VMWs	Village Maintenance Workers
WAD	Women and Development
WASH	Water, Sanitation and Hygiene
WASH SDP	Water, Sanitation and Hygiene Sector Development Plan
WATSAN	Water and Sanitation
WDO	Women Development Officer
WECS	Water and Energy Commission Secretariat
WGP	Water Global Practice
WHO	World Health Organisation
WID	Women in Development
WISP	Women Involvement and Sanitation Programme
WPE	Women, Poor and Excluded
WRA	Water Resources Act
WRR	Water Resources Regulations
WSMB	Water Supply Management Board
WSP	Water and Sanitation Programme
WSSCC	Water Supply and Sanitation Collaborative Council
WSST	Water Supply and Sanitation Technician
WSUC	Water and Sanitation Users' Committee
WTO	World Trade Organisation
WUA	Water Users' Association
WUC	Water Users' Committee
WUSC	Water Users' and Sanitation Committees
WWC	World Water Council
WWF	World Water Forum

Foreword

I have been in the development sector working with a number of national and international organisations as well as academic institutions for nearly 25 years. During these years I had the opportunity to travel to many places both inside and outside Nepal. The ultimate outcome of these exposures was the establishment of Measures for Intervention, Training, Research and Action (MiTRA) Samaj, an NGO, to do research, training and program implementation. My hunch was that the programme can be effective only when it is designed and implemented based on reliable data about the people for which the program has been aimed, and it is only through profound research that we can generate reliable data needed to design and implement an effective programme.

It was in the context of running MiTRA Samaj that I happened to meet with Dr. Shibesh Chandra Regmi, a well-known figure in the development sector in Nepal. In one of our conversations, Dr. Regmi told me that he was thinking of upgrading his research on gender and water conducted for his Ph.D. about 20 years ago into a book. Despite being in the development sector for so long, I was hardly able to see any connection between gender and water at that time! However, my limited knowledge of the relation between gender and water gradually changed once my brainchild saw the light of the day in the form of an initiative called "Mitini" which primarily focuses on an innovative approach to address menstrual hygiene issues. With an increased understanding of the intersectionality between water, gender and menstrual hygiene management, I then shared my interest with Dr. Regmi to be a part of his contemporary research and also offered the support of a couple of staff of MiTRA Samaj for the same. The members of MiTRA Samaj that assisted Dr. Regmi in the review of the policies and publications of various international donors, the Government of Nepal, bilateral funded projects, NGOs, scholars, development practitioners and agencies engaged in the WASH sector from January 2017 to March 2018 were: Ms. Barada Regmi, Researcher and Ms. Arzu Rana, Programme Assistant.

The book has been structured into three parts. Part I sets the context for the book bringing forward the discussion on the evolution of gender in the Water sector and the analysis of existing gender and development frameworks for choosing an appropriate framework to conduct a gender analysis of any development projects, including that of the water sector. Part II presents the findings of the research undertaken 20 years ago from 1997-2000 that consists of study context and research methods, gender analysis of the water policies at international and national levels, gender mainstreaming at institutional and projects levels, and the meeting of women's practical and strategic gender needs at the community level. Part III presents gender transformation in international, national, bilateral project and NGO level water policies, gender integration in Nepal's development plans- all for post-2000, and policy implications for all stakeholders to make their water/ development policy and interventions gender-sensitive for achieving gender equality and women's empowerment, thereby sustaining the benefits arising out of such water/ development projects.

The beauty of this book is that it gives a comprehensive understanding of the evolution of gender in the water sector and gender issues involved in its management along with rich information regarding the importance of water as a finite resource and the need to treat it as profoundly as possible. Another feature of this book is that it presents a comprehensive overview of the various gender and development frameworks and their comparative strengths and weaknesses for use not only while designing a gender-sensitive development project but also while assessing the impact of such projects in meeting women's practical and strategic gender needs. The outcome of this comparative analysis of the various GAD frameworks is the recommendation of a new contextualized GAD framework for use in any GAD research projects, academia and evaluations- which is the other milestone of this book. An equally important contribution of this book is the sharing of the findings of the earlier research showing the inability of gender-insensitive water policies and practices in meeting women's practical and strategic gender needs. The final contribution of the book is the overview of the gender transformation in policies and practices of international donors, national government, agencies engaged in the WASH sector in the last 20 years and policy implications as a way forward to make the WASH/ development sector fully gender-aware and sustain the practical and strategic benefits. This book thus can be useful for everyone involved in programme design, implementation, evaluation; designing gender studies; conducting research and academic courses; formulating GAD policies and plans by donors, government and non-governmental agencies; studying GAD courses; and conducting GAD training; among others.

Finally, I would like to extend my sincere gratitude to Dr. Regmi for giving MiTRA Samaj such a wonderful opportunity to be a part of this important initiative both in assisting the research and supporting the publication of the book. MiTRA Samaj feels honoured and will always remain indebted to Dr. Regmi for giving us this amazing opportunity to get involved in this timely and profound research work which opens a scope of work towards a new development discourse. On this occasion, I would also like to express my heartfelt appreciation to Barada for her sincerity and dedication in facilitating the entire research work on behalf of MiTRA Samaj to support Dr. Regmi during the entire book writing process. Last but not the least my sincere thanks to Adroit Publishers, New Delhi, India for editing and publishing the book.

Vivek Singh Thakuri
Executive Director
Mitra Samaj

Acknowledgements

Before acknowledging the people who have contributed to the realisation of this book, I would like to briefly describe, without repeating what has already been said about it in the Foreword, that the main beauty of this book is its comparative review of the water policies and practices observed over the last 20 years at all levels- international, national, institutional and project levels- using a gender lens and the assessment of the impact that those policies and practices have made in meeting women's practical and strategic gender needs at the community level. This comparative analysis, which has provided an opportunity to offer policy implications along with a detailed chart showing the areas that need to be gender-sensitive at all levels to make the sector more gender transformative, is another principal feature of the book. The book, after making a critical review of the strengths and weaknesses of the existing gender and development frameworks, also suggests a new contextualised gender and development framework for conducting a gender analysis of the policies and practices both at the agency and community levels- another major contribution of the book. The anticipation, therefore, is that the book can be immensely useful for everyone interested and needing to do gender related works in any sector, including that of the WASH sector.

Despite the book's immense usefulness to all engaged in gender works, one way or another, I could not prioritise my time in publishing the book, due to my full-time professional commitments, until I shared my interest in this subject with Vivek Singh Thakuri, CEO of MiTRA Samaj (a national NGO), during an event held to mark the second anniversary celebration of their menstrual hygiene initiative called "Mitini" in 2017. Given his intense involvement in health and menstrual hygiene programme, Vivek immediately understood both the academic and programmatic values of this book and thus showed interest to provide a team from MiTRA Samaj to work with me to conduct the contemporary research.

I, therefore, first of all, would like to express my sincere gratitude to Vivek for his understanding of the importance of the book and for providing the support of a team of MiTRA Samaj to update the earlier research and meeting the editorial costs. Similarly, I also would like to extend my genuine appreciation to Barada Regmi, Researcher, MiTRA Samaj, who worked very profoundly in undertaking the review of the latest literature on gender and water, both at an international and national level, and collecting the required information from various sources at different levels. Likewise, I would like to extend my sincere appreciation to Arzu Rana of MiTRA Samaj for ensuring administrative and logistical support as required during the research period.

I also would like to extend my sincere appreciation to Dyuti Baral, Ankeeta Shrestha and Prakash Dahal for spending time discussing various aspects of the book and helping me sharpen my analysis. Similarly, I remain grateful to Tripti Rai, Country Director, WaterAid Nepal; Jasmine Rajbhandari, Social Development Specialist, the World Bank; Umesh Pandey, Director, NEWAH; Pratik Gurung, Monitoring and Evaluation Officer, Gurkha Welfare Trust/ Nepal; Bhoj Kumar Shrestha, Librarian, New ERA; for helping me in finding the most current water-related publications of their organisations, as well as others included in this book; and Dr. Dina Mani Pokharel, Senior Advocate, in tracing some important WASH policies of the Government of Nepal. Similarly, I would like to express my sincere appreciation to various individuals – women, men, and elected representatives from the research communities; I/NGO and project staff/ officials from the agencies selected for the research, and government officials, planners and policy-makers whom I met during the course of the research; Ben Fawcett, who guided me during my Ph.D. research; Nicky May and Simon Trace from the research management team of the University of Southampton who provided constant feedback during the course of the Ph.D. research; Dr. Frances Cleaver, Dr. Tina Wallace, Dr. Bal Gopal Baidya, and Kiran Bhatiya who took their valuable time in reading the Ph.D. research report and providing useful feedback; Sushma Sharma for assisting me in conducting fieldwork during my Ph.D. research; and my brother (Dhrubesh Regmi) for being committed to my family when I was busy with my research both in Nepal and the UK; and son-in-law (Sujal) for making my stay comfortable while writing some chapters of the book in the USA.

Last but not the least, I would like to express my heartiest gratitude for the patience, moral support, love and encouragement provided to me by my mother

(Sanu Baba), wife (Bhawana), daughter (Barada), and son (Lokesh) during the entire course of writing the book.

I would like to dedicate this book, as a token of my deep respect, to the memory of my beloved father, late Professor Satish Chandra Regmi, who has been the source of my inspiration, and without whom, neither this book nor any other life achievements, would have been possible.

My sincere gratitude is to Mr. Akhil Sharma of Adroit Publishers, New Delhi for his interest in publishing this book.

Shibesh Chandra Regmi

PART I
Setting the Context

Part I presents an overview of the evolution of gender in the water sector and an analysis of existing gender analysis frameworks for choosing an appropriate framework while assessing the status of a development project, including that of the water sector, in meeting women's practical and strategic gender needs.

CHAPTER 1
Evolution of Gender in the Water Sector

Water, the Global Scenario

Water is the source of life on earth. The human body is made up of 70% water. People begin to experience thirst even after a loss of only 1% of bodily fluids and risk death if fluid loss nears 10%. Human beings can survive for only a few days without fresh water. This reality exists amidst the scarcity of water resources, which is both a natural as well as a human-induced phenomenon. A mere 2.5% of the earth's water resources is freshwater, of which 69% is stored in glaciers and ice caps, 30% in groundwater and only about 1% in surface water, which serves most of life's needs (US Geological Survey, 2016; Regmi, 2000; Population Reports, 1998). Some other sources report that 'if a bucket contained all the world's water, one cup of that would be freshwater, and just one teaspoon of that would be available for people to use, from lakes, rivers and underwater reservoirs as groundwater. Consequently, 844 million people in the world – one in nine – do not have clean water close to home, just under two-thirds of the world's population- 4 billion- live in areas of physical water scarcity, where for at least part of the year demand exceeds supply and 2.3 billion people – almost one in three – do not have a decent toilet of their own. As a result, around 289,000 children under the age of five die every year from diarrhoeal diseases caused by poor water and sanitation, which is almost 800 children a day, or one child every two minutes (Water Aid, 2017; WHO & UNICEF, 2017 and Mekonnan and Hoekstra, 2016 in WaterAid, 2019).

Diarrhoeal diseases and other water-related diseases such as filariasis and schistosomiasis - an acute and chronic disease caused by parasitic worms contracted as a result of exposure to contaminated water- and intestinal worms, which are largely attributed to poor water quality, sanitation, and hygiene, have been killing hundreds of thousands of people every year (WHO, 2019; Prüss-

Üstün et al., 2014). In fact, diarrhoeal disease is the leading cause of malnutrition, and the second principal cause of mortality among children under five years of age (WHO, 2017a & 2017b). In 2012 alone, unsafe water, inadequate sanitation and insufficient hygiene were responsible for 842,000 deaths from diarrhoeal disease (Mills and Cumming, 2016; WHO, 2014). Even after five years, the disease, which can be largely prevented by improved water, sanitation and hygiene, has been resulting in about 525,000 deaths of children under the age of five (WHO, 2017a & 2017b; Mills & Cumming, 2016). Moreover, 443 million school days are lost each year around the world due to water-related illnesses (The Water Project, 2016; UN News, 2010a & 2010b; UNDP, 2006), and the absenteeism due to diarrhoea alone is 272 million (UNICEF, 2010; Hutton & Haller, 2004). In addition to diarrhoeal diseases, it is estimated that almost 240 million people all over the world are affected by schistosomiasis (WHO, 2018a & 2018b). This is mainly because 2.1 billion people, according to the Joint Monitoring Programme report of the WHO and the UNICEF 2017, lack access to safe, readily available water at home (WHO & UNICEF, 2017a & 2017b) and over two billion people use faecal contaminated sources of drinking water (WHO, 2018a & 2018b). The effects of waterborne diseases in developing countries are even more noticeable, with almost 80% of people in these countries suffering from a health problem caused by improper water and sanitation at any given time (The Water Project, 2016; Malik, Yasar, & Abubakar, 2012; United Nations, 2003). Nearly half of all people in Sub-Saharan Africa, and one-fifth in Southern Asia use dirty unprotected water (WHO and UNICEF, 2015).

In the backdrop of an estimate that by 2025, 1.8 billion people worldwide will be affected by absolute water scarcity, and two-thirds of the world population could be under 'water-stressed conditions' due to water shortages (UN Water, 2018; UNESCO, 2012), the deprivation of freshwater which is, furthermore, disproportionately distributed and managed across the globe, is worrisome. For instance, in the developing world, one in five people do not have access to a suggested minimum of 20 litres/day of clean water; whereas, the average water consumption in Europe and the US ranges from 200 to 600 litres/day (Lerner & Lerner, 2011; UN Water, 2007; Howard and Bartram, 2003). Likewise, the 2011 Human Development Report (UNDP, 2011) illuminates that the domestic per capita water consumption rate in high Human Development Index (HDI) countries accounts to 425 litres a day, which is six times more than the low HDI countries, where the average rate is 67 litres per day. This wholly unacceptable situation causes untold suffering, holding back human and sustainable development to a large extent in developing countries. It particularly affects women, who carry the burden of collecting water and caring for sick children, and girls who often fail to finish their education because their schools lack decent toilets and they are also expected to help their mothers in carrying water from distant sources (WaterAid, 2017; WHO & UNICEF, 2017 and Mekonnan and Hoekstra, 2016 in WaterAid, 2019).

As a result of the depleting water resource, on the one hand, and increasing demand for it, on the other, the concept of water to be treated as an 'economic good' emerged. Realising the danger that the economic value given to water resources can provoke the corporate sector to maximise its use for profitable activities even at the cost of drinking water purposes, the parallel concept of water to be seen as a 'social good' emerged soon afterwards. The discussions around water to be treated as an economic good, a social good or both, took place in the UN Summit of 2000, one of the major target-setting events, which set the Millennium Development Goals (MDGs): 2000-2015. Among the MDG targets, target 10- 'halving the proportion of people without access to safe drinking water and basic sanitation by 2015'- was directly relevant to water; nevertheless, water's potential contribution to all of the MDGs, and not just those that refer explicitly to water, was also supported by several other documents (UNICEF & WHO, 2012). Unlike the first water decade, which failed to meet the quantitative goal, the world, however, partially met this MDG target well in advance of the MDG 2015 deadline because of the profound commitments made by the national governments to fulfil the MDG targets realising the negative impact that the scarcity of water can have among the general population.

Since 1990, 2.6 billion people have gained access to improved drinking water and 1.9 billion of those gained access to piped drinking water within their premises. In 2015, 91 per cent of the global population was using an improved drinking water source, compared to 76 per cent in 1990. Sanitation, however, remained a significant global challenge despite 2.1 billion people worldwide having gained access to improved sanitation since 1990 (United Nations, 2015). The MDGs' sanitation goal of halving the proportion of the population without basic sanitation and extending access from 54% to 77% of the global population was not met (WHO, 2015). According to the WHO report of 2015, only 68% of the world's population used an improved sanitation facility, which was 9% points below the MDG target of 77 per cent. About 50 per cent of people living in rural areas lacked improved sanitation facilities, as compared to 18 per cent of people in urban areas (United Nations, 2015). Various studies indicated that targets, such as those in the MDGs relating to water, were unlikely to be achieved unless gender perspectives were integrated into planning and implementation activities (United Nations, 2005; Lenton et.al., 2005).

Over the last couple of decades, there have been galvanised and concerted actions undertaken by the international community to remedy this issue. The UN Water & WHO Report (2014) indicates that although the global aspirations and efforts towards universal access to clean drinking water and sanitation have improved in the form of increased aid commitments and targeted national financing for water supply, sanitation and hygiene (WASH), there remain critical gaps in the capacity to formulate, implement and monitor related plans (UN Water & WHO, 2014 & 2013). UNICEF and WHO (2015) also report that the world indeed has witnessed some progress in the water sector over the last two decades, although the rate of progress has varied among geographical regions and locations. Globally, 2.6 billion people have gained access to an improved drinking water source since 1990. However, regions like Caucasus & Central Asia, Northern Africa, Oceania, and Sub-Saharan Africa have fallen behind in meeting the MDG targets. Even though Sub-Saharan Africa, the Caucasus & Central Asia, and Oceania missed the MDG target, the proportion of the population in these regions with access to an improved drinking water source between 1990 and 2015 increased by 20, 2 and 5 per cent respectively. Regarding the geographical variations in accessing the water sources, the WHO (2015) also acknowledges that there exist substantial disparities between rural and urban populations in terms of using improved drinking water sources, with 96% of the global urban population using improved sources, as opposed to 84% of the rural population.

Interestingly, the timeframe for meeting the MDGs coincided with another significant global event - the second International Water Decade - Water for Life Decade (2005 - 2015), which aimed to promote efforts to fulfil international commitments made on the water sphere by 2015. The relevant international commitments include contributing to achieving the water-related MDG targets, such as reducing by half the proportion of people without access to safe drinking water and basic sanitation by 2015. Another important area of focus of the Water for Life Decade was attaining the goal for all countries to stop the unsustainable exploitation of water resources and to develop integrated water resource management and water efficiency plans by 2005 as agreed at the World Summit for Sustainable Development in Johannesburg in 2002. Water for Life Decade also put a special emphasis on the participation of women in water-related development efforts. The Sustainable Development Goals (SDGs) adopted at the United Nations Sustainable Development Summit on 25 September 2015 further built on and went much farther than the MDGs. It covered broader sustainability agenda and addressed the root causes of poverty and the universal need for development that worked for all people. The SDG Target 6.2 stipulated achieving access to adequate and equitable sanitation and hygiene for all, ending open defecation and paying special attention to the needs of women and girls and those in vulnerable situations by 2030. Attaining this goal required considering all dimensions specific to women and girls on board and involving them directly in the water management and related development processes.

Similarly, the Seventh World Water Forum held in Gyeongju, Republic of Korea, in 2015, welcomed the proposed water-related SDGs by the Open Working Group of the United Nations General Assembly (UNGA) and further recognised that sustainable management of water resources is a collective responsibility of all stakeholders (WWC, 2015). As a result of the concerted efforts of all concerned international and national stakeholders, in 2017, 90% of the world's population (6.8 billion people) used at least basic drinking water services, rising from 82% (5 billion people) in 2000. If the current trends continued, global coverage will be around 96% in 2030. The corresponding figures for sanitation in the same year were: 74% (5.5 billion people) compared to 56% (3.4 billion people) in 2000 indicating that there is a need to double the current annual rate of increase (one percentage point per annum) to achieve the universal coverage by 2030 (UNICEF and WHO, 2019).

These discussions highlight that there is a need for countries to streamline fragmented international efforts to mobilise resources and galvanise political action by putting water and sanitation upfront on the development agenda. The national governments must draw up credible plans and strategies for tackling the crisis in the water and sanitation sector based on their local contexts and scenarios. Water scarcity and poor sanitation are silent emergencies, especially experienced by people in the developing countries, and just like in the time of war, natural disasters and hunger, collaborative international action, financial resources, better technology, human capital and political will are required to alleviate this problem.

Water - the South Asian Context

The countries in Eastern Asia, Southern Asia and South-Eastern Asia have all achieved the MDG target of improving drinking water coverage, by reducing the population without access to improved drinking water by half (UNICEF & WHO, 2015). However, access to sanitation is not as satisfactory, with almost 2.6 billion people in the world, including about 1.8 billion in Asia, still without access to proper sanitation facilities. It is unlikely that the proportion of people without access to improved sanitation will be halved by 2015 (ADB, 2011 referring to a WHO and UNICEF Update, 2010). Even concerning the improved access to safe water, the management of water has forever been a story of an unfolding disaster in South Asia. Millions encounter growing water stress as a result of over-exploitation, climate change, inadequate cooperation, and growing population in the region (Price, 2014). Moreover, there are many millions, especially from the rural areas in South Asia, who only have access to unprotected surface sources and unimproved sources (WHO & UNICEF, 2015). The 7th South Asian Conference on Sanitation (SACOSAN-VII) Declaration made in 2018 has acknowledged that rapid urbanisation and growing inequalities in accessing WASH, especially around geographical areas, vulnerable groups and income levels, present challenges in sanitation and hygiene service provision in South Asia. It also recognised the progress made towards reducing open defecation in the region and the growing attention given towards building sustainable and safely managed sanitation systems, calling for a renewed commitment of the countries to align their national and sub-national policies/ strategies with safely managed sanitation services and hygiene as outlined in the SDGs. Despite the progress, 558 million people in the region still practise open defecation and about 177,000 children die of diarrhoea each year (NEWAH, 2020).

In Bangladesh, India and Nepal, where high levels of arsenic contamination have been found, even water from improved water sources is not guaranteed to be safe (The Guardian, 2016). While the coverage of improved drinking water sources in Bangladesh and Nepal ranges from 87 to 96 per cent, the proportion of the population using improved drinking water sources free of faecal contamination is significantly lower (WHO & UNICEF, 2017a & 2017b). Research conducted in some urban areas of Nepal also confirms that the water supply sources are contaminated with faecal coliform, and bacteria, including heterotrophic bacteria (Pant, Poudyal, and Bhattacharya, 2016).

In terms of the coverage and functionality of the public water supply system, the statistics of South Asia still look depressing. The experiences from the late eighties and nineties have revealed the non-functionality of up to half of all water supply systems within five years of installation in the rural areas. Though designed to operate for about 20 years, the majority of the schemes ceased to function before reaching even half of their design life (Dixit and Crippen, 1993; Simpson-Hebert, 1989). What is worse, the statistics look grim even after almost twenty years, as the public water supply system is becoming increasingly non-functional due to breakdowns, lack of maintenance, and dwindling water sources triggered by climate change. In Pakistan, for instance, 39% of the water supply systems in public schools need extensive repair or replacement. The situation is much worse in Afghanistan with nearly 50% of the water supply systems in schools needing extensive repairs (UNICEF, 2012). Moreover, a nationwide survey conducted in Nepal in 2011 to capture the coverage and functionality of water supply projects also illustrates that only 17.9% of the total piped-water schemes are in well-functioning condition. The remaining 82.1% of the drinking water projects are in a non-functional state or need minor or major repairs that are either within the capacity of community users or need technical support from external experts for rehabilitation and/or reconstruction (NMIP & DWSS, 2011). Several other reports published recently also put it in the picture that more than 50% of the water points are malfunctioning implying that the quality of the operation and maintenance has not improved significantly in the last 25 years (NEWAH, 2020; UNICEF, 2019; GoN, 2015; GoN 2014).

These experiences depict that the international donor community, as well as the national governments, need to pay serious attention to not only meeting the post-2015 water and sanitation goals but also eliminating the socio-economic and political inequalities that perpetuate inaccessibility among vulnerable and marginalised groups. Despite various international efforts to establish access to water as a basic human right, the current international human rights instruments/laws do not oblige nation-states to safeguard this in their legislative policy frameworks (Albuquerque, 2014). Consequently, not all countries have taken concerted actions or made legal provisions that entitle every citizen to sufficient, safe, acceptable, physically accessible and affordable water for personal and domestic use.

Water as a Human Right

Given that water is so fundamental for human existence, it is almost axiomatic to define water as a human right although the acknowledgement of water as a human right has been a comparatively new feature of the international legal system. While the human right to water and sanitation has not fully received the status of customary international law, the General Comment No. 15 adopted by the Committee on Economic, Social and Cultural Rights in November 2002, the 2010 General Assembly Resolution 64/292, and 2010 Human Rights Council Resolution 15/9 have nevertheless brought the right to water and sanitation within the scope of the rights recognised under the International Covenant on Economic, Social and Cultural Rights (ICESCR). This makes the right to water and sanitation legally binding rights for the signatory states of ICESCR.

It was only in 2010 when the UNGA explicitly recognised the Human Right to Water and Sanitation (HRWS) that it propelled the awareness of the global water and sanitation crisis to new heights. Though 41 countries abstained from the Resolution 64/292, including the USA and Canada, expressing some procedural concerns (such as, 'there does not exist any right to water and sanitation in an international legal framework as described by this resolution', 'the Human Rights Council had yet to complete the legal examination of the matter making the current resolution premature', 'the resolution appeared to have declared a right without setting out its scope', etc.), yet it was endorsed by the UNGA on 28 July 2010 with 122 votes in favour (Murthy, 2013; UNGA, 2010a & 2010b). This Resolution acknowledged the right of every human being to have access to sufficient, safe, acceptable, affordable, and physically accessible water for personal and domestic use (United Nations, 2010). The Resolution recognised the Right to Water and Sanitation as being fundamental 'for the full enjoyment of life and the realisation of all human rights', and further urged all states and international organisations 'to increase assistance, particularly to the developing countries, to deliver safe, clean, accessible and affordable drinking water and sanitation for all' (UNGA, 2010).

That same year in September, the United Nations Human Rights Council (UNHRC) also affirmed access to water and sanitation as human rights by consensus through the adoption of the Human Rights Council (HRC) Resolution 15/9. The 2010 HRC Resolution is more specific than its predecessor- UNGA Resolution 64/292. It successfully confirms that the rights to water and sanitation are derived from 'the right to an adequate standard of living', which is enshrined, among other instruments, in Article 11 of ICESCR, and, therefore, are legally binding human rights. By grounding the scope of the legal obligations associated with the human right to water and sanitation in rights recognised by the ICESCR, the HRC resolution seems to have addressed the concerns of the countries that abstained from voting during the earlier General Assembly discussion on this matter (Murthy, 2013). Additionally, the HRC Resolution also recognises that the human right to water and sanitation is 'inextricably related to the right to the highest attainable standard of physical and mental health, as well as the right to life and human dignity' (UNHRC Resolution 15/9, 2010). The resolution also includes clauses that directly address the debates around the privatisation of water, affirming that the right to water and sanitation is not incompatible with private sector participation, and further asserts that States may choose to involve non-state actors in the process, provided that the principal responsibility for ensuring the realisation of human rights are maintained by the State itself (Murthy, 2013; UNHRC, 2010).

These milestones add up to important signs of progress made in the past in terms of water and sanitation rights, especially the adoption of General Comment No. 15 in November 2002 by the UN Committee on Economic, Social and Cultural Rights (CESCR), which is responsible for interpreting and clarifying the provisions of the ICESCR. Though a non-binding interpretation, the Committee determined that under the ICESCR, the right to water is contained within the right to an adequate standard of living (Article 11.1), "inextricably related" to the right to the highest attainable standard of health (Article 12.1), and the right to adequate housing and adequate food (Article 11.1) (UN CESCR, 2002). It further stated that the human right to water is indispensable for leading a life with dignity and that it is a prerequisite for the realisation of all other human rights (Article I.1). General Comment 15 also recognised the entitlement of everyone to "sufficient, safe, acceptable, physically accessible and affordable water for personal and domestic uses" (UN CESCR, 2002).

Though the right to water and sanitation has been recognised in international law through human rights treaties, declarations, and other standards, the earlier instruments such as the Universal Declaration of Human Rights (UDHR)-(ICESCR- 1966; United Nations, 1948) only implicitly recognised water rights. The idea of human rights to water first emerged at international environmental conferences, in response to water justice struggles around the world. However, the United Nations Water Conference at Mar del Plata, Argentina, in 1977 is considered to be an important benchmark in the history of water resources. This two-week conference (14-25 March 1977) was devoted exclusively to water, which underscores the attention that the international community was offering to this issue. This is also because it was during this period that the international community accepted water to be one of the major cross-cutting links having a direct influence on other areas, such as food, environment, population, human settlements, science and technology, renewable energy, etc. (Biswas, 1988). This water conference is also considered to be among the first few conferences that explicitly documented the role of women in the management of water and sanitation. The Mar del Plata Water Conference further called for the declaration of the decade 1981-1990 as the International Drinking Water Supply and Sanitation Decade (IDWSSD). The IDWSSD highlighted the significance of drinking water as a basic need for human survival, and also stated that everyone should have access to an adequate amount of safe drinking water.

Since the IDWSSD, various other human rights treaties and commitments have emerged, which have played an important role in the evolution and strengthening of water and sanitation rights. Some of them include- the 1992 International Conference on Water and Sustainable Development or the Dublin Conference, 2000 Water Forum, 2001 Ministerial Declaration of the Bonn International Conference on Freshwater, 2002 World Summit on Sustainable Development or the Johannesburg Summit, 2005 Draft Guidelines for the Realisation of the Right to Drinking Water and Sanitation, MDGs: 2000-2015, Water for Life Decade (2005-2015), A Post-2015 Global Goal for Water of 2014, the SDGs: 2015-2030, etc. Many of these subsequent conferences and meetings also called for gender-equitable governance in water-related projects- providing space for both women and men to voice their specific concerns, as well as broaden their participation. Moreover, using a 'Gender and Development (GAD)' approach, these international commitments made efforts to understand the different gender roles, relations, and inequalities that affect men and women differently in the water sector.

Building on the previous achievements and commitments, the international community has made noteworthy headway in terms of progressively strengthening the international efforts on water rights. The recognition of water and sanitation as a human right has expanded the international community's political, legal, and moral will to address the serious need for water and sanitation. Moreover, a growing number of good practices have been witnessed in the implementation of these rights, which include many countries recognising the human rights to water and sanitation in their constitution, laws, development plans, and policies. Some have voiced that increasing emphasis on human rights to the water and sanitation sector could side-track resources from other development programmes, displacing the policy priorities across competing priorities such as food security, education, health, infrastructure, and employment. Nevertheless, the human right to water and sanitation has now been recognised as fundamental rights necessary in realising other human rights, and are also grounded within the ICESCR and maintained by Article 2 Obligation, which requires States to achieve progressively the full realisation of all rights recognised within the ICESCR.

Women, Gender and Water

> *"In the overall water sector, the sub-sector of drinking water supply has got the longest history of appreciating women's role and involving them initially at the construction phase in supporting roles, and gradually bringing in the gender dimension in it taking into account the changing social structures and the way the availability, or, for that matter, the lack of water, impacts women and men"* (GWA, 2003).

Since the evolution of human settlement, water has been an integral resource, and women since then have been the major users, providers and managers of water. Despite women playing such a pivotal role, the policy-makers, public health specialists, engineers and development experts seem to have failed to recognise the importance of women's participation and contribution in community water supplies. This is true when, in turn, such acknowledgement could have enhanced and encouraged the better management of water resources. It was only after the feminist movement started to gain momentum in the seventies, more so with the beginning of the United Nations Conference on Women held in Mexico in 1975 and the declaration to consider the 1975-1985 period as the International Women's Decade, followed by profound debates on female emancipation, that the recognition of women's role in the development efforts, including water-related initiatives, started to receive impetus. Simultaneously, the United Nations Water Conference at Mar del Plata 1977 is considered to be one of the first conferences that documented the role of women in the provision and management of water (UNDESA and UN Water, 2014; UNWC, 1977). This

Water Conference further called for the declaration of the decade 1981-1990 as the IDWSSD and aimed at providing safe water and sanitation for everyone by 1990. The intersection of two important world events: The United Nations Decade for Women (1975-1985), which recognised women to have equal rights as men and also as an equal partner in development, and the IDWSSD (1981-1990), which focused on providing safe drinking water and sanitation to underserved urban and rural areas, brought forth the much-needed attention to the two important areas- women and water, and also emphasised on the symbiotic relationship between the two.

Although various other conferences aiming to assess the global situation and drawing up long-term action plans took place since then to address the water and sanitation problem, the role of women in this sector was discussed and addressed only in the Ninth Meeting of the Steering Committee, held in April 1982. This was the result of the resolution passed at the UN Mid-Decade Conference on Women held in Copenhagen in 1980, which demanded that all international and national agencies should pay serious attention to involving women at all stages of drinking water projects. Accordingly, this meeting set up an Action-Oriented Inter-Agency Task Force for fostering women's participation in activities of the IDWSSD. The mandate of this Task Force was to:

1. develop a strategy for the enhancement of the role of women within the IDWSSD,
2. assist in activities in support of the IDWSSD programmes concerning the role of women,
3. act as a mechanism for collaboration in the development and implementation of activities at international and national levels,
4. monitor, evaluate and report on the implementation of IDWSSD policies and programmes related to women, to ensure that they adequately reflect women's concerns, needs and contributions, and
5. recommend further action in this regard (Population Reports, 1998; Wakeman et al., 1996).

In turn, it was decided at the 10th Meeting of the Steering Committee and endorsed at the 11th Meeting held in late 1983 that a strategy document should be developed on the promotion of women's participation in water supply and sanitation activities. However, by 1985, it was realised that the targets set were not achievable. Despite their commitment to reach as many people as possible, many developing countries participating in the IDWSSD had failed to realistically aim for 'Water and Sanitation for All'. Although the first water decade was successful in delivering water to over 1.2 billion people and sanitation to almost 770 million, many countries were unable to keep up with the desired results due to the growing population, rapid urbanisation, and low public awareness about health (WHO and UNICEF, 2006; Mullen, 2004; Srinivas, 2004). The major reasons highlighted for the low performance in achieving the desired results were: too much focus on technical aspects, lack of proper understanding of the local community, and lack of people or agencies responsible for operation and maintenance of completed projects. Since the effects of these failed projects had to be faced by women in general, and more so by those among the poor and marginalised population, it was realised that a proper understanding of the community dynamics, including the socio-economic and cultural aspects, was highly needed. It was also felt that the technology of the water systems needed to be simpler so that the local community could manage them better.

Accordingly, the involvement of people from other sectors, especially the social sciences, was felt necessary to deal with the social, cultural, economic and environmental aspects of the drinking water projects as they determined their sustainability. It was also a period when there was a growing realisation that the international strategies and interventions that were relying on a 'welfare approach', as resonated by the then Women in Development (WID) and Women and Development (WAD) approaches of the seventies, that considered women as just the primary beneficiaries and recipients of improved water supplies, needed to be changed following the support for rights which were reverberated by the Gender and Development (GAD) approach in the 1980s.

Although the IDWSSD was able to: i) appreciate the need for comprehensive and balance country-specific approaches to address the water and sanitation-related problems; ii) acknowledge that the water-related goals can be fulfilled only with more money and time than what it was initially thought of; and, iii) admit that the fulfilment of the goal requires revisiting the approach, strategy and efforts made for it (United Nations, 2003; Choguill, Franceys, and Cotton, 1993), a body called "External Support Agencies (ESA) Collaborative Council" was formed in 1988 to tackle the water-related shortcomings. The ESA's goal was to help the national governments in formulating appropriate sector policies. The attempts of the ESA were further stressed in the Global Consultation Forum held in New Delhi in 1990 which set out four basic principles related to water as guided by the new slogan: 'some for all rather than more for some'. One of the principles is related to the full participation of women in sector institutions. This forum also changed the role of managing the water sector at the country level from ESA to national governments themselves. Consequently, the name of the ESA Collaborative Council was changed to Water Supply and Sanitation Collaborative Council (WSSCC). The first meeting of the WSSCC, held in Oslo in 1991, focused on seven key areas related to improved planning and management of water supplies, one of which was 'gender and sustainability'. The other emphasis of this forum was on the role of national governments as facilitators rather than providers, unlike in the past (Wakeman et al., 1996).

The International Conference on Water and the Environment held in Dublin in 1992 was one of the conferences that focused on the economic value of water, women, and poverty among other things. The four Dublin Principles that were set out in the conference but continue to be relevant to date are:

- Principle 1- 'Freshwater is a finite and vulnerable resource, essential to sustain life, development and the environment';
- Principle 2- 'Water development and management should be based on a participatory approach, involving users, planners and policy-makers at all levels';
- Principle 3- 'Women play a central part in the provision, management and safeguarding of water';
- Principle 4- 'Water has an economic value in all its competing uses and should be recognised as an economic good' (United Nations, 2003; WMO, 1992).

Further, the UN Conference on the Environment and Development (UNCED) at Rio de Janeiro in 1992 produced Agenda 21, which, with its seven programme areas for action regarding freshwater, helped mobilise change and heralded the beginning of the still very slow evolution in water management practices. This conference, along with the Dublin Conference, was influential in that these conferences placed water at the centre of the development agenda and highlighted the importance of involving women in water management. Similarly, the Fourth UN World Conference on Women in Beijing in 1995 focused primarily on gender issues and while doing so, it also remained dedicated to ensuring the availability of and universal access to safe drinking water and sanitation and emphasised to put in place effective public distribution systems as soon as possible (United Nations, 1995). The Second World Water Forum in Hague in 2000 and the International Conference on Freshwater in Bonn in 2001 continued to position water at the centre of the sustainable development debate and the Third Water Forum- the International Year of Freshwater- held in Japan in 2003, further raised awareness of the need to protect this precious resource (IISD, 2003).

Subsequently, the Fourth World Water Forum held in Mexico in 2006 and the Fifth World Water Forum held in Istanbul, Turkey in 2009 reaffirmed the importance of women in the planning and management of water services and decision-making processes (IISD, 2009a & 2009b; IFRC and RCS, 2006). The Sixth World Water Forum held in Marseille, France in 2012 affirmed the commitment of the governments to achieving the MDGs related to clean drinking water and sanitation, highlighted the contribution of water to a green economy, and called for incorporating water in all its economic, social and environmental dimensions in a framework of governance, financing and cooperation. This Forum installed a new commission- the Grassroots and Citizen Commission- to ensure the full participation of women, youth, NGOs and indigenous peoples, and to ensure the mainstreaming of their inputs in the Forum deliberations (Schulz, 2012; WWF, 2012). Despite the growing attention paid by the international forums in involving women in the water sector in the '80s and '90s, there was a serious lack in the understanding of the intensity of gender issues and in developing the strategies that could help address the engendering of the water sector. This gender gap in the water sector has been continuing even post the year 2000 and despite the 15 years spent talking about the MDGs and one-third of that time spent on the SDGs, as discussed below.

"Access to and use of water has been 'gendered' throughout history and in every culture. The roles and identities resulting from being female or male determine who has ownership, control and use of water, and access to it. Gender, therefore, is central to any work that is done to increase the supply and use of water, or to improve access to it" (Wallace, 2003). Due to the influence of historical, economic, religious and cultural realities, women and men are affected differently by water-related problems, therefore, understanding gender roles, relations and inequalities, in line with water-related matters is crucial. Gender roles, in the water and sanitation sector, refer to the different roles, unequal relations, the division of work, different responsibilities, and skills, and different rights between women and men undertaken and shared while performing water-related activities.

Often the work and attributes of men are valued more than those of women, whilst women are usually tasked with collecting water for daily consumption, household use and agricultural purposes (Regmi and Fawcett, 2001; Regmi 2000). Even though there is no natural, biological reason why women should fetch water while men get educated as water engineers, the water world has historically been male-dominated. Men, mostly higher educated than women, hold important positions on local, national and international policymaking bodies, and make decisions about water-related matters, including the structure of the water supplies and sanitation facilities, irrigations systems etc. The task of water collection, however, is one such issue that has disproportionately affected women. In developing countries, women and children, especially girls are primarily burdened with the task of hauling water every day. It is estimated that they spend 200 million hours collectively each day fetching water, which is 8.3 million days or over 22,800 years (UNICEF, 2016). The United Nation's SDGs for water and sanitation (Goal 6) calls for universal and equitable access to safe and affordable drinking water by 2030. In line with this, the initial step is for everyone to have the provision of basic water service within a 30-minute round trip, and the long-term goal is to ensure the availability of safe water at home for everyone. The whole idea behind this is to help improve the lives of the people of countries like Sub-Saharan Africa where 29% of the population are still 30 minutes or more away from improved drinking water sources (UNICEF, 2016).

In the absence of readily available water, women and girls have to bear the opportunity costs of collecting water, which have far-reaching and severe effects on many of their activities, including educational, economic, socio-cultural and political, even in the post-2000 period. Moreover, due to the transportation of water over long distances, serious implications on the physical and mental health of women have also been witnessed. The health consequences are heavier for women who carry small children and those who are pregnant. Medical research conducted over the years has reported many cases of injuries to women because of carrying heavy loads of water. These include spinal and pelvic disfigurements, head, neck and back pain, chronic fatigue, and effects on reproductive health, such as spontaneous miscarriages (Huber, 2017; Drop in the Bucket, 2016). Recent reports on Kenyan women of West Pokot County, encountering negative effects such as miscarriage due to carrying heavy loads of water over long distances, also validates this claim (KBC, 2017). The WHO research also affirms that risks for unborn children of pregnant mothers include inadequate water, sanitation and hygiene (WHO, 2017a & 2017b). Lack of safe and sufficient water also causes damaging mental health effects, such as anxiety, worry, and even stigma and shame for not being able to provide water for the family. A FASEB Journal discloses that many Kenyan women thus feared the risk of miscarriage and early labour etc. as a result of transporting heavy loads of water (Collins et al., 2017).

The gender issue related to water hauling reported above has been overlooked by the agencies involved in the water sector in many other societies as well. For instance, the WHO (2016) recommends 20-50 litres of clean, safe water per day for drinking and hygiene which amounts to hauling between 44 and 110 pounds of water daily for use by each household member. However, even the average container for water collection in Africa, the jerry can, weighs over 40 lbs. when full, which is nearly the same amount checked luggage on most passenger airline flights would weigh (NPR, 2016; WaterAid, 2016; The Water Project, 2016). Constant lifting and carrying of heavy load over long distances can result in physical injuries, such as strained backs, shoulders and necks, as well as pelvic deformities that may result in childbirth problems. Moreover, the reality that water has to be transported from a distant location and then stored, increases the risk of it being polluted with microbiological contamination, faeces etc. by the time it is consumed, even though it is collected from a safe source (UNICEF, 2016; IOM, 2009). This, in turn, leads to an adverse health effect for the whole family, and more so for the women.

Likewise, for women and girls, the effects of not having a safe source of water and toilet nearby are categorically damaging. Having to travel longer distances at an average of six miles round-trip (WaterAid, 2016), to collect water increases their risks of facing conflicts, and physical and sexual assaults on their way and at water points. For example, in Kenya, 90% of reported rapes befell while women were collecting water and other natural resources (UNESCO, 2016). Moreover, water crises and other water-related natural disasters like drought also affect women and girls more, since it amplifies their time to search for water. It also leads to an increase in harmful practices against women and girls, such as domestic and sexual violence, trafficking, child marriage, and courtship rape (UNESCO, 2016; UN WOMEN, 2016).

Apart from encountering enormous health-related challenges, the women and girls, who mostly fetch the water, also have to take their time away from education and sometimes even have to miss their schools (UNICEF, 2016). Many girls are forced to drop out of school when they start to menstruate, as it is considered to be a highly stigmatised issue in many communities worldwide.

Moreover, this issue is exacerbated due to the lack of water and sanitation facilities such as the availability of toilets, sanitary pads, facilities for disposing of used sanitary pads etc. in schools despite that these amenities are extremely essential for young girls to manage their menstruation in a dignified manner. This gender bias arising from the water crisis- i.e., not being able to offer girls the same schooling opportunities as boys- is estimated to cost less-developed nations $92 billion every year, which amounts to $1 trillion per decade on missed out salaries (Drop in the Bucket, 2016). Between collecting water and searching for toilets, considerable time is lost- for instance, it is estimated that each year women and girls collectively spend 97 billion hours looking for a place to urinate or defecate because of the absence of toilets (WaterAid, 2016). This time could, however, have been spent on other valuable activities such as pursuing skills outside of the traditional roles, receiving an efficient education, engaging in income-generating endeavours etc. which, in turn, could have resulted in increased autonomy, confidence, empowerment, and the ability to choose for herself.

As primary providers, managers, and users of water, women are often in an optimal spot to help drive productive change in the design, operation and maintenance of water systems, water distribution, and policymaking activities, which include the information on reliable water sources, location of the water points, technology to be used, and other health, hygiene, sanitation and income-generating activities which are to be introduced etc. However, there have been many instances even during the post-2000 period where women were rarely offered roles in water improvement programmes and initiatives resulting in the negative impact on many water and development projects, even failing, at times, due to the exclusion of women (Nguyen, 2018; Mommen, Humphries-Waa, & Gwavuya, 2017; Kilsby, 2012; Ray, 2007; Regmi & Fawcett, 2001; AusAID, 2000; Regmi, 2000). Even when women were involved in the management of water points, either in the key positions or as members of the WUSCs or as caretakers or maintenance workers, they could not be as effective in their roles and in making decisions - because of their small number- as opposed to the number of their fellow male colleagues.

To illustrate, a study in northern Kenya revealed that although women held positions in the local water management committees, they were neither invited to nor allowed to speak in meetings. As a result, the women, at times, would get into conflict with the men- be it on matters related to the selection of water points or the overall management of the project. Because the women's participation was in smaller numbers, the chances that men would bypass them in several committee decisions were high. This situation not only discouraged women from engaging actively in committee activities but also questioned the performance of the water project as they started to lose their interest in it (Yerian et al., 2014). Similarly, the findings of another study revealed that although it was promising to see many women undertaking technical education at various levels and being involved together with men in all aspects (technical and non-technical) of water supply management over the years, the relatively small proportion of women, which was less than 17% of the WASH labour force, was unable to influence organisational policies and practices (IWA, 2014).

It is, therefore, essential that women's increased involvement in water boards, water user committees, water associations, and other community-based water organisations in many developing countries, gained as a result of affirmative actions, is not perceived as a tokenistic involvement. Since women's symbolic involvement will neither help sustain the project benefits nor will it be able to help women meet their practical and strategic gender needs, the concerned authorities should take every step to ensure that an extensive number of women are involved in the management of water projects and they get to play meaningful roles holding key positions as well. The evidence of substantial improvement in the outcomes, effectiveness and efficiency of water projects has been discovered when women's involvement is noted. It is estimated that women's involvement in water projects, including planning, financing, and upkeep makes these projects six to seven times more effective (Water.org, 2018; Chapman, 2016; Water for People, 2016). This is because women, as primary customers and managers, have valuable insights to offer regarding the needs and preferences about the design, operation, usage, maintenance and overall management of water projects.

Researchers in Baluchistan, Pakistan, who initially deterred consultation with women members of the community, had to eventually collaborate with an all-women group after a year, since the water project constructed without women's involvement, did not succeed. The suggestions provided by the women's group later on, such as repurposing a new water tank on vacant land to provide water for non-functioning public standpipes, appeared to be more cost-effective than the original plan devised by the men-only group. Moreover, it also resulted in better management of water and enhancement in the quality of life due to the provision of hygiene education which was taken care of mostly by women. A couple of years later, the community not only established a new school for girls but also invested in the empowerment of women, resulting in the inclusion of more women in policymaking roles (Thompson et al., 2017).

From their experience with the Centre of Rural Studies and Development (CRSD), Jansz and Wilbur (2013) report that women's grassroots involvement in advocacy provides an impetus in the success of drinking water projects. The local women beneficiaries involved with the CRSD were able to actively and successfully influence the Rural Water Supply Department to make the local government stakeholders more effective, responsive and accountable to the communities. Thus, women's activism in creating support groups and employing advocacy tools such as local media changed the community's perception, especially that of men, in relation to women taking up leadership positions. Furthermore, the women's leadership had not only improved drinking water facilities in their communities but had also reduced the time women spent in water collection by almost 20 per cent. Citing an experience from several African countries, UN Women (2012) also presents that at the macro-level, an increased number of women as ministers of water and environment can enable gender-responsive policies in the water and sanitation sector. Women ministers in South Africa, Lesotho, and Uganda used affirmative actions to encourage other women to take up water and sanitation-related careers such as repair and maintenance.

All in all, the last few decades have witnessed a changing emphasis on the role of women and gender relations in general, in many development efforts including water-related initiatives. It is optimistic to observe the expansion of women's role from being just the beneficiaries of a water supply system, to different others, including in the management, operation, distribution, technical field, advocacy, policymaking, and the like. What is, however, needed for this to continue is the constant focus on issues around gender inequality along with the stigmas associated with their bodily functions, and not just the focus on addressing the WASH need in isolation. All the while, it is also imperative to acknowledge the role of men and boys, and increasingly engage them, together with women and girls in all water-related matters. This is crucial not only in attaining gender equality but also for carrying out all other development efforts, which require participation from both genders. It is also essential to realise that because women's water needs arise based on many factors such as culture, caste and ethnicity, economic status, and/or whether she is an urban or a rural dweller etc., all of these factors should be taken into account while devising targets, programmes, plans and legislation. Hence, this book, instead of trying to synonymise gender with 'women', aims to bring a holistic perspective by assessing the implications of water-related planned actions, including legislation, policies, programmes etc., for both women and men. The discussions, at times, however, will seem to revert more to women and their issues, since they are the hardest hit by the scarcity of water, especially in developing nations like Nepal.

❍❍❍

CHAPTER 2

Selecting An Appropriate Gender Lens

This chapter dwells on various Gender and Development or GAD frameworks that can be followed to analyse the gender issues involved in the development sector, including the water sector. Also presented in this chapter are reviews of the most commonly used GAD frameworks, tips for modifications in these frameworks for their effective use in analysing the gender issues in the water sector and the hybrid version of the frameworks suggested for gender analysis of agencies engaged in the water sector and of their impact at the community level.

A Review of Existing GAD Frameworks

Since GAD is generally preferred over other approaches for gender analysis, it is presumed that this approach will provide an impeccable lens to see through gender issues with an accurate perspective. The GAD approach emerged in the 1980s as an alternative to the earlier Women in Development (WID) approach. March et al. (1999) underline that 'the WID approach aims to include women in development projects to make them more efficient while the GAD approach aims to address inequalities in women's and men's social roles in relation to development.' Moser (1989) states 'the GAD approach tries to link the productive and reproductive roles presuming that the social construction of these two roles is the basis of women's oppression.' She further argues that 'the gender issues emerged because the problems of women were attributed to biological differences between women and men rather than the social relationship between those two sexes which made women subordinate to men. Gender should, therefore, be understood as a system of socially ascribed roles and relationships between men and women, which are determined not by biological but by social, political and economic context.' Seed's (1991) addition to this argument is that gender roles are learned and they can change over time. It is the analysis of these roles and relationships which shows the imbalance in power, wealth, workload etc., between women and men and it is this analysis that may then lead to the possibility as well as the necessity of change.

Given the argument of the GAD practitioners that any development activity such as water supply, should be taken as an entry point for the improvement of women's condition, both practically and strategically, it is relevant to use the GAD approach to unearth gender issues in this sector. However, the task of arriving at a decision over which one of the available GAD frameworks suggested for gender planning and gender analysis- for example, the Harvard Analytical Framework, Moser Framework, Gender Analysis Matrix (GAM), Empowerment (Longwe) Framework and Social Relations Approach– is the best fit is always challenging. There has been a lot of debate about the potential and the limitations of these frameworks. Hence, a review of these frameworks is always useful to decide which, one or more of them, could best serve the purpose and also to develop ideas for some modifications in one or more of these frameworks if needed. The introduction of the various GAD frameworks along with their potential uses and limitations presented in this section comes mainly from the following authors, March et al. (1999), Kabeer (1994a), Moser (1989 and 1993), and Longwe (1991), and the author's understanding of these frameworks and their applications in various contexts. Although there are a few other GAD frameworks such as People-Oriented Planning Framework, and Capacities and Vulnerabilities Analysis Framework suggested for gender planning and analysis, they have been left untouched because these frameworks have been suggested mainly for planning and analysing refugee and vulnerability situations, which lay outside the purview of the discussions made in this book.

Harvard Analytical Framework: This framework, brought out in 1985, was developed by researchers at the Harvard Institute for International Development, USA. This is one of the first GAD frameworks proposed for gender analysis. This framework has four main components namely, The Activity Profile, The Access and Control Profile, Influencing Factors, and Checklist for Project-Cycle Analysis. The users of this framework claim that it is simple, practical and helpful in finding out the details of the activities that women and men in a community are engaged in. These tools are suggested for use mostly at the micro-level and present the gender division of labour between women and men and their access to and control over various resources. This framework is considered to be gender-neutral. Hence, the results of the framework can be a good basis for development projects to plan the project activities without threatening the existing structures, including the patriarchal structure.

The critics, however, argue that the Harvard Analytical Framework is more concerned with increasing the efficiency of development projects rather than addressing the issues of inequality and imbalance in power relations between women and men and finding out the reasons behind it. This framework has also been criticised for its lack of focus on the analysis of women's and men's existing roles in the community and the imbalanced access to and control over resources between them due to its over-reliance on a tick-the-box approach. Given these limitations, it is argued that this framework, will be more relevant for use in combination with the Moser Framework and the Longwe Framework. To illustrate, this framework argues that women's participation is necessary for the effectiveness of a development intervention such as water supply but it does not properly explain how their participation can be increased without increasing their burden, how they can adjust their domestic workload to engage in community activities, and how their interests towards the project activities can be maintained for a longer period since the sustainability of those interventions depends entirely on their effective participation, which is all, however, addressed by the Moser and Longwe frameworks.

Moser Framework- Practical and Strategic Gender Needs: The Moser framework developed by Caroline Moser (1989 and 1993) includes: women's triple roles- productive, reproductive and community roles, practical and strategic gender needs, and categories of WID/GAD policy approaches. Moser developed this framework initially for gender analysis and later with further emphasis on gender policy and planning as a challenge to the dominant WID approach in the early 1980s when she was with the Development Planning Unit at the University of London, UK. Those in favour of this framework claim that it is user-friendly, action-oriented, and suitable for determining the project impact at the community level through a practical and strategic gender needs approach. The framework also answers why project results are positive or negative so that the planners can understand the whole project picture easily and can act accordingly. Moser argues that the focus on practical and strategic gender needs can lead to a proper analysis of the issue of inequalities and imbalance in power relations between women and men and come up with appropriate plans to address them, which can eventually improve the gender relations, sustain the practical benefits of any development project in a community, and empower women vis-à-vis men.

Maxine Molyneux first coined the terms 'practical' and 'strategic' and distinguished them by suffusing them with gender interests in 1985 (Molyneux, 1985) and Caroline Moser then adopted this distinction in her gender works. Moser (1989 and 1993) defines practical gender needs as the needs women identify in their socially accepted roles in society. These needs do not challenge the gender division of labour or women's subordinate position in society, although they arise because of them. They are a response to an immediate perceived necessity, identified within a specific context. These gender needs are practical and often are concerned with inadequacies in living conditions such as water provision, health care, and employment. Though these needs, when fulfilled, are shared by all family members, women generally presume that these are their specific needs as the responsibility of fulfilling these needs has traditionally fallen on them.

Strategic gender needs, on the other hand, are the needs women identify because of their subordinate position to men in their society (Moser, 1989). They are the needs that arise from the analysis of women's subordination to men. These needs vary according to particular contexts. The strategic gender needs when met would allow women to improve their imbalanced power relationships with men. They relate to the abolition of the sexual division of labour, the alleviation of the burden of domestic labour and child care, freedom of choice over childbearing, the removal of institutionalised forms of discrimination, power and control, and may include such issues as legal rights, domestic violence, equal wages and women's control over their bodies. Meeting strategic gender needs helps women to achieve greater equality. Moser (1993) further states that the main objective of gender analysis and planning is to relieve both strategic and practical gender needs to emancipate women from their subordination, and to embrace equality, equity and empowerment. Hence, the focus of GAD work should be on recognising women as active participants in development by looking at practical gender needs. Such work should also recognise that women do not participate in development on equal terms with men because of their subordinate position. Thus, there is a need to address their strategic gender needs as well. This framework is recommended for use in conjunction with the Harvard Analytical Framework.

Despite the strong justifications provided in favour of practical and strategic gender needs approach, the term 'needs' has come under criticism as it tends to imply that women are passive recipients of assistance determined by external planners. In contrast, 'interests' is a more active concept, because it implies that women themselves define their demands (Kabeer, 1994b in March et al. 1999). The critics of this approach also opine that this approach does not give much emphasis to inequalities caused by caste, class, race etc. It is also said that this approach is more concerned with women's strategic gender needs, and not with men's strategic gender needs, which might invite resistance from men to researchers' or agencies' work, and it can also invite resistance from people working in an agency whose goal is not the emancipation of women from subordination. Similarly, this framework has also been criticised for reasons that the division between the practical and strategic gender needs is artificial as there is a continuum between these two, and the framework is more focused on finding out women's and men's activities rather than the interrelationships between them, which govern how decisions are made.

Women's Empowerment (Longwe) Framework: This framework, developed by Sara Hlupekile Longwe, claims that empowerment of women will arise by bringing them into an equal position to that of men so that they can participate in the development process and have control over resources which is equal to that of men. At the heart of this framework is the idea of five hierarchical levels of equality- welfare, access, conscientisation, participation and control (Longwe, 1991). Longwe describes welfare, the first level of equality, as women's access to material welfare, relative to men, in matters such as food supply, water supply, medical care etc. Access, the second level of equality, refers to women's access to factors of production such as land, labour, capital, credit, training, market opportunities etc. in relation to men, and suggests that reform in legal and administrative procedures is needed if women do not have equal opportunity as men do to have access to these factors of production. Conscientisation, the third level of equality in the hierarchy, has been defined as a process of understanding the difference between sex roles and gender roles, and that the latter are cultural and thus can be changed. It also refers to the need for the sexual division of labour to be fair and agreeable to both sexes and not decided by one's domination due to economic and political factors. Participation, the fourth level of equality, has been defined as a process where women get equal opportunities, together with men, to participate in decision-making processes at all stages of a project. Finally, control, the fifth and the highest indicator of women's equality and empowerment is the level where women are in a position to control and to make decisions about the use of factors of production and the subsequent benefits arising out of them. As women's position moves forward from welfare to control, the higher is their equality with men, indicating their greater empowerment.

The Longwe framework is considered to have much in common with Moser's framework of practical and strategic gender needs but, it moves one step ahead of the Moser framework in that it treats the move from practical to strategic gender needs as a progression of women's empowerment. The supporters of this framework claim that it is a useful tool for planning, monitoring and evaluation of a project to translate commitment of empowerment into action. The other claim of this framework is its emphasis on women's inequality with men in every respect so that corrective actions could be taken on time to achieve equality between them.

The critics of the Longwe framework argue, however, that it tends to focus more on women than on men which might invite problems while planning a project. It also fails to address inequality caused by differences in caste, class, race etc., and it can invite resistance from those who are not committed to women's empowerment. Its hierarchical levels of equality and empowerment can make the users confused and its use is limited since these levels may not necessarily follow the same order all the time. The other criticism of this framework is that it does not explain well the difference between women's control over a small resource like an allowance received from participation in training and their lack of access to a big resource like land, building and other valuable family assets. The other limitation of the Longwe framework is that the level of 'participation' has been placed way beyond the levels of 'welfare' and 'access' which gives an impression that women's 'participation' has to be sought only when the first three levels of equality have been achieved, since all these are presented in a hierarchical order. The large gap between the levels of 'access' and 'control' is also confusing since these two levels complement each other and thus make more sense if they are put together. Given these limitations, it makes more sense if the Longwe framework is used in combination with the other GAD frameworks like Moser's practical and strategic gender needs approach rather than using it as a standalone framework.

Gender Analysis Matrix (GAM): This framework, developed by Rani Parker, is recognised as a systematic community-based technique to be used by field workers to find out the impact of development interventions on four levels- women, men, household and community- in terms of four areas- labour, resource, time and culture. This tool is used in a matrix form and is claimed as simple, quick and participatory with the representation of both women and men in the process, thereby fostering bottom-up planning to increase the chances of higher acceptance of a project by a community.

However, this approach has also been criticised for reasons such as it is less suitable for macro-level analysis; the use of various categories can be confusing, leading to the loss of some important data in the process; it demands a lot of skills and patience on the part of facilitators and it is difficult to find such skilled people, and its emphasis on collecting information from mixed groups may lead men to dominate the discussions. For instance, while it proposes the category of 'household' as one major element when collecting and analysing information, the framework also proposes two other categories for 'women' and 'men', which, can encompass all household-related activities within one of these two categories. If so, what is then going to be recorded under the category of 'household' becomes confusing. As a result, the possibility of recording the same variety of information in one or more categories and missing out on other useful information is high while using this framework. Similarly, the other limitation of this approach is its emphasis on 'resource' as a separate category when it already has two other categories for 'material' and 'labour', which are also resources.

This framework is also criticised for its inability to deal with structural aspects of unequal relationships and unequal access to and control over resources between women and men. Further, this framework also does not shed enough light on the consequences of women's and men's lack of participation in projects such as water supplies and the mechanisms that need to be followed to sustain the benefits, both practical and strategic, accrued from such interventions. Though this framework is quite effective in disaggregating the collected data by sex to know the level of the impact of the development interventions on women and men, this does not appear to be more concerned with the issue of women's empowerment, and thus fails to explain properly why the impact on the two sexes are different and how best they can be improved.

Social Relations Approach: The social relations approach developed by Naila Kabeer at the Institute of Development Studies, Sussex University, UK, in 1994, has three main elements: the goal of development as human well-being, the concept of social relations and institutional analysis. This framework, proposed more in the form of concepts rather than tools, focuses on people's relationships with each other and with resources through institutions such as the state and the market. It tries to analyse the inequalities between women and men in the distribution of resources, power, rights etc. and helps create an environment where women can act as change agents in the development process. This approach is considered to give a holistic picture of poverty by describing processes of impoverishment and empowerment. It is recommended for use at various levels, for analysing institutions with linkages at different levels, and to dig out the connectedness of women and men through their social relationships.

The limitations of this approach are, however, that it is complicated, demands a lot of work from the practitioners and requires a lot of skills on the part of users to develop a proper linkage between various levels. The lack of proper understanding of complex concepts such as 'institution' and 'organisation' makes it unsuitable to use them in a participatory way at the community level. Its focus on institutional relations can lead to the overlooking of crucial gender issues at other levels. Because of the existence of various smaller groups formed for various purposes even within a community, it is difficult to define the boundary of a community as an 'institution'. Likewise, this framework is difficult to use in contexts where the roles of various actors such as household, community, market and state- the important layers of the framework- is not fully established.

Tips for the Prospective GAD Frameworks

It appears from the earlier discussions that none of the GAD frameworks is free from criticism, resulting in difficulty to decide which GAD framework works best over the other while undertaking a review of a development activity like a water supply. In such situations, understanding the perspectives of some scholars with enormous experience in this sector can be helpful.

The book 'Gender in Water Resources Management, Water Supply and Sanitation Roles and Realities Revisited' written by Christine van Wijk-Sijbesma (1998) and published by the IRC, both of whom have done enormous work on gender concerning water and sanitation, suggests an approach for the analysis of gender in water resources development and management which is based only on six questions disaggregated by gender. They are- the way people are using resources, the way people are contributing to the development and management of water resources, the decision-making and controlling of implementation, types of beneficiaries in particular jobs and training that results from the programme inputs, types of people having access to and control over various project benefits, and the distribution of benefits among the people of various social and ethnic divisions. This approach suggests that one can still carry out a gender analysis even without applying any established GAD framework as long as the objective of empowering women is clear and all relevant information is disaggregated by sex.

March et al. (1999) argue that one does not need a formal GAD framework to work well or innovatively on gender issues, to reduce gender inequality or to support women's empowerment. The purpose of the various GAD frameworks is to help the users to go one step further in understanding gender issues, but they will not be useful if the users find them confusing. Because a framework selects a limited number of factors, those felt to be important by the users, each framework can only produce a crude model of reality. On the other hand, each person can also have her/his own sets of values and assumptions. Hence, these authors further suggest that the users can interplay between their sets of values and assumptions and those of the existing frameworks to determine which approaches and interventions to consider. Further, one can also combine gender frameworks designed by others to create one's hybrid version, adapting different components of separate gender frameworks and adding one's own ideas to them.

The message, therefore, is that a new perspective can be taken by combining one's ideas with those of others if that is deemed necessary. It is, however, necessary at the same time, to be clear on the GAD framework(s) to be combined so that it can lead to an effective analysis of the facts gathered in the field as well as provide a better direction to the fieldwork. To develop ideas on the appropriateness of a framework, a review of literature on gender integration in various sectors will be useful. Such reviews will show whether the development projects, including the water projects, have succeeded in sustaining practical benefits (availability of an adequate amount of drinking water, for instance) to women and men of their project areas. This kind of review will help identify the reasons for the success or the ineffectiveness of the development projects.

In the context of water and sanitation, though women are the primary actors and users of these resources, the experiences show that they have been involved only to fulfil the project requirements (token involvement) rather than to improve their overall living conditions. The main argument of the GAD framework for women's active involvement in development projects, however, is not only to foster the sustainability of project benefits but also to ensure overall societal development through women's empowerment and gender equality. van Wijk-Sijbesma (1998) argues that balanced attention to involving both women and men in water and sanitation projects optimises social and economic development. On the contrary, the projects which bypass women not only endanger the efficiency and effectiveness of the project itself but also will harm development. Some others (Hannan-Andersson, 1995 and Mlama, 1994 in van Wijk-Sijbesma, 1998) argue that the effective involvement of women in water supplies enables them to give direction to their lives and circumstances, while in the absence of such involvement, they keep doing secondary activities where they have no say and do not share control of the resources on which their livelihood depends.

Moser (1989), talking about her empowerment approach, claims that the involvement of women in development interventions is to give them the same rights as men so that they can determine choices in their lives and influence the direction of change. Highlighting the need for addressing women's strategic involvement in development interventions, Moser (1993) from her other experiences also argues that because women, more than men, face the consequences if projects fail, they will be more concerned about their sustenance. Their active involvement in decision-making roles also gives them a higher status in the family and the community, which is essential to increase their confidence. The Institute of Development Studies (1995) claims that active involvement of women can improve their position vis-a-vis men which can make a significant contribution to overall development. Mosse (1993) also supports that women's strategic roles in projects can increase the efficiency of the projects as well as the growth of societies.

Documenting the experiences of several countries, van Wijk-Sijbesma (1998) notes that the reason why women, despite being the primary users and managers of water resources, protectors of family health and educators of the new generation, have few opportunities to participate in decision-making roles in water projects is that they have many strategic constraints. These include unequal rights both in the household and the community, lack of freedom over their own bodies, lack of access to and control over resources, lack of recognition for their work, inability to make independent choices due to lack of other skills and lack of self-respect. On the other hand, addressing these strategic issues such as control over resources can improve their status in their own eyes and the eyes of their husbands and other male members of the family and this gives them more decision-making power in the household. It also enables women to take up health education and organise savings and credit groups to initiate other income-earning activities. These economic and social changes also create spaces for them to get recognition from men in public decision-making.

The other argument in the GAD literature is that though there has been a lot of emphasis on soliciting women's meaningful participation in development activities, women find it difficult to participate because they are already over-burdened (Bilgi, 1998; May, 1997). These authors argue that the projects should not only be concerned about increasing women's participation but also about understanding prevalent gender roles and how a compromise can be made between these two so that the projects can easily meet women's genuine needs and interests. Some others (Regmi, 2000; Van der Laan, 1998; Frischmuth, 1997; Curtis, 1986) argue that a better understanding of the gender division of labour between women and men in the project community, which is a strategic need of women, can yield many advantages such as improvement in women's health, increase in project efficiency, and more time for women to participate in other productive activities. The fulfilment of this need can give women opportunities to earn more income, which can have multiplier effects in the improvements of the lives of all family members, including women themselves (Regmi, 2000; Jazairy et al., 1992).

'A Gender Reference Guide' prepared by UNDP (1998) also suggests many gender-sensitive strategies to address the gender inequality between women and men. They include increased participation by women in all activities, a shift in women's traditional roles and responsibilities, improvement in access to and control over resources- and increase in women's bargaining power, positive changes in women's and men's attitudes at all levels: household, community, field staff and project management, and increased initiatives by women and men from different interest groups in project activities.

Since the arguments made in the GAD literature have shown a clear linkage between the importance of involving women in all stages of project activities and the effectiveness/ ineffectiveness of water supplies in meeting women's practical and strategic gender needs, the author used Moser's framework of practical and strategic gender needs in the earlier research he conducted 20 years ago as will be presented in Part II of this book. The positive sides of the Moser Framework, despite some limitations, are that it is highly recommended for judging the gender impact of a development intervention at the community level. Further, as per Moser, women's empowerment is possible only by addressing their strategic gender needs, which can help women to be on an equal footing with men- another reason to use her concept. Because Moser sees meeting women's strategic gender needs as the process of women's empowerment, borrowing some concepts from Longwe's Empowerment Framework was thought to be relevant while deciding about a GAD framework for the research which the author led. Though there is a lot of debate going on about women's empowerment, as can be found from the work of Jennifer Harold, Srilatha Batliwala, Nira Yuval-Devis, Kate Young and Jo Rowlands (all in Rowlands, 1997), Longwe's Empowerment framework is better structured and more user-friendly, and thus a more widely used as a GAD framework than others. Similarly, since the tools 'Activity Profile' and 'Checklist' of Harvard Analytical Framework can better guide in finding out the details of how women and men participate in various stages of the selected projects and what the impact of such participation would look like in the household division of labour, their application in conjunction with Moser's practical and strategic gender needs approach and Longwe's empowerment framework proves meaningful.

While these concepts of practical and strategic gender needs are well-known to development practitioners trained in gender analysis, they remain outside the conventional framework for planning and designing water projects. Drinking water projects are mostly carried out by engineers - most of the men - whose goal is the simple and laudable one of bringing adequate quantities of drinking water closer to the homes of the target communities. These male engineers do not perceive any direct relationship between their traditionally understood objective- to fulfil people's primary need for safe water, and many of the strategic gender needs as they have been emphasised by Moser. Though some of these engineers would agree that their work is ultimately concerned with the twin aims of enabling women and men to meet their practical needs, and enabling the marginalised groups within communities, including women, to fight against oppression and exploitation, the difficulty for them is to find how Moser's understanding of women's strategic issues, such as the right of women to exercise control over their bodies and to decide whether or not they want to bear and rear children, to own land and property, fight against domestic violence etc. can be addressed in the drinking water projects.

Hence, the present need is to derive such indicators of women's strategic gender needs which might not conflict with the traditionally perceived objective of the development of water supplies, which are less challenging for male engineers to tackle in the beginning, and which can help to prepare a platform to meet the above-mentioned strategic gender needs of women to develop a society where both women and men can thrive equally. This is where Longwe's Empowerment Framework appears to be useful for consideration, as her indicators of women's empowerment are more specific and are close to the reasons for the ineffectiveness of development projects, including water supplies.

Framework Suggested for Gender Analysis at the Institutional Level

Since the effectiveness of drinking water projects in meeting women's practical and strategic needs depends on the institutional environment in which the projects are designed, planned and implemented, it is equally important to look at the policies and practices of the selected agencies from a gender perspective. Accordingly, a review of the literature on institutional studies was carried out to find out the important gender issues at the institutional level which can influence the outcomes of agencies' activities/projects (Regmi, 2000). The other main reason behind such a review was to suggest a framework, though a baffling task for sure, that could be adopted while analysing gender issues at the institutional level be it the water sector or some others. An overview of the findings that came out from the review is as follows:

Swieringa and Wierdsma (1992) identify four aspects of an organisation that determine its behaviour. They are: i) **strategy:** the organisation's goals and the ways it seeks to realise them; ii) **structure:** the division and grouping of tasks, authority and responsibilities; the relative positions of, and formal relationships between, members of the organisation; iii) **systems:** the conditions and agreements relating to how processes (information, communication and decision-making) proceed; and iv) **culture:** the combined sum of the individual opinions, shared values and norms of the members of the organisation. Along similar lines but being more specific, Macdonald et al. (1997) suggest to breakdown the concept of an organisation into component elements, in which gendered structures and processes can be identified. Their suggested components of an organisation are i) the shape of the organisation in terms of the distribution of decision-making power; ii) the balance of women and men in the composition of the staff members, and particularly in management and policy- or decision-making roles; iii) organisational culture and style; iv) the day-to-day functioning of the organisation - is it women-friendly, or even people-friendly?

Similarly, a review of the works of some others (May, 1997; Macdonald, 1997; Goetz, 1997a and 1997b; Wakeman et al. 1996; Hadjipateras, 1996;

Goetz, 1995; Macdonald, 1994) has highlighted some more specific issues to be looked at while engendering an institution. They are organisational ideologies and goals, management style and organisational values, organisational structure, practical arrangements and facilities, resource commitment, gender training, expressions of power, presence of change agents etc. While some of these issues are complementary, some overlap with each other.

Given the key gender issues prevalent at the institutional level and the arguments of various authors about the framework to be considered for a gender analysis at the institutional level as discussed in the literature, it was thought to be useful to develop a new framework consisting of all issues suggested as important and examine them in the assessment of the selected agencies from a gender perspective. The institutional framework suggested, therefore, for the gender analysis are:

- Policy formulating mechanisms
- Objectives and strategies
- Personnel policies
- Organisational structure
- Organisational culture and management style
- Provision for gender training
- Provision for human and capital resources
- Role of change agents

Based on these indicators, a gender analysis was carried out in the selected agencies as presented in Part II of the book to examine the extent to which the policies and practices of the selected agencies were supportive of meeting women's practical and strategic gender needs at the community level. Because in Nepal, almost all the agencies engaged in the drinking water sector, whether they are governmental or NGOs or running bilateral or multilateral projects, are mostly funded by international donors, and they have to follow the norms set out in the water legislation and national plans and policies, it was also essential to analyse the water policies at these levels from a gender perspective as they could impact upon the gender outcomes of the projects undertaken by the selected agencies at the community level. This task has been presented in Part II and Part III of this book.

Framework Suggested for Gender Analysis at the Community Level

From the arguments put forward by the GAD practitioners, the reasons cited for the ineffectiveness of drinking water projects in providing sustainable benefits to women and men in their project communities, and the emphasis put on various women's strategic needs and empowerment in each of Moser's and Longwe's Framework, a number of women's strategic issues have emerged for consideration while carrying out a gender analysis of the outcomes of drinking water projects (Regmi, 2000). A summary of these issues is as follows:

Experiences of various drinking water projects implemented in different parts of the world show that women's participation, to men's, is limited in the implementation of those water projects. Even in projects where women have been involved, their involvement is limited to contributing labour and other secondary activities that neither improve their status in the household and the community nor their relationships and bargaining position with men. Such a tokenistic involvement of women has only furthered the demotivation of women towards the proper protection and management of water resources. As a result, many such projects have been ineffective to provide long-term practical benefits to women and men in their project communities as well as empowering the former to fulfil their various other genuine needs. What, therefore, appears from these experiences is that women's active participation, together with that of men, is a key indicator of a project's effectiveness in sustaining practical benefits and of women's empowerment which can eventually lead to the fulfilment of the former and many of their other genuine needs and concerns.

These experiences also show that though some projects have sought to solicit women's active participation in the wake of women's willingness to participate, the load of household chores on their back has hardly allowed them enough space and time to avail themselves of the opportunity. This finding is an indication that the water projects have only emphasised the involvement of women in the project activities, but they have not laid the groundwork to create an environment where men are motivated to share women's traditionally assigned activities. Further, even in projects where more women got the opportunity to participate in various project activities, their roles have been very similar to what they have been performing in their households and other communal activities. The result is that there is no advancement in women's status, no reduction in their work burden, no improvement in their relationships with men, and no success in improving projects' effectiveness in providing long-term benefits to its beneficiaries. Hence, a change in the traditional gender division of labour appears to be an important indicator to be looked at while analysing the outcomes of a drinking water project from a gender perspective.

An extensive review of the relevant literature has also shown that in many water projects studied, women, in relation to men, have limited access to various project resources such as timely information, choice of technology, selection of the location of water points, training, especially technical ones, paid positions, etc. Moreover, when it comes to the issue of control over those resources, they don't have any. The literature further shows that the projects, where women have better access to and control over the project resources, were more effective in meeting women's and men's needs and concerns and in improving the relationships between these two sexes than in the projects where women had limited access to and control over such resources. From these experiences, the issue of women's access to and control over project resources has appeared as an important indicator to be considered while analysing the results of a water project from a gender perspective.

Similarly, a review of literature on gender issues in the development sector in general and in drinking water projects in particular highlights the equity in sharing of benefits as one important issue to be taken into consideration while analysing water projects from a gender perspective. These experiences show that to receive everyone's attention towards the better management of project resources, the latter should provide equal benefits to all in the community, irrespective of their sex, ethnicity, class, etc.

The literature on GAD also argues that development interventions, including that of water, need to be profound in addressing the issue of equity not only for the sustainability of practical benefits to women and men but also for observing principles of distributive justice to those who are poor, vulnerable, and marginalised in most cases. And, finally, the other important issue that can be drawn from the past experiences is that the development projects such as water supply should provide training on skill development, technical aspects and basic literacy to women together with men so that the former can feel confident of their roles not only to undertake the given project activities but also to initiate new development ventures in their communities. These efforts can also help to minimise the gap between the women and men in the project areas and to develop a society with sustainable human development.

In view of these major women's strategic gender issues drawn from the literature and the current analysis of gender issues in the water sector, a new framework, consisting of five indicators of women's strategic gender needs vis-à-vis women's empowerment, has been drawn up to carry out a gender analysis of the outcomes of the development projects, including that of drinking water, which is as follows:

- women's participation in project activities
- changes in the traditional gender division of labour
- women's access to and control over resources (higher bargaining power)
- equity in sharing of benefits, and
- women's increased status and new development initiatives

A brief description of what each of these indicators refers to is presented below:

Women's Participation in Project Activities: In this book, participation, as one of the indicators of women's strategic gender needs in water supplies, refers to women's equal participation, in relation to men, in all stages of a drinking water project- pre-construction, construction and post-construction. Because women are the primary users of water resources just like what they are of other several resources, any gender analysis should attempt to find out whether women are involved from the very first stage of negotiation that took place between the community and the project, to monitoring and evaluation of the project progress. The gender analysis should explore issues related to women's participation with an assumption that their participation in project activities needs to be sought not only in terms of their higher number but also in terms of the opportunities given to them to make decisions about the activities that affect their lives.

Changes in the Traditional Gender Division of Labour: This is the second indicator of the framework proposed for a gender analysis of the water projects. This indicator refers to a sharing of women's traditional responsibilities by men so that women can have more time to participate in project activities, without which there is less chance of the sustainability of water supplies. Any gender analysis, therefore, should focus on the analysis of the efforts made by the selected development projects, water projects included, in sharing of women's work by men since this mechanism gives the former opportunities to be actively involved in many other productive activities which can have multiplier effects in the household, community and nation.

Women's Access to and Control over Resources: This third indicator of women's strategic gender needs, which needs to be considered while doing a gender analysis in water supplies, refers to women's equal access to the use of water resources and control over the use of those resources, to that of men, by having decision-making authority over them. Because the decision-making power comes through an increase in women's bargaining ability, the gender analysis should explore the projects' efforts to increase women's access to and control over income, which strengthens their bargaining position both in the household and the community.

Equity in Sharing of Benefits: This fourth indicator of women's strategic gender needs, to be considered while analysing the impact of water supplies on gender aspects implies the extent to which the water supplies have considered the issues of sex, caste, class, etc. while providing benefits to the people in the project areas. Because the sustainability of the water systems as well as of other development projects depends on the interests of all segments of the community towards the protection and management of those systems/ projects, the issue of providing equal benefits to all in the project areas is crucial. Some aspects that need to be explored under this indicator are the types of benefits received by women and men, caste/ethnicity and class of women and men that benefited from the project, project requirements to be met by women and men for them to benefit from the project, types of people directly concerned with the management of water resources, etc.

Women's Higher Status: This indicator of women's strategic gender needs in water supplies refers to opportunities given to women, in relation to men, to increase their self-esteem, confidence, social skills (training on literacy, numeracy and project management) and technical skills (for instance, training on repair and maintenance of the water systems and construction in case of a water project), and their involvement in higher decision-making bodies responsible for the management of the projects. The gender analysis should, therefore, explore the efforts made by the selected projects to increase women's status to men's since the former can lead to many positive effects both in the household (for example, control of domestic violence, emphasis on children's education) and the community (for example, women can organise themselves in groups to initiate other forms of development activities in the community).

PART II
Gender Integration for Meeting Practical and Strategic Gender Needs

Part II presents the findings of the research undertaken during the period 1997-2000 that tried to examine the gender issues involved in the water sector at various levels- international, national, institutional and project- and their impact in meeting women's practical and strategic gender needs at the community level. Chapter three presents the study context while chapters four and five offer gender analysis of international water policies and national water policies, respectively. Similarly, chapters six and seven dwell on the status of gender mainstreaming at the institutional level and implementation level of selected water agencies, while chapter eight bestows on the success of selected water agencies in meeting women's practical and strategic gender needs.

CHAPTER 3

Study Contexts and Research Methods

This chapter provides an introduction to Nepal and the gender situation and the social context of Nepali villages where the research was undertaken during 1997-2000. Also described in this chapter are the agencies and the communities selected for the research, research methods, selection of informants, and types of information collected as well as their analysis.

Introduction to Nepal

Situated on the southern slope of the Himalayas between India to the east, south and west and the Tibet region of China to the north, Nepal, with a total area of 147,181 sq. km., extends from 26 22'N to 30 27'N in latitude and 80 4'E to 88 12'E in longitude. Topographically, it is divided into three ecological belts, mountains occupying 15%, hills occupying 68% and Tarai, the flat plain land in the South, occupying 17% of the total land area of the country. For administrative purposes, the country was further divided into five development regions namely, eastern, central, western, mid-western and far-western regions, till Nepal got a new Constitution in 2015 which created a basis for Nepal to become a federal state. While the earlier administrative structure of five development regions included 14 zones and 75 districts consisting of about 3,915 Village Development Committees (VDCs) and 58 municipalities (CBS, 2011), the new administrative structure includes one central (federal) government, seven provincial governments and 753 local governments within a total of 77 districts.

Nepal has a clear diversity of weather and climate as it has great variety in its topography. It has tropical, mesothermal, microthermal, taiga and tundra types of climate. The average annual rainfall is 1,600 mm. Nepal's population was estimated at 26.5 million in its 2011 census and has been projected to be more than 30 million in 2021 (the next census time) with an annual population growth rate of 1.40%. The population census of 2011 reported that of the total population, about 7% lived in the mountains, 43% lived in the hills and the remaining 50% lived in the Tarai. As of 2011, 17% lived in urban areas (CBS, 2011). As there are many ethnic groups in Nepal, there are many dialects spoken in the country. Nepali is the first language and it is used for official purposes. While 81% of the population observe the Hindu religion, the rest practice Buddhism, Islam and Christianity (CBS, 2011). Mount Everest, the highest peak in the world, and the Lord Buddha, the symbol of peace, are the pride of Nepal.

Social Context of Nepali Villages Prior to 2000

This section presents the main features of the Nepali village economy and gender roles, gender division of labour and decision-making power of women and men before 2000.

The Village Economy: The Nepali rural community was an agro-pastoral economy in the past. The community functioned to meet the basic survival needs of its people rather than produce for market outlets or cash income. As reported by Acharya and Bennett (1981), Nepal's rural economy was subsistence oriented with 85% of the average household production consumed by the family that produced it. Agriculture and allied sectors were responsible for more than 80% of the total household income while only about 19% was generated outside the household. On average, about 70% of the household income was generated in the subsistence sector and only 30% through market intervention. This household subsistence production in which women played a major role, emerged as the backbone of the Nepalese rural economy. However, as Joekes (1991) reports, only about 90% of food-grains requirements and 60% of national income were derived from agriculture. The farm production was not able to keep pace with the growing population compelling the rural population to make up the rest of the household needs by engaging themselves in various off-farm activities.

A World Bank (1991 in Joekes, 1991) Report notes that in both hills and the Tarai, small farmers worked a higher proportion of their time off-farm but were penalised by earning lower hourly wage rates than members of larger farm households. The food deficit in the hills compelled nearly 1.2 million people to move to the Tarai region in the 1960s and 1970s but this resulted in the availability of only a little scope for further settlement since 20% of the Tarai population were already estimated to be landless. Nevertheless, a study carried out by Shtrii Shakti (1995) in 10 rural villages and 5 urban centres notes that agriculture was still the main source of income for all rural sites. The massive movement of the hill population, mostly males, to the Tarai (as well as outside Nepal), led the sex ratio to be in favour of males in the urban areas and to increase the number of female-headed households who had limited access to resources but more responsibilities in rural villages.

Gender Situation: Various studies conducted in several Nepali villages report that the situation of Nepalese rural women before 2000 was depressing since many socioeconomic indicators were not in women's favour, as opposed to men's, as summarised below (Baidya, 2000; Acharya, 1997; UNICEF, 1997; Singh, 1995; Acharya, 1994; Joekes, 1991; Acharya and Bennett, 1981).

The girls and women in rural areas of Nepal were discriminated against in all spheres. The girls would get less food, be educated to a lesser extent and take part in household chores from an early age. Since boys were preferred over girls, the latter faced discrimination right from their birth causing them to be the poorest of the poor when they entered into womanhood because they virtually had no ownership of land or other assets. In many castes/ ethnic groups, women were given a lower value than men. In turn, the other important indicators such as infant and child mortality rates, under-five mortality rate, crude death rate and life expectancy were also not in women's favour signifying the social neglect of female infants and children since it is a scientifically proven fact that female children are stronger than male children during their infancy and early childhood. Because the girls were considered as a burden, the literacy and educational qualification, as well as the age of marriage, were also not in their favour. For instance, the illiteracy rate was 75 per cent among women while it was only 46 per cent among men. The average age of marriage was also detrimental as the parents wanted to see girls married off by an early age of 16 and even after marriage they were treated in a worse manner if they were unable to bear a child or if they gave birth only to girls.

Those studies also reported that despite women's substantial contribution in providing labour, only 48 per cent of rural women, as compared to 70 per cent of men, were reported as being economically active in the 1991 census. In the industrial sector, the 1991 census reported three per cent of male employment as against only one per cent of women's employment. While males were employed in high paid and skilled jobs women held low paid and unskilled jobs. Women's participation in politics was also negligible, as it was in the bureaucracy, where

Nepalese women lagged far behind their menfolk. Women's representation in the judiciary and other constitutional bodies was also extremely low. The sex ratio, one of the most important indicators explaining women's status, was also in favour of men in the population censuses of 1971 and 1981. This is also true of the census of the year 1991 when the sex ratio is broken down by ecological regions such as the hills and the Tarai (plain flatlands), and rural and urban areas unlike in many developed countries where the sex ratio is usually in favour of women. Similarly, fertility, another important indicator of women's empowerment, was also found to be very high at 5.6, the second-highest in South Asia. In case a woman in Nepal failed to be fertile, she had no security, as her husband could legally marry another woman.

Although the Nepalese rural women put in substantially more time than men into the family farm enterprise and their contribution to total family income through their input into the local market economy and employment outside the village was also significant, these were not considered to be of high value as men's contribution to the total family income was higher than women's. The findings of Shtrii Shakti (1995) corroborate with these results as it reports that rural women contributed 67% to the family farm economy, 41% to the local market economy and 25% to the short-term employment sector while these figures were 33%, 59% and 75% for men respectively. Though women's participation in economic activities had gradually moved beyond traditional agriculture to the local market economy, they had been further circumscribed with an additional work burden, less mobility and no proportionate access to and control over financial gains. On the other hand, men were spending more time in cash crop activities and less time in traditional agriculture.

As per a World Bank Report (1991 in Joekes, 1991), the Nepalese rural women neither in general owned land or other assets, including those used for production purposes nor did they have adequate access to agricultural resource inputs (improved seeds, fertilisers, credit, training) as compared to men. Nepal South Asia Centre's findings (1998), in such light, are that the income distribution, job opportunities, wage rates, working hours, working conditions were all in favour of men due to the patriarchal mindsets which considered only males as the primary actor, earner and decision-maker. Regarding the reasons why men were able to spend considerably more time in the market economy than women, the studies mentioned above report that men's higher socialisation, greater mobility and greater access to education and capital followed by the full assurance that whatever land and livestock resources the households had, they were fully utilised to provide as much of a subsistence base as possible since the female labour was available free of cost within the family.

Gender Division of Labour: Acharya and Bennett (1981) reveal that the rural women in Nepal spent 10.8 hours per day in activities categorised as domestic, expanded economic and conventional economic as against 7.5 hours per day spent by men. These rural women spent only 5.2 hours per day for social maintenance and leisure while their menfolk spent 8.5 hours per day for the same. This time use pattern was almost the same in all eight villages that the authors had included in their study. This imbalance in the gender division of labour between rural women and men not only showed men's bias not to participate in non-economic activities but also indicated how over-burdened the Nepalese rural women were and how exposed they remained to various health risks. A World Bank report (1991 in Joekes, 1991) also depicts that rural women in Nepal provided the major labour input into agriculture, livestock keeping and natural resource use. They worked an average of 9.6 hours daily, compared to men's 8.9 hours in the Tarai, and 10.5 hours daily, compared to men's 7.9 hours, in the hills and mountains. On the same lines, girls worked proportionately longer than boys- 7.7 hours compared to 4.4 hours.

Another study carried out by Shtrii Shakti (1995) also reveals that despite some changes in women's traditional roles women worked much longer than men, 10.9 hours daily as against 7.8 hours daily. As before, women continued to engage in 'invisible' labour, i.e., non-market subsistence labour and undervalued public wage labour in the export-led economy. The economic contribution of women in terms of hours of work was much more than that of men, and women's working hours per day in rural areas were longer than those in urban areas. Although women's participation in economic activities was gradually increasing, it had also led to different kinds of exploitation of women. For instance, the large numbers of young women between the ages of 12 and 25 migrating to the cities to take advantage of purported economic opportunities were faced with the reality of exploitation and commodification. There were indications of the increasing abuse of such women in the cities in the forms of rape, trafficking, prostitution etc.

Decision-Making: The first comprehensive study on the status of women in Nepal (Acharya and Bennett, 1981) shows considerable variation in the decision-making power of women and men of various ethnic groups at the household level. While women in the economically defined non-dichotomous ethnic groups (such as Lohorung Rai, Baragaonle and Kham Magar) had considerable decision-making power both outside and inside the household, the women in the dichotomous ethnic groups (such as Maithili, Parbatiya and Tharu) had lesser power; in the remaining ethnic groups (Newar and Tamang), women's decision-making power fell in between the earlier two categorisations. This study further reports that: while women appeared to be the principal decision-makers in activities related to crop seed selection, use of organic manure, choice of food for daily consumption, giving small gifts and loans, and vegetable gardening and sales, men held the primary decision-making power in matters that involved cash such as the use of chemical fertiliser, shopping for food, household necessities and clothing, education and medical treatment, sale of small animals, major household loans, and sale and purchase of land and major animals. Interestingly, women and men had equal decision-making power about religious and social obligations and disposal of household production. A study conducted by Shtrii Shakti (1995) also reports similar results, with the 'inside' (private domestic sphere) characterised as the proper domain of women and the 'outside' (sphere of politics, commerce and wider public concerns) mostly ascribed to men. Nonetheless, the Shtrii Shakti study further notes that because women were showing remarkable disagreement with the choices and decisions made by men as indicated by 58% of women showing such dissatisfactions in rural areas, it could be expected that through gaining more power or status, they would be able to increase control over decisions in the future.

Unlike women's relatively influential roles in decision-making at the household level, the rural women's decision-making power at the village level was insignificant. This was mainly because the village level decisions were mostly made by the then Village Development Committee (VDC), which consisted of 11 members elected by the local people, where the chances of women being elected were bleak due to their poor education, lack of experience of similar work in the past, and thereby the lack of confidence, and lack of access to and control over family property and other resources that could be used for contesting elections, as has been explained in greater detail in Chapter V. As NSAC (1998) reports, low income earning opportunities together with the absence of the right to property limited the role of Nepalese women in decision-making not only about the allocation of household income but also at the level of the village development activities. This ultimately undermined the women's access to gainful employment opportunities, participation in professional jobs and their mainstreaming in the developmental and political processes.

Factors Influencing Gender Roles and Power Structures: Gender occupies a central space in Nepal's socio-cultural context as in many other South Asian countries. Caste, ethnicity, class, age, region, etc., normally mould the construction of gender and gender relations, which usually put men in an advantageous position over women. These elements are reinforced by the patriarchal structure prevalent in Nepal contributing to an unequal level of life opportunities and attainments between women and men. As per the 'Nepal Human Development Report' (NSAC, 1998), the ideologies of patrilineality and patrilocality prevalent in Nepal before 2000 manifested high rituals and other values, including the right to inherit family property and access to household productive resources, income, off-farm employment, schooling, public decision-making structures and public facilities, to sons over daughters. The situation, however, started to be in favour of women as a result of the strong women's movement taking place progressively over the years.

Given such poor future images of Nepalese women, the poor and uneducated parents from rural Nepal did not expect their daughters to earn an independent living and to support them during their infirmities and old age. This bitter reality resulted in their lack of motivation to invest their limited resources in their daughters' schooling. Some consequences of this scenario were: girls were engaged more in household chores while boys were mostly sent to schools. As per the NSAC (1998) report, 'the girl child spent approximately 1.4 times as much as a boy in household chores, including sibling care and farm work. Even in cases where girls got to go to school, their educational participation ratios and rates got skewed at the higher levels of schooling and colleges.' Consequently, girls were married off at an early age which, in turn, led to early childbirth, high fertility rate, limited employment opportunities and the lack of access to and control over income and other resources. The Nepalese rural women's involvement in the government civil service and politics was also a distant dream for these very reasons. Further, as in her childhood at the parental home, the woman would not get proper health care even in her affinal home. As per the MoH (1997), 'only 10% of all the mothers received professional help during child delivery - with another 23% being assisted by local traditional birth attendants who had varying, often questionable levels of skills; 44% of all the new mothers did not receive any professional antenatal care, and at least 539 mothers died per 100,000 live births.'

Realising the need to address such imbalance power relationships between the women and men, by supporting self-employment among the former and making them more productive, the then His Majesty's Government (HMG) of Nepal initiated nationwide programmes such as Production Credit for Rural Women (PCRW) Project and the Women Component of the Small Farmers Development Programme (SFDP) in the early 80s. Similarly, Rural Development Banks were also established to provide production credit to poor rural women. However, as the NSAC (1998) reports, because these interventions were peripheral, they did not address the larger economic, political and cultural issues which continued to subordinate women. Illustratively, a policy emphasis on income generation among women necessarily produces limited results without a concurrent legal and cultural emphasis on the personal property rights of women.

Overall, the patriarchy perpetuated by the religion and culture prevalent in Nepal prior to 2000 viewed women's lives as 'incomplete' without entering into a life-long dependent relationship with particular categories of men, principally a father and a husband. The process of making a woman fully dependent on men starts from early childhood. While a male child is socialised giving images of future independent work-life, a female child is socialised giving images of dependent married life. These images are further crystallised and concretised with the advancement of childhood through formal education, work routine, social interaction, valuations, and above all, male-female relationships. The formation of gender identities sharply diverges by the end of childhood and let girls enter into a dependent adulthood relationship with men who hold all the power that shape women's and men's lives.

Selected Institutions and Research Communities

This section introduces the agencies selected for the research and the communities where the fieldwork for the research was undertaken.

Description of the Selected Institutions: A review was carried out of the significant institutions which were active in the drinking water and sanitation sector in Nepal and, using criteria presented in the box below, four projects from three institutions were selected for the research. These were: Nepal Water for Health (NEWAH)- a Nepali NGO funded by the British NGO WaterAid (labelled as International Non-Governmental Organisation (INGO) in Nepal) at that time; Rural Water Supply and Sanitation Project (RWSSP), funded by the Finnish International Development Agency (FINNIDA)- a bilateral agency; and the Asian Development Bank (ADB) funded Fourth Rural Water Supply and Sanitation Sector Project (FRWSSSP) of the HMG Nepal's Ministry of Housing and Physical Planning (MHPP)/ Department of Water Supply and Sewerage (DWSS).

Process followed to select institutions

- Listing of International and National NGOs, Bilateral and Multilateral Agencies, and government units involved in assisting/ implementing the drinking water and sanitation projects
- Segregating the agencies which had water and sanitation projects both in the hills and the Tarai of Nepal
- Listing of the institutions that followed a participatory methodology in their projects
- Stratification of the institutions which had a GAD or WID policy and objectives related to undertaking water and sanitation projects
- Identification of the institutions which had a separate women's cell or office to promote women or gender-related activities in the water and sanitation sector
- Verification of the interest of the potential institutions to collaborate in the research work and their categorisation

A brief description of the selected institutions and of the projects that the selected agencies supported are as follows.

NEWAH: Nepal Water for Health or NEWAH, a non-governmental organisation (NGO), was established in 1991 through the initiative of WaterAid, a British charity working towards better hygiene and safe water for people in developing countries. WaterAid began its operations in Nepal in 1986 with a joint project known as "Decade Cell" in collaboration with the then Social Service National Coordination Council (SSNCC). In 1991, following Nepal's return to multiparty democracy in 1990, the joint project could not be continued due to the SSNCC's effectiveness being limited by the bureaucratic muddle and political machinery. Consequently, WaterAid, with support from some Nepali development practitioners, initiated the formation of NEWAH, as an NGO, to carry out its activities. NEWAH, run by an executive committee composed of seven members, who were elected by the general council, was receiving major funding from WaterAid, and partial funding from UNICEF at the time of the research. With crucial changes in policy within UNICEF, its support to NEWAH had been drastically curtailed since 1995. On the other hand, the Department for International Development (DfID), formerly the Overseas Development Administration (ODA), of the British Government had started to fund NEWAH during this time.

The construction of gravity flow systems and protected springs in the hills, and installation of shallow or deep tube-wells and hand-dug wells in the Tarai were NEWAH's major activities together with sanitation promotion, awareness campaigns for health and hygiene education, and construction of domestic latrines. In addition, other environmental sanitation measures, such as drying racks, garbage disposal pits, washing platforms and proper wastewater facilities, were also made available to project beneficiaries. It implemented water supply projects in selected rural areas of Nepal through its regional offices located in four out of the five then regional development centres of the country namely, Biratnagar, Kathmandu, Pokhara and Nepalgunj in the Eastern, Central, Western and Mid-Western Regions, respectively. NEWAH had about 145 staff comprising technicians, health workers, project management specialists and administrators. Initially, NEWAH implemented its projects itself and later through local NGOs. The cost per capita led NEWAH to fund more tube-wells than gravity flow schemes. Till the time of research in the period of 1997-2000, NEWAH had assisted approximately 103 local NGOs and 41 SFDPs and benefited more than 0.3 million people through gravity flow schemes, hand-operated tube-wells, hand-dug wells, and domestic latrines. About 300 people per day were also benefitting through seven public latrines in semi-urban areas. It had trained over 10,728 people from NGOs, SFDP groups and community groups in health-related matters, and system operation and maintenance (NEWAH, 1997).

RWSSP: The Rural Water Supply and Sanitation Project or RWSSP, funded by the Finnish International Development Agency or FINNIDA, was implemented in two phases. Phase I was a joint effort between the MHPP/DWSS of the HMG of Nepal and the Ministry of Foreign Affairs/ Department for International Development Co-operation of the Government of Finland. Phase II, however, was implemented through collaboration between the FINNIDA and the Ministry of Local Development (MLD)/District Development Committee (DDC) of the HMG of Nepal. Phase I of the RWSSP started in January 1990 and ended in December 1995. In this phase, the District Water Supply and Sanitation Office (DWSO) of the DWSS was responsible for the "hardware" while the consultant team was responsible for "software", in particular the extensive training programmes. The total cost of Phase I was Finnish Mark 50.54 million (6.06 million Sterling Pounds that time) (RWSSP Work Plan, 1997/98; RWSSP, December 1996; RWSSP, June 1996; RWSSP, 1989).

The focus of Phase I was to strengthen the institutional capacity of the DWSOs in health education, community participation and sanitation along with the provision and promotion of the use of safe, sustainable water supplies and improved sanitary facilities to 100,000 people. This target was later changed to 175,000, covering all six districts of the Lumbini zone in the Western Region of Nepal. To achieve this target, the project had set out five components: district water supply development plans, physical improvements, socio-economic studies, hygiene education and sanitation, training and human resource development, and community involvement. By July 1996, a total of 234,052 beneficiaries received improved water supply facilities. The population coverage was over 230% of the original target. Although the RWSSP focused on WASH, almost half of the project cost (47.42%) in Phase I was spent on physical improvements and implementation (RWSSP, 1996).

The development of a step-by-step approach for systematic community involvement in all phases of projects, including the planning, implementation, operation and maintenance of community schemes, was one major outcome of Phase I. Similarly, the initiation of health and sanitation programmes, to change the knowledge, attitude and practices of the inhabitants for improved health and hygiene benefits, was another outcome of this phase. Finally, the project was also able to learn extensively about training and capacity building at the community level from the activities included in the step-by-step approach. However, the two very weak parts of Phase I, as reported by Tiwari (1998), were the lack of its institutionalisation in the DWSS, which had the mandate to plan, coordinate and manage the water supply and sanitation sector, and the low investment/ limited progress in the capacity building of beneficiaries and of their representative institutions. These were then made the focus of Phase II with additional effort for the involvement of private-sector agencies.

Phase II started in July 1996 and ended in June 1999. This phase aimed to i) strengthen DDCs' and NGOs' capacity in planning, coordination and management of the water supply and sanitation sector in the district, ii) provide community water supply and sanitation services through NGOs within the framework of decentralisation and privatisation, and iii) complete the remaining work of Phase I. Implementation had been planned on a district-by-district basis for maximum impact. The project targeted the hardship areas which were defined in terms of service level criteria. A demand-led participatory process of scheme-identification was followed. Community involvement in all activities was assured through a step-by-step approach. Environmental sanitation and gender concerns were included as an integral part of the project planning. Local NGOs assisted users' committees to make them capable of private sector service delivery. The total budget of Phase II was Finnish Mark 17.42 million and Nepali Rupees 58 million (a total equivalent to 2.67 million Sterling Pounds at that time).

FRWSSSP/DWSS: The Fourth Rural Water Supply and Sanitation Sector Project or FRWSSSP, funded by the ADB, was managed by the DWSS of the HMG Nepal. The DWSS was formed in 1972 when the community water supply function was separated from the Department of Irrigation. Since 1986, the DWSS had been formally appointed as the lead sector agency and made responsible for overall sector planning, coordination and technical standards. Its nominal mandate in water supply was planning, design, procurement, and construction of water supply schemes covering areas with 500 or more people. To help the DWSS meet the national goal of providing safe drinking water to the people of Nepal by 2002, the ADB had given it four soft loans. The First and the Second Sector Projects, which consisted of 187 sub-projects, were commenced in 1985-86 and the Third Sector Project, which consisted of 385 sub-projects, was commenced in the year 1992-93. The projects which were completed under the First, Second and the Third Sector Projects had already been handed over to the respective Water Users' Committees (WUCs).

The FRWSSSP, which consisted of 335 sub-projects, was commenced in 1996/97. The FRWSSSP aimed to address and improve potable water supply and sanitation deficiencies in about 1,500 rural communities in 40 districts from three development regions, namely Eastern (15), Mid-Western (16) and Far-Western (9). The project period covered January 1997 to December 2001. Partners involved in the implementation of the FRWSSSP included 1,500 socially and economically disadvantaged rural community groups, DWSO Engineers, Overseers and Technicians, Members of the DDC, and NGOs where applicable. The project was assisted by a multidisciplinary group of 17 national advisors in social science and technical fields, including sociology, economics, public health, and engineering. All but two of these advisors were located at Regional Project Management Offices (RPMOs). Each RPMO was staffed by a team of seven professionals in engineering, sociology and other fields. The total cost of the project was US$ 26 million i.e., 17.68 million Sterling Pounds at that time (HMG, 1996a).

The FRWSSSP placed special emphasis on capacity building both at community and organisational levels, sustainability, community awareness, water use, hygiene education and sanitation, and institutionalisation of the process. Regular monitoring and assessments were designed to ensure timely performance and timely remedial measures to improve performance. Hence, participatory monitoring and evaluation were also important aspects and an integral component to the FRWSSSP. The major programme components of the FRWSSSP included: community awareness and education, water supply and sanitation development, and institutional strengthening.

Description of the Research Communities: This section describes the criteria following which the research projects were selected as presented in the box below.

Criteria for Selecting Projects

The following factors were considered while selecting the project(s) from the three institutions selected for this research:

- ❖ A project which had both rural water supply and sanitation components
- ❖ A project which had WUC with women as its members
- ❖ A project which was started after 1990 to ensure that gender issues were considered while designing it
- ❖ A project which was in operation for at least a year or near completion to be able to find out the details of women's and men's participation at all stages of the project
- ❖ A project which was accessible, safe to travel to, required relatively limited travel time and had no disputes.

Motipur and Magaragadhi Drinking Water Projects: These projects lied in Motipur and Magaragadhi VDCs respectively in Tarai of Bardiya district in the then Mid-Western Development Region of the country. While the

Motipur project covered all wards apart from Ward 2 in the Motipur VDC, the Magaragadhi project covered all nine wards in the Magaragadhi VDC. These VDCs were located at a distance of 35 to 55 kms. from Nepalgunj, the then regional headquarters of the Mid-Western Development Region where there was a plane service from Kathmandu, the capital city of Nepal. Gularia, the district headquarters, was three hours on bicycle from Motipur, and six hours on foot during summer and two hours by bus during winter from Magaragadhi (Table 1).

Gajedi Drinking Water Project: This project of RWSSP was situated in Gajedi VDC, in the Tarai of Rupandehi district in the then Western Development Region of Nepal. The research was carried out in Belbhariya, Ward 2. The VDC was located at a distance of 23 kms. (19 kms. to Basgadhi on the East-West Highway and 4 kms. to the VDC passing via a motorable dirt road) from Butwal, where the main office of the RWSSP was located. It takes one and a half hours by bicycle to reach Butwal, the nearest town to the village (Table 1).

Hile Drinking Water Project: This project of FRWSSSP covered Ward 1 (known as Hile) of Dhankuta Municipality of Dhankuta district in the hills of the then Eastern Development Region. Hile is located at a distance of 13 kms. from Dhankuta, the district headquarters. A blacktop road that connects Hile with Dhankuta passes through it. The bus was the only form of transportation in Hile during the time of the research. It takes about 45 minutes from Hile to Dhankuta by bus. The climate in Hile is semi-tropical. The average temperature was 31 degrees centigrade while the average annual rainfall was 1,850 mm. especially from June to September. Tamang was the major ethnic group occupying nearly 75% of the households. The literacy rate for Dhankuta Municipality including Hile was 39% (Table 1).

Table 1: Background Information of the Research Communities

Information/ Site	Motipur	Magaragadhi	Gajedi	Hile
Altitude	300m	300m	Not Available	1,160-1,350m
Area	132 sq. km.	118 sq. km	1,400 ha.	Not Available
No. of Households	3,069	2,822	1,530 (275)	860 (360)
Population	16,880	15,520	9,515 (1,577)	5,160 (2,160)

Ethnic Groups	Tharu, Brahmin, Chhetri, Blacksmiths, Tailors	Tharu, Brahmin, Chhetri, Goldsmiths, Magars	Magar, Tharu, Chhetri, Blacksmiths	Tamang, Chhetri, Magar, Brahmin, Tailor, Blacksmiths
Major Occupation	Agriculture	Agriculture	Agriculture	Agriculture and business
Major Crops	Rice, mustard, wheat, maize, gram	Rice, wheat, maize, oilseed	Rice, wheat, maize	Rice, wheat, maize, millet
Language	Nepali, Tharu	Nepali, Tharu	Nepali, Tharu	Tamang, Nepali
Major Means of Transport	Bicycle and bus	Bicycle and bus	Bicycle and bus	Bus
Project Type	Point source	Point source	Point source	Gravity flow
Types of WUC	Women only	Mixed	Mixed	Mixed
Offices	Agriculture, bank, children's home, post office, health, veterinary, police, tele-communication, schools, VDC and NGOs like BASE, Help/Nepal, GSS	Health post, forest, police station, bank, tele-communication, 3 each of public and private schools, VDC, and MPS (an NGO)	RWSSP, NGOs such as Nirdhan, REDO/CAPT, Red Cross, NEWAH, Swabalamban, 7 public schools and 3 private schools, VDC	Bank, post office, police station, army camp, 3 schools and Reukai (an NGO)

Note: The figures in parentheses are only for the area covered by the projects in these two communities.

Gramin Sewa Sangh **(GSS):** The GSS, an NGO based in Motipur VDC, was established in 1992. It was registered at the HMG's District Administration Office. There was a total of 110 general members of whom 12 (11%) were women. For the daily routine activities, an executive body of nine members, which included one woman (11%), had been formed. It was reported that only three male members, who all came from within the VDC, were active in running the NGO. Since its formation, the GSS had undertaken a number of activities including, adult literacy classes, goat raising, pig raising, distribution of smokeless stoves, a savings and credit programme, a co-operative programme, drinking water, health and sanitation, literacy classes, etc., mostly with a focus on women. The basic objectives of the NGO were as follows:

- To raise general awareness among women
- To involve women together with men in development activities in the community
- To organise women to contribute directly to social, economic, political, educational and cultural matters
- To facilitate social change in the community
- To implement women's and children's health education programmes

***Mahila Punaruthan Samuha* (MPS):** The MPS, located in Magaragadhi VDC, was established as an NGO in 1994. The MPS was registered at the District Administration Office to implement literacy classes, skill development activities and general village development activities focusing especially on women. There were 252 general members and 7 executive members- all women. The idea of opening a woman-led NGO came from the insight of 6-7 women who worked for an NGO called Rural Reconstruction Nepal (RRN). While working with RRN these women realised that most Nepali NGOs were male-dominated and hence, women's issues were not prioritised. These women thought that by opening a women-only NGO, they could perhaps meet the genuine needs of poor rural women, make them more aware of their potential and prepare them to be involved in various activities to improve their status. MPS' motto of empowering women-led NEWAH to select the former as their local partner.

Research Methods

Taking into account the nature of the research topic that demanded some lengthy, relaxed and open-ended conversations with women and men in the research communities and the conceptual framework chosen to guide the fieldwork, participatory rural appraisal (PRA) approach, a well-known qualitative research technique, was used to collect information as required for the research.

The following section discusses briefly the use of qualitative and quantitative research techniques, including PRA tools and techniques, for use in collecting information for research, planning, implementation, monitoring and evaluation of development projects, including those of the WASH sector.

Qualitative vs. Quantitative Research Technique: Regarding the usefulness of qualitative and quantitative research techniques, Nichols (1991) notes that quantitative research techniques have been mainly suggested at times when someone wants more precise, statistical answers to carefully defined questions on topics that are thoroughly understood. They are powerful tools for collecting a broad range of standard information on a large population. These research techniques can give precise estimates because of the use of statistical methods and hence can be used to assess the reliability of the results as well. On the contrary, qualitative research techniques are often chosen when time and money are short. They are essential in exploring community attitudes and priorities and when dealing with socially sensitive topics in depth. They can provide a rich understanding of community life, beliefs and norms. These techniques are useful for learning from the people in the community. Some others also suggest that quantitative approaches could best be followed in studies that seek more numbers, counts and quantities and that need more statistical validation while qualitative approaches are suggested more widely in cases where the focus is on finding people's attitudes, behaviours, norms and values that cannot be quantified or are hard to quantify (Pratt and Loizis, 1992; Berg, 1989; Dabbs, 1982; Bogdan, 1972 in Berg, 1989).

The authors mentioned above further report that while quantitative research techniques provide quantifiable facts, counts and measures of things, the qualitative research techniques provide facts such as people's understanding and perceptions; meanings, concepts, definitions, characteristics, and description of things; as well as answers to the what, how, why, when and where of a thing.

Since this research was exploratory, requiring a series of interactions with the local women and men, it aimed for the application of qualitative research techniques. Similarly, because the research had to collect information on sensitive topics like gender issues that demanded formal and informal conversations both at the household and community levels, the application of the qualitative research technique was found to be more appropriate. Finally, the need to verify the validity of the information collected from secondary sources with those collected using primary sources also justified the use of the qualitative research technique.

Since PRA tools and techniques meet all the features of the qualitative research technique described above, this research used them for collecting the required information. Similarly, since much of the analysis of the collected information has to be done at the local level itself demanding a good amount of their time, the need for building a good rapport with the local women and men was essential. The use of tools such as social mapping and transect that generate a lot of enthusiasm and curiosity among the local women and men to participate actively in the data collection and analysis processes; and flexibility that PRA provides in simplifying and skipping the questions as needed as well as in changing the informants, time of the visit, and the tools to improve the quality of the research as relevant, are the other reasons for using PRA tools and techniques.

To ensure that the information collected following PRA in combination with several GAD frameworks is reliable, trustworthy and correct, some of the pitfalls of the PRA reported in the literature (Sarin, 1998; Cleaver, 1997; Regmi, 1995; Chambers, 1994a and 1994b) were also reviewed and measures were taken to address them. The pitfalls of the PRA, as reported, are i) it lacks reliability, quantification, and precision so there is a danger of generalising from individual circumstances; ii) it requires skilled facilitators who are not readily available; iii) some people in the group may dominate discussions; iv) poor and vulnerable people, especially women, might be reluctant to participate in the process due to socio-economic differences with others. To address these pitfalls, the following steps were taken: extensive secondary information was collected to supplement the primary information; a female research assistant, who could speak the local dialect, was hired, trained and placed in the research communities to collect the sensitive information on gender issues as required by the research following both the formal and informal conversations; the principle of triangulation of tools, locations, informants was thoroughly followed; and the dominant participants in the group discussion were respectfully tackled so that the other participants could freely speak and express themselves.

The PRA tools used to collect the information were: social map, activity calendar, access and control profile, group discussion, semi-structured interview, transect walk, observation of the social settings, the status of water resources, and WUC meetings, holding of workshops, key informant interviews, and desk review. The bulk of the information required by the research was collected between July 1997 and August 1998. Nonetheless, the task of visiting the institutions to clarify and validate the collected information and to collect some additional information, as required during the analysis stage, went on until July 1999.

Selection of Informants

The sources of information at the institutional and project levels were head office, regional office, and project office staff (Table 2). Similarly, at the community level, the local women and men, local WUC members and advisors, NGO officials, VDC officials, caretakers, female motivators and female health volunteers (FHV) were the sources of information. While the local women and men were selected from among the users of the tube-wells and the tap-stands installed in the research communities, the others were selected based on their involvement in the project activities. Since the number of women was much less than men in all agencies, almost all of them as available were interviewed in the research (Table 3).

At the national level, though the analysis was made on information obtained through secondary sources, three each of male and female senior development practitioners and policy-makers were interviewed for verification of the analysis.

Table 2: Number of Interviews held at Head Office and Project Office of the Selected Agencies

Types of Interviewees\Agencies	NEWAH	RWSSP	FRWSSSP
Head Office-Male Staff	7	6	7
Head Office-Female Staff	6	4	8
Regional/Project Office-Male Staff	7	6*	14
Regional/Project Office-Female Staff	2	1*	4
Woman Engineers	NA	NA	4
No. of Group Interviews with Males	4	3	3
No. of Group Interviews with Females	3	2	3

*Notes: *Includes the staff of the DDC and DPU NA: Not Applicable*

Table 3: Number of Group and Individual Interviews held at Community Level by Site

No. of Interviews\ Sites	Motipur	Magaragadhi	Gajedi	Hile
Men's group Interviews and the number of participants	6 (5-7)	9 (5-8)	7 (5-12)	5 (4-8)
Women's group interviews and the number of participants	6 (5-7)	9 (5-8)	7 (5-9)	5 (4-8)
Male PMC members interviewed	2*	3	11	6
Female PMC Members Interviewed	9	9	3**	2
Male Caretakers Interviewed	5	NA	2	2
Female Caretakers Interviewed	6	9	7	NA
VDC Officials Interviewed	2	2	3	2
NGO Officials Interviewed	3	4	NA	NA
FHV/Motivators Interviewed	2	2	3	3
Tube wells/Tap stands Observed	6	9	30	11

*Notes: i) * refers to male advisory board members, ii) ** refers that since there was one female WUC member and two female advisors, all three were interviewed, iii) NA: Not Applicable, iv) PMC: Project Management Committee; v) FHV: Female Health Volunteer; vi) number in parenthesis indicates the number of participants*

Types of Collected Information and Their Analysis

At the international and national levels, information was collected on the water policies of some international donors that influenced the water sector in developing countries, including Nepal. At the institutional level, information, following the institutional framework discussed earlier, was collected on policy formulation mechanism, objectives and strategies, personnel policy, organisational structure, organisational culture and management style, provision of gender training, funds and human resources allocated for GAD activities, and role of change agents, if there were any. At the project level, information was collected about the procedures followed while implementing projects. Finally, at the community level, information was collected following the conceptual framework of the five indicators as discussed in Chapter II: women's participation in project activities, changes in the traditional gender division of labour, women's access to and control over resources (higher bargaining power), equity in sharing of benefits, and women's increased status and new development initiatives. Checklists were used to collect the information. All the checklists were first developed in English and later translated into the Nepali language for convenience while collecting information.

Being qualitative in nature, the focus of the research was on 'what', 'how' and 'why' aspects of each phenomenon while analysing the information collected at all levels. The preliminary analysis of the collected information took place at the research site itself by cross-checking and verifying it with the other sources, a feature of triangulating information. To enhance the reliability of the information, the multiples lines of sight, data collection procedures, theoretical perspectives, and/or analysis techniques were considered as suggested by Berg (1989) and Denzin (1978 in Berg, 1989) while collecting and analysing the information. Accordingly, in situations when conflicting information was reported by two sources, attempts were made either to bring the two conflicting groups together for an open discussion on the conflicting matters or a third source was explored to increase the weight of the information provided by one of the two groups. The findings of research studies carried out elsewhere were referred to support or question the findings of the research.

CHAPTER 4

Gender in International Water Policies Prior to 2000

Context

Despite women in many countries being the only existing "water supply system", as they are the ones who carry the water required by their family for drinking, cleaning and even irrigation, often from distant locations, they are commonly kept at the outskirts when it comes to water-related decisions. The lack of effective involvement of women has led to the increasing number of malfunctioning water points, thereby the scarcity of drinking water for the general population. Accordingly, the main thrusts of the discussions made during the various international water conferences held towards the late '80s and '90s were: how to ensure the effective involvement of women at all stages of a water project for its sustained use; who should control water- the donor agency, the national government, the community or a combination of these actors for its rational use; how to improve efficiency and effectiveness in the delivery of water services by ensuring effective mobilisation of the private sector, since water is an economic good?

Although a parallel thought that water should also be considered as a social good, given that it is a basic human right, was also being floated in the international water arena in the late '90s, the water paradigm happened to be influenced more by the idea of water to be perceived as an economic good. This idea promoted the concept of a demand-driven cost-recovery concept among the donors and this is what they expected the national governments to adopt in their water and sanitation projects during those years. The following section, therefore, presents a review of the policies formulated before 2000 of selected international actors such as the World Bank, the ADB, FINNIDA and WaterAid since they were the major donors in the water sector of Nepal where the research was undertaken and also the ones promoting the engagement of the private sector in the delivery of water services for its rational use.

Demand-driven Approach and Gender

Beginning in the early '90s, the international community encouraged the involvement of the private sector intending to control the unaccounted use of water since it was being described as a finite, vulnerable resource and hence, one to be given only when there was a genuine demand for it. The post-IDWSSD period had been influenced by the Dublin and Rio Principles and all efforts, both at the international and the national level, had revolved around the concepts of demand-driven approaches and cost-recovery aspects. The main reason for the shift from a supply-driven to a demand-driven approach was to improve efficiency by making the beneficiary communities accountable to meet some capital costs and the full cost of operation and maintenance of water supplies. Those in favour of this approach argue that 'users will be willing to pay a considerable proportion of their household income for improved water services if they perceived that they were adequate, better, and more reliable than the traditional sources'. A review of some sample international policy documents (ADB, 1998; FINNIDA, 1994; World Bank, 1993) showed that the international community was looking at water from a more demand-led cost recovery perspective and less so from a rights-based perspective though the latter would have encouraged agencies to further understand water as people's basic right and one without which the rural livelihoods of poor and marginalised people cannot sustain.

Although Agenda 21, the perspective document of the Rio Earth Summit 1992, aimed to strike a balance between the two views- on the water as an economic good and as a social good, some dilemma in the donor community could be seen between the two views. The gist of Agenda 21 was that water needs to be prioritised for the satisfaction of basic water needs and protection of the eco-system, but beyond these requirements, water should be treated as an economic good, with appropriate commercial charges for its use. Accordingly, ensuring the right to water to its people is the obligation of governments which should thus progressively extend access to sufficient, affordable, accessible and safe water supplies and safe sanitation services. However, a careful look at the water sector after 1990 indicated something else.

Since the early 1990s, when the water was started to be perceived as an 'economic good', a conglomerate of 'water lords' (water transnational corporations or TNCs), international institutions and governments started exerting increasing pressure to privatise water across the globe. The World Bank and the IMF, arguing along the lines of efficiency and investment, also imposed privatisation of water as a condition on the national governments that were cash-strapped and debt-ridden, to be qualified for loans from the former. In the official text of the WTO on General Agreement on Trade in Services (GATS), water was mentioned as a service provided in the exercise of governmental authority, and the rights of the governments to ostensibly decide which services to liberalise. In practice, however, all services were assumed to be open for inclusion under GATS, unless the government specifically kept them out. The governments from developing and least developed nations could not, however, resist the pressure from the powerful nations because of the financing power of the latter. For example, since 2000, the EU and the US (representing the interests of water TNCs) began to demand free and open market access to public services so that the management of essential goods, including water too, went into the hands of TNCs that represented their interests; this would eventually lead to the failure of poorer governments to protect the interests of their people (ActionAid, 2004).

To understand the impact of a market-led demand-driven approach based on the cost-recovery concept on women in meeting their practical and strategic gender needs in the water sector, a gender analysis of its basic premises was done in the research undertaken in 1997-2000 which is as follows.

Premise 1: Improved water services lead to higher income: One argument put forward in favour of the demand-driven approach is that local people can achieve higher income from the improved water services, due to their adequacy, quality, accessibility and multiple uses for domestic, agricultural and commercial activities, hence, people will be willing to pay for the services (ADB, 1998; World Bank, 1996 and 1993). However, because the households in general and women, in particular, are so poor in the rural areas of countries like Nepal, the idea that they will be willing to pay for the improved water services does not hold even if the services are better. Further, the argument that access to higher income resulting from multiple uses of water should enable users to pay for the improved water services applies only to water used for irrigation and other commercial purposes, which is possible in urban and semi-urban areas, but not to the water used for household consumption in rural areas as it does not directly lead to higher income.

In the Hile village in east Nepal, a thriving commercial centre attracting people from adjoining villages and districts, the improved water supply was used for commercial purposes, such as running tea shops, hotels and restaurants, and thus women and men were able to increase their income from the time saved from water hauling. This was not, however, the case in three villages in west Nepal namely, Gajedi, Motipur and Magaragadhi, where improved water supply was used simply for household consumption. As a result, the women from these areas experienced difficulty in paying even the water tariffs collected for the operation and maintenance of the water points. Discussions with these women suggested that they were very likely to go back to their unhygienic traditional sources if the payment of water tariff was made mandatory to use the water service, indicating the failure of water projects in ensuring equity in project services (Regmi, 2000).

Another experience from the ADB itself also confirms that because the local people, including women, did not have substantial income from the improved water supply and sanitation projects, these projects had a lower success rate.

An assessment of water schemes based on 122 project performance audit reports and 18 project completion reports showed that the success rate, which was determined based on a number of indices, including economic internal rate of return, declined in the drinking water and sanitation projects between the periods 1968-1979 and 1980-1990. In contrast, the success rate in hydropower and flood control and irrigation and drainage assignments either increased or remained constant for the same period (ADB 1998).

In turn, there are high chances that the women from such rural areas will return to their unhygienic traditional sources, resulting in many damaging health implications not only in their own lives but also in the lives of their family members. Because the poor rural women, in general, do not have adequate skills, access to credit and market, and enough time to do productive work, the notion of improved water services alone leading to higher income and increasing their ability to pay the water tariff needs to be re-examined as there are many experiences from various parts of the world of such women going back to their traditional unhygienic water sources for not being able either to earn income or even to pay for the water tariff (Regmi, 2000; van Wijk, 1998; Boesveld, 1994).

Premise 2: Payment increases the feeling of ownership towards the water supply: The demand-driven approach which emphasises the cost-recovery concept argues that because users have to contribute to both the capital formation, and operation and maintenance stages of a drinking water project, they will have increased feeling of ownership towards the project, which will eventually lead to the sustainability of project benefits (ADB, 1998; World Bank, 1993). These arguments, however, do not highlight the need to distinguish who in the family, men or women, are responsible for the payment of water services and consequently, whose - men's and/or women's - ownership towards the project needs to be increased. It has been reported in many studies (Ahmed and Raza, 1999; van Wijk, 1998; Fong et al., 1996) that because women undertake most of the water-related activities in the household, the men in the family attach lower value on water spending, taking it for granted that women should be responsible for this expenditure. These studies have also shown that men, in general, expect their women to pay the water tariff and that women have been taking this responsibility in many projects around the world. However, the studies also report that there are many cases where women are unable to do so, though they are willing, due to their lower access to and control over family income.

Cleaver and Elson (1995) have noted that 'the mismatch between the willingness to pay and the actual ability to pay puts women in a vicious circle- without improved water supplies they have no spare time for income-generating activities, but without the income, they cannot pay for new facilities'. This lack of gender sensitivity in the water policy means that women are under pressure either way- if they want to use the services, they have to work hard to pay for them; if they do not use the services, they have to walk long distances even to collect unhygienic water. Hence, it is not wise to expect that the demand-driven approach can raise people's, especially women's, feeling of ownership towards the improved water services. This raises doubts about the sustainability of the projects since women, as the main drawers of water for domestic supplies, are also seen as the 'natural' domestic water managers.

> *In one meeting held over the collection of water tariffs amongst the user households in Gajedi village in west Nepal, it was discovered that the water tariffs were mostly paid by women and among the 28 defaulters, 22 were women whose husbands had either died or gone to other places as migrant workers. One decision taken in the meeting was that if the defaulters did not pay their dues in two weeks, their use of improved water services would be curtailed. Two of these defaulters were contacted as a matter of curiosity. Both these women were shocked at the decision as both of them were ultra-poor and surviving with their several children on wage labour. Once the decision went into effect, they will have no choice but to revert to their unhygienic traditional sources located far away, requiring them to spend a lot more time and energy in water collection and increasing the risks of getting exposed to many water-related ailments (Regmi, 2000).*

The fact that a majority of Nepali rural women are illiterate, lack confidence, and cannot give voice to their needs and concerns under the existing socio-cultural practices which are always in favour of men, this issue of demand-based cost recovery concept needs to be revisited while aiming its application in the rural areas of countries like Nepal. On the other hand, what is also alarming is that this concept is being gradually promoted not only in the water sector but also in the other sectors such as health, education etc. without making any attempt to address the fundamental issue of how would the poor and marginalised people, especially women, as they are the permanent residents of the households, meet the cost-recovery demands.

Premise 3: Private sector involvement leads to effective services: Another argument put forward in support of the demand-driven approach is that the delivery of water services should be delegated to autonomous and accountable private agencies for an appropriate fee (ADB, 1998; Vikman (1998) discussing FINNIDA; World Bank, 1993) as they can be more efficient than the government departments. However, because the private sector normally runs for profit, it will be least bothered about the financial limitations of poor people, women in general, and poor women from female-headed households in particular, to pay the water costs both for construction and for operation and maintenance. By being known for charging "appropriate fees for appropriate services", the private agency will easily stop serving people who do not pay for its improved services. This means that women, who take care of meeting the household need for water, will be excluded from the benefits of improved water services and compelled to go back to their traditional sources, which are not only unhygienic but also present difficulties as they demand more time and energy.

It is, hence, essential that the demand-driven approach highlights how the private sector can be made accountable in continuing their services to the poor who have problems in paying for the services. As DfID (1998) comments "for the private sector to be accountable to the poor is to monitor in great detail against appropriate indicators the level of service provided to the communities, both before and during private sector participation. Appropriate clauses need to be included in the contract".

Though the international agencies such as FINNIDA (Vikman, 1998) and the ADB (1998) had briefly stated that there is a need in particular cases to subsidise services to the poorest among the projects' beneficiaries, they did not make clear how such subsidies should be provided nor who should provide them. There are numerous cases where the benefits of subsidies are reaped by the well-off households rather than the poorer ones, in the absence of proper mechanisms (van Wijk, 1998). As a result, poor rural women cannot come forward to demand the benefit from the better services that the private sector provides. If in some cases, they do, this might be at the cost of reduced water consumption and consequently, giving up some requirements that are essential for their survival. van Wijk (1998) has documented several experiences from different parts of the world, where poor households in general and women, in particular, have tremendously reduced their domestic use of water for health and hygiene purposes, resulting in many implications on their health. DfID (1998) has also confirmed that high water tariffs may result in cutting food consumption, and hence, reduce nutritional status, inviting health risks. For these reasons, the poor need to be subsidised and the government also needs to ensure that the private sector makes provisions for the same in their agreements and that the implementation of such agreements is carefully monitored. Otherwise, the involvement of the private sector can easily put the poor and marginalised women and men through a state of uncertainty and confusion which can even lead to the sacrificing of their basic sources of livelihood.

Premise 4: Commoditisation of water: Water, before 2000, was regarded as a resource to be treated efficiently in its multiple uses. To control the unaccounted use of water, emphasis was laid on seeing water as a finite, vulnerable resource and thus for it to be treated as an economic good (ADB, 1998; Garn, 1998).

Wakeman et al. (1996) note that an economic analysis of water from a gender perspective, which shows the gender differentials in activities, resources and benefits of household water use, can be very useful while preparing plans. They further report that as women and girls are often the primary managers of water facilities, determining what kinds of services they prefer, as well as those that men prefer, will be essential. This should lead to the control of the misuse of water.

However, once water is considered as a commodity, those who could use it for multiple productive purposes for greater economic benefit, such as large industries and big landholders, would have the power to pay for unlimited use. This can lead to a severe curtailment in the supply of domestic drinking water. Documentation of these experiences can be found in a technical report written by van Wijk (1998). Even though the international stakeholders have appreciated, at least in their policy documents, that priority in the supply of water should be given for drinking purposes, this might not happen in reality once the private sector took on the responsibility for water supply, as has been highly encouraged by donors. The effect is that women, who are responsible for managing water in the households, are hard-hit by such a situation as they have little voice with which to justify the need of their families for water for basic survival, as they are less capable of paying for it than other high earning consumers. Since the donor community and the national governments, till the time of the research, had neither been strict in developing a clear mechanism to monitor the functioning of the private sector nor in following up the effectiveness of the monitoring plan in cases where it was developed, the notion that the commodification of water can benefit the user community did not hold when looked at from the perspectives of poor, excluded and disenfranchised people, especially women.

Furthermore, the concept of the economic good of water can also create conflicts between women and men at the micro-level i.e., at the household level. Experiences show that while women are more concerned with its household use, men are more interested in the use of water in agriculture- for irrigation. Some other experiences also revealed that women in developing countries had very little decision-making power on household matters, especially those related to economic aspects. Hence, women's varying roles need to be recognised and both women and men need to be involved in discussions about protecting water resources for their efficient use for various purposes (Regmi, 2000; Mustanoja, 1998; van Wijk, 1998; Shtrii Shakti, 1995).

> *In four villages studied in Nepal, namely, Hile in the east, and Motipur, Magaragadhi and Gajedi in the west, it was found that the local women had considerable participation in making decisions about agriculture-related activities, but not in those related to cash crops. Similarly, they were much less involved in making decisions about household expenditure and their participation was almost zero when it came to making decisions about capital-oriented expenditure (Regmi, 2000). Another study carried out in Nepal threw up the similar fact that of the total household decisions, 88 per cent were made by men and only 6 per cent by women. In the same way, in taking decisions on domestic expenditure and disposal of household products, and capital transactions, the men's share was 86 per cent and 89 per cent as against 7 per cent each for women (Shtrii Shakti, 1995).*

As a result, men can divert the use of water for their purposes, leaving women to continue using their traditional sources, located at some distance. Because of the diversion of water for these uses, the domestic use of water receives lower priority, which, in turn, can have several effects on women:

1. they will have to walk longer distances spending lots of energy to fulfil the domestic need for water which can, in turn, have serious implications on their health;
2. women will continue using their unhygienic traditional sources which will affect the lives of millions of poor rural people and also demand them to spend a significant amount of money on medicines and treatment; and,
3. women's established role as caregivers for family health will be ignored affecting the employment of millions of women worldwide who are currently employed in the health sector (Cleaver and Elson, 1995; van Wijk, 1985).

The basic argument is that the shift in emphasis from health to economic aspects of water can undermine the recognised role of women as informal hygiene educators at the household level. This shift affects women more than men as the former is more active in the health sector than the latter. With this shift, there is a likelihood that the number of women working in this sector will be reduced. The ultimate result is that the possibility of women contributing to the formulation of gender-aware water projects and water policies becomes less.

Premise 5: Possibility of higher health benefits: Drinking water has a significant impact on the health of human beings. One WHO estimate claims that 80 per cent of sickness and disease in the world is due to inadequate water supply and sanitation. Hence, one strong argument put forward for the cost-recovery approach to water services (ADB, 1998; World Bank, 1993) resulted from the enormous health benefits to the family, especially to women and children, which arise from more efficient and effective water services. Tadle's (1990) argument is that 'the strongest and the most frequent argument put forward for expenditure on domestic water supplies is the observed correlation between better water and health; several studies have shown that differences in water quantity or quality are associated with differences in morbidity.' Wakeman et al. (1996) note that because women and girls are so closely involved in household water supply, they often benefit the most when the village supply is improved. In principle, when water quality and quantity improve, and water is available closer to home, girls and women take shorter trips carrying heavy containers, which can have tremendous positive effects on their health. Women can save their energy for many other productive activities and for leisure, which will have compound positive effects on the health of other family members, and girls can have the time to go to school and in fact, spend more time there.

However, improvement in women's health as a result of the reduction in their water fetching time will not arise so easily in the absence of mechanisms for women's work to be shared by men. As experiences (Regmi and Fawcett, 1999; Mustanoja, 1998; Wakeman et al., 1996) showed, the consumption of water tremendously increases in correlation with its proximity to the home:

> *In the lowlands in Gajedi village in west Nepal and Motipur and Magaragadhi villages in mid-west Nepal, the women contacted for focus group discussions reported that in the past they collected water 4 or 5 times a day, amounting to a total of 80-100 litres per family per day before their villages were given improved water services. But, after water came near their homes, the collection frequency increased to 10-15 times per day, with the use of nearly 200-300 litres of water a day. This was due to the very high temperature in the lowlands, and thus, everyone wants to drink and wash in the fresh and cold water straight from the tube-well rather than that stored in the house, which was mostly warm. Similarly, in the uplands in Hile village in east Nepal, which is often very cold, women carried water all the way to their homes, several times each day, spending significant amounts of energy to bathe freely and wash the clothes used during menstruation comfortably. They were unable to carry out these activities freely at the new tap-stands, which were located along the roadside, where there were higher chances of men and boys seeing them performing these activities. The women said they did not have this problem while using the more distant, traditional sources, where there was no chance of men being in the vicinity (Regmi 2000; Regmi and Fawcett, 1999).*

Further, the fact that women are not able to pay for the capital costs or the operational costs of improved water services because of their lack of access to, and control over, financial resources, would naturally distance them from health benefits. The lack of access to safe and clean water due to the inability to afford it may again lead to negative effects on the health of all the family members increasing women's burden as they take care of sick persons in the family. This is the origin of the opinion that water should not only be regarded as an economic good but also as a social good.

Premise 6: Local participation in decision-making: Donors who support the demand-driven approach also argue that water supplies are more likely to be sustainable when communities made decisions themselves about the services they wanted (ADB, 1998; FINNIDA, 1998; World Bank, 1996 and 1993). They also note that since women usually manage household services, they need to be involved in decision-making about these services. As women are often the managers as well as the direct users of water facilities, involving them as well as men in management and decision-making helps ensure that systems met women's needs. Women use water supply systems frequently and are in a good position to provide accurate, up-to-date reporting on the functioning of a given system. If a system broke down, it is women, not men, who would most likely be the ones to travel further to get water. Women, therefore, need to be involved in making decisions about the water supply (Wakeman et al., 1996).

However, the weakness in this argument is that it does not explain how this should be done, especially in the case of women from developing countries where the patriarchal structure and other social biases are very strong against allowing women to be involved in activities outside the home. Because these women are quite vulnerable in the communities, due to the lack of education, reduced access to and control over resources, and other social and cultural factors, the chance of their involvement in the management of water resources is bleak. Even when they are involved, their number and voice would be so small, as seen in many water committees around the world, that they would not be able to voice their concerns effectively (Regmi, 2000; Mustanoja, 1998; van Wijk, 1998; IRC, 1994; Carloni, 1987; IDRC, 1985). The chance of women from female-headed households being involved in the management of water supplies is even less, as they have to struggle with their meagre resources to meet the various family needs; hence, there is no question of their being able to pay the costs of water or their getting involved in the management of water supplies.

> *In a local water committee that consisted of 11 members in Gajedi village in West Nepal, only one woman was included as a member by the local men. Similarly, in Hile village in East Nepal, two women had been included by men in a committee of 13 members. All these women who had made it to the committee were relatively better off than many other women in these villages. Because these women had not experienced the difficulty of collecting water, spending hours of walking, unlike many other women in the community, they seldom attended the committee meetings. Even when they attended, they had inhibitions to speak before the committee which was composed of almost entirely of men. Interestingly, in the case of Hile village, the two women nominated to the committee, did not know for months that they had been selected by men to be in the committee. The reasons that men cited for disfavouring women in the committees are: they are illiterate, they are good only at household chores, they lack experience, they do not have exposure, and hence, lack the decision-making ability.*

In turn, the lack of women's involvement raises questions about the sustainability of water supplies, as experienced in many countries (Regmi and Fawcett, 1999; van Wijk, 1998; Fong et al., 1996; Mathew, 1991). This issue also raises doubts about the long-term benefits that people could enjoy from the massive investment that had been pumped into the drinking water sector in the '90s and early '00s by various international agencies, should women continue being bypassed in the management of water supplies. Therefore, such a principle must be further elaborated to clarify the 'how' aspects of women's participation rather than simply saying that women's participation will be sought, because the danger is that women's participation can be misinterpreted only as their involvement as project beneficiaries but not as active change agents in society. For this situation to improve, changes are needed in the organisations that promote new policies.

For example, many international agencies stressed the need for women's incorporation in professional, managerial and technical positions at all levels so that water projects could be more effective, not only in meeting people's needs but also for women's economic and social development (IRC, 1994 referring to UNICEF; UNCED, 1992 in IRC, 1994; UNDP/PROWWESS, 1990 in FINNIDA, 1993). But, at the same time, the 'how' part was not always explained well resulting in fewer benefits on the part of women. For instance, UNCED and the World Bank singled out women as a special category within

Chapter 18 of Agenda 21 of their policy paper instead of integrating them into the mainstream. The policy paper took account of women's role as providers of water for domestic consumption, but not as those who were active in productive activities as well (Green and Baden, 1994a and 1994b). The authors further argue that this kind of compartmentalisation of women distances them from their relationships with men and reinforces the gender gap even if they have been mentioned in the policy document. These agencies have neither felt the need to discuss women's needs and roles as against those of men nor have they defined how the system of social relations (including gender relations), within which they operate, determined women's participation in the management of water projects.

Premise 7: Gender-neutral words can benefit women and men equally: The sector strategies as well as the publications of the donors that advocated the demand-driven approach mostly used gender-neutral terms, such as 'people', 'users', 'community', 'stakeholders', 'beneficiaries', 'poor', etc., assuming that women and men have the same needs and concerns and can benefit equally when new water supply systems are implemented in their communities (ADB, 1998; World Bank, 1996 and 1993). However, experiences have proven that women and men have different needs thus they need to be dealt with separately. For example, in its section (policy doctrine, directives, principles, strategy paper) on capacity building, the ADB (1998) has not specified the need for building the capacity of local women more than that of men, though the former's involvement in operation and maintenance of water systems is proven to be an effective means of achieving success (Fong et al., 1996; IRC, 1992). The same was true in the case of WaterAid (1996) which talked about the role of women very briefly in its strategy document despite the latter's unquestioned role in all stages of water supply schemes. The implication that can be drawn from the use of terminologies that appear to be gender-neutral, but which are hardly so in reality, is that they keep women away from meeting not only their strategic needs but also their practical needs since all training, skill development, capacity building and decision-making activities were centred only around men (Regmi, 2000). Some others also argue that in many cases, the donors' policy statements tend to be vague and confusing with catch-all phrases that offer little concrete guidance at the implementation stage. Project staff who have technical expertise are unfamiliar with these catch-all phrases, and therefore, lack the skills or willingness to put policy recommendations into practice. This is made even worse by project documentation which continues to talk in gender-neutral terms referring to the 'community' or the 'users' and the 'consumers.' The brief discussion below attempts to show the implications of the use of gender-neutral terms for women by donors in their policies formed before 2000 though the readers must be cautioned that certain changes are gradually taking place in all of these agencies over the years.

In general, the vision, aims and objectives of several donors and development agencies discussed above did not mention anything specific about improving women's lives or meeting their strategic gender needs. Although these agencies highlight the need for engaging partner agencies in the implementation of water and sanitation projects, they do not see the need for providing training on gender analysis to the partner agency staff. The strategic documents of these agencies talk about people's willingness to pay for improved water services but they do not feel the need to talk about how the local people, more so the women, would be able to pay. Similarly, these agencies emphasise the technology to be people-friendly but again, they do not focus on such technologies to be women-friendly as the latter are the primary users of the water systems in many rural contexts be it in Nepal or elsewhere. These experiences indicated that the strategic frameworks in the water sector were mostly designed by male engineers and technicians who had little empathy towards women and the problems they encountered in the absence of improved water services resulting in the use of generic terminologies.

The above discussions indicate that the thinking of the international donors prior to 2000 about managing the water sector within the frameworks of demand-driven, cost-recovery, economic good and privatisation had a lot of implications on poor and marginalised people, including women in general and the female-headed households in particular, in terms of the latter's ability to benefit from the improved water services. The argument that women and men can generate extra income from their time saved from water hauling, which can then be used to meet the water costs did not hold in the absence of the promotion of such activities as a complement to water projects, and lack of other opportunities available locally. Because the policies of the donor agencies can influence the policies of their partner organisations and the other stakeholders, including the government, the lack of gender insensitivity in their policy documents can influence the policies of the latter also to be gender-insensitive. Chapter IX in Part III discusses the changes which have taken place in international donors' water policies from 2000 to 2020.

CHAPTER 5

Gender Focus in National Water Policies Prior to 2000

The research undertaken during 1997-2000 conducted an extensive review of Nepal's water legislation, plans and policies formulated prior to 2000 to get an idea on gender integration in those policies with an expectation that such gender-aware policies would influence the other actors engaged in the water sector which, in turn, will yield gender-responsive results. The topics covered in this chapter are the status of rural water supplies and women's role, gender analysis of Nepal's water legislation, plan and policies and donors' role.

Status of Rural Water Supplies in Nepal

Nepal, being on the slope of the Himalayas, is naturally endowed with an abundance of water resources. The total length of rivers and rivulets exceed 45,000 km. The average annual surface water availability is about 225 billion cubic meters (bcm) and the per capita water availability is 10,000 cubic meters. However, the uneven spatial and temporal distribution of the water over a year makes the management of water use imperative. For example, 78% of the average flow of the country is concentrated in four major river basins (Koshi, Karnali, Gandaki, and Mahakali) which accommodate 42% of the population, while the medium river basins with only 6% concentration and small river basins with 16% concentration accommodate 19% and 39% of the population respectively. In turn, although the major river basins will be in a comfortable situation with more than double the water requirements to avoid water stress situation, the people living in medium and southern basins will suffer water stress for at least seven months a year as about three-quarters of runoff is available during the monsoon between June and September (JVS, 2002).

It was estimated that almost 60% of the population would suffer water stress by 2025 even though- about 8.5 bcm out of 13.2 bcm of groundwater was economically exploitable annually; only 0.2% of economically feasible hydroelectricity generation (42,000 megawatts) had been installed; only 1 million hectares out of 2.2 million hectares of net irrigation potential area had been brought under irrigation command; and existing total withdrawal for all human activities was limited to 2.5% of the resources (JVS, 2002). This indicated the urgency to develop a vision for utilisation of water resources which would lead to its efficient and rational use, consequently saving the Nepali population from the water stress situation. Accordingly, Nepal Water Vision 2025 was released in 2002.

In Nepal, the traditional drinking water sources are ponds, streams, rivers, springs, stone spouts and wells. However, depending upon origin, many of the surface and spring sources vary considerably in yield and many dry up in the pre-monsoon period. It was only in 1895 that the first piped water supply systems were initiated in the Kathmandu valley to serve the urban population. Although the oldest written legislation of Nepal- the Country Code 1963 (*Muluki Ain,* 2020 BS) touched upon the development and conservation of water supplies with a primary focus on the management of water resources, its major focus was on irrigation. The need for rural piped water supplies was first recognised by the HMG/ Nepal only in its Third Five-Year Development Plan (1965-70). In 1966, the Department of Irrigation was created and given the responsibility to manage the water supply and sanitation. However, given its failure to attend to this matter well, the Department of Water Supply and Sewerage (DWSS) was created in 1972 to take up that responsibility. In 1971, the Local Development Department (LDD) of the Ministry of Home Panchayat, with a mandate to undertake small self-help development projects, embarked on a plan of implementing small water supply schemes in communities willing to provide voluntary labour. This work continued with the addition of a shallow tube-well programme in the Tarai after the Department was upgraded to the status of a Ministry of Panchayat and Local Development (MPLD) in the early 1980s.

The population with access to piped water supply remained very low until 1980, with only 2% of the rural population having access to this facility by the end of the Fourth Five-Year Development Plan (1970-75) and 7% by the end of the Fifth Five-Year Development Plan (1975-80). In response to the campaign of the IDWSSD to draw up a decade plan for providing drinking water supplies and sanitation to its population, the HMG of Nepal prepared a plan covering the period from 1981 to 1990, corresponding with the Sixth (1980-85) and the Seventh (1985-90) Five-Year Development Plan periods. A review of the performance of this sector during the decade shows that a total of 5.93 million of the population in rural areas was served with piped water supplies as against the target of 11.83 million. The population served during the decade plan was 38% as against the target of 69% for the entire country. The reasons for this poor performance were: poor organisational, managerial and environmental aspects which mainly included low community involvement, inappropriate project implementation procedures, weak mobilisation of local resources, poor operation and maintenance systems, and a lack of proper coordination among sector organisations (New ERA, 1990).

Realising these limitations and having made a commitment to provide the entire Nepalese population with safe drinking water, one of the basic needs, by the end of 2000, a separate Ministry of Housing and Physical Planning (MHPP) was established in 1988, and the DWSS was included under this Ministry. For being the lead agency in the water and sanitation sector, the DWSS was further strengthened and reorganised, and all the sector activities conducted previously under LDD were transferred to it. In turn, the Decentralisation Act of 1982 made the DWSS responsible for providing all necessary technical support to its district offices for the implementation of rural water supply schemes (New ERA, 1990).

Taking into consideration the drawbacks of the Seventh Five-Year Development Plan, the Eighth Five-Year Development Plan (1992-97) aimed to provide drinking water to 72% of the population by the end of 1997. However, the water supply coverage achieved by the end of 1996/97 was estimated to be 61% and 62% of the total population living in rural and urban areas respectively. To improve the situation, the Ninth Five-Year Development Plan (1997-2002) set the target of providing access to piped or protected water facilities for 100% of the Nepalese population (Government of Nepal/ GoN, 1998a) though this target seemed somewhat ambitious given the past performances. In fact, the government committed to provide high-quality drinking water to 25% of the population, medium quality to 60% and low quality to 15% during this plan period. As mentioned above, the Nepal Water Vision 2025 was also released in 2002 with the following objectives to keep up with the spirit of the Ninth Plan (JVS, 2002):

- Self-sustained and export-oriented development of hydropower and its integration with the national economy
- Year-round irrigation development for food security and improvement of livelihood
- Provision of potable water and sanitation facility for entire population ensuring the control of the quality of effluent water for industries
- Watershed management, conservation of water quality and overall conservation of environment
- Integrated water resource management through the coordinated development and management of water, land and related resources.

Accordingly, several components, vision drivers, instruments and targets were also developed to help achieve Vision 2025. Despite the government claiming that they would serve 100% of the population with basic freshwater by the end of the plan period, it was only 71.6% of the population that the Ninth Plan was able to serve by that time. Realising from the failures of the past, the Tenth Five-Year Plan thus made a target of serving only 85% by the plan period (2002-2007). Since women's mobilisation was instrumental in realising the target, the following section presents the history of Nepalese women's role in this sector before 2000.

Women's Role in Nepal's Rural Water Supplies

Nepalese women, whether urban or rural, have traditionally been viewed as the basic managers of water systems. Women and girls in all regions of Nepal are deeply entrenched in water-related activities that revolve around their daily household activities. Women and children, especially girls in rural communities, often have to walk for miles to collect water. When the taps run dry or water is scarce, it is women who bear the brunt of the difficulties. Many studies conducted prior to 2000 have shown that since women in Nepal are the predominant managers and users of domestic water, their involvement in the planning and management of water supply programmes can greatly improve the sustainability of the resulting system (Regmi 2000; Mustanoja, 1998; CMS, 1996; New ERA, 1997 and 1991). These studies note that decisions about how much water to use, from which source, and for what purposes, are critical in controlling almost 80% of the water-borne diseases commonly causing mortality and morbidity among infants in Nepal. The studies further report that these decisions are influenced by learned behaviour and largely fall on women because of their responsibilities for household management and child care.

In Nepal, the important roles of women in the water supply were mainly realised since 1985, the time when UNICEF was supporting the LDD, in executing the Community Water Supply and Sanitation Schemes (CWSS), with local community involvement in their preparation, construction, and operation and maintenance (New ERA, 1991). This realisation could be attributed to the appreciation of women's role that formally took place at the international level in the early '80s, the beginning of the IDWSSD. Accordingly, some institutions in Nepal also officially appreciated that women's involvement can increase the effectiveness of the water system, improve women's status and considerably help to assure the continued benefits of the system to the whole user community and thus, started involving women formally in the management of water projects. They were: Helvetas, a Swiss government-funded institution in 1985, UNICEF in 1986, and Nepal Red Cross Society (NRCS) in 1989.

Helvetas began its Women Involvement Programme in the Western Region in 1985 with a Woman Development Officer (WDO), a few women workers and a part-time expatriate advisor. The programme goals were to educate women on hygiene and sanitation, to strengthen their position in society and to develop their self-confidence to publicly voice their views on water supply. Formal "involvement" was the keyword of this approach whereby local women trained by the women's team were made to be gradually involved in planning and decision-making relating to water and sanitation issues. Local water user committees (WUCs), including two women, were formed; this was the first event of women's formal inclusion in water management in Nepal. The idea was to train these women on issues related to health, sanitation and water supply systems and to spread the knowledge through them to fellow women and consolidate the learned behaviour in their daily lives. These women were then expected to become responsible voluntarily for the activities in the village after handing over the programme to them (New ERA, 1991). This approach got continued in all water supplies designed and implemented in Nepal after 1991.

UNICEF assisted a Women Involvement and Sanitation Programme (WISP) carried out as a pilot activity in Chaurjhari in Rukum district in the Mid-Western Development Region of Nepal in 1986. This programme was later extended to the Dolakha district in the Central Region in 1988 and Ilam and Makwanpur districts in the Eastern and Central Region respectively in 1989.

The objectives of this programme were similar to those of Helvetas i.e.: train representative women from each tap-stand community, and through them spread the health message to a larger body of women to improve the health of the rural population; improve the quality and the effectiveness of the gravity flow water supply system, and strengthen the social status of women in the community. This approach was developed with a conviction that women could not voice their needs because of the lack of self-awareness, self-esteem and self-respect, and their excessive respect towards men. Hence, the key concept in this approach was awareness building about one's capabilities through organised training that disseminates information, helps women develop their own ideas and encourages them to express opinions about water issues without being shy in public (New ERA, 1991).

Though UNICEF/Nepal had been quite concerned about women's active involvement in its water supply projects, it stopped its direct investment in the water supply sector since 1997. The approach after that had rather been to complement the water projects implemented by other I/NGOs, bilateral/multilateral agencies and government through health and hygiene activities and link them with its other thematic engagements. While integrating gender into all its programmes had always been UNICEF's major concern, the focus remained, for a long time, only on meeting the practical needs of people in the project community. Nevertheless, it released a 'Gender Mainstreaming Guide' to ensure that their projects meet both the practical as well as the strategic gender needs of women during the same time.

Becoming more aware of diseases spread through contaminated water, the **NRCS** started to work on the water sector (with tube-wells in the beginning) in 1983. The NRCS included women workers in its sanitation programme and assigned female Village Health Leaders (VHLs) since 1989. These female VHLs, together with their male counterparts, were given one-month training on primary health care and assigned to work in the then VDC to implement a health programme that focused on oral rehydration therapy (ORT), immunisation, sanitation, nutrition and growth monitoring.

An evaluation study on women's involvement in water and sanitation programmes concluded that the lack of interest shown by the DWSS towards WISP, the lack of a national policy on sanitation leading to poor coordination among various agencies working on sanitation-related issues, the lack of emphasis on linking water and sanitation through the education and involvement of women, and the lack of incentives provided to women volunteers who were supposed to carry out the programme after the women workers left the area, were some key factors affecting the WISP (New ERA, 1991). The same evaluation study, however, also reports that women's involvement in water supplies created a positive change in the general status of women, assured the protection of water sources and the areas surrounding them, led more and more people to use latrines, and reduced the incidences of diarrhoeal diseases among infants and children. The study further concludes that though it appeared that the provision of women workers and the training of women volunteers and women committee members required an additional cost, the support of women in the long-term upkeep and maintenance of the water supply systems would greatly increase the life of the water system as well as improve the health and quality of village life.

The need for women's involvement in the drinking water sector, at the government level was, however, realised only in 1989 when the MHPP initiated a policy guideline and directive. This policy, which was later revised in 1991, called for involving user groups, including women, at all stages of water supply schemes including need identification, planning and construction (Bajracharya et al., 1997). The ADB, the major donor in the water sector in Nepal, started funding in this sector in 1984. According to an evaluation carried out by Bajracharya et al. (1997), though community involvement was emphasised in the documentation for both- the first project (1985-1993) and the second project (1989-1995)- real community involvement, including some involvement of women, was achieved only in the third project (1992-1997). The project documents of the fourth project (1997-2001), appeared to be more concerned in terms of soliciting women's participation in various project activities.

The other agency with an exclusive focus on water supply and sanitation- **Rural Water Supply and Sanitation Fund Board (RWSSFB)**, under an agreement between the GoN and the World Bank- also had its focus on women. This agency, which aimed to benefit 550,000 people from 900 communities in a period of five years (1997-2002), had a budget of Rs. 1. 21 billion (USD 10.75 million at the rate of September 30, 2019), of which 86% was from loan support of the World Bank, 3% was from the GoN and 11% was through community contributions. One of the major activities of this agency included technical services and informal education with more focus made on women for their effective participation in water supply and sanitation activities.

Nepal's Water Legislation, Plan and Policies from a Gender Perspective

Water Legislations: Nepal Water Supply Corporation (NWSC) Act, 1989 (BS 2046) was introduced concerning the establishment of the Nepal Water Supply Corporation as a perpetual, autonomous government-controlled corporation to supply drinking water on a regular basis and make appropriate arrangements for the sewerage system. This Act, among others, also instituted a provision of the involvement of two women representatives to serve as members on its board of directors- perhaps, the first formal engagement of women in the higher level of a government-managed water organisation.

However, the other principal water policies- Water Resources Act (WRA) 1992, Water Resources Regulation (WRR) 1993 and Drinking Water Rules (DWR)1998 released after the NWSC Act 1989 (GoN, 1999), which dealt with provisions made about the use and control of water by the people of Nepal, were not found to be adequately covering women's role in the management of water resources.

Clauses 5 and 6 of the WRA (1992) talk about the formation of autonomous Water Users/Consumers Association for collective benefit on an institutional basis. However, these clauses do not lay down any minimum mandatory requirement for women's involvement while constituting such associations. Despite this gender insensitivity found in the WRA 1992, Rule 3 of both the WRR (1993) and DWR (1998) have made provision for two women in such consumers' associations which are provisioned with nine members. Given that women are the primary managers of the water resources as they traditionally carry out almost all water-related activities, especially those which are drinking water-related, the provision to include only two women in a nine-member committee was unlikely to make any significant impact on major decisions. Moreover, because the language in the provision is 'at least two women', there were hardly any WUCs in the government system that had more than two women as their members.

Because of the notions prevalent in most Nepali rural societies that women's priority is in the household and that they should not be involved in activities outside the home, that women are illiterate and thus not capable of making decisions, that men are superior to women so that the former should be in such associations, and that women lack the confidence to participate in such activities, the chances of more than two women being members of such associations is almost nil. Moreover, since none of these important policies mention penalty clauses for not including women in the consumers' associations and that no women's involvement has been made mandatory in any other subsequent activities – registration of the application, licensing, formation of committees at the district level, among others, it is possible that consumers' associations can be registered without women's involvement in them.

Though the WRA 1992, the WRR 1993 and DWR 1998 appear gender-neutral by using the word 'consumers'/users' association', they are implicitly gender-biased. The critical gap in these policy documents is the absence of a clear definition of how users are to be selected as representative members from within households, and whether a household identified as a legitimate user or consumer can be represented by one adult member or more. When the statement is not clear, it may be interpreted that any member of the household, normally assumed to be a man, can represent the needs of other members within the household. It fails to acknowledge the well-researched reality that men and women within a household have different needs and constraints and are not necessarily homogeneous. Another underlying assumption of these policy documents is that the household should be represented by the head of the household which, in the majority of cases, is the man.

The other gender bias seen in Nepal's legislation was in the formation of the District Water Resources Committee (Rule 8 of WRR 1993) and of the Water Resources Utilisation Conflict Resolution Committee (Rule 28 of WRR 1993 and Rule 23 of DWR 1998). These committees are formed, respectively, to issue licenses for the utilisation of water resources and to resolve conflicts, if any, in the water resources claimed by any consumer association. Even though women are more knowledgeable than men in activities related to domestic water resources, none of these rules sought women's specific representation in such committees. Though it could not be assumed that women's representation in such committees could protect the interests of women of all categories, it could be expected that their presence, as against the presence of only men, could be more favourable for other women as they understand women's problems and needs better than men.

An even more serious gap in the DWR 1998 can be seen in Rule 38 which describes the formation of Service Charge Fixation Committees consisting of five members. Rule 38 does not mention that the committee should have both women and men as its members. It is clear, as mentioned above, that women, more than men, can better evaluate the women users' economic status and their ability to pay for the water services since they have gone, in one way or another, through the same experience. This rule lists several factors to be considered while fixing the charge for the water services; but, none of the factors is related directly to women. There is no mention in this rule of important factors such as: who in the household is responsible for the payment of water services, whether the local women have any income-earning opportunities, whether the local women have access to and control over resources - all related to the payment of the water tariff and women's strategic gender needs. The presence of women in the committee can answer these questions and can help achieve a more equitable charging system which could be helpful to improve the lives of rural women in general and hopefully of poor vulnerable women in particular. On the contrary, the men in such committees such as the Local Development Officers, VDC officials, the DWSO officials, hold the impression that because men are the breadwinners, they will be the ones to pay for the water services. Accordingly, they decide the amount of water tariff based on the earnings of the men. The Schedules 1-7 enclosed with the DWR 1998 that mostly talk about application procedures to be completed for registration of a consumer association to get water supply are equally gender-blind as none of these schedules mention even a single word about women.

National Plans: During the time of the research undertaken in 1997-2000, Nepal was in the middle of its Ninth Five-Year Development Plan (1997-2002). The sectoral policies are normally developed based on such long-term development plans. The Ninth Plan aimed to provide all Nepalese with water supply facilities of basic service level by the end of 2002. Several strategies were formulated to fulfil this objective (1998a).

Like the WRA 1992, WRR 1993 and DWR 1998, the Ninth Plan, which guided the development activities of the country, also did not specify a breakdown of roles by gender in its objectives, policies and strategies. Moreover, it used confusing terminologies such as "local communities" and "users" and nowhere in its activities did it mention why women together with men needed to be incorporated in the water supply processes. Despite the Ninth Plan's focus on underprivileged, minority groups and poorer communities and involvement of user groups in the operation and maintenance of the completed water schemes, it did not mention women's roles in whichever case. The Ninth Plan did have a separate section on women, with emphasis on three major components, mainstreaming women into national development, elimination of gender discrimination and women's empowerment. However, from the fact that the issue of women was dealt with separately and was not integrated into other sections, it can be surmised that the gender-weak sectoral activities will fail to produce gender-sensitive results, including those in the water sector. The gender-weak sectoral plans and policies cannot address gender issues at the time of implementing those policies and plans.

National Water Policy: Following the DWR 1998, Nepal formulated the National Water Supply Sector Policy (NWSSP) in 1998 (GoN, 1998b), focusing mainly on rural water supplies. This policy was a major shift in recognising women's pivotal role in the management of water resources since it had a separate section on Gender Equality and Service Development encouraging women's participation in all aspects of a water supply scheme. Nevertheless, this policy was still inadequate in ensuring gender integration in many aspects of the water sector. For instance, the NWSSP was silent about gender in general and women's role in particular in many sections, including strategic objectives, technology, water quality, and operation and maintenance. Despite the reality that the presence of only two women in a 9-to-13-member committee does not bring about any major change, this policy still had provisioned for only two women. Moreover, although in its strategy on "gender equality and service development" the NWSSP talked about social reforms and improving the present condition of women, it did not mention anywhere in its programme activities, strategic objectives and strategies how it aims to do so or if any gender training should be provided to the concerned staff for the same. The use of the so-called gender-neutral terminology like 'community' presuming that both women and men have the same concerns regarding water and sanitation was another flaw in the policy. This scenario simply indicated that gender was taken as an ad-hoc topic without any systematic backup to integrate it into the national policy.

> *A senior government official in Nepal remarked, without showing an understanding of women's various roles, that the drinking water sector should not expect much from women staff as they never have time to be serious on official matters. They do not want to go to the field and they do not want to stay after office hours. Even when they are in the office, half of their time goes in gossiping about their family matters. Despite this, he proudly said, the government has mentioned women here and there in the policy documents such as the Ninth Plan and the NWSSP and also made provision to include two women in the local water committees. In a sarcastic tone, he further said, "I wish I were a woman so that I could also have all the attention towards me." Similarly, a male VDC official said "how can one expect women to be in the planning and policymaking bodies since they have their brain under their feet", which meant they cannot do wise things as they have no brain in their head* (Regmi, 2000).

As Wakeman et. al (1996) note, Tanzania's National Water Policy 1991 included explicit statements about equal gender involvement in village water committees which led to outstanding socio-economic impacts of the water projects on women and children, with women having more time in their fields and for their children because they could influence the project design and implementation. Similarly, the national water policy of the Philippines made provisions for calling at least 5% of funds from international donors to support programmes that included mainstreaming gender concerns into development and this percentage was expected to increase to between 10 and 30% in the future. As a result of such gender-aware policies, the women from the central Philippine province of Capiz were so encouraged that 10 of them with help from two men built their own Ferro cement rainwater tank. In another project in the same province, women built a 10,000-litre water tank over seven days using a manual that conveyed necessary information. After the engineer approved it, the women were very proud, and at the same time, astounded that they could build a tank. "Now, they are saying, give us a manual on how to construct a house and we will." Levy's (1998) experience is also along the same lines.

Regarding the reasons for the lack of gender integration in national legislations, plans and policies formulated prior to 2000, some major reasons are as follows:

1. A lack of proper understanding among the national policy-makers about gender issues in rural water supplies;
2. A patriarchal structure that always considered men as the primary actors and breadwinners and women as simply the housewives;
3. The makers of legislation, policy and plans, in general, were virtually males who had a hidden attitude of maintaining male supremacy in the development sector, including the water sector. On top of this, there was a tendency to label the water sector as the 'technical sector suitable only for men' resulting in parents' reservation to not send their daughters to study civil engineering and this will be discussed in Chapter VI.

About the composition of Nepal's parliament which formulates the Acts and legislations, the situation before 2000 was as follows: 8 (4%) women were elected in the first parliamentary election in 1991, 7 (3%) women in the second election in 1994 and 12 (6%) women in the third election in 1999, out of a total of 205 members in the parliament. In the case of the Upper House also, the situation was the same with three women holding 5% and eight women holding 13% of the total 60 seats in 1994 and 1999 respectively. Though it was made mandatory in the Upper House that at least five per cent of the total seats should be for women, there was no such provision made in the Lower House. Because the political parties were least bothered about promoting the political participation of women, they did not propose more than five per cent women candidates, which was the minimum constitutional requirement, in all three general elections of the Lower House. In fact, the five per cent reservation for women was no reservation in any valid sense, because this reservation demanded political parties to propose five per cent of their total candidates to be women in the election. But it did not guarantee or demand the same number to be elected in the parliament. The tendency of the political parties had thus been that they proposed women candidates in areas where they knew they would lose. This showed the male parliamentarians' hidden attitude towards continuing to hold their control on the legislation-making bodies. Had there been an adequate representation of women in the parliament it was likely that the constitutional requirement, of proposing only five per cent women in the general election, would have been challenged.

In Nordic countries, where women's status is much better than in many other countries in the world, women occupied an average of 36% of seats in the parliament. Even in Sri Lanka and India, where the status of women is better than Nepal, a quarter of seats and one-third of seats were occupied by women in the parliament, respectively (Samath, 1998). These experiences reinforce the argument that the higher the women's representation in the parliament, the greater are the chances of the country's legislation to be gender-focused. As per Regmi (2000), though it was difficult for Nepalese women to contest elections and to increase their representation in the legislation-making body, given their literacy rate of only 35% (HMG, 2002) and their lack of access to the parental property, or even to that of their husband, except in some special circumstances, a mandatory provision to increase women's representation in the parliament could resolve the gaps disclosed in Nepal's legislations.

Regarding the access of the Nepalese girls and women to schools and resources, it was considerably low as discussed earlier in Chapter III and this scenario would not change until the government takes some bold steps to change it, thereby achieving women's increased participation in the parliament.

> *One of the women focus group participants in Gajedi village in the Tarai of west Nepal said, 'I wish I could send my two daughters to school so that they did not have to go through the same pain that I have gone through. Because I am not educated my husband always tells me that I can never talk wisely. I know why he is saying this. It is all because he can read and write and talk with outsiders when it is necessary. He is proud of the fact that we are surviving because of the money he brings home. As a result, he thinks he can do anything and no one will say anything to him. Despite my request to send our daughters to school, he says that there is no point in spending money on daughters as they will go to their husbands' homes after marriage. All men in our community are like him. If I were literate and had some money, he would probably listen to me'.*

Similar experiences are reported by Aziz and Halvorson (1999) from their research in Pakistan. While the control over property could help women to overcome many socio-cultural barriers that men had imposed on them, the timely education of daughters could, in the long run, solve the problem of under-representation of women in all aspects of society including the parliament and the other law- and policymaking bodies.

As in the parliament, women's representation was notably low in the composition of the plan and policy implementing/ coordinating bodies like the VDC and District Development Committee (DDC) at the political level, and DWSO, DWSS, MHPP and NPC at the bureaucratic level. The VDC and the

DDC, which planned, implemented and coordinated programmes, including those for the water sector at the local and the district levels, were regulated by the then VDC Act 1991 and the DDC Act 1991, respectively (GoN, 1991). However, those Acts, formulated by the parliament which had limited women's representation as discussed earlier, provided for only limited political participation of women if they failed to be elected for VDC level and DDC level elections as can be seen in Tables 4 and 5. Acharya's (1994) findings confirm the limited chances women have in getting elected at these levels. For instance, there were 11 women chairpersons (0.27%) and 18 vice-chairpersons (0.45%) among 4,004 chairpersons and vice-chairpersons individually. As the members of the VDCs, there were altogether 210 women (0.58%) out of a total of 36,093 members. At the DDC level also, the findings of this research are in line with the findings of Acharya who reported that of the 75 chairpersons of the DDCs none was a woman. There was only one woman who served as vice-chairperson at the district level. As the members of the DDCs, only six women were elected while the figure for men was 924.

Table 4: Composition of VDC and VC by Study Site and Sex in 1997/1998

Research	Site	Motipur		Magaragadhi		Gajedi		Hile*	
		VDC	VC	VDC	VC	VDC	VC	VDC	VC
Male	Members	12	39	11	42	12	43	12	41
Female	Members	1	10	1	9	1	10	1	12

*Notes: *As Hile fell under Dhankuta Municipality, the VDC and the VC here should be understood as Dhankuta Municipality and Dhankuta Town Council (Regmi, 2000).*

Although another provision of the VDC Act could increase the chances of more women's representation at the VC level, the fact that VC did not have executive power unlike the VDC, the higher representation of women at this level made little sense. At the DC level, however, women's representation was even weaker than their representation at the VC level since this representation was subject to women's winning of elections for various positions at the VDC level. There was provision for one advisory committee at the VDC, to suggest activities to be implemented in the VDC, but again the chances of forming such a committee and of women being nominated to this committee were bleak as such nomination was not mandatory. Indeed, it was reported in all VDCs studied that such a committee was not formed.

Table 5: Composition of DDCs and DCs by Study Districts and Sex in 1997/1998

Members/	Districts	Bardiya		Rupandehi		Dhankuta	
		DDC	DC	DDC	DC	DDC	DC
Male	Members	13	77	20	167	14	90
Female	Members	2	2	1	1	1	3

Source: Regmi, 2000

The presence of 1-3 women at the VDC and the DDC, the executive bodies, as against the presence of 11-20 men, confirms women's limited power in influencing decisions made at these levels implying the gender blindness on the part of the people, mostly males during those times, who provided inputs to the drafting of the two important Acts- the VDC Act and the DDC Act. What could be inferred from such poor participation of women in the VDCs and DDCs is that the development activities, including those of water, initiated by these agencies would not meet the needs and concerns of the local women.

Similarly, at the district government level, the involvement of women in making plans and policies was nil. It was reported by the concerned government officials, at the time of this research, that there was only one-woman engineer in all of the 75 DWSOs in the entire country. As at the local and the district levels, the NPC, the highest-level body, which is mandated to consolidate national plans and programmes also never had women members since its formation in 1956 till 2000. Similarly, at the DWSS and the MHPP, there were only five women engineers. Because these five women were at different levels in the hierarchy, they could hardly contribute to the formulation of plans and policies. It could thus be concluded that the water projects planned, designed and implemented by these male technicians would have limited chances of meeting the genuine needs of women as can be witnessed in Chapters VII and VIII.

Donors' Influence on National Policies

The international agencies/donors play an effective role in shaping the national policies due to their financing power. Often the donor agencies demand their recipient governments and their partner organisations to adopt their policies and strategies. In fact, changes that take place amongst the international donors compel the national governments to adopt the same, because of the former's financing power. There are examples which demonstrate how the real commitment showed by donors in addressing gender issues compels recipient governments and other agencies to formulate gender-sensitive policies (ADB, 1998; Macdonald et al., 1997; Oxfam, 1997; World Bank, 1993).

Table 6 shows that every time that an event related to water took place at the international level, it impacted the water plans and policies in Nepal. The reasons are: as a member of the United Nations, it has to ensure its compliance with international policy instruments and as two-thirds of the national development budget is generally met by the international community, it has to follow the international norms. For example, the policy documents of some donors such as the ADB (1998) and the World Bank (1993) have provisions that they want national governments to design their water programmes by stating clearly the approaches that respond to demand, mechanisms to ensure full cost-recovery both in capital costs and operation and maintenance costs, and commitment to phase this policy in as soon as possible in their water projects. Accordingly, after the Dublin Conference in 1992, which emphasise water being treated as an economic good, the GoN and the NGO sector built in this provision in their policies and plans formulated thereafter (Regmi and Fawcett, 2000).

Table 6: Major Events in the Water Sector in Nepal in Relation to International Water Events, 1997/1998

International Level		National Level	
Year	**Event**	**Year**	**Event**
1975	UN Conference on Women declared 1976-1985 as Women's decade	1976	Equal Pay Legislation
1976-1978	Conferences held on the water sector during this period decide to declare 1981-1990 as IDWSSD; the limited role of women	1975-1980	No specific WID policy in the Fifth Development Plan (1975-1980)
1980	UN Mid-Decade Conference on Women demanded all governments involve in women in water supplies	1980	WID policy mentioned for the first time in the Sixth Development Plan

1982	Action-oriented Inter-Agency Task Force formed for fostering women's participation in activities of the IDWSSD	1985, 1986, 1989, 1989	Women's formal involvement in the water supply programmes by Helvetas, UNICEF, Nepal Red-Cross Society, and the government, respectively
1991	UN Convention on Elimination of All Forms of Discrimination Against Women	1992	WID policy included in sectoral programmes of the Eighth Development Plan (1992-1997),
1992 1992-1998	Dublin Conference on Water followed by several conferences emphasising women's role in the water sector; Various other water-related international conferences held supporting demand-driven approach	1992 1993 1997 1998	Formulation of Water Resources Act; Formulation of Water Resources Regulations; Gender issues addressed in the Ninth Development Plan (1997-2002) A separate section on GAD is included in National Water Supply Sector Policy.

Source: Regmi, 2000

The fact that changes in the water sector in Nepal have taken place after every major change had already taken place internationally confirms that external support agencies have ample opportunities to exert subtle pressure on the government because of their global experience and the weight of their financial backing. Hence, it is essential in cases of countries like Nepal that the funding to the government is made subject to the preparation of gender-sensitive plans, programmes and policies in the water sector as well as in other sectors. At the same time, national and international NGOs should also exert pressure by lobbying government delegates to pay attention to gender issues in the international fora.

❍❍❍

CHAPTER 6

Gender Mainstreaming in Water Agencies Prior to 2000

Mainstreaming gender in organisational policies and practices is essential to bring equality between women and men. As per the discussion made in Chapter II, the areas where the service sector institutions need to focus on mainstreaming gender in their policies and practices are policy formulating mechanisms (procedures and mechanisms for setting policies, rules, and norms); organisational goals, objectives, strategies, and activities; and personnel policies that include recruitment policy and working facilities and conditions. Equally important areas that the service sector institutions need to consider from a gender lens are organisational structure, organisational culture, gender training, adequate financial and appropriate human resources, space for change agents, and programme implementation and management. This chapter presents the gender status of the selected agencies in these areas. It is essential to mention that the institutional issues discussed in this chapter make little sense if treated in isolation from each other, while their consideration in a composite form gives a better picture of gender sensitivity in any organisation in terms of their commitment to meeting women's strategic gender needs along with their practical gender needs.

Policy Formulating Mechanisms

Concerning policy formulation, the process is as important as the outcome, and the more participatory the process, the better the experience of hammering out a policy and the result (Macdonald, 1994). In the case of any institution, how it sets out its policies and rules is a strong basis to find out whether the institution is committed to gender equality. If the institutional norms and procedures are formulated by involving both women and men taking into consideration the gender relations between them and appreciating that they have different needs and concerns, the implementation of those norms can help achieve gender equality. If the organisational objective is not gender equality backed up by gender-sensitive policies and practices, whatever it does in the name of women's wellbeing will only look like paying lip service to the cause.

Bangladesh Rural Advancement Committee (BRAC), a leading NGO in the development sector in the country, maintained a strong commitment to gender equity in its anti-poverty programmes which resulted in having over 700,000 members, of whom 70% were women; by 1995, women made up 85% of its total borrowers (Rao and Stuart, 1997 and Goetz, 1997a). However, as Goetz (1992) argues, even in institutions such as the BRAC and Grameen Bank which claim themselves to be gender-sensitive, the credit given to the women was non-proportional to their representation as members. Individually, women received credit in much smaller amounts than men, training was for low profit, sex-stereotyped activities, and unlike men, women's programme membership was made conditional on their acceptance of family planning measures. This could be due, in part, to the fact that the women staff turnover in BRAC was high, with women occupying about 25% in 1991/92, 16% in 1993 and 20% in 1996 of the total staff and the majority being in low (field-based) positions with almost no opportunities to provide meaningful inputs to the policy formulation; only four of BRAC's 20 senior managers were women (BRAC, 1997). It is, therefore, important to understand if gender equality is the objective of the organisation and whether the current norms and procedures have been well analysed and modified as relevant to meet the objective (DAC Sourcebook, 1998).

Hadjipateras (1996), with her experience of the international NGO ACORD, also argues that while the number of women on the staff as a whole is critical, female participation and representation at senior management levels is also critical, as is the commitment of all senior management to gender equity. In ACORD, some of the most ground-breaking programmes in terms of gender were those managed by female staff with a strong commitment to gender equity. Moser (1993) also comments that it is important to recruit women professionals into management positions for the institutional policies to be in favour of meeting gender needs. However, this will help local women only if such managers are gender-aware. Similarly, Hamerschlag and Reerink (1998) from their experience of a survey of 30 Inter-Action Member Agencies note that while some men demonstrated and incorporated gender sensitivity in their decision-making processes, it was mostly women who raised issues that were of particular concern to women. Further, both in the field and the headquarters, the organisation's gender work was greatly strengthened by recruiting and hiring women with a gender perspective into senior management positions.

Ironically, neither the policymaking bodies nor the bodies which made operating guidelines were gender-balanced in any of the three institutions studied in Nepal. In NEWAH, only one woman (as against six men) and in RWSSP, no woman (as against 10 men) was present in the policymaking body (executive committee in NEWAH and steering committee in RWSSP). In the case of FRWSSSP, there was only one woman each at the central level (as against seven men) and regional level (as against 11 men), and none at the district level (as against three men). Though there were four women in the General Council, the highest decision-making body, in NEWAH, it did not have much meaning since this body had delegated its authority to the executive committee, where there was only one woman. Similarly, in the bodies making operational guidelines - senior management team consisting of 11 members in NEWAH, an advisory body consisting of five members in RWSSP and the central project management team consisting of eight members in FRWSSSP - there was only one woman present in each of those three institutions.

Despite the commitment made by the senior staff of NEWAH and RWSSP that they would convince the Board in case of NEWAH and senior expatriates in case of RWSSP to change the scenario, no change was observed either in the executive body of NEWAH or in the project support unit (PSU) and district support unit (DSU) of the RWSSP. In fact, despite the commitment of the senior staff, NEWAH's new strategic plan for 1998-2002 was still silent about this matter (NEWAH, 1998). There was even less enthusiasm in FRWSSSP/DWSS towards increasing women's participation in the policymaking bodies at any level, either district, regional or central. Out of the five women engineers in the DWSS only two, one each at the 'second class' and 'first class' levels, had any chance of being involved in policy formulation meetings.

The possibility of the women staff, together with their male counterparts working at junior levels, generally making meaningful contributions to policy formulation in any of the three institutions, was also bleak due to the existing hierarchy. In RWSSP and FRWSSSP the junior staff had not attended any meetings for months while in NEWAH, they did attend some meetings which used to take place between the period of one to three months but these were only to inform the junior staff, mostly women, the decisions taken by the management, but not for consultations. Though the SMT of NEWAH said that the policy decisions are all kept in files and anyone could look at them, the junior staff, especially women, said that because the minutes were in the English language, they faced difficulties understanding them.

The above discussions show that the policy formulating mechanisms of the agencies under study did not appear to be gender-sensitive. The reason for this is that there was strong male domination in all three agencies leading to the involvement of more men than women in the policymaking bodies. Because of the presence of more men, most of whom were technicians, the men interviewed in these agencies put a lot more emphasis on the technical aspects of water supplies than on their social and gender aspects. It was completely ignored that while the emphasis on the technical aspects would ensure the supply of water, the emphasis on the social and gender aspects would ensure proper protection and maintenance of the water supply systems and regularity in the supply of water.

Though it is not inevitable that the provision of gender-sensitive policy formulating mechanisms will always lead to the betterment of women as it entirely depends upon how the policies are translated into action, experiences have shown that women's participation in policy formulation together with gender-sensitive efforts of the donors plays an important role in creating such an environment. For instance, the decision about hiring a gender consultant at NEWAH was initiated by WaterAid and it was only after this consultant joined NEWAH that the latter started implementing activities such as GAD training, GAD workshops, forming GAD poverty units etc. The efforts to recruit women technicians were also made after the comments from a team of expatriates from WaterAid/UK that came to evaluate NEWAH activities in early 1997. In RWSSP also, the decision about carrying out a gender study and increasing the number of women was suggested by the missions that came periodically from the FINNIDA Headquarters to evaluate the activities of both Phases I and II. The fact that the project documents of Phase III were more gender-sensitive than the other two phases was the result of these external suggestions, supplemented by the recommendations of a gender study by an expatriate. The situation was similar in FRWSSSP too.

> *A mission from the ADB/Manila recommended to the government that posts of women workers at DWSOs be created by rationalising positions within the organisation and existing budgets. The mission also advised that DWSS should improve the balance between women workers and engineering staff. The government confirmed that it saw the inclusion of women workers in DWSS as important and would ensure that DWSS complied with the Bank's recommendation as follows: i) complete the recruitment of 75 women workers to fill in the then-vacant positions by 31 July 1996, ii) draw up a programme to increase the number of women workers in DWSOs at a scale of 2 in every DWSO with one engineer and 4 in every DWSO with 3 or more engineers, iii) ensure that of the pool of 40 technicians to be maintained at the regional level effective October 1996, at least 25% would be women workers, and iv) draw up a programme of training of women workers commensurate with their recruitment (HMG, 1996a).*

Goals, Objectives, Strategies and Activities

Another area where the literature suggests that an organisation should be gender-aware is in its overall development goals, areas of work and the strategies that it adopts to fulfil those activities and goals. Most policy-makers tend to think that because their goals, areas of work and strategies are gender-neutral they can benefit both women and men equally. What these policy-makers, however, fail to realise is that because gender is a political issue as it is about power and also because it seeks to bring the private sphere into the public arena of debate and action (Macdonald, 1994), benefitting men and women equally needs added attention and effort. For example, the institutions, on the one hand, claim to benefit people by providing them certain services but on the other, they also expect the local people to contribute in cash or kind for those services without understanding the fact that women and men do not have the same level of access to and control over resources, and yet it is the women while talking of the water sector, who are expected to be meeting all kinds of costs if they needed the services.

The DAC Sourcebook (1998) mentions that many policy-makers assume that their work is gender-neutral and that it will have the same impact on all people. They do not, however, see the overlap between their objectives and inequalities between women and men. As per Macdonald (1994), project planning and implementation from a gender-based perspective should have only one ultimate goal of contributing to changing the balance of the sexual division of labour and resources to make it more equitable. This goal applies to various stages of the project cycle. Some others (Macdonald et al., 1997) further argue that once an organisation has accepted a move towards gender sensitivity and gender equality, it should have an array of strategies that it can deploy to carry this aim forward. From the literature, the objectives such as a shift in the gender division of labour, gender parity in staffing at all levels, and making the workplace and work style more women-friendly, and strategies such as gender-sensitive policies (programme, personnel, project etc.) have been found as those that an institution can develop to address the gender needs of both sexes at various levels, institution, project and community. GAD practitioners further argue that gender can be fully imbibed onto the formal agenda of the agencies only by making gender awareness a strategic objective along with a commitment for training on gender analysis to all staff and ensuring adequate resources for gender work.

May (1997) also states that it has become increasingly clear that poverty and social exclusion affect men and women differently, and interventions that do not reflect this difference have in many cases reinforced structural inequalities for women. As Mosse (1993) suggests, if those who plan projects and programmes were better able to understand women's gender interests, they would be in a much better position to ensure that their gender needs are met. In turn, Longwe (1991) recommends three points that the policy-makers need to consider while formulating gender-sensitive plans, programmes and objectives. They are as follows: women have different and special needs, women are a disadvantaged group in terms of their limited access to and control over resources, and women's development entails working towards increased equality and empowerment for women, relative to men. However, if agencies think of benefiting women by using gender-neutral words in their policies, objectives and strategies, and do not necessarily mention women as constituents, they are likely to fail at the objective despite their best intentions. Kabeer (1994a) also argues that the use of gender-neutral terms like 'members', 'communities' etc. in policy documents is usually misinterpreted to benefit only men.

One of the key assumptions underlying a GAD analysis is that women and men, because they have different gender roles and power, also have different gender interests. If the policy-makers understand this reality, they can design objectives that can help to meet the needs of both sexes. However, a review of the objectives and the strategies of NEWAH (1998), RWSSP (1996a & 1996b) and the FRWSSSP/DWSS of the HMG/Nepal (1996a), shows that all these institutions were concerned about meeting only the practical needs of women and men (the need for water) but not women's strategic gender needs. None of the agencies incorporated in their written objectives and strategies that they will aim for a reduction of women's labour, change in women's income, improvement in women's condition, etc. by involving them in the decision-making of project activities and providing them with opportunities to participate in various training programmes, among others. In turn, the project benefits are reaped more by men than women.

In RWSSP and FRWSSSP, they mentioned in their strategy that users from the community will form a WUC and the members of the WUC will be provided with the training. Taking undue advantage of these so-called gender-neutral terms, only one woman in the RWSSP and two women in the FRWSSSP were included in the WUC of 11 and 13 members respectively. Accordingly, more men received training in both cases as compared to women. There were many other examples similar to this in which women were deprived of or provided fewer opportunities compared to men - while selecting people for paid and unpaid positions while going on observation tours while giving skill-oriented training etc.

Amongst the three institutions studied, only the FRWSSSP briefly stated in its objectives that improving the quality of life and the living condition of children, women and men was its goal. However, because the other objectives and strategies of the institution did not coincide with this goal, it could be argued that this goal would only be partially fulfilled as seen in its water project implemented in Hile village.

The women in Hile drinking water project (FRWSSSP) had access to safe water near their home, still, there was no change in their quality of life and living conditions as expected. When the water had to be collected from a farther distance, the women were helped by men in this task. However, later, because the water was near the house the men expected more water to be available at home but had completely stopped fetching it. Moreover, due to the unviable location of tap-stands, women were obliged to carry water to their homes to perform their private ablutions, whilst they previously had privacy at the old water sources. This all had meant more burden on women's part (Regmi, 2000).

A couple of reasons can be attributed to the gender-unaware objectives and strategies of the selected agencies. They are:

1. The agencies' use of the gender-neutral terminologies (although they are not so in reality) like 'community', 'poor', 'people', etc. as a result of the same gender-unaware language used in donor and national water policy documents which the agencies considered as their guidelines.
2. The reluctance of the male bureaucrats and policy-makers to put the gender-sensitive ideas and policies in black and white since they were afraid of loosening their patriarchal grip on the whole system to continue maintaining a male-dominated culture in their institutions.

Personnel Policies

From a gender perspective, two important issues about the personnel policies of an institution involved in water supplies are important to be analysed. They are recruitment policy and working facilities for men and women employees.

Recruitment Policy: The recruitment policy of an institution is one of the major indicators of whether the institution is gender-aware and is committed to gender sensitivity in its activities. A review of the recruitment policy and the discussions with the senior staff of all three selected institutions showed that none of the institutions had a gender-sensitive recruitment policy. Normally, in all three agencies, employees were hired either through personal contact (through selected recommendations followed by interview) or through vacancy announcement (this was slightly different in DWSS where this could happen only when recruiting project staff but not the case of the regular employees for whom there was a separate mechanism). In NEWAH and RWSSP, the senior officials reported that the criteria they mostly used in an advertisement were: the minimum qualification of the applicants, their age, working areas, job responsibilities and a line such as "women are encouraged to apply" to attract women. After the applications were received, they were first sorted to make sure that they met all the minimum criteria set by the institution. Those who met the criteria were then interviewed by a team of senior staff, which usually meant male staff, as the numbers of women in senior positions were low in all cases. Such a recruitment procedure had several implications which are as follows:

1. When the same academic qualification is expected from both men and women, the women applicants are bound to be outnumbered by men as their number is much less than that of men in all fields in the market. In

such a situation, even the fillip "women are encouraged to apply", put by NEWAH and RWSSP did not appear to be more than lip service since the number of women applicants was much less than the male applicants in both the agencies. As Macdonald et al., (1997) note, public service might have a policy of equal opportunities and targets for numbers of female staff at professional or managerial levels but effectively exclude women from applying for jobs by setting gender-biased qualifying examinations. Macdonald (1994) suggests the inclusion of gender sensitivity as a criterion for recruitment and selection in all jobs instead of technical qualifications all the time since the gender-sensitive staff work towards a gender-sensitive programme. May (1997) further stresses that offices should struggle with the need to balance the numbers of women and men in the team at every level. Hamerschlag and Reerink (1998) also confirm that by including gender issues in interviews, job descriptions and performance reviews, organisations will attract and retain employees who are more likely to pursue gender-sensitive practices.

2. Because of their domestic responsibilities, girls start and finish their school and college education later than boys. Even at times when they start at the same age, the girls finish late as they often miss school and college since they have to help their parents, especially the mother, in household chores and also during the menstrual period due to the social taboo associated with it. When this fact is not considered, women always find themselves too old to apply for vacancies. Age restriction thus appears to be an important issue to be taken into consideration if the purpose is to encourage more women to join the formal sector/ institutions.

3. The advertisement which does not indicate what facilities men and women staff receive will always attract fewer women applicants as experienced by the selected agencies since women's needs and concerns are different from those of men due to society's expectations of women to be performing almost all household chores in addition to their official responsibilities. When there are fewer women staff, it not only affects the institutional objectives and strategies but also influences project implementation and the achievement of women's strategic gender needs. Macdonald et al. (1994 and 1997) stress that gender equality should be a priority not only in the organisation's mission statement, general objectives and policies but in its internal regulations (recruitment procedures, terms and conditions

for workers, etc.). Hence, to keep women in the institution, the agencies should clearly outline in their advertisements the facilities and conditions they offer, such as childcare, flexibility in working hours, maternity leave, openness to job sharing, part-time work, and working from home, based on the recognition of their responsibilities to their household as well as to their paid work.

4. An interview panel with more men will tend to select more men than women since it is no exaggeration that in general, men in Nepal tend to be less gender-sensitive than women because of the heavy influence of patriarchy that shapes and conditions their mind-sets. Men usually perceive the biological responsibilities of women as the latter's personal problem. Further, men also tend to think that men are suitable for technical jobs and women for 'software' jobs such as health and sanitation, administration, etc. The higher number of male staff in all selected institutions and a majority of women in the health and administration sectors confirm this argument (Regmi, 2000). Such gender insensitivity seen in recruitment also affects the conditions of service and the criteria set for promotions, which put women in a disadvantaged position. As pointed out by Longwe (1995), the lack of seriousness seen in these aspects indicates an institution's willingness to maintain the tradition of male domination, male culture and that of a male club atmosphere.

Working Facilities and Conditions: Working facilities offered by an institution determine whether it can attract and retain its employees, especially women, as they have to share their time in the household, community and office. As Hamerschlag and Reerink (1998) put forward, family-friendly work policies enable workers - both women and men - to balance their work and family responsibilities more easily. Since women are often the primary caregivers in families, providing family-friendly work options often has a greater impact on women, enabling them to take on more senior-level positions in an organisation without negatively affecting their ability to care for their families. NEWAH, RWSSP and FRWSSSP had offered several facilities to their men and women employees at different levels. Among the three institutions, NEWAH had a greater number of appropriate facilities for its employees than the other two. Aside from the various facilities provided to both sexes, it also provided paternity leave of seven days for its men employees. Though, in general, the NEWAH employees were happy with the types of facilities and conditions that were being provided to them, it still had not addressed women's issues such as an increase in maternity leave, provision for some additional expenses to meet the cost of helpers hired by women staff to look after their small children while undertaking field work, and allowing the women who were on maternity leave to use their accumulated annual and sick leaves from the previous year since they were not getting these facilities despite their request to the management to consider it.

RWSSP, funded by FINNIDA, a bi-lateral agency, also had some appropriate facilities for its men and women employees but it was startling to learn that the RWSSP did not even provide maternity leave for its women employees and crematory leave for its men employees though both were common facilities provided in almost all, national and international, institutions working in Nepal. This was the reason why there were fewer women staff in the RWSSP than the other two and there were only two women applicants as against 38 men applicants for the post of District Support Advisor in 1998 (Regmi, 2000). The junior women staff also complained that when there was a gender study carried out by a foreign consultant they were not consulted. All these issues showed the lack of attention of the senior officials as well as the management of RWSSP in understanding gender concerns.

In FRWSSSP, the staff were provided with facilities in accordance with the *Nizamati Sewa Niyamawali* (Civil Service Regulations). Aside from various leaves offered to both women and men employees, women got maternity leave of 60 days (twice in their working period) and the men employees received crematory leave of 15 days. The married women employees were also allowed to use the crematory leave if their husbands were using it. Regarding the placement of the employees also, the government had a provision that if both the husband and the wife were in the civil service, they should be placed in the same area as possible (HMG/ Nepal, 1996b). Similarly, as stated in the Gazette (HMG/ Nepal, 1998c), there were different age barriers for men and women to apply for different posts at the government service, but in the case of women who had been working in government service temporarily for a consecutive period of five years, there was no age barrier to be a candidate. This was not, however, the case with men. The probation period was also in favour of women as it was only six months for them while it was one year for men. Likewise, the government had set a certain number of years to be served by men and women employees to be a candidate for promotion. However, here also, the women employees were considered for promotion even if their service period was one year less than the minimum criterion; this though was not the case with men employees.

Despite such facilities, one of the major issues related directly to the situation of women employees of the FRWSSSP/ government service concerned the age of retirement which was the same for women and men. Given the fact that Nepalese women, in general, start their careers later than men due to their delay in starting school and completing their studies, their age of retirement needs to be different from that of men. Similarly, the other substantial bias seen in the government agency was related to the attitude of the senior officials about not sending women water supply and sanitation technicians (WSST) to the field, presuming that they are not capable of doing the necessary technical work. Since there are several examples from different countries (van Wijk-Sijbesma, 1998 and 1985; Fong et al., 1996; Baden, 1993; Bilqis et al., 1991) showing women successfully undertaking the role of maintenance workers, such attitudes of the male officers towards women's ability simply indicated their interest in maintaining a male culture of undermining women.

Another point which emerged from the research was that the senior officials of all three institutions had shown considerable understanding to women employees by being flexible in working hours, for matters like going to the field when they were pregnant or breast-feeding their child and fulfilling household chores etc., taking into account women's triple roles. However, it is an irony that nothing had been written about it. The problem with a verbal understanding is that as an institution grows bigger and there is a substantial increase in the number of women employees, such understanding may not continue to exist among the senior staff, for various administrative and managerial reasons.

> *One junior female member of staff had to return to the office within 22 days of her delivery in RWSSP, which was rare in the Nepalese context. As a result, she had to ask her other family members to bottle-feed the child as she could not come to breastfeed the baby herself though it was essential for a new-born baby. Some others in NEWAH and the FRWSSSP had to resign as their maternity leave was not adequate for them and they could not take extra leave, as they were temporary staff (Regmi, 2000).*

The reasons that came out for the insensitivity in the personnel policies as discussed above are:

1. Lack of understanding of the senior male policy-makers about women's biological needs and concerns and how addressing them could help achieve gender equality;
2. Lack of seriousness about the contribution that women could make in meeting the agencies' GAD objectives;
3. Men's biased attitude against women that the latter should always be subordinated by putting them in a lower profile; and
4. Lack of political will and commitment on the part of male decision-makers to introduce gender-transformative activities, including affirmative action and positive discrimination, to change the work environment which is historically established to be in favour of men.

Organisational Structure

The gender ratio between women and men employees and the types of work they are assigned is a strong indicator showing an organisation's willingness and commitment towards engendering itself. To understand the current situation and facilitate changes, it is important to know who holds what position within the institution. Women are most often placed in jobs that are related to women's reproductive functions - either biological or social. As a result, institutional activities fail to address the genuine concerns of women and men in a given community. As Goetz (1992) points out, women bureaucrats are to be found most often in institutions in the service sectors such as nursing, community care, nursery and primary education, involved in activities often modelled on an extension of women's domestic work. Further, unable to guarantee the same quantity of time and emotional and physical energies to the organisation as men can, women are penalised by exclusion from promotional opportunities, if not by exclusion from the working world altogether. On the other hand, experiences have shown that in many institutions, gender-specific policy concerns such as child care, equal pay, maternity benefits etc., which determine the retention of women in the organisations, have been voiced mainly by women policy-makers.

Hence, the literature on institutional studies recommends increasing the number of women staff members in general and in senior positions in particular, along with the provision of a number of facilities that are necessary to retain them. For example, because of the high turnover among women staff, BRAC introduced a policy of three months' maternity leave and six days' special leave a year for women. It adapted the organisational culture to the participation of women, made efforts to increase women's presence in the organisation and their participation in decision-making, and facilitated their physical adjustments to the demands of the workplace and their role within it (Rao and Stuart, 1997; Goetz, 1997a and 1997b). However, what is also important is that the institutions do not make just ad-hoc changes to address women's needs without paying attention to formalise those proposed changes. Otherwise, it can lead to many negative situations. As Macdonald et al. (1997) argue, if an organisation waits until one of its workers becomes pregnant before it works out a policy and procedures for maternity/paternity leave, it will probably already have lost many valuable potential women because it has made no provision in the case of its workers becoming pregnant. Alternatively, women working in the organisation may either avoid becoming pregnant until they are ready to leave or leave if they become pregnant.

From her experience of ACORD programmes in Gao (Mali) and Gulu (Uganda), Hadjipateras (1998) notes that a programme in Gao, with virtually all-male staff, was very resistant to the gender policy, while in Gulu, where the programme was headed by a woman for many years with equal numbers of male and female staff, the programme was proactive in adopting a gender policy confirming that commitment on the part of staff to integrating gender into institutional activities is positively associated with the level of female representation and their seniority. On the contrary, the numbers of women employed in the three institutions studied were disappointing. There were only 17% women (22 out of 128 staff) in NEWAH, 8% women (5 out of 64 staff) in RWSSP and 14% women (21 out of 146 staff) in FRWSSSP (including RPMO, CPMO and all permanent and temporary staff at DWSO), indicating an imbalance in gender ratio in all of the three institutions. The other gender issue of concern was that none of the selected institutions was able to break the traditional gender division of labour among its men and women employees since men were seen mostly in the technical positions while women in 'software' roles i.e. health and sanitation. There was only one female technician (overseer) against nearly 25 male technicians in NEWAH, no female technician as against eight men technicians in RWSSP (DDC) and five female engineers and six overseers as against thousands of male engineers and technicians in the DWSS.

As Goetz (1992) remarks, according to feminist institutional analysis, the under-representation of women serves as an obstacle to the institutionalisation of WID/GAD concerns. Macdonald (1994) further argues that agencies need not just more women staff but more gender-aware women in senior positions and more women (and men) experienced in gender work at all levels. May (1997) also adds that unless there are gender-aware women and men in senior posts, awareness of gender issues in an organisation will be slower to develop. From their other experiences, Macdonald et al. (1997) also note that the only guarantee of gender sensitivity in the organisation is the presence of a significant number of women, constituting a critical mass, and among whom are strong, gender-sensitive women, who are committed to women's empowerment and gender equality. They further write that according to the UN, such a critical mass threshold is 30 to 35% of the organisation's staff. Once this threshold has been attained a process of change becomes self-sustaining. This process will speed up considerably if women are not only present at top management levels but are also committed to gender equality. The experiences of Novib and NCOS are some cases in point. Their affirmative action policies contributed to a strong increase in women at middle and higher management levels - 12% in 1991 to 40% in 1996 in the case of Novib and 12.5% to 50% in the case of NCOS. Staff reported that as a result, gender considerations were placed at the core of the organisation's management.

In the case of the selected agencies, although the number of female staff was increasing over the years in NEWAH, it did not mention this commitment under its strategy on "conditions of employment" in its strategic plan 1998-2002. Moreover, although NEWAH had attempted to recruit men to the post of health supervisor, which used to be exclusively women's sphere of activities, it was also important that they made efforts to hire women in the male-dominated technical positions or else, women would get left out even from the health sector. In the case of the RWSSP (including Phase III) and FRWSSSP also, it was hard to envisage that there would be a substantial increase in the number of women engineers and technicians, given the opinion of the senior officials that they could not commit to any special consideration for women over men if the former could not compete with the latter. With such an attitude of the selected agencies, it can be said that they cannot attract the limited number of women technicians being produced by Engineering Colleges. Regmi (2000) reports a case in point as presented in Table 7.

Table 7: Numbers of Boy and Girl Students Applying for Civil Engineering Courses at the Nepal Engineering Campus in 1997 and 1998

Number of Students	1997/98			1998/99		
	Boys	Girls	Total	Boys	Girls	Total
Applicants	856	108	964	1261	203	1464
Entrance Test Passers	282	27	309	875	154	1029
Actual Enrollers	92	8	100	131	13	144

Source: Regmi (2000)

Given the necessity of more women engineers to work in sectors such as drinking water for it to be effective in sustaining benefits to people and their small number receiving an opportunity to study this subject, with 8 girls against 92 boys in 1997/98 and 13 girls against 131 boys in 1998/99, the following issues need to be given further attention:

1. expansion of the civil engineering course by the government so that both the boy and the girl applicants passing the entrance test could study this subject,
2. preference to girl students if there was only a marginal difference in their performance as compared with that of boy students unless the government could absorb all the girl applicants passing the entrance test. This required an increase in the quota of 10% allocated at the time of research to girl students passing the entrance test to 33% as has been proposed in the electoral posts to redress the historical imbalance.

In general, because of the limited supply of women engineers and their high demand, they had better choices of joining the employment institutions that they preferred. If institutions like NEWAH, RWSSP and FRWSSSP offered good facilities to women employees, created an environment where women could feel comfortable and secure, and assured them that women have at least the same career opportunities as men, they could attract more women technicians. Berger (1984) and INSTRAW News (1997) offer several recommendations, including preparing a career guide for women technicians in this regard, so that women could be attracted to work in technical positions. Kardam (1989) reports a case of the Ford Foundation where inclusion of a gender policy in development was accepted as a major agency goal, with 6% of agency funds to be directed to women's programmes in the mid-1980s. However, this shift in agency priorities did not occur until women staff became the majority (53.2%) of agency employees.

In the case of the selected agencies, several reasons came out for a gender imbalance in their staffing structure: i) there were only a few women in senior posts meaning men were the principal decision-makers who preferred to select more men over women as they thought they could get more work done by men than by women whose performance was considered to be affected by their biological limitations; ii) the male senior staff believed that water sector being technical was appropriate for men as against women, who were best placed in health and sanitation-related work; iii) the senior management were holding the view that if women could compete with men they had equal opportunities to join their agencies; iv) the lack of emphasis put by the donors on their policy documents since the selected agencies viewed their donors as their role model (Regmi, 2000).

These discussions raise the question of whether it is essential that the institutions working in the water sector, where women's role is central, specify in their policy documents that a certain number or proportion of their staff will be women so that they provide scholarships to encourage the girl students to study civil engineering. A condition tag that such institutions may attach to the scholarships is that the latter will have to work with the agency for a number of years - perhaps three to five. It is also essential that such women, once hired, are immediately given on-the-job training so that they feel competent to work together with their male colleagues. These discussions conclude that among the various issues that need proper attention to translate gender-related policy matters into action, one concerns the need for a sizeable number of women in the institutions working in the water sector. Also important are the issues of women's adequate representation in senior positions and the necessity for a change in the tendency of recruiting only women for work in the soft sector and men for the technical sector.

Organisational Culture

While analysing the institutional aspects from a gender perspective, the literature on institutional studies further emphasises looking at the culture of an organisation. As per Macdonald et al. (1997), organisational culture is the personality of an organisation; if the organisation's structure can be thought of as its body, its personality or soul is the way people deal with each other and the values and beliefs that are dominant. Organisational culture determines the conventions and unwritten rules of the organisation, its norms of cooperation and conflict, and its channels for exerting influence. They further report that there are in general five categories of obstacles that most organisations face: ignorance or misunderstanding of what gender is about, cultural resistance by partners and donors' reluctance to question that resistance, gaps between rhetoric and real practice, the slowness of change, and women with less power.

Similarly, Nicky May in Alan Fowler's book (1997) reports two categories of obstacles, covert and overt, to a gender-fair organisational culture. The covert obstacles include: assuming that women are best for support roles, applying male norms for everyone, treating female authority as something to be marginalised, disrespect for femininity etc. The overt obstacles include too few women in positions of authority, tokenism where women are assigned mainly to administrative and secretarial jobs, defensive action for arguing that biases against women are an inviolable part of the culture, the majority of women in low paid positions, working hours and facilities not matching with the various roles that women play in the household and the office, etc. Nevertheless, May also suggests some steps to overcome those obstacles: starting a process of diagnostic analysis, introducing frameworks and tools for gender analysis, identifying prejudices between men and women staff, developing a friendly organisational culture, introducing training, identifying outside allies who can support the direction of change and inside staff that can play the role of change agents, etc. DAC Sourcebook (1998) also suggests that the informal and formal rules that guide the functioning of institutions are important. A policy that aims to change people's work priorities, to incorporate equality considerations, stands little chance of being effective if the policy is generally not respected. The factors that might increase the likelihood of the successful integration of equality considerations include flexibility and openness to new ideas in general, willingness to change and incorporate from diverse constituencies, accountability structures within the institution to ensure that staff comply with policy directions, and recognition and value given to a wide range of professional skills.

Informal norms that reflect the organisational culture determine whether the formal rules and procedures related to gender issues will be adopted. Wakeman et al. (1996) note, if the employees are open, they might be positive towards applying new ideas, but, if they are not, they will be resistant to the testing of the new ideas. An organisation may have formal rules that promote gender issues, but in practice, informally, staff remain sceptical and discourage those who wish to work in this area. In such a situation, the pressure from an outside group can be effective. For example, if an institution wants to be seen as credible or even as a leader in the field, its staff will start developing a positive organisational culture. In general, most development institutions are dominated by men. Hence, the working hours, facilities, norms for field visits etc. are all set as per the men's behaviour. Goetz (1997a & 1997b)) observes that the everyday aspects of the way organisations structure their work is a feature of their culture; they will be reflected in performance criteria, rewarding people who flourish within the physical and social boundaries of the organisation. Rao and Stuart (1997), with their experience of research, carried out with some profit corporations in the USA, reveal that one set of characteristics and behaviour that was unconsciously valued in these organisations was heroism and the features that describe this are mostly in favour of men.

> *In all institutions studied, someone who will stay at the office working for long hours when a report is due, who can respond to an emergency and solve the problem, is labelled as a "hero". Since a woman cannot be this person given her triple roles, this so-called 'hero' in the organisation is always a 'man'. His work is noticed, he is given a high profile, and feels valued and is promoted. On the other hand, skills such as preventing crises, building relationships, coordinating, thinking in advance, and helping things to move smoothly, where women have particular strengths, are all invisible. As a result, women do not see any space for them in such institutions and thus either they do not join, or they quit once they find another institution in which they feel more comfortable (Rao and Stuart, 1997).*

Chigudu (1997) notes that an organisational culture helps to create standards of what is acceptable and what is not. In general, mainstream management models are patriarchal and eliminate respect for individuals, flexibility and differences. In comparison, a 'feminist' culture can be characterised as challenging the idea of patriarchal control although, in this culture, everybody would feel needed and respected, with their talents used and recognised. Macdonald et al. (1997) also write that every organisation should introduce some practical strategies that are friendly to women. Such strategies can involve a fair distribution of power and authority between the women and men employees, reorganising working hours to allow workers to attend to family responsibilities, formulation of policies on maternity and paternity leave, childcare facilities on-site, and proper planning which gives adequate notice of field trips. Though many organisations have already given attention to some of these issues they are still, too often, on an ad-hoc basis rather than as a part of institutional policy. This is dangerous as it increases the chances for the organisation of losing out on women staff.

What comes out from these discussions regarding the indicators of organisational culture that are relevant to gender are understanding of gender concepts both of the women and men employees; conducive physical environment for women; men employees' attitudes towards women employees; opportunities provided to women to express their concerns/ideas; the extent of consultation that takes place between the management and the other employees, both women and men; the way staff greet each other; the career opportunities that both women and men employees have in the institution; and the respect that is shown by the women and men employees on the institutional policies etc.

In all three agencies, it was reported by the women interviewed that they felt less powerful than their male counterparts working at the same level. They had the impression that because they had to be absent from the office from time to time because of their reproductive roles, and as their number was small, leading, of course, to their negligible representation at the policymaking level, the management, which was, of course, male-dominated, listened more to the male staff than to themselves. This fact was implicitly supported by the male staff as well, as most of them had the attitude that they were more useful for the institution and also more effective than their female counterparts since they were ready to serve the institution at any time, unlike the female staff. This situation not only indicated a lack of trust on the part of the women employees towards the management but also the lack of understanding of women's additional roles and responsibilities among the male staff and the management, which is a negative factor in institutionalising gender aspects. Macdonald et al. (1997) write that a people-friendly organisation should take account of women's reproductive roles and plan them into its structure, administration and physical arrangements. Every organisation must recognise that women have public, as well as private lives, and the events in one, affect their role in the other.

Also, about other factors that might indicate the gender sensitivity of an organisation's culture such as the types of work that men and women are involved in, the value given to women's perspectives and the opportunities that women have to express their interests etc. (Goetz 1995 in Macdonald et al., 1997), none of the three agencies had a positive organisational culture as almost all women were in the 'software' sectors and at lower levels though NEWAH was making some efforts both to bring women into the technical sectors as well as into the senior levels and to introduce men into the health sector. In terms of opportunities for women to express their feelings, the female staff at NEWAH had more possibilities than their counterparts in RWSSP and the FRWSSSP. Concerning the staff's level of understanding of gender issues in the development sector in general and in water supplies in particular, which is another significant determinant of the culture of an organisation working in social development, it was found to be poor among the majority of the staff of all the institutions studied; this was more marked at FRWSSSP and less so at NEWAH. Even among the staff who had heard of gender issues in these agencies, their understanding was limited only to the fact that gender referred to women's issues. Out of the many staff interviewed in these agencies only three people (2 women and 1 man) at NEWAH and two people each at RWSSP and FRWSSSP (1 woman and 1 man in each) appreciated women's involvement as a means to their empowerment. Some others thought that women can get involved in some income-generating activities in the time saved from water hauling which can bring many positive changes in the household, but again, they were not clear how women could do so since none of the agencies had such provisions and there were very few such opportunities available locally, especially for women, in the rural areas of Nepal.

An equally important determinant of the culture of an organisation, about gender, is whether it is willing to change in terms of gender equality. If a majority of the staff in the organisation are willing for this kind of change, the change becomes an institutional goal and it can be achieved in a relatively short period. On the other hand, if the need for such a change is felt by only a handful of people, especially women, then institutional change is either impossible or takes a long time. From her experience with ACORD's programme in Gulu and Gao, Hadjipateras (1998) notes that because gender objectives were accepted as a collective staff responsibility in Gulu, a gender committee comprising representatives of all programme components was formed and thus, the gender awareness of the staff here was much higher than that of the staff in Gao, where a woman's officer post was created to take on chief responsibility for gender with little support from the rest of the staff.

In NEWAH, a majority of the staff were seen to be in favour of a change, which led to the undertaking of several gender-related activities, such as gender workshops, gender training, review of the strategic plan from a gender perspective, gender-sensitive project implementation procedures and personnel policy, the establishment of GAP units, and implementation of some pilot projects with a focus on GAP. However, a certain level of fear was also observed among some male staff regarding how the change would affect them in terms of the power and the facilities that they were enjoying. In FRWSSSP and to a lesser degree in RWSSP, gender had been taken as a token by a majority of the staff and hence these organisations were not keen on a rapid change in the present working style. The senior management in RWSSP was evidently not prepared for this kind of change as they could not decide whether they would introduce even such basic facilities like maternity leave for women and crematory leave for men in their organisation. Both in RWSSP and FRWSSSP, the concern was more centred on completing the projects and less so on women's empowerment (though the second and the third phases of RWSSP appeared to have addressed women's issues more than the first one, as could be seen from the project documents). Nonetheless, some staff working in the FRWSSSP were slightly more positive about gender issues than those working in the main government structure as was noticed from their curiosity in knowing how their activities could be made more gender-sensitive. This positive attitude was the result of their close interaction with the consultant teams, which was, however, not as distinct in the case of the staff working in the main structure of the DWSS.

The provision for separate lavatories, childcare and transportation facilities for all women staff regardless of their seniority etc. is another determinant of the organisational culture. However, the lack of these provisions for women staff in the selected agencies indicated that they did not have a culture where differentials between men and women were thoroughly considered. Similarly, the roles and behaviour of the women and men staff expressed while having lunch, greeting each other, participating in meetings etc., are also relevant determinants of the organisational culture. The relationship between the senior and junior staff was formal and official in the FRWSSSP, where everything was done based on one's position in the organisational hierarchy. On the contrary, the staff at NEWAH seemed very friendly with each other, as they were observed having lunch together and making jokes about each other. The situation in RWSSP was rather different, as the people in the management were expatriates and hence there existed a different kind of relationship between them and the Nepali staff. While the senior staff were observed to be relatively friendlier with the management, a large gap existed with the lower staff. Even amongst the senior staff, the male staff members had a closer relationship with the RWSSP management than the only senior female staff member.

The management style (participatory vs. top-down) of an institution is also a determinant of its culture. Because NEWAH was following a participatory approach in the implementation of its water supplies, there were more interactions between the senior staff and the lower staff resulting in more women staff, including senior positions, formation of GAP units with both men and women as their members, more facilities for women etc. In the case of RWSSP and FRWSSSP, because the practices were still guided by a blueprint approach (though not on paper), there were fewer interactions between the senior staff and the junior staff- the junior staff had not attended any meetings for months, there were fewer women staff in general and in policymaking bodies in particular, etc. All of this had led the women staff in RWSSP and FRWSSSP to experience more problems in terms of the lack of various facilities when contrasted with those enjoyed by the women staff in NEWAH. This was obvious in FRWSSSP where the management was keen to recruit women more as temporary staff than as permanent staff.

The possible reasons for the lack of gender-sensitive objectives in both cases were: the organisational environment had historically been in favour of men resulting in the small numbers of women staff and male senior staff's inability to see the connection between the women-friendly culture and the presence of more women and positive project results.

Gender Training

The provision of gender training for people involved at all levels in an institution - policymaking, projects, and communities - is another gender-related issue. Gender training is important both to raise awareness of the issues and to provide concepts and techniques for programme staff. Citing her experience of gender training in ACORD's London Secretariat, Hadjipateras (1997) notes that such training conducted using tools of gender analysis such as the Harvard Framework helps to reveal subtle forms of gender discrimination and can help improve and potentially transform gender relations not only within the office but also in programme activities. Moser (1993) suggests three types of training for this purpose: gender analysis training, gender planning training, and gender dynamics training; each of these should have one or more of the following four objectives: sensitisation or awareness-raising, skill transfer in gender analysis and diagnosis, translation of skills into planning practice, and motivational factors. Likewise, drawing on her experience with Oxfam and several other institutions, May (1997) further argues that such training should be provided to all employees as well as to men and women from the project communities since it can build up confidence in all parties and help them realise the importance of each other's role in development efforts. Such training is useful but its impact is sufficiently reduced if only a few male individuals are trained.

Many other authors, based on their experiences with several organisations, also suggest that training on gender should first be given to the people in senior positions so that the institutional objectives, strategies, policies, norms, procedures etc., which all are formulated by these people, can address gender concerns and inequalities. The next step is then to provide gender training to the people implementing the projects so that they can address all gender concerns that can otherwise affect the success of the project in terms of meeting both the practical and strategic gender needs of women. And, finally, provision should be made for gender training for women and men in the project communities. Such training should include the cases where women have successfully built, maintained, and managed water supply systems as site caretakers, maintenance workers, construction workers, treasurers, committee members and chairpersons etc. Moreover, the agencies also need to ensure that they create a favourable environment for use of the skills acquired by their staff so that the new skills do not become a waste in the long run (Levy, 1998; Macdonald, 1994; IRC, 1991; Poluha et al., 1990 in Baden, 1993; SIDA, 1990; ADB, 1990; and PROWWESS/ UNDP, 1988).

For women to participate in such training, whether it is on gender or other related topics, careful attention, however, needs to be paid to the venue and the timing of the training so that they are convenient for women. As Hannan-Andersson (1990) and Baden (1993) confirm: "many women have been bypassed in terms of human resource development in water supply and sanitation because of the timing and location of training and due to biases in the selection of candidates. A carefully planned gender analysis, on the other hand, can help to understand the burden of women's activities, the kind of training programmes appropriate for women and men in the community, and the time they can spare to participate in the training. In order to be effective, training programmes should use a variety of methods to sustain the attention and involvement of participants. For example, in a five-day training programme in Nepal organised for female sanitation volunteers, the methods included posters, non-directive questioning, short walks in the locality, role plays, demonstrations, street theatre, puppet shows etc. These methods not only helped to attract more women to come to the training but also to retain them throughout the training period (Morgan, 1992 in Baden, 1993).

Some key issues that emerge for extra attention from the above discussions are the frequency of training (one-off or regular), contents of the training (whether poverty is a focus since it is a major gender issue); types of training - formal, in the form of workshop or meeting, or group discussions or orientation; beneficiaries of the training – policy-makers, senior staff, men or women or both, project staff, project beneficiaries - women and/or men; duration of the training; timing of the training; credibility of the people providing the training; and availability of financial and human resources regularly for the training.

In the case of the selected agencies, only six staff, four females and two males, at NEWAH had received training on gender issues. In January 1999, a five-day-long gender workshop (the first in NEWAH's history) was organised by NEWAH for its senior staff (6 women and 12 men) and a week-long training of future trainers on gender was held for its 31 staff (7 women and 24 men) in June 1999. Even though the donors of the selected agencies such as WaterAid had mentioned several capacity-building activities for its staff and partner agencies in its strategic plan, gender was not on the list. Cleaver and Jobes (1996) note that despite its acknowledged importance, FINNIDA's in-house training programme had been severely curtailed and was no longer obligatory for all staff due to budget constraints, although it remained so for field staff. The lack of emphasis given by the donors on gender training in their organisations and policy documents led, in turn, the selected agencies not to make any long-term resource commitment for gender training. This resulted in a situation where even when these agencies wanted to organise some gender training for their staff, they did not have the adequate funds for it. The lack of a definite plan and policy on gender training led to difficulty on the part of the staff to be able to look at their activities critically. They had the feeling that the way they were implementing water projects had no better alternative. Their understanding of 'development' was limited to making water available near people's homes, but without much focus on what it meant in terms of changing women's and men's lives by meeting their strategic gender needs. The lack of a plan for gender training had also blocked institutional learning in terms of systematising gender-related experiences, critical review of the work culture of their institution and the realisation that they have a long way to go in engendering their institution if the ultimate goal is sustainable development.

These discussions reveal that the main reasons for the lack of planning for gender training in the selected agencies are: the small number of women in general and in decision-making positions in particular, lack of seriousness about gender issues among the senior men staff in management positions, lack of ability to judge the positive impact of the GAD work that could be undertaken after the gender training, lack of ability to understand that women and men in the project communities have different needs and concerns and thus cannot be addressed with one single approach, the general notion that men can easily represent women and their needs and problems and the lack of focus on donors' policy documents on this matter.

Resource Commitment

Financial and human resources: In most development institutions, budgets for gender-related activities are either nil or very small though they may talk about bringing gender equality between women and men. As a result, the institutions end up doing virtually nothing about addressing gender issues at any level. As Wakeman et al. (1996) note, resources are key to implementing policy. Without appropriate resources, little can be accomplished. Budgets for WID/GAD activities have often been small, notwithstanding rhetoric that might suggest otherwise. This kind of double standard can be seen even in international institutions like the UN which write and talk so much about gender equality. For example, the development agencies of the UN - the system which sponsored the Women's Decade (1975-85) - allocated just 0.2% of their overall budget to projects which benefit women. Similarly, less than one per cent of FAO projects specified strategies to reach women farmers (Goetz, 1992).

Hadjipateras (1997) reports that most of the problems observed during her review of gender work in ACORD were compounded by the lack of resources for the promotion of gender work. The two factors that she thus stressed for the implementation of an effective gender plan in ACORD were the need for the strong commitment of its staff and the provision of adequate resources. Macdonald et al. (1997) also emphasise, based on their experience of reviewing several Eurostep member agencies, that to create the scope for gender-sensitive organisational development in any organisation, real support for change and dialogue about gender requires real resources, and budgeting is most often the point at which the rhetoric of equality is put to the test. Whether the management of an agency and its donors, if any, are prepared to commit sufficient funds and support for a long-term change process in all organisational activities is key to the effective implementation of GAD activities in the institution.

Similarly, the human resources available to deal with GAD issues are usually inadequate in many development institutions. As Wakeman et al. (1996) write, in many agencies most staff working on these issues are not regular agency staff but consultants, lacking the authority, access and continuity that regular staff have. GAD positions have often been at a junior level. Macdonald et al. (1997) also report, based on their experience with many Eurostep member agencies, that the people that were so-called gender persons did not have real power to push on this issue in the organisation. As a result, the gender issue was not only side-lined in their own organisations but also in the institutions that they were funding. Hence, they recommend that if any institution is committed to gender activities it must nominate a senior person to take on this role and this person must have both the personal commitment and enough power to fight for it.

Among the three institutions, NEWAH had more money available for GAD activities through various sources though it had not allocated any funds for this activity in its annual budget. WaterAid/UK had allocated £15,000 for various training activities for NEWAH in 1998/1999; WaterAid/Nepal had a budget of £7,500 for local consultants, half of which was for gender and socio-economic studies; NEWAH also had access to £5,300 allocated by the PAR/IRC project for dissemination of the project outcome which could also have been used for gender training within the GAP unit and other GAD activities as was reported by the senior staff. Similarly NEWAH could have used some funds from a relatively big project that it was going to sign with the DfID for GAD activities. In addition to all this, NEWAH could also use part of its regular budget which was £630,889 (£445,760 from WaterAid and £185,129 from DfID) for 1998/99 for GAD activities (NEWAH, Project Summary for 1998/99 by Region and personal communication). Despite all these funds, only £3,200 (0.5% of the total NEWAH budget) was used on GAD activities - a gender sensitisation workshop and training of trainers on gender, both in 1999.

In the case of RWSSP, the total cost of the project was Finnish Mark (FM) 50.53 million in Phase I and FM 17.42 million and Nepali Rs. 58 million in Phase

II. Out of FM 50.53 million in Phase I, FM 0.85 million was allocated for human resource development, but, not even a single mark of this budget component was spent on any GAD related activities. Unfortunately, in Phase II, this component was not even mentioned either in the main budget sheet or in the year-wise work plan. The only activity that was directly related to GAD, carried out by the RWSSP with support from its donor (FINNIDA), was the undertaking of a GAD study of the project areas by a Finnish Consultant in 1997. In the project document prepared for Phase III, provision was made for a separate component on GAD with a specific budget. This component also included the cost of a gender specialist and training on GAD for all concerned individuals including the staff from the partner organisations such as government, NGOs etc.

Similarly, in the case of FRWSSSP, the project had a total budget of US$ 26 million over five years (1997-2002), out of which $19 million (73%) had been allocated for hardware/water supply and sanitation, $6 million (23%) for 'institutional strengthening' through consultants, and $1 million (4%) for software/ community awareness and education programme (CAEP). The CAEP included activities such as WUC training, project management training, village maintenance workers training, health and sanitation training etc., but not any GAD activity. Under the institutional strengthening budget of US$ 6 million, only US$ 0.25 million had been allowed for social components. A review of the breakdown of this amount showed that only US$ 0.02 million (8%) had been allocated for training such as health and sanitation training, teachers' training, WUC training etc., but not on gender training.

The main reasons for not using even the budget available for gender training by all three agencies studied were: lack of a clear understanding about gender issues in the water and sanitation sector and lack of seriousness compounded by the male senior staff's biased attitudes to work on GAD activities.

Regarding the provision of human resources to look after gender works, none of the selected agencies had been serious on this matter though this need was felt much earlier by NEWAH than RWSSP and FRWSSSP. The staff at NEWAH were also of the opinion that instead of employing a separate gender specialist, the organisation should rather provide gender training to all the staff and integrate a gender approach in all their activities. Though this seemed to be a good idea in the long run, the danger with this approach was that in the absence of a person with specific responsibilities on gender issues and a strategy explaining how gender gets integrated into the organisational activities, the

GAD activities might lose focus as was what happened in NEWAH where the staff had not been able to do much even with the GAP units. The other reason for this danger is that when all are made responsible for one activity it turns out to be no one's responsibility in the long run, as it ceases to be anyone's priority.

In RWSSP, though funded by FINNIDA, which was considered to be relatively better aware of gender issues, there was no one to ensure gender sensitivity in their work either in Phase I or Phase II. Accordingly, even if the project documents demanded that there should be two women in a local WUC, water supplies were implemented even with only one or without any woman in the WUCs. For example, the WUC of Belbhariya (Gajedi), where the field work of the research was undertaken, had only one woman member. In the other eight WUCs in the Gajedi VDC, only two had women (one had one woman and the other had two women). It was reported by the RWSSP DSU staff that this was common in other WUCs too. Because this weakness was also pointed out by the FINNIDA evaluation team and the gender consultant who carried out a gender study in the project area, the provision for a gender specialist was made in Phase III.

In FRWSSSP, a consultant team of five people had been hired to undertake work on social components which though had only a partial focus on GAD activities. The discussions with some of the consultant team members revealed that it was difficult for them to inject the importance of social and gender dimensions into the minds of the government staff, mostly engineers and overseers, who thought the water sector needs technical minds, not social or gender minds. In turn, even the sociologists, who were hired to give continuity to the consultant team's work on gender once they completed their involvement in the project, did not get adequate support from within the team to continue the gender work. One of the main reasons for the inability of the sociologists to mobilise support from the technical staff was their limited power and authority since most of them were on temporary contracts. Nevertheless, the DWSS officials thought that the fourth project had addressed gender issues more seriously than the first three sector projects.

As Jahan (1995) and Hadjipateras (1997) note, the lack of resources leads to agencies' failure to promote gender work including an increase in the number of women staff members, implementation of gender-sensitive policies etc. They, along with Macdonald et al. (1997), further argue that the type of human resources, especially the consultants used for social and GAD activities is also part of the problem, as they often lack authority, access and continuity, unlike the regular staff. As Cleaver and Jobes (1996) note, in the presence of a gender unit or a gender person, there is a risk that staff may not involve in gender work saying that 'it is not their department'. Conversely, a system whereby all individuals are made responsible for gender policy implementation may result in no one being accountable. It would, therefore, seem important to institutionalise an accountable gender strategy. Hence, Hamerschlag and Reerink (1998) from a survey of 30 InterAction Member Agencies including ADRA, Save the Children, and Oxfam America, suggest that though there is a debate about which kind of structure is most effective, institutional experiences indicate that it is important and necessary to adopt both strategies. By including both a separate gender officer or unit as well as a specialised gender person in each department, organisations will be more successful in mainstreaming gender equity concerns.

The key issues that appear, therefore, from the above discussions are the need for allocating adequate financial resources specifying that they are for GAD activities, including allowances for the field staff who have to work with local people, including women, that takes longer time, and making provision for appropriate human resources who are permanent staff, with authority and power, and who can push gender onto the agenda of the agencies. An equally important issue concerns developing a vision for integrating gender in all institutional activities in the long run backed up by a provision of an adequate budget. This is more relevant in the case of agencies that are funded by donors since the guidance provided to integrate gender into agency activities by the latter does not mean anything if there is no increase in funding at the same time.

Role of Change Agents

Change agents are those who are willing to assist and can be instrumental in bringing about reforms in terms of gender in an institution. According to Macdonald et al. (1997), such change agents need three things: modest aims and ambitions since changing the personality - the soul - of an organisation can be a very difficult and painful process; an understanding of the organisational culture to find out clues on how it can be changed; and flexibility in strategy, to determine which among the following three, persuasion, pressure and 'win-win', works best. These authors describe three types of change agents in an institution, the lone pioneer, the fighter, and the player. Depending on the gender status of the organisation, such as gender-blind (the ones that reinforce biases in favour of existing gender relations and therefore, tend to exclude women), gender-aware (the ones which recognise both women and men as active partners and beneficiaries in the development process) or gender-redistributive (the ones that intend to transform the existing power imbalances between women and men to a more balanced relationship by focusing on strategic gender needs and interests), these change agents can initiate different strategies.

The people, known as change agents, will have different roles to play and different effects depending on where they are located and what kind of person they are. These might involve putting gender on the agenda by explaining facts and figures; holding arguments based on ideology and values; building planning, monitoring and evaluation systems, and mechanisms for learning and accountability; and promoting innovative practices. The authors further say that the change agents thus need to find people inside the organisation, and outside if necessary, with whom to work on building consensus around the issue. The people external to the organisation could be friendly consultants or trainers, but they need to be people who know the organisation well.

In NEWAH it was more the Director, a male, and the three senior women staff working in the health section who were keen to see gender-related changes. They were the staff members who had been raising gender issues in official meetings. One example concerned the transportation problem faced by women staff to and from the office. This issue, along with other issues concerning women, while raised by the senior female staff, was supported more by the Director who was the most instrumental person in supporting GAD activities due to the power he had. The women, on the other hand, felt uncomfortable while raising their issues themselves instead of some men raising the same for them. In this regard, the NEWAH Director thought that gender change is a gradual process and it would take time to change the attitude of the male staff. He wanted to formulate the GAD policies without antagonising the male staff but rather convincing and motivating them to be supportive.

In RWSSP, it was the male institutional advisor and the female health advisor who saw themselves as change agents in terms of introducing GAD activities. Even between these two, the role of the institutional advisor was more crucial as he was involved in the preparation of project documents and writing reports. In the meetings, it was the female health advisor who raised GAD issues, normally supported by the institutional advisor; the other senior male staff were not, however, so keen on this matter. Consequently, these two still had difficulty in increasing the presence of more women in the PSU and DSU team and the WUCs, organising gender training for staff, hiring a gender person, etc. The main reason was that the RWSSP, being a bi-lateral project had expatriates in the management playing key roles in making major decisions; unfortunately, these expatriates were not so concerned about gender issues, including the lack of provision of maternity and crematory leave despite these being continuously raised by the two Nepali advisors.

Contrary to the situation of NEWAH and RWSSP, no change agents were observed and their presence was not reported in FRWSSSP. The relatively young male officers, especially those working at the CPMO, RPMO and the DWSO, and the female staff, were positive about gender issues, as they said, 'one major reason for the failure of more projects implemented by the government than those run by NGOs was the lack of attention towards gender aspects in the projects.' However, because they were located lower in the hierarchy, they were not in a position to influence policy matters nor even to raise gender issues, as they did not have any suitable forum for this. Hence, gender continued to be an issue of little concern in the FRWSSSP, among all staff, unless and until there came more pressure from its international donors - ADB, the World Bank - and national pressure from NGOs (e.g. NEWAH), and women's groups. Following the classification of Macdonald et al. (1997), the change agents in NEWAH and RWSSP could be termed as 'players' as opposed to 'lone pioneer' or 'fighter' - as they were diplomatic and pragmatic and trying to build alliances and strategies both with the staff and the management, and were negotiating gender policies not just for the benefits of one group of people but for the overall organisation.

One major issue that emerged from the above discussions is that the higher the level of the 'supposed to be change agents' the greater is the possibility of addressing gender concerns in the agency. As Hamerschlag and Reerink (1998) comment, the literature as well as member agency experiences affirm that for principles of gender equity to be fully integrated into an organisation's programme and policies, there must be support from the leadership and the senior management particularly the chief executive officer.

Conclusion

To conclude the review of institutional policies and practices, it should be noted that all the institutional issues discussed in this section are complementary to each other and none of them on its own will succeed in making an institution gender-sensitive. There can be provision for gender training for the employees, but if there is no change in the organisational structure and culture, making them more conducive to women, the training alone may not be able to make any major change. Hence, the need is to look at all institutional activities in totality when the purpose is to engender the agency for achieving a society with equality between women and men. It does not, however, mean that if an agency is not in a situation to address all these issues together it should not address any. The message is rather that in such a situation the impact will be limited as against the impact that can be seen when all issues are properly addressed.

The learning that has come out regarding the relevance of the institutional framework suggested earlier in this book taking into account the analysis made in this chapter are that: the use of the institutional framework that consisted of eight useful indicators discussed above has given a good understanding of the gender issues at the institutional level of the selected agencies. Hence, this framework can be recommended when carrying out a similar type of gender analysis at the institutional level. Nevertheless, one critical issue that has come out from the analysis of those indicators is related to the degree of 'power' that women and men staff were able to exercise in the agency and the reasons why they had different degrees of power. Because this power came from various sources, such as the nature of the job (technical or social) of women and men staff, positions held by them in the organisational hierarchy, their levels of income, presence of peer groups to support them, etc., which are strong determinants of respect that one receives from the others, this appears to be the crux of women's and men's empowerment at the institutional level. Hence, the author feels that instead of addressing the issue of power under several other indicators, where it might get mixed up with other issues and thus might lose its essence, this issue of power should be dealt with as a separate indicator while carrying out a gender analysis of any agency.

Similarly, the analysis made in this chapter also highlights one other important indicator that shapes the gender sensitivity in any agency which is its relationship with various national and international agencies. Recognising the importance of this issue, it was dealt with mainly under two indicators, policy formulating mechanisms, and objectives and strategies. However, given the fact that more than two-thirds of the development budget in Nepal comes through external donors, and all NGOs and INGOs need to work under the government policy in any sector, including that of water, it appears that the national government agencies and international donors play a crucial role in shaping the policy of any agency working together with them. The donors' influence is even more evident in the water sector where all agencies, including the governmental ones, rely heavily on external funding. As a result, the emphasis put by these national and international agencies on gender aspects and their relationships with the implementing organisations, such as the ones selected for this research, can determine the priority that the latter gives to gender aspects in their policies and practices. Hence, it appears that agencies' external relationships should be treated as a separate indicator at the institutional level while examining gender issues at the agency level.

All of this means that the institutional framework followed in guiding this research should now be expanded for its future use as follows:

1. policy formulating mechanisms,
2. objectives and strategies,
3. personnel policies,
4. organisational structure,
5. organisational culture and management style,
6. provision of gender training,
7. provision of human and capital resources,
8. role of change agents,
9. sharing of power between women and men staff, and
10. relationships with external agencies.

CHAPTER 7

Gender Mainstreaming in Water Projects Prior to 2000

This chapter analyses the efforts made by the selected agencies to mainstream gender in various project activities during the late '90s with a belief that the higher the integration of gender lens in project activities the greater the possibility of the success of the project in terms of meeting women's practical as well as strategic gender needs.

Almost from the beginning of its operation in Nepal, NEWAH used participatory rural approaches or PRA techniques while carrying out its pre-feasibility/feasibility and detailed surveys. Most of its staff were trained in PRA techniques. In RWSSP, though the participatory approach was said to have been adopted in Phase I (1990-95), the fact that this was implemented by DWSO staff, who did not have any background in using PRA techniques at that time, led to their overlooking the importance of involving local people, especially women, in project activities. In the FRWSSSP, a participatory approach, under the name of Rapid Assessment Procedures (RAP), was in use since the Third ADB funded project. It was reported that the DWSS ran nearly 100 projects every year and it was, therefore, impossible for the agency to look after the operation and maintenance aspects of so many projects, due to limited time and other resources. Hence, the reason for adopting the participatory approach was that the government wanted the local community to take up responsibility for the completed projects. However, because the RAP technique is rather rapid, with more focus on the collection of information than on the process, there is always a risk that the local women are bypassed by the project activities, because of the notion that it is time-consuming to work with women for reasons such as their illiteracy, lack of experience, restrictions to come out of home etc. Considering the varying experiences of the selected agencies in their application of the participatory approach, the following sections describe the process followed and the outcomes achieved by those agencies while implementing their drinking water projects.

Pre-construction Phase

This section analyses the major steps followed by the selected agencies during the pre-construction phase of their water projects studied from a gender perspective.

Request for Water: Local women were not involved while finalising the request for water in any of the three institutions, as all the local people contacting and visiting the concerned authorities in these agencies and signing the applications were males. Yet, the requests were considered for follow up activities instead of being sent back with a message that women too should be involved in these stages. As a result, it became common for the local people and the project staff to overlook the presence of women in various project activities in the later stages as well. One of the main reasons for this situation was the lack of clarity provided in the project cycle management procedures about how gender sensitivity could be achieved at this stage of the project. In a patriarchal society such as the one in Nepal, institutions involved in the WASH sector need to make extra efforts and introduce several activities to help men understand the contribution that women can make in this sector; this does not happen overnight. The other reason was that the decision whether to act upon the request was made based on the technical aspects with little or no attention given to the social or the gender dimensions of the project such as what changes will the water project bring into the lives of men and women, will it change the gender division of labour since water will be more easily accessible, will men and women have more income-earning opportunities from this project etc. all of which have direct relevance in changing the lives of people, especially women, and the effectiveness of the project.

Since this step is the beginning of the interaction between the local community and a drinking water project, this is the best time to encourage the local men to realise the importance of women in water supplies. Similarly, the other advantage of involving women right from the beginning is that this would enable them to get more clarity about the procedures to be followed in getting the water project, the purpose of the project, and the requirements, formalities and responsibilities to be fulfilled both by the local women and men during and after the project is done etc. This will not only help to raise women's confidence to actively participate in the project activities throughout and to organise themselves for putting out requests to other agencies for development assistance but also to avoid any confusion and conflict with regard to whether the project can meet the needs and concerns of both women and men.

Selection of Implementing NGOs: In Nepal, the use of local NGOs in implementing development activities on behalf of INGOs, donors or government departments has become a common phenomenon. The understanding is that since such NGOs are locally based, they can understand the local people and their practices better than outsiders, and hence, can help to implement all stages of the project activities effectively. As explained by Fong et al. (1996), NGOs can act as partners to mobilise local communities. Projects can often take advantage of the presence of existing NGOs that have expertise and experience in working with the local women in the project area and can thereby help project staff in reaching out to them. Accordingly, the involvement of NGOs was given high priority both in NEWAH and RWSSP Phase II, on the assumption that it will enable active community participation and help to sustain the project. The FRWSSSP was also thinking along these lines. The agencies had developed several selection criteria such as having relevant experience in the drinking water and sanitation sector and community development, being locally based, being registered with the government etc., but gender dimensions such as the gender balance in staffing, experience in gender work, the presence of people who have received gender training etc., were not considered as relevant criteria.

As a result, the tendency of local NGOs to bypass women in project activities seemed high. In the case of NEWAH projects, the NGOs played a dominant role in the selection of women to the PMC, in sharing financial matters with the women PMC members, in leading the discussion in meetings etc. Conversely, even in two years from the time the project was started, women were not empowered in a real sense, as will be discussed in greater detail in the next chapter. The reasons for the NGOs' oversight in using a gender lens in the project activities are i) the lack of awareness on gender issues in water supplies since the NGO staff had not received any formal training to get an understanding of gender issues in any sector, including the water sector; ii) the NGO members thought that they could represent other people on their own, including the women in the community resulting in the lesser attention of the project staff to mobilise the latter; iii) the lack of confidence in their skills and abilities due to the lack of prior experience of involvement in such project works;

iv) the sweeping influence of the project staff, who were not aware of gender issues in the water sector, in all activities, led the NGOs to be dependent on the former.

Fong et al. (1996) argue that it is not safe to assume that an NGO is by definition gender-sensitive. Care will be required in determining which NGOs can facilitate greater gender balance in programmes and projects, taking into account such information as their overall track record on gender. Macdonald (1994) also notes that the choice of partners is influenced by the extent to which the partner organisation is committed to changing the existing balance of power between women and men in favour of women. As an alternative, the lead agencies can also provide gender training to the local NGOs before working with them. For example, highlighting the role of NGOs in the implementation of development projects, a report prepared by Shtrii Shakti (1995) suggests that the concerned institutions should raise people's awareness in support of NGOs on improving gender relations so that the projects can be more effective in meeting the requirements of women as well as those of men.

Hence, institutions focused on the WASH sector must include a gender dimension as one criterion while selecting NGOs so that their projects address gender inequalities while meeting practical needs. The gender dimension can include information such as the organisational background of the local NGOs, the composition of membership, number of men and women staff, organisational objectives that include gender equality, commitment towards improving the status of women, employment of people with exposure to gender issues or at least to women's issues, willingness to participate in women's development activities etc.

Feasibility Study and Detailed Survey: This is one of the most important steps in the management of a project cycle, as the fate of the project is decided in this phase. The types of information collected at this stage, the people involved in collecting information, the time spent doing this survey, among others, are all critical to making the project effective. However, in all cases, more in RWSSP and FRWSSSP and less so in NEWAH, these aspects were given inadequate attention. The project documents showed a greater focus on technical information than on social dimensions. The only social information emphasised in the documents was that concerning health and sanitation. There was no attempt to identify the target group - men and/or women, the caste and class of the target group, the gender relations in the target community, women's role in activities related to the proposed project and their access to and control over relevant resources, nor to define strategies to integrate gender concerns and to identify people participating in and benefiting from the project etc. May (1997) notes that institutions should have a policy framework, with a requirement to place gender analysis centrally in design and evaluation. Others also have highlighted the importance of gender analysis before implementing water supply activities (Fong et al., 1996).

Gender analysis was, however, lacking in the work of all three institutions, as the field staff were contacting men for technical information and women for health and sanitation information. Among the three institutions, NEWAH was more concerned about involving women in the technical meetings and men in the social meetings. Nevertheless, even in NEWAH, the lack of gender analysis, especially concerning information about the access to and control over different resources in the household and the community, affected the projects in various ways and this section will be dealt with in greater detail in Chapter VIII. Green and Baden (1994a) also confirm that gender blindness caused by the lack of gender analysis at the project planning stage is difficult to rectify later since this will carry through into project objectives, design, implementation, management, monitoring and evaluation.

Another important aspect concerning the feasibility study and the detailed survey concerns the sex of the staff carrying out the preliminary work. The project cycle guidelines of all institutions mentioned that the feasibility study and the detailed survey will be carried out by a team consisting of several persons. However, there was no mentioning of whether the team should include women.

Unfortunately, it is clear that when women are not mentioned, men usually constitute such teams. For example, both in RWSSP and FRWSSSP, the people who were involved in doing the feasibility study and the detailed surveys were men. When only men are involved, there is a danger that while holding meetings they may not follow the correct processes which could increase women's participation. On the other hand, women surveyors can be more sensitive than men about where, when and how such meetings are to be conducted. For example, the number of women present in various meetings in RWSSP and FRWSSSP was much lower than in NEWAH (Regmi, 2000). Because women have several responsibilities to fulfil, they cannot attend meetings that are held far from their homes and at times that are not convenient for them. van Wijk-Sijbesma (1985) also stresses the presence of women in such survey teams to work with women from the target population. Alternatively, a gender specialist of either sex can also be included in such teams. As May (1997) argues, the presence of a gender specialist in any team conducting research and analysis can ensure more accurate knowledge of the different needs and interests of the population to be served. Further, even when meetings are held close to women's homes and at an appropriate time, they may not still be able to express themselves if they are not allowed to sit at the front and are encouraged to express their views. Female project staff are known to display greater sensitivity about these issues than male project staff and utilising this aspect can yield positive project results.

In the case of NEWAH, because the survey team consisted of both men and women, the factors such as venue and timing of meetings and the seating arrangement were all considered by the project staff and this led to the presence of relatively more women at meetings than in the case of RWSSP and FRWSSSP. These women were reported to be more vocal than women from the other two projects. As a result, in NEWAH projects, PMCs consisted mainly of women and more women were given the position of caretakers. Moreover, even illiterate local people, especially women, did not have any problem in participating in the information generation process; both in Motipur and Magaragadhi, more women participated in this process than men. On the other hand, in the case of the RWSSP, the WUC included only two women initially and later, only one, and in the case of FRWSSSP, no women initially and only two women later, since no woman was involved in the survey team in either case. There were also no women selected initially for the position of caretakers in the RWSSP village and no women were selected at all for the position of village maintenance workers (VMWs) in the case of FRWSSSP. The process of empowering women was completely overlooked in both the RWSSP and FRWSSSP (Regmi, 2000). Many other studies also support the need for the presence of women in survey teams to increase local women's involvement in the planning stage (Hadjipateras, 1997; WASH, 1990a and 1990b in Baden, 1993; van Wijk-Sijbesma, 1985). Highlighting the need for women's presence in the survey team Moser (1993) also comments that in many societies, unless women speak, data will only reflect men's view of the world. Therefore, a precondition of gender diagnosis is the involvement of women researchers in data collection.

The length of time spent by the survey team in carrying out the feasibility study and the detailed survey in the project community is another important factor to determine whether the project can be gender-sensitive in its implementation. The time spent by the project team was 9-13 days to cover the whole VDC, in the case of NEWAH; 3-5 days in the case of RWSSP; and less than a week in each phase of feasibility, detailed survey and appraisal in case of FRWSSSP. Given the area covered by these agencies, the dispersed settlement pattern that required more time to contact the households, and the social and cultural factors that constrained women from coming out easily from their homes, it could be said that the time spent was not adequate to explore gender issues, including an investigation of people's willingness to pay for services, which is crucial to the effectiveness of water supplies.

During the survey period, the project staff informed the communities of the criteria to be met by them to have water supplies in their communities, but no time was spent to analyse whether the people, especially women, were in a position to meet those criteria. In some cases, this was seen to make the local people's lives even more difficult than before. Similarly, several households in NEWAH projects and in RWSSP had to borrow money from others to meet the project criterion of contributing cash, which led them to work very hard to pay the money back. Such a requirement was met by the municipality in the case of the FRWSSSP, as not all people were in a position to contribute the required amount. Further, the lack of adequate time spent for social analysis also affected the operation and maintenance of tube-wells in NEWAH and RWSSP villages, as not all people in the community, especially the female-headed households, were in a position to pay the same amount of water tariff as others. This also created conflicts among the user households which halted the collection of the water tariff in both NEWAH projects and in the initial phase of the RWSSP leading to considerable uncertainty about the sustainability of benefits from the projects (Regmi, 2000).

These discussions confirm the importance of the three points raised at the beginning of this section that the agencies, such as NEWAH, RWSSP and FRWSSSP, engaged in water supplies need to include gender analysis as an essential component in their feasibility study, the survey team should comprise both women and men to increase women's participation, and adequate time should be spent to explore all relevant gender issues before implementing projects.

Selection of Technology and Location: All three institutions made use of pre-determined technologies and standardised tube-well/tap-stand and platform designs. The community, especially the women, who were the primary users of the tube-wells and tap-stands, had no inputs to offer at this stage as they were not consulted either about the appropriateness of the designs or the building of platforms. One complaint that was made by the women of NEWAH projects and of the RWSSP was that they had to bend their bodies more to the front while pumping the tube-wells which caused discomfort in their waist and back. This was mainly because they found the handle of the pump a little long for their height. Emphasizing women's involvement in the selection of appropriate technology, Fong et al. (1996) share that women from project areas in Bangladesh, Guinea-Bissau, Malawi and Tanzania have rejected some types of facilities, such as foot and hand pumps, because of the difficulties that certain users, such as children, pregnant women, and the old, had in operating them for activities such as bathing. As a result, users resorted to unsafe but easier-to-use water sources. DfID (1998) also argues that because the technology is used by women, they need to be involved in its selection – for instance, the height of taps and handles need to be suitable to women as they are the primary users.

Regarding the selection of locations of tube-wells and tap-stands also, the local women were not encouraged to contribute much in any of the selected projects. Among the three institutions, more women were involved in the case of NEWAH projects while deciding about the sites for tube-wells, but, the major role while deciding about the location was played by the women members of the local NGO in the case of Magaragadhi and the men members of the local NGO in the case of Motipur. In the case of the selected projects of RWSSP and FRWSSSP, the decision about the siting of tube-wells and tap-stands was made mainly by the WUC, composed mostly of men. The cluster-wise and area-wise meetings to solicit women's participation in this stage of project development, as described in the project cycle guidelines of these agencies, did not take place in their projects while making decisions about the siting of tube-wells and tap-stands. As a result, the tube-wells and tap-stands in all cases were built facing the roadside, giving limited scope for women to use them whenever they liked. Similarly, in NEWAH and RWSSP, the tube-wells were not located at the centre of the group of user households, requiring poor and disadvantaged women to walk further to fetch water. Such glaring lack of involvement of women in the crucial selection method of the location for tube-wells and tap-stands can eventually lead to the failure of the projects, as happened in Thailand, where women users did not pay attention towards the maintenance of hand pumps. Likewise, in Tanzania, the hand pumps dried up as they were located in places that women did not suggest (Fong et al., 1996).

Formation of PMC/WUC: The importance of involving women in the PMC/WUC, set up for local project management, seemed to have been understood more by NEWAH than by RWSSP and FRWSSSP. While NEWAH encouraged its project staff as well as the community to include a significant number of women in the PMC, RWSSP and FRWSSSP advised that at least two women should be included in the WUC. Accordingly, the PMCs formed initially in NEWAH projects had only women as their members while in the case of RWSSP there were two women initially, and only one afterwards, in a committee of 11 members; in FRWSSSP, there were no women initially and only two afterwards in a committee of 13 members. In both cases, because the instruction was to include at least two women, the projects did not include more than two in the PMCs thus clearly reflecting men's bias against the involvement of women in such committees.

In NEWAH's Magaragadhi project, because only women were included in the committee, they had difficulty in doing the required paperwork, organising the committee meetings, and keeping minutes of meetings and records of financial matters due to their lack of education, experience, and thereby, confidence. This led them to be heavily dependent on men advisory members, who were not always cooperative, as their interest was directed more towards the status derived from being part of the committee than being helpful. As a result, the WUC of Magaragadhi was reconstituted after about a year to include men in the committee. The same problems were felt by the women members of the WUC in Motipur and thus, they too were on the verge of reforming their committee. Because of these limitations of the committee women, the project staff were also found to have been consulting the men, advisory members, in both communities as well as the male NGO coordinator in Motipur to a greater extent than the women in the PMC. These factors did not help increase women's confidence.

In RWSSP and FRWSSSP, where there were only one and two women respectively in the WUCs, the women members were not able to contribute extensively to the project. From the discussions with the male WUC members and the project staff, it was understood that the women were included only as a token since without showing their names on the paper the staff could not proceed with the project activities. Accordingly, some men just randomly picked two women, unlike in NEWAH projects where a mass meeting, including a large number of women and men, was held to select the WUC members. Such a biased attitude against women was even higher in FRWSSSP, where the women were invited to only two committee meetings in the last 12 months. No woman was included in the sub-committee/working committee formed since all the members were only men. Though all these activities took place in the presence of the project staff they never advised the local men to include more women in those activities, as the staffers themselves did not acquire a proper gender orientation. This kind of poor representation of women seemed to be a common feature in many FRWSSSP projects, as reported by the project staff. The reasons provided for such weak participation of women were as follows:

1. given that the seniors would question the project staff for the delay in the completion of the project but not for the exclusion of women, the project staff didn't display sincerity towards the latter since they thought the process of involving women would delay the project completion; and
2. the project staff did not have any incentive/ allowances for staying longer in the field site and so they did not bother about involving women which on the contrary, could have increased the chances of prolonging their stay in the field.

Because the lack of women's involvement can lead to many disadvantages to the users, especially women, as they are the main actors in water supplies, Hadjipateras (1997), Fong et al. (1996) and van Wijk-Sijbesma (1985), with their experiences of various countries, strongly support the presence of as many women and men as possible while forming the water committees. They also stress that such committees are better if their composition is mixed, with equal numbers of women and men since it can give women and men a good opportunity to accurately understand each other's roles and functions in water supplies and the overall development of the community. Similarly, although the project documents of all three institutions stressed the need for appropriate ethnic and geographic representation in the PMC/WUC, these two factors were considered only while selecting men but not women. Further, when women were selected to be in the PMC/WUC they tended to be from relatively wealthier sections in the community. Moreover, the selection process was not as democratic as was required in project guidelines. In the case of the NEWAH projects, the local NGO played a key role in selecting women. In the case of the RWSSP the local leaders, who were, of course, men, decided which women should be in the WUC and in the case of the FRWSSSP the selections of both men and women were based on more political criteria. In no case were the project staff able to protect the interests of women in general and poor vulnerable women in particular.

Regarding the involvement of women of all categories in terms of ethnicity, age, socio-economic status etc. the project staff of all agencies disclosed with frustration that it was not possible to look for all women's higher participation in the project activities unless there was a change in present project management practices. They said the time and the resources (both human and capital) that were presently allocated to complete the projects were not enough even for a non-gender approach. If the projects were to be planned, designed and implemented, and managed following a gender approach, the present time and the resources needed to be increased. Otherwise, it would not be fair to expect the project staff to address the issues of gender equity without a change in the thinking of the senior management about being flexible in the time and resources allocated for their projects. The senior management in all agencies clearly understood the paradox in their present approach and the flexibility required in this approach if gender concerns were to be addressed by their work. However, because all their funding came from donors, they said they needed to convince the latter about the advantages they could have with the extra cost incurred for the same work. What this shows is simply the reluctance of the senior male engineers in integrating gender concerns in the project since there would be no objection from the donors to adjust the project funds, provided it leads to making the project gender-sensitive both in its implementation as well as sustenance. Again, here also, NEWAH was one step ahead of the other two agencies since it had already decided to initiate five projects, one in each the then development region, following a GAP approach and it had already got additional funding support from WaterAid, its donor, for this piloting work.

Selection of Caretakers/VMWs: Another important aspect in the project cycle management is the selection of people to take responsibility for the operation and maintenance of the project. Because those involved in this phase receive technical skills, which can increase the chances of their saleability in the market, this aspect can be considered as a strategy related to meeting local people's, especially women's, strategic needs. Accordingly, both NEWAH and Phase II of RWSSP (not Phase I which had only male caretakers in the beginning) were concerned to fulfil strategic gender needs as they were encouraging women, together with men, to take on the position of pump caretakers. The FRWSSSP was not, however, concerned about this aspect, as the tendency in all its projects, including the selected one, was to recruit men as VMWs. The general impression of all male engineers and technicians was that women cannot play this role, as it demands more travel and extra physical labour.

However, the local women, along with many others from their varied experiences, did not agree with this view as there are many examples where women have performed this kind of role effectively (van Wijk-Sijbesma, 1998; Fong et al 1996; Wakeman, 1995; Green and Baden, 1994a). Such a bias among the officials of FRWSSSP/DWSS could inhibit women's progress and development to a great extent since the DWSS covered the entire country and ran hundreds of projects every year. Hence, its decision to recruit women in the position of VMW would make a big difference in improving the status of large sections of women in the country.

Training to NGO/PMC/WUC Members: In a male-dominated society like that of Nepal, gender training to the people in the community is important to help men and women to understand each other's role and contribution in the water sector. Good gender training can greatly help the project staff to help the local men and women to appreciate each other's roles and to begin to change the existing gender relations in the water sector. It also helps to overcome the cultural and social barriers that may prevent local women from participating in water projects. Such training should be targeted mainly to local men so that they can fully appreciate what their women can do in a water project and what it means to the whole community.

However, although NEWAH and Phase II of the RWSSP had provision for providing training on community development issues and PRA techniques to their partner local NGOs, neither was gender training planned nor was gender as an issue included as a component of other training packages. This led the local NGOs to play a dominant role in the formation of PMCs resulting in the full dependence of the women PMC members on the NGO staff even for a minor activities such as calling meetings. In such a situation, it was meaningless to think that these women would concern themselves with meeting their strategic gender needs. Hence, drawing on the experience of Oxfam, May (1997) argues that 'gender training should be provided to NGOs to change their attitudes and practices, not just to add to their skills.' As in the case of NGOs, the training given to PMC/WUC members and the other people in the communities, by all three institutions, did not include gender, either as a separate package or as a component of other training packages. The lack of gender training to the

NGO, PMC members and the local community, mainly men, led the latter to be reluctant to pay the water tariff, a key factor for sustaining the water schemes, as they thought it was a women's project. As experienced in other areas too, training on gender orientation can help to motivate local men to extend their support to the women (Baden, 1993; IRC, 1991; PROWWESS/UNDP, 1988).

It is imperative that the institutions like NEWAH, RWSSP and FRWSSSP involved in the water sector provide gender orientation to the NGO personnel as well as to the PMC/WUC members plus the local men and women so that they could understand and think of meeting both the practical and strategic gender needs of women, together with men's, for their better future. Furthermore, it is also important that whenever training, irrespective of whether it is related to gender or not, is provided to any of the project staff or the community, the materials given in the training must be gender-neutral otherwise they will further reinforce the traditional gender division of labour, giving a wrong impression to the trainees. To illustrate, the handbook on operation and maintenance of water facilities given by NEWAH and the FRWSSSP to the caretakers was gender-biased, showing pictures of male caretakers only. It is equally important to enhance women's confidence to come out of their homes to attend training sessions. This may require pre-training and more training, and provision of an appropriate budget in the project documents (May, 1997). This also demands a substantial amount of time from the project staff to sit together with the male members of the community to carry out gender sensitisation activities so that they recognise the benefits of women's participation in water supplies and encourage female members to come out of the home to attend training sessions, meetings and all other project activities. Informal discussions, which can also be called informal training, can be conducted by inviting both women and men to discuss issues such as who pays the water tariff and why only women have been perceived to be taking this responsibility while it is the need of all in the family, among others.

Signing of Agreements: In all three institutions, the contract agreements focusing on the roles and responsibilities of the concerned parties in the project activities were purely technical. There was nothing mentioned in the contract agreements about the qualitative aspects such as improvement in the quality of life, especially that of women as they are hit hardest by the lack of water supplies. The contract agreements did not bind any parties to pay special attention to the strategic gender needs of women such as improvement in their status, in their bargaining power, in their life through meeting their genuine needs and concerns etc., which are essential not only for the sustenance of the practical benefits of the projects but also for overall societal development. A study of the contract agreements indicated that project activities in all cases could be completed without considering gender aspects at all. The lack of reflection of gender needs and concerns in the contract agreements was a further indication of the lack of concern of all three institutions in making their activities gender-sensitive.

Construction Phase

Programmes in the implementation phase are most likely to be gender-sensitive when there has been adequate gender planning, when project workers have a gender perspective, and when gender issues are discussed among project participants (Hamerschlag and Reerink, 1998). A review of the project guidelines and project activities in all three agencies showed that unlike in the pre-construction stage, which involved a lot of background work to initiate the project work, the activities that were proposed at this stage were limited to the management of financial and construction materials, involvement of various parties to complete the implementation work and the supervision of the work progress. The review also showed that the activities proposed in this stage were quite general and did not address any gender issues. The project documents did not have any provision to alter the design if women felt that the final output of the construction work would not address their needs. This situation was likely to occur when women are not involved in the planning and design of water supplies, as experienced in all selected projects.

Theoretically, the management and the supervision of the construction was the responsibility of the local WUC. Since the WUC was supposed to include both men and women, it implied that both these groups got involved in the implementation process. However, in reality, it did not happen in this manner and the management of the construction stage, which included both finance and materials, was mostly under the control of men. In NEWAH projects, it was the NGO Coordinator and the NEWAH project staff both of whom were men (except in Magaragadhi where the NGO Coordinator was a woman and thus consulted with the male advisory board members more), who handled the project money, construction materials that came directly from NEWAH, and the payment of skilled workers. In both Motipur and Magaragadhi, the women PMC members reported that they were not involved much in financial matters as they did not understand the paperwork and hence, whenever they (especially the chairpersons) were asked by these persons to give their signatures on any paper they did so. The same was true in RWSSP where the management of finance and construction materials was all done by the WUC male members and the project staff, a man, of course; the only woman present in the WUC did not have much to contribute to this activity.

One improvement that had taken place in Phase II of the RWSSP was that the project money was transferred to the account of the WUC, which then used the money to purchase construction materials, upon consultation with the VDC and the RWSSP project staff. However, because the number of women in the WUCs in Phase II was not more than two in many projects, as reported by the DDC officials, the women did not have sufficient involvement in this new mechanism, though it showed the decentralisation of power from RWSSP to the local WUCs. In FRWSSSP also, since all this activity was the responsibility of the sub-committee of six people, all men, the women members of the WUC did not know anything either about the financial matters or the construction materials that were sent to their project. As a result, the supervision of the construction work was also done mostly by male WUC members in RWSSP and FRWSSSP, and the NGO Coordinators in NEWAH projects.

In all projects, the construction works generally began after the monsoon was over i.e., in September/October. The local women reported that this was the time when they were busy harvesting crops. As a result, their life became miserable during this period, partly due to their fieldwork, and also due to the necessity of providing labour to the project work. The implication of this was more serious for women from female-headed households, who had to do wage labour for their survival since it was during this season that they found more paid work for themselves. In contrast, the labour contribution to the project work deprived them of such seasonal earning which was so essential for their survival and for that of their children. This problem was reported more in FRWSSSP, where the local people, both women and men, had to contribute a significant amount of their labour due to the nature of the gravity flow schemes that demanded a lot of manual work.

The traditional gender division of labour had been further reinforced in all projects while initiating the construction work since the project staff had the feeling that women, in general, are technically incompetent. Hence, all the skilled labourers hired for both the water supply and latrine construction by the projects were men. Wherever women were hired, they were paid less than men. The women of all four projects also complained that during construction, they resisted the idea of installing water points along the roadside as they will not be able to use them comfortably for various purposes. However, the project staff and the male WUC members did not pay attention to this matter, saying that they cannot alter the design. On the other hand, the findings of studies carried out by New ERA (1991) and Fong et al. (1996), among others, report that women's involvement during the construction phase would not only lead to ensure the sustained use of the water systems and make them cost-effective in the long run, including the operation and maintenance stage, but also contribute to improving women's status by giving them new opportunities to increase their skill, income, and decision-making power.

Post-construction Phase

The major post-construction activity is the effective operation and maintenance of the completed water supplies, and proper supervision, monitoring and evaluation of that activity. This stage is as important as any of the other stages in a project cycle as it indicates the improvements in people's lives as envisaged by the project. If it is a gender-sensitive project, its importance is even higher since this can tell the project managers and the policy-makers on time whether their goal of improving the quality of women's lives, both practically and strategically, is being fulfilled. As Fong et al. (1996) note, even when projects are well designed concerning gender, it is not safe to assume that they will necessarily have a positive gender impact. Experience shows that gender perspectives may fade away if the progress is not regularly tracked. The project lead person has a crucial role in keeping alive the issue of gender and correcting deficiencies through timely supervision and monitoring of the progress.

In all projects, the task of operation and maintenance was the responsibility of concerned caretakers and VMWs. However, the monitoring of operations and maintenance, which was the responsibility of the local PMC/WUC, and evaluation, which was to be done by the support agencies such as NEWAH, RWSSP and FRWSSSP, was found to be weak in all cases. In fact, there was no further regular contact between these agencies and the partner communities once the project was handed over, or a letter of ownership was given to the concerned PMC/WUC. Among the three agencies, NEWAH was the only one, which had developed a system, that required NEWAH staff to visit the recipient community for two years at an interval of six months and to hand over the responsibility of the management of the system to the local community. However, even in this case, NEWAH staff had not visited Motipur and Magaragadhi projects regularly nor had they formally handed over the management responsibility to the local PMCs till the end of the fieldwork. Nonetheless, NEWAH expected a report on the status of the project every quarter from the local PMCs during this period. This was to be done by filling out a monitoring form developed by NEWAH. There were, however, two problems with this form. First, the form was not simple enough to be filled easily by women PMC members and hence this had again made them dependent on their NGO partners. Second, the form was too general and the information required was not gender-specific.

Fong et al. (1996) recommend that gender-specific monitoring and evaluation should address three issues such as effective utilisation, sustainability and replicability of systems; and to achieve these, should seek information by gender on access, use and acceptability of new facilities, increase in coverage, attitudes of users about the efficiency of the system, repair skills, willingness to pay water tariffs and their collection, representation and decision-making in committee activities. Also, to be explored are the emergence of women community leaders, women's higher access to training and income, an increase in women's status and bargaining power, and women's confidence in initiating other development activities. Many of these issues that are related to measuring women's empowerment are also recommended by Hamerschlag and Reerink (1998). During the research, the form designed by NEWAH did not answer any of such gender concerns resulting in NEWAH's inability to say the impact its projects made in improving the lives of women and empowering them.

The situation in RWSSP was worse than NEWAH since the former had not developed any monitoring tool and there was no further contact between the RWSSP and the local WUC regarding what these two parties expected from each other after handing over the project. Nonetheless, the WUC was meeting every month and collecting water tariffs, though lately, for the operation and maintenance of the tube-wells. In the case of FRWSSSP, the project studied had just been completed, with the provision of two VMWs for operation and maintenance of the tap-stands. No monitoring and evaluation forms had yet been introduced to the WUC. Though the project had designed a monitoring form, this was mainly to know the progress during the implementation phase, not for the post-construction phase; a review of this form showed that it was not gender-specific. Though one of the activities proposed in the project guidelines was regular interaction between the WUC and the DWSO, the project staff were not yet clear how this was to be accomplished.

The above discussions show that the outside agencies are often weak in carrying out proper and timely monitoring and evaluation of their project activities. Therefore, there is perhaps a need for a system that can be initiated at the local level itself. This system, which is known as participatory monitoring and evaluation (PME), is normally less costly and can give timely and accurate results as even the people with basic education can apply it. Fong et al. (1996) and UNDP (1998) have proposed several steps concerning the use of such gender-based PME systems, which can be useful for institutions such as NEWAH, RWSSP and FRWSSSP if they want to reduce their local partners' over-reliance on them. There are several other experiences of PME adopted in other sectors such as forestry, income generation programmes and agriculture (ICIMOD and FAO, 1998; IIED, 1998). Since these experiences of the implementation of PME have been found to be positive, they can be drawn upon to initiate a PME process in the water agencies as well.

Overall, the project implementation procedures in all selected agencies were not gender-focused though the situation was slightly better in NEWAH than others. The following are the major reasons for such gender-weak project implementation procedures:

1. The gender-unaware institutional policies that guided the project implementation procedures, which again was the result of gender-weak international and national water policy documents.
2. Patriarchal thinking that women's place is the home, not outside the home, reinforced the notion that the water sector is technical - where women have less to contribute.
3. Men's opinion that to maintain their domination and exploitation of women, and their control over the system as a whole, they have to preserve the patriarchal structure to prevent women from being at the same level as men.
4. Difficulty among the men in the project areas and the male staff in projects in acquiring a proper understanding of the gender issues in development in general and in water supplies in particular.

5. The lack of clarity between the donors and their partner agencies, concerning whether it was the number of projects and the number of beneficiaries or the quality of those projects that they should be more concerned with. The trade-off is that the concern with the former can bypass women's meaningful involvement since it takes more time to work with women due to their low levels of literacy, lack of exposure to similar work, and lack of confidence, all of which can increase the chances of the unsustainability of project benefits; while the concern with the latter can ensure the sustainability of project benefits but can take a longer time.

CHAPTER 8
Meeting Practical and Strategic Gender Needs

This chapter presents the analysis of the process and the outcomes of the selected drinking water projects based on the five indicators of women's strategic gender needs such as women's meaningful participation in project activities, changes in the traditional gender division of labour, women's access to and control over resources, equity in sharing of benefits, and changes in women's status and new development initiatives, as explained earlier in this book. The assumption behind the assessment of these five indicators is that if the projects do not meet these needs of community women, the projects will not only fail to contribute to better development through greater gender equality between women and men but also will fail to sustain the practical benefits of the projects. It is hoped that this analysis will not only confirm the relevance of the new gender analysis framework but also help the agencies engaged in the development sector in general and the water sector, in particular, to be able to meet women's practical and strategic gender needs, together with those of men.

Women's Participation in Project Activities

The findings presented earlier in this book show that women's participation in the selected projects was limited to inviting some women to attend meetings, to be nominal members of water committees and, at the most, to take the tedious job of treasurer, in which she ends up spending a lot of time struggling to collect the water tariff. The women from all project communities were involved mainly to provide voluntary labour for various tasks during the construction, and operation and maintenance stages. However, they were not involved in the essential planning and designing activities such as deciding the technology to be used, selecting which water source to exploit, choosing the location of hand pumps or tap-stands, and recruiting people for paid jobs. They were also not invited to attend skill-oriented technical training, to perform skilled work, nor to be in paid positions, all of which could have offered women decision-making power and income-earning opportunities, two strong indicators of women's empowerment.

The community women's knowledge of the selected drinking water project was limited in all cases. Most of them got to know about the project only at the time of providing labour for construction work. There was no women's involvement at the time of conceptualising and negotiating the projects with the implementing agencies. Even the women who were in the PMC or WUC got to know about the project only at the time of formation of the committee. Among the community women in general and the women PMC or WUC members in particular, women from the well-off and so-called higher ethnic groups had a relatively better understanding of the projects than women who were poor and from the other ethnic groups as evident from the discussions below:

The PMCs of Motipur and Magaragadhi in the case of NEWAH and Gajedi in the case of RWSSP were chaired by a Brahmin woman, a Chhetry woman and a Brahmin man respectively (so-called higher caste people), and they had a relatively better understanding of the project than others. The NGOs in the case of the NEWAH projects in Motipur and Magaragadhi, which played a key role in the selection of women members in the PMC, were headed by people from higher social groups and thus they recommended their own women relatives to be in the PMCs. In the case of the WUCs of Gajedi (RWSSP) and Hile (FRWSSSP) also, the women selected in the WUCs were the relatives of other influential male WUC members (or well known to them through their husbands or fathers). As a result, these women had more interactions with their men relatives either in the committees or back home in their families which, in turn, gave them more opportunities to know about the project than the other women who did not have such contacts.

Even in the positions of FHVs, motivators and caretakers of tap-stands or tube-wells, a majority were from the ethnic groups other than those who were from minority groups, the marginalised and the economically weak. This finding, concerning women's limited access to information about the project in general and of the particularly poor communication with women of minority groups, was also reported by Mustanoja (1998) in her study carried out in four RWSSP districts.

Regarding the community women's participation in project planning meetings also, this was higher only in NEWAH projects, Magaragadhi project (which was due to the involvement of a women-led NGO and more women's presence in the PMC) followed by the Motipur project (due to a women-only PMC), but poor in RWSSP and FRWSSSP villages. Though the presence of women in the survey teams of NEWAH helped to increase the number of women in the planning meetings, the timing of such meetings vis-à-vis the volume of work to be done at home and the lack of another person to share this work constrained many other women from coming to attend these meetings. This reason, followed by the lack of presence of a woman in the survey team, was the main reason for women's poor participation in planning meetings in RWSSP and FRWSSSP villages.

Likewise, in all projects, the participation of women PMC/WUC members in committee activities was not so encouraging. In NEWAH projects, the women PMC members relied on NGO staff, mostly male, and the male advisory board members for almost all committee activities including, calling meetings, filling up forms, selecting technicians for construction work, making other major decisions such as the selection of locations for tap-stands and tube-wells; the choice of PMC/WUC members, caretakers, and persons to attend training; the design of the platforms; fixing of water tariff etc. Though, in principle, it is the women PMC members who had to take all the decisions related to the projects, the actual power of making decisions laid with NGO Coordinators and the male advisory board members. In RWSSP and FRWSSSP villages also, the women members' participation in WUC activities was discouraging. The only woman member in the WUC of the RWSSP attended WUC meetings regularly but she was easily dominated by other males during the discussion. There was provision for two women advisors in the WUC but they seldom attended meetings. The situation was even worse in FRWSSSP.

> *In Hile village (FRWSSSP), the two women in the WUC said that they did not know for months that they had been selected to the committee. Because the male members of the committee were instructed by the project officials that there should be two women in the committee, to activate the process of implementing the water project, they put forward their names as a token. As a result, these women were never invited to participate in any meetings nor were they included in the sub-committee formed to monitor the project progress. For this reason, they said there was no question of them being able to do anything that could improve the lives of women in the community.*

In all cases, the committee women were only asked to volunteer in activities such as the collection of water tariffs and cash contribution to meet the capital costs, and in contributing labour, which was both difficult and time-consuming. This lack of women's involvement in key decisions about the project activities resulted in significant losses of their time and energy in collecting water. Almost all women interviewed in NEWAH, RWSSP and FRWSSSP villages complained that their water collection time significantly increased (nearly 4-5 times) after they received the improved water services. This was because the tap-stands and the tube-wells were located along the roadside where they could not bathe freely or comfortably wash the clothes that they used during menstruation, for the shame of being seen by males. In turn, women in Hile village (FRWSSSP), which is in the hills and therefore is cold, carried water all the way up to their homes, several times each day spending significant amounts of energy to do this. In the other three villages, in Tarai, they waited till dark to undertake these activities. They said they did not have this problem while using the more distant traditional sources where there was no chance of men being around. They complained that this was mainly because the people who came for the surveys did not consult women while designing the platform and selecting the locations for tube-wells or tap-stands. This situation had pointed out the danger of the community women and their families, especially children, falling into the trap of various water-borne diseases due to the use of unhygienic practices resembling what happened in the hills of Uttar Pradesh (Joshi, 1999).

Regarding women's participation in project management training also, more women were given this opportunity in NEWAH projects than in RWSSP and FRWSSSP. However, in the case of training on technical aspects, like latrine construction and masonry, no woman from any selected communities was able to attend such training, which was given only to males. Similarly, in another technical training (operation and maintenance), no women got this opportunity in the FRWSSSP (where the trainee got paid both during and after the training) and in RWSSP (in the initial stage) while more women got this training in NEWAH projects (where there was no provision for payment at any time). In leadership development also, some women in the NEWAH projects and one woman in the RWSSP (but no one in the FRWSSSP) got to be in the position of chairperson, vice-chairperson, treasurer or secretary, but, all of them were fully dependent on male advisory board members and other male members of the WUC/PMC, as they could not organise any PMC/WUC activities without consulting them, due to their illiteracy and lack of confidence resulting from not having previous experience of doing similar activities.

The above discussion shows that community women's participation in various project activities was not encouraging in any of the cases studied though it was slightly better in NEWAH projects than in others. Several reasons were identified from the discussions held with local women and men, NGO personnel, PMC or WUC members, field-based project staff, women and men caretakers, FHVs, and women motivators for such poor participation of women in the selected project areas. These are as follows:

1. The male staff of the selected agencies and the local men harboured biased attitudes against women suggesting that the latter are unable to move around as demanded by the project activities since they have to attend the household chores and children and look after the wellbeing of the other members of the family.
2. Women's limited literacy resulting in a lack of confidence not only in making major decisions but also in carrying out routine works like keeping records, preparing the minutes of the meeting, and doing the official paper works.
3. A majority of the agency staff, mostly males, both at the headquarters and the field, presumed that water is a technical activity thus it is a male domain.
4. The misconception among the agency staff and community men that women are preordained for health and sanitation activities and men for water-related activities.

5. The heavy reliance on the use of terms like 'community', 'people', 'users', etc. in the agency policy documents, which, though they look gender-neutral, cover up the role of women due to various social and cultural factors.
6. The small number of women in general and in decision-making positions in particular in all agencies (more so in RWSSP and FRWSSSP and less so in NEWAH) led the men to decide the activities as per their interest with less consideration of women's practical and strategic needs.
7. Despite community women's poor education, lack of experience, and multiple roles to play, the project did not allow adequate social preparation time for women to be fully familiarised, motivated, convinced and prepared regarding the roles and responsibilities which they needed to take in the project. The field staff were neither provided gender training nor were they given any incentives to spend additional time in the field for preparing women for their new roles and responsibilities in the water project.

The key issues that appear to be relevant from the above discussions to increase women's meaningful participation in project activities both for project's success in ensuring practical benefits and acknowledging women's right to participate are:

1. provision of adequate social preparation time,
2. provision of adequate resources,
3. basic literacy skills,
4. proper gender orientation on the part of agency staff at all levels concerning the importance of addressing gender issues,
5. higher number of women in general and in decision-making in particular both in the agency and the community,
6. holding of meetings at a time and place that are convenient to women, and
7. creation of an environment where men prepare themselves to share women's traditional work so that women can find more time for project activities.

The experiences reported earlier from the works of Hill (1998), DfID (1998), Fong et al. (1996), Mosse (1993), Moser (1993), INSTRAW and UNICEF (1988), and van Wijk-Sijbesma (1985) also confirm that if women, representing all groups within a community, do not fully participate in project activities, those projects will not be effective in the long run. In fact, they increase more burden on women. There will also be disproportionate sharing of benefits between women and men and among women of various categories, but more remarkably, they will contribute to widening the existing gender inequality between women and men as well. By involving women, particularly in the planning, design, and operation and maintenance stages, as well as in complementary health education programmes, drinking water projects can, on the other hand, greatly increase the chances of their acceptance, use, maintenance and sustainability.

Changes in the Traditional Gender Division of Labour

For drinking water projects to have a chance of being effective and of improving the lives of poor rural women, a focus on changing the traditional gender division of labour is essential. The change in the gender division of labour can lead to many advantages as follows:

1. It can give women more time to become involved in other productive and income-earning activities and the increased income can have multiplier effects in the family and community (Van der Laan, 1998; Curtis, 1986).
2. It can have positive effects on women's health which can lead to many other social and economic benefits for all the members of the family. They feel less mental and physical stress because they have more time and energy for their daily work. They can also minimise many sicknesses and disabilities, such as malnutrition, backaches, energy-sapping anaemia (among pregnant women), and poor quantity and quality of breast milk among breast-feeding women resulting from their continued heavy work, including water carrying, when combined with a poor diet, which is very common among poor women in rural areas (Van der Laan, 1998; Curtis, 1986). Given that there has been a massive reduction, both in terms of quality and quantity, of health services provided from the public sector to the people in the poor rural communities in recent years, the best option for women is to avoid being sick (Jazairy et al., 1992). Changes in the gender division of labour can make a significant contribution to meeting this option.
3. Sharing of women's work by men can bring improvements in children's nutrition and health, resulting in more time spent in food preparation and more emphasis on child-care (Jazairy et al., 1992).

4. As children see wider benefits of their parents sharing domestic work, a society with greater gender equality will evolve.
5. Women can find more time to participate in various other development activities taking place in the community, which increases the chances of those projects being more effective in meeting women's and men's practical and strategic gender needs (Van der Laan, 1998; Jazairy et al., 1992).
6. The sharing of women's traditional activities, such as carrying water by men, can increase the possibility of girl children going to school, since in many societies girls are kept away from school when there is a lot of work, including water hauling, to be done at home, which normally falls under women's domain. This hypothetical argument has been raised in several studies (Aziz and Halvorson, 1999; DfID, 1998; Curtis, 1986) though no study has been carried out yet exploring this kind of a relationship. One reason for the lack of such a study could be that in many societies, men have not yet prepared themselves for sharing the burden of women's work and thus the impact on girls' schooling is not yet evident as a result of the absence of an alternative scenario.

Several other authors (IRC, 1994; Davis et al., 1993; Simpson-Hebert, 1989) also argue that the lack of change in the traditional gender division of labour does not empower women, does not do justice to women, impedes the process of developing a society with balanced power relationships between the two sexes, and demotivates women from being active in the protection and management of water resources. This kind of situation results from the excessive burden on women, which increases the chances of the unsustainability of project benefits. As Moser (1993) argues, many governments and the personnel recruited into their women's bureaux, do not acknowledge that whilst welfarist measures may help low-income women to meet their practical gender needs, they reinforce their subordinate gender position. These approaches are unlikely to reach women's strategic gender needs. Agreeing with this idea, van Wijk and Francis (undated) also note that a shift in the gender division of labour can lead to an effective and sustained water and sanitation sector, a condition for and a part of wider socio-economic development, which cannot be attained when one half of the population is either passed by or overburdened.

Despite the numerous benefits arising out of the changing division of labour in a given family and community, the women, in all communities studied, worked much longer hours and performed more activities than men, and all their activities were related to reproduction and unpaid farm and community work. The collection of water in the villages studied fell entirely under women's domain; men collected water only when their womenfolk were sick, menstruating (traditionally women are considered impure to do certain activities during menstruation), or away from home. In these communities, when the water source was very distant from the village, demanding hours of walking, men used to help their women so that they would feel more secure. However, after these communities had access to the use of improved and more accessible water facilities the men stopped helping them, arguing that the water supply is now nearer to the home. The men had not realised that because the water source is nearer to home the use of water had increased tremendously among the family members, requiring women and their girl children to fetch water many times a day. The time and energy spent were often almost the same as before.

In Motipur, Magaragadhi and Gajedi villages, women worked up to 15-18 hours a day, while their men counterparts normally worked up to 12-13 hours. There was hardly any regular activity (except ploughing which was considered to be a male reserve) that was not performed by women, but there were many activities that were not undertaken by men. Even in their supposed-to-be rest-hours women knitted, weaved and sewed, while men spent their time drinking alcohol, playing cards or gossiping politics. Men felt that their agricultural work, which was mainly ploughing and preparing the fields, was much more difficult than that of women. They did not realise that in totality women worked much longer hours than them and some of their activities, such as spending hours every day collecting fuel-wood and fodder, and fetching water, were at least as labour intensive as theirs. In all communities, the women reported that they used to collect water 4-5 times a day amounting to a total of 80-100 litres per family per day before they got the improved water services, but, after they got the water near their homes, the collection time increased several folds with the use of nearly 200-300 litres of water a day, due to the very high temperature in the lowlands, and thus, everyone wanted to drink and wash in the fresh and cold water straight from the tube-well rather than that stored in the house, which is mostly warm.

The above situation of the gender division of labour between the women and men of the project communities was no different than that of other rural villages of Nepal as shown by several studies and discussed in the earlier chapters as well (Mustanoja, 1998; New ERA, 1997; CMS, 1996; WECS, 1995; Shtrii Shakti, 1995; New ERA, 1994; World Bank, 1991 in Joekes, 1991; Acharya and

Bennett, 1981). Experiences from other countries also confirm that the improved water facilities led to a 25 per cent reduction in women's water collection time but an increase in water use from 10 to 30 litres (three times) per capita per day. Such a workload of women, which was not shared by their husbands or other male family members, was hindering their participation in the water supply activities although experiences from all over the world have shown that their active involvement is essential (Wakeman et al., 1996). Indeed, this was one major reason reported by the local women in RWSSP and FRWSSSP, and by women PMC members in NEWAH projects, for not attending and holding community and PMC meetings, respectively, though these meetings were necessary for the smooth operation and maintenance of the tube-wells which had experienced some problems afterwards.

Not recognising women's multiple roles, which leave them with very limited time and energy to participate in project activities, the project staff thought that women were not interested so no woman was included in the construction committee formed in FRWSSSP; only one woman, as a member, and two as advisors, were included in the WUC of RWSSP; no women were chosen to work as VMWs in the FRWSSSP; no women were included while negotiating the project with NEWAH, RWSSP and FRWSSSP. Men members as well as the male project staff had the feeling that even if these women did not attend the meetings or take part in any activity (which is what happened in all cases), it would not affect the project.

The two women advisors of the local WUC in Gajedi village (RWSSP) reported that they attended only one out of ten meetings of the local committee held last year as the meeting place was far and there was no one to share their work at home. The women said that though their husbands supported them to participate in such meetings, the latter did not realise that their wives cannot do so if the husband did not share their work at home. The suggestion that came out from these two women was that the projects should focus more on how to motivate men to share women's work rather than spending time involving women in project activities which is never meaningful without men's sincere cooperation.

Indeed, the small number of women attending project meetings, the absence even of the few women members in the WUC meetings in RWSSP and FRWSSSP, the lack of seriousness in calling meetings by the women PMCs in NEWAH projects to discuss the status of the tube-wells, and the increasing numbers of malfunctioning tube-wells in RWSSP (8) and NEWAH (9) projects causing inconvenience to women in general and the poor women, in particular, confirmed that the lack of women's time was the main reason behind the situation. Even when women could participate, they were involved in stereotypical secondary activities like attending meetings, providing voluntary labour, preparing food and feeding people during construction, collecting cash contribution for capital costs and operation and maintenance costs, cleaning and maintaining health and hygiene in and around water sources etc. Men, on the other hand, were involved in activities such as negotiating the project, contacting the implementing agencies, selecting the skilled workers and fixing their remuneration, selecting the PMC or WUC members, caretakers, CHVs, motivators, and other people for various training, selecting the location of tube-wells or tap-stands, and in making many other major decisions.

Many reasons can be attributed to the lack of focus of the selected agencies in changing the traditional gender division of labour between women and men of the project communities which are as follows:

1. The focus of all projects was, basically, on meeting the water needs of people rather than on creating an environment where women together with men could participate in the decision-making of various project activities. Though one can argue here that changing the gender division of labour between women and men does not fall within the scope of water projects, what has to be clear is that without women's strategic involvement, water projects cannot sustain practical benefits, and without men sharing women's work, the latter cannot participate.
2. Though the implicit objective of the selected agencies was to reduce women's burden of fetching water, changing the traditional gender division of labour between women and men was not their objective.
3. The organisational culture of the selected agencies' headquarters and regional offices which deemed that women should be involved in non-decision-making secondary activities led to creating the same dichotomy between the roles of women and men in the project communities.
4. The lack of proper gender orientation to the people involved in the planning, design and implementation of water projects on the importance of changed division of labour between women and men.
5. The lack of adequate time for the field staff to use a gender lens to socially and mentally prepare the local men and women regarding the benefits

which the family could have from the changed division of labour between the two.

6. The lack of supplementary income-generating activities in which women could have invested the time that they saved from water hauling could have motivated men to start sharing women's work.

The issues that appear to be important for consideration in this regard are clarity on institutional objectives and strategies, proper gender orientation of agency staff at all levels, provision of adequate time for gender analysis and gender sensitisation activities along with the provision of adequate resources, provision for income-generating activities, the commitment of the field staff to involve women in decision-making activities, and a positive organisational culture in which women are not seen differently from men in terms of their ability, skills and competence. Experiences from different parts of the world also confirm that this kind of activity can help clarify the several advantages that the family and community can have from the sharing of each other's roles (Bilgi, 1998; Frischmuth, 1997; Chibuye, 1996) as well as appropriately address men's concerns that they are not suitable to take care of domestic work, including child care, and resistance to taking part in women's work as there is a low value attached to it since it is not counted in national statistics such as the Gross National Product (May, 1997).

Because the gender division of labour directly impacts women's and men's access to and control over resources and benefits, the next two sections deal with these two issues.

Women's Access to and Control over Resources

In water supplies, while access refers to the availability of water resources (a practical gender need), control refers to having decision-making authority (a strategic gender need) concerning those resources. By giving women adequate decision-making power, their interest in the projects can be maintained, assisting their effective operation and maintenance. The decision-making power usually comes through an increase in bargaining ability which, in turn, arises through increased access to and control over resources such as income, skills, information, knowledge etc. Stressing the need to increase women's income to raise their bargaining power, Moser (1993) argues that in many societies the starting point for the subordination of women is the family, one of the most powerful and pervasive mechanisms of control. The entry point for debate and negotiation at the intra-household level for women can come at an individual level from increased economic independence. Elson (1991) also supports the argument that an increase in women's income lessens their economic dependence upon men, increases their economic value, and may increase their bargaining power within the household. Access to an income of their own tends to be highly valued by women, not only for what it buys but also for the greater dignity it brings.

An increase in women's income can also lead to many other advantages such as: i) paying water tariff which is considered to be women's responsibility (van Wijk-Sijbesma, 1998; Wakeman et al., 1996); ii) meeting education expenses, including those of daughters', as women do not want to see them going through the same pain as themselves mainly due to not acquiring proper education (May, 1997; Jazairy et al., 1992); iii) spending on children's food and nutrition, both in terms of quality and quantity, which leads to improved health of their children whereas increases in men's income tend to go in productive investments, consumer goods and entertainment (Mosse, 1993; Jazairy et al., 1992; Wallace, 1991); iv) basic survival of the family as this responsibility falls completely on women, who are the permanent residents of the households, unlike men who regularly travel in search of work and for various other reasons (May, 1997; Mosse, 1993; Jazairy et al., 1992; Elson, 1991); v) multi-dimensional contribution to overall growth and development, including an increase in demand for goods and services, enhancement of the quality of life in the family, and unemployed husband's dignity if the latter is unemployed since women, unlike men, have got the tendency to share their income with the family members, especially the husbands (May, 1997; Jazairy et al., 1992).

Despite the numerous experiences showing a strong relationship between women's increased income and decision-making power on the one hand, and sustained use of water supplies, family health and overall family and societal development, on the other, women's situation in the selected research communities was completely different. The fact that men played an active and dominant role, more so in RWSSP and FRWSSSP villages and lesser in NEWAH villages, in all project activities implies that the projects failed to create an environment where women could participate in making important decisions. Even in situations when women got some space to make decisions, it was in areas that involved less capital/ cash matters implying that only men are capable of making decisions on financial matters. The women in all project areas had considerable participation while making decisions about agriculture-related activities, but much less so concerning decisions about household expenditure and almost none when it came to making decisions about capital expenditure. Among NEWAH, RWSSP and FRWSSSP, the women from NEWAH project areas had higher participation while making decisions about both agricultural matters and household expenditure followed by the women from FRWSSSP areas and RWSSP areas. The finding that once the decision-making pattern moved from activities that have less cash involvement, to activities that involved more cash, women's decision-making power gradually decreased in all project communities, follows the findings of the studies carried out by Shtrii Shakti (1995) and Mustanoja (1998). This situation revealed by the research communities confirms that the selected projects were unable to raise community women's decision-making power because they did not secure an increase in income.

All of the projects studied have indeed made certain attempts to give some control over water resources to women. The examples are attempts to: include women in the PMC/WUC (though the number was very small in RWSSP and FRWSSSP villages as compared to NEWAH villages), to gather more women in community meetings, to recruit women together with men in the position of caretakers (though not in FRWSSSP) etc. However, the point is that this level of control given to women is not enough in the process of empowering them given their small number in decision-making positions and the lack of involvement in producing income. Even in NEWAH projects, though a large number of women were present in the planning meetings and PMCs, indicating women's higher control over water resources, the fact that the PMC of Magaragadhi was later reorganised to include men to take up half the seats in the committee indicates local men's and project staff's (all male) biased attitude of giving the control over water resources back to men. Because the other project of NEWAH in Motipur was also going through the same process, this further supports the general tendency of Nepalese men to vest all the power in themselves.

Despite income being the crux of the power, all the selected projects tended to include women in the position of PMC/WUC members, health motivators, CHVs, pump/tap-stand caretakers etc. which were unpaid positions. Similarly, in all projects, it is only men who were hired as skilled workers for the construction of tube-wells or tap-stands and latrines, the paid positions because they were the ones who were provided training in these areas. Further, the training that was provided to the community women was usually non-technical, such as in health and sanitation, cleanliness, record-keeping etc., none of which provided income though there is an adequate experience reported from elsewhere of women taking on these activities satisfactorily (Thresiamma, 1998; Cleaver and Jobes, 1996; WATSANNEWS, 1996; Fong et al., 1996).

> *In the district water supply office in Dhankuta in east Nepal, three women were recruited as WSSTs. But, due to the biased attitude of the senior officers, that women cannot undertake labour-intensive activities in the field, they were assigned to perform administrative jobs, like typing and other clerical works. Similarly, in most of the gravity flow schemes of NEWAH, RWSSP and FRWSSSP, only males were hired as maintenance workers, who were paid initially by the agencies themselves and later by the beneficiary communities. However, in the point sources that include tube-wells and hand pumps in Tarai (the plain flat land), NEWAH and the RWSSP were encouraging women to be in the position of caretakers which was an unpaid position. The argument is that the job of a caretaker in a point source is easier than the job of a maintenance worker in a gravity flow scheme; this argument is not completely true since the tube-wells also can demand the same amount of time once they become older.*

Another serious aspect of the selected projects is that even when they hired women and men as wage labourers the normal tendency was to pay men higher wages than women.

> *In one project of FRWSSSP in Hile village of Dhankuta district in east Nepal, the local women who were hired to work as wage labourers during the construction phase complained that they were paid less than their male counterparts even though the total working hours was the same for both of them. As a matter of fact, the women even said that the men should have been paid less than them as the men spend a lot of time chatting and smoking cigarettes while women are sincere in their work. When the project staff and the male WUC members were enquired about it they said that men do more labour-intensive work than women thus it is normal for them to receive more wages.*

A number of reasons have come out for the lack of agencies' focus to increase women's income, thereby their decision-making and bargaining power in the selected communities:

1. Increasing women's income was neither in donors' policy documents nor that of the Nepali government's, the documents that the agencies had to refer to.

2. Despite the claim that the time saved from water hauling can be used for productive activities, none of the policy documents from- the donors, the government and the agencies'- explained how this could be done.
3. The small number of women in the selected agencies in general and in senior positions, in particular, led to a gender-unaware environment in the field.
4. None of the selected agencies made any commitment to increasing local women's skills through appropriate training sessions, allocating extra time to build up women's confidence and providing inputs to start new initiatives to earn income.
5. The lack of orientation to the staff working at various levels in the selected agencies regarding the linkage between women's increased income and their increased ability to meet their other strategic needs as discussed earlier.

The implication was that as long as the community women were getting sort of social or economic incentives such as observation tours and/or training, they were seen to be active in the operation and maintenance of the water supplies and inactive when such incentives, as compared to those provided to men, did not exist. As a result, there was an increase in the number of malfunctioning tube-wells in the NEWAH (9 tube-wells) and RWSSP (8 tube-wells) areas over time. Further, the husbands and the other family members of the women PMC members were also not so happy that the women members were not getting any monetary benefits despite spending so much time in the project activities. This situation indicated questions on the sustainability of the project benefits. Green and Baden's (1994b) and IRC's (1992) findings are also along the same lines that in the absence of economic benefits, women may not be interested or able to continue taking up project responsibilities including those of operation and maintenance of the water system, especially when it is old and demands more time from them.

> *The women members of the PMC in Magaragadhi village and WUC in Gajedi village expressed in frustration that "what changes have we personally felt in our lives by putting extra time and making special efforts to the project. As long as we do not earn income, our husbands and/ or male family members will not appreciate our opinions. Since we have been asked only to do the non-technical activities that do not provide any income, unlike the men, who have received training on latrine construction and masonry and are thus making income even after the completion of the water supplies, we are demotivated to continue as volunteers."*

This is where there is a need to think about whether a tube-well or tap-stand at the household level is more effective than the tube-well or tap-stand at the community level to maintain the interest of the users towards the protection and the management of water resources, though the issue of meeting women's strategic gender needs will still have to be considered in either case for women's empowerment, for justice to them and in favour of overall development. From these discussions the key issues that appear to be important for consideration while planning and designing a water supply project from a gender perspective are:

1. whether women together with men get opportunities to earn income from their added responsibilities;
2. whether projects create opportunities, along with providing water services, for women to increase their income by using the time saved from water hauling;
3. whether projects provide technical training to women, together with men, so that the former can use their technical skills to earn income;
4. whether the projects pay equal rates to both women and men whenever they are hired so that the projects do not widen the economic gap between them.

Addressing these issues, along with increasing women's decision-making power, an important strategic gender need of women, the projects can facilitate the women to think of fulfilling their other strategic gender needs that do not directly fall within the mandate of such projects.

Equity in Sharing of Benefits

The issue of equity in the sharing of benefits that local women and men receive from water supplies is related to both the practical and strategic gender needs of both sexes. The projects are concerned with practical gender needs when they fulfil the perceived immediate necessity of the local people, especially women, as they are traditionally considered to be responsible for fulfilling those needs. On the other hand, the same projects can lead to meeting women's strategic gender needs when they ensure equity in those benefits by empowering women from all spectrums of society with skill, appropriate training, confidence and income. Experiences from this research and elsewhere show that failure to meet the strategic gender needs of women can affect even the practical benefits to women and men. For women to benefit fully from the water projects, their various genuine concerns, along with water, need to be met. Such concerns can be related to the following issues:

1. whether the projects have included all the women in the community who genuinely need water, regardless of their ability to meet the project criteria,
2. whether the projects have paid extra attention towards fixing appropriate positioning of tap-stands/tube-wells so that all women, irrespective of their socio-economic status, can have easy access to improved water facilities,
3. whether the projects have made extra space in the tube-well/ tap-stand locations for women to freely and comfortably bathe and wash their private clothes,
4. whether projects have taken measures for the smooth operation and maintenance of the installed tap stands/tube wells.

The findings of the research show that the selected projects failed to ensure equity in the sharing of practical benefits, as there were still about 125 households in Motipur, 200 households in Magaragadhi and 26 households in Gajedi (Belbhariya) not benefiting from the projects, mainly because these households could not meet the project criteria as well as due to some technical reasons such as lack of aquifer and poor discharge of water. Among these households, 15 per cent each in Motipur and Magaragadhi and one-third in Belbhariya were female-headed and had genuine problems of water and were not in a position to have their own hand pumps. These female-headed households mainly belonged to the lower ethnic groups such as blacksmiths, tailors, cobblers, and Mallah. As these families were still using the traditional source, the health situation of their children was reported to be poor due to frequent dysentery, diarrhoea, eye infections and other stomach ailments. Further, the girls from these families were not going to or continuing at school as they had to help their mothers in household matters including water collection.

> *A Mallah woman from Belbhariya village of Gajedi drinking water project said that she still has to rely on a traditional pond to fulfil her water needs as she is far from the areas where improved water services have been provided by the project. She, along with some others, could not manage to install a tube-well in their area as they could not form a group of 10 households, a project criterion to get the tube-well. Because she is poor and comes from a lower ethnic group, her husband is mostly out of the village in search of work due to their poor economic condition and because she could not build a house in the centre of the village which is mostly occupied by rich and so-called higher ethnic groups, she could not voice her concern while the tube-wells were distributed in her village. The use of the pond water has resulted in frequent stomach ailments of her children. She felt that the people who are in the centre perhaps have first access to benefits as they are the first point of contact with the project staff rather than those who are on the periphery and who hardly know what is going on in the village.*

Moreover, even among the beneficiaries, the poorer women from the lower ethnic groups still had to walk approximately 10 minutes more than the well-off women who would walk only 2-5 minutes as the former could not voice their concern while locating the tube-wells. Many other examples like this show the lack of concern of the water projects towards benefiting as well as empowering poor, marginalised women. Accordingly, such women are understandably less interested in protecting the newly installed water supply, which may hasten the failure of such water supplies.

> *A widow in Magaragadhi village whose husband had died years ago expressed her anguish over the fact that she was never invited to participate in any of the meetings including those which dealt with the sitting of tube-wells. Since there was no one to speak for her and she could not voice her concern due to her poor economic status, the tube-well in that community was installed without considering how much further she has to walk. As a result, while other women could collect water just in 2-5 minutes she had to toil for a longer duration, which affected her time available for wage labour without which she would not be able to help her three children to survive. She then remarked, "will there ever be a time when such poor women who cannot voice their concerns are also treated equally in the community?"*

Another poor woman from the lower ethnic group called Mallah in Gajedi village similarly remarked with frustration that she and many other women from her ethnic group still spent one hour collecting water in one stretch while the women from the higher ethnic groups were able to install the tube-wells right in front of their homes. She further said with immense frustration that such discrepancies made her and her contemporaries, who were not receiving benefits from the project, feel like "doing something wrong" to the project tube-wells so that all were then on an equal footing in the community.

The other negative sides of the selected projects regarding the equity in their benefits were that the women in the lowland had not been able to benefit much from the improved water services as the use of improved tube-wells with hand pumps had caused them pain in the back and around the waist due to the pump-handle being too short for their height. Similarly, in gravity flow schemes the project benefits were accrued more to men as they were preferred over women for wage labour work. Similarly, all the selected projects failed to make extra space in places where tube-wells or tap-stands had been installed so that they could perform their washing of private clothes, especially those used during the menstruation period, and for bathing freely. Hence, as reported earlier, these women were either carrying water back home (in FRWSSSP) or performing these activities at the tube-well site itself when it was dark so that there was no chance of them being seen by males while performing these personal activities (in all NEWAH and RWSSP villages). This situation compels one to ask the agencies involved in the water sector whether they have been able to save women's water hauling time, whether they have been able to improve the quality of women's lives by reducing their burden, whether they have been able to meet the needs of all people in their project communities, and whether their project outcomes can be sustainable when they, in a real sense, have not been able to benefit all women, though the latter are expected to take the responsibility of protecting and managing the water resources.

The issue of equity in benefits is also related to whether a provision is made for a regular collection of water tariffs from user households to lead to a smooth operation and maintenance of tube-wells and tap-stands, and whether the rates of the water tariffs are decided to take into account the ability (socio-economic situation) of the user households. Concerning the collection of water tariffs regularly, which is one key factor determining the sustainability of water supplies, only the WUC of the RWSSP was active, but not the others. However, even in RWSSP, the problem is that the WUC was attempting to collect a similar amount from all the user households, without considering factors such as the number of water users in the family, the total income of the family, female-headed households, the person responsible for paying the water tariff etc. In all selected projects, as in many communities elsewhere (Ahmed and Raza, 1999; van Wijk-Sijbesma, 1998; Wakeman et al., 1996; Green and Baden, 1994b; IRC, 1994; IRC, 1992), paying the water tariff was considered to be women's responsibility for reasons as follows:

1. Because women mostly deal with water, women, as well as men in the household, assume that all water-related activities, including the payment of tariff, fall under women's domain,
2. Women are the permanent residents of the households as men keep moving to other places in search of work as there is a clear dichotomy between the inside and the outside home activities in Nepali villages. Thus women are considered responsible for all household responsibilities including paying the water tariff,
3. The formation of women-only water committees in projects such as NEWAH gives an impression to men that the water supply is a women's project and thus women should take care of all responsibilities that arise out of such a project.

The problem with considering the payment of water tariffs as women's responsibility is, however, that because they do not have control over income, they have difficulty in paying the fee, though they are willing to do so. This problem is made even worse among the women of female-headed households, as they have difficulty running their family as well as meeting the water tariff, with their meagre resources. Fong et al. (1996) go on to say that in discussions with the community in one project it was revealed that 80 per cent of those who could not afford the planned flat fee were female-heads of households. Giving further evidence about the difficulty of women-headed households in paying the water tariff, Wakeman et al. (1996) also argue that in areas where women have access to land, credit and other resources, they use the time gains for income generation. In turn, part of that income goes towards paying for the maintenance of the water system. However, one-third of the women - most of them heads of households - do not benefit because they cannot pay the water tariff.

In the selected project of RWSSP also, though a majority of the users were paying their contributions at the time of this research, it was found that there were some late payers (28 out of 282), among whom many were women (22) whose husbands had either died or gone to other places in search of work. Neither the PMC/WUC members nor the project staff had thought of subsidising the cost of water tariffs for those who could not afford it. As a result, there is a danger that these women may go back to their old unhygienic water sources, increasing again the chances of detrimental effects on the health of the whole family (Evans, 1992 in Baden, 1993). On the other hand, the provision of subsidies can increase poor men's and women's interest in the protection of the system, as experienced in Mali and Niger (FEMCONSULT, 1998).

> *In one meeting related to the collection of water tariffs from the user households in the Gajedi village (RWSSP), it was found that the water tariffs were mostly paid by women and among the defaulters, a majority were women from female-headed households. The decision that was taken in the meeting was that if the defaulters do not pay their dues within the next 15 days, they will not be allowed to use the tube-wells. As a matter of curiosity two of such defaulters were met to find out the reasons for their default. Both of them turned out to be very poor and had the problem of a hand to mouth existence. One had two children and the other, three. The small piece of land that they had was not enough for their survival. As a result, they had to work in others' farms or houses for wages in kind. Once they heard the committee's decision, they were wondering what they were going to do if they were indeed not allowed to use the tube-well.*

Further, even among the timely payers, who were mostly women, there was still some dissatisfaction about the equal amount to be paid by all. Thus, these factors, along with the fact that women did not have control over family income, could lead to the discontinuation of the collection of water tariffs. Indeed, the NEWAH projects were all facing this problem and it was likely that this situation might have also arisen in RWSSP. In the FRWSSSP also, since none of these issues were considered concerning the collection of water tariffs from the users of 11 public tap-stands, it was difficult to ensure the sustainability of the system. The original idea of subsidising the cost of the public tap-stands from payments made by the private connectors was not yet finalised, as there were still some conflicts concerning this proposed arrangement among the private connectors themselves.

The above discussions show that the selected projects in Nepal had failed to take into account the particular needs of women and other marginalised people even though several benefits such as initiation of kitchen gardening, use of improved water leading to fewer incidents of water-borne diseases, timely preparation of rice seed-bed with the availability of water even before monsoon, more opportunities for children to go to school etc., were enjoyed by some households in NEWAH and RWSSP villages. The projects' ineffectiveness to address the issue of equity had questioned not only the assurance of the long-term benefits from the project but also the fulfilment of the immediate concerns of many women and to relieve their increasing burden. This had raised dissatisfaction among women caretakers and women PMC members to continue working hard during the post-construction phase which increased the numbers of malfunctioning tube-wells in both NEWAH and RWSSP villages. The reasons that came out from the discussions with people at various levels for the lack of focus on the equity aspect are:

1. lack of clarity in the agency regarding the practical and strategic benefits that the projects should aim to provide equally to the local people;
2. lack of clarity among the field staff regarding the need for exploring the genuine needs of women and men of all categories while planning the project activities;
3. the lack of commitment of resources to invest to increase women's skills, confidence and income as per their interest and socioeconomic status;
4. lack of understanding among the agency staff that even among the women and men beneficiaries there are various categories due to their class, ethnicity, social structure, and hence, their requirements and concerns need to be dealt with separately;
5. the notion among the agency staff that the benefits arising from the project will trickle down equally to all women and men of the project communities;
6. the lack of clarity among the agency staff on gender roles, responsibilities, power structure, etc., of the local women and men which determine their access to and control over various project benefits;
7. agencies' inability to see a connection between practical gender needs and strategic gender needs (equity and empowerment in this case);
8. even when some women were involved in various project activities, the project staff assumed that these women can represent all other women in the community, regardless of the differences in their social status, economic class, ethnicity etc.

Hence, from the above discussions, some issues appear to be important for consideration by water agencies while planning, designing and implementing their water supplies so that they can achieve equity in the sharing of project benefits, sustainability in those benefits and a balanced power relationship between women and men - a strong indicator of sustainable human development. They are:

1. a better understanding of gender issues in development in general and water supplies in particular,
2. a clearer opinion on women's strategic gender needs and how they impact equity and sustainability of project benefits,
3. a better picture of the differences in gender roles, responsibilities and power between and within women and men of various categories in terms of class, social structure, ethnicity, and how these determine women's level of access to and control over various resources,
4. creating a mechanism for an equitable sharing of information, knowledge, and other benefits among all women and men in the project communities,
5. a better consideration of the social and the gender aspects, along with the technical ones, while determining the needs of women and men, recruiting caretakers so that women from the poorer sections with appropriate training and remuneration also get to be hired, and paying both the women as well as men for their extra responsibilities,
6. initiation of a process to make provisions for alternative activities with the necessary training to increase women's skills, status and income, decide the amount of water tariff based on the economic status of the household, the number of members in the family and the person paying it, and develop a mechanism of subsidising or exempting water fees from those men and women who cannot afford it.

Changes in Women's Status and New Development Initiatives

An important strategic gender need of women that development projects, like those in the water sector, should address is an improvement in women's self-esteem, in their confidence to initiate new activities in their communities, thereby in their quality of life. Even if projects can have a direct impact in improving the lives of only a few women this can have multiplier effects in the long run, both in the family and the community, as these women can be seen as role models by others. Experiences reveal that the lack of improvement in women's self-esteem, confidence and skill can adversely affect projects (Moser, 1993; Mosse, 1993). On the other hand, talking about the SIDA experience, Cleaver and Jobes (1996) mention that equipping women with new skills, and providing them with both practical and strategic tools are instrumental to their confidence, status and ultimately their authority. These authors further argue that women's increased status will not only prepare them to continue taking up their assigned responsibilities in water supplies but also lead to many other advantages as follows:

- Women can think of initiating or at least discussing the possibility of running new activities related to improving their lives in the communities and the increased status can also motivate women to start new ventures to increase their income which, in turn, can give them a higher status with control over more income.
- Women can organise themselves for meeting their various strategic gender needs, the absence of which makes their lives vulnerable. For example, domestic violence which is common in the rural parts of many developing countries can also be minimised/ stopped by increasing women's confidence and self-esteem.
- Because women are the permanent residents of the households, are in maximum contact with their children and deal with water-related activities which affect people's health, their increased confidence can have multiplier effects on aspects such as better education for children, better health for the family, and acting as better sources of information for many other fellow women in the community.

Mentioning their experience of a survey of women beneficiaries of Grameen Bank loans in Bangladesh, Jazairy et al. (1992) highlight that all the women interviewed reported that relationships with their husbands, relatives and community improved as a result of their individual economic contributions to family welfare. Several other authors (Joosten, 1998; Hill, 1998; Chibuye, 1996; Mosse, 1993; and Penny, 1991) also note that formal and non-formal education programmes and technical training aiming to increase various skills can offer both practical skills and a chance to increase confidence and self-esteem, thereby making women's empowerment a basis from which to challenge the apparent rigidity of social structures.

However, as the following discussions reveal, none of the selected projects had much success in this respect. Because a large number of women were involved in various phases of the NEWAH projects, and a good number of women were in the PMCs and the position of caretakers, these women were observed to be relatively more knowledgeable and enthusiastic about talking with the author than the women of the RWSSP and FRWSSSP villages. Even in the RWSSP and FRWSSSP projects, the women who were in the WUCs and the position of caretakers were relatively more active than others in the community. During the discussions, many of them revealed that they received good exposure to the development sector after being in PMCs/WUCs, receiving training, being in the position of caretakers etc. This gave them a measure of confidence in conversation with outsiders, something that they did not have before. But, because the number of such women was small in all projects and particularly in RWSSP and FRWSSSP, and that they were not able to impact other women yet in the project communities, it can be said that the selected projects were able to make only a little change in the status of women in general.

Further, as a majority of the women in the PMCs/WUCs and the position of caretakers were from relatively well-off households, and this was precisely the reason why they got selected for those positions, it cannot be claimed that the limited activeness, enthusiasm and confidence they had shown during the project works were the results of the projects alone. This is also supported by the fact that none of them was involved in income-generating activities though had some more free time as compared to the women who lived a little farther from their tube-wells. Also, the fact that the women PMC members in NEWAH projects thought that the concerned NGOs could exchange them for other members anytime they wanted, was another indicator of the women's lack of confidence in themselves.

Similarly, the women PMC members in NEWAH projects had not held monthly meetings after the projects were handed over to them about two years ago for not having enough confidence although the meetings were necessary to discuss the remedies for an increasing number of malfunctioning tube-wells, the inadequacy of water, sandy water, additional time spent to collect water from other tube-wells etc. Further, the meetings were also necessary to discuss how the local PMCs/WUCs in general, and the women PMC/WUC members in particular, could organise themselves to translate their confidence into implementing other drinking water projects in the vicinity, especially for the people who were deprived of water facilities, mainly in NEWAH and RWSSP villages, where there were still a significant number of households suffering from the shortage of safe drinking water.

Although the women PMC members had the right to make decisions about the project related activities themselves, they did not have the confidence to do so in absence of the NGO personnel and the male advisory board members. Moreover, it was true that a few women in NEWAH projects displayed a degree of satisfaction from being part of the PMC in the positions of caretaker and in conflict mediation. Yet it is significant to note that whenever there was a conflict between family members in some households, there was no sign of either these women members or many other women in the community organising themselves for community development activities or taking self-initiative for the fulfilment of their other strategic gender needs like changing the traditional gender division of labour, increasing access to and control over income, increasing their stake in household and community decision-making, and acquiring technical skills, all of which could have increased their status and confidence further.

The main reason for the low confidence and weak status of women was their inability to generate cash income for the family although they were working much longer hours and their level of contribution to the survival of the family was much higher than that of their male counterparts. The activities where women were involved simply geared them towards increasing the efficiency of the water projects but not to empower the former by providing income, knowledge and status. This often led to bypassing women and their activities in the project activities. In turn, women, including those in the PMCs or WUCs never had a clearer understanding of their new roles and responsibilities. The analysis of the collected information also revealed that the PMC/ WUC members were never provided on-the-job training or gender orientation to increase their understanding of the symptoms and causes of prevalent social, cultural, legal practices rooted in most patriarchal societies. In this regard, some senior staff of the selected agencies argued that addressing these activities will involve additional cost and increase the cost per capita of the project, increasing the chances of the project not getting funding from the donors, as this is one major criterion for the latter to decide on this matter. However, the point is that if these issues are not addressed on time, there remains a danger that the projects might not be sustainable in the long run as they can neither fulfil the practical benefits nor the strategic aspects of women's lives resulting in the lack of women's interest towards the project.

Further, any development intervention such as water supply should be considered as an entry point for the initiation of other development activities locally and this will be possible only if the concerned people, including women, feel confident of their ability, improved through their active participation in the water projects. Moreover, the issue of addressing justice to women is another aspect that also needs to be considered by development agencies. Hence, because of all these reasons, even if there will be some extra cost involved while addressing the aspects of empowering women, they will, in the long run, be fruitful to the local people as well as the country. An equally important aspect is that owing to a majority of women staff in the selected agencies being in lower working levels and in non-technical positions resulting in their inability to influence the planning and policy formulation, the issue of improving the status of the community women did not appear as a priority in the minds of the senior male colleagues involved in making policies and planning, designing and implementing the water projects. As a result, neither the project objectives nor the project management guidelines highlighted this issue. Similarly, the other reason reported for the lack of focus on improving women's status is the agencies' inability to realise the interconnection between improvement in women's status and the efficiency of the water projects.

Although NEWAH was about to implement several water and sanitation projects focusing on women's empowerment on a pilot scale to judge how the latter impacts the sustainability of project benefits, what can be inferred from the above discussions is that the selected projects, in general, were not able to improve women's status in the project communities. Had the agency staff been provided proper orientation focusing on gender planning, gender analysis and gender strategies along with the practical and strategic benefits of a gender-sensitive project, be it water or any other sector related, the results in terms of women's status would have been different. Such an orientation of the agency staff would have led them to introduce various activities which would help to build up women's confidence, income, and status. On the other hand, as reported by many scholars, the failures not only divert women away from more productive activities but may also disillusion them from attempting any new ventures (Acharya, 1997; Mosse, 1993; Kamminga, 1991 in Baden, 1993; Mayoux, 1991; Puganosa and Amuah, 1991; Wadehra, 1991).

Conclusion

The community-level framework of women's strategic gender needs that are discussed in this chapter provides an effective understanding of the gender issues that have prevailed and continue to do so at the community level of the selected agencies. It can thus be said that these indicators appear to be useful and relevant for consideration in the future when carrying out a similar type of gender analysis at the community level. Nevertheless, the discussions also suggest that some of these indicators need further breakdown for this framework to be more realistic, user-friendly and comprehensive. The indicators that need further breakdown are 'women's participation in project activities' and 'women's access to and control over resources'. There is no doubt that the information presented under these two indicators are useful and provide a clear and comprehensive picture of the status of women in terms of their level of empowerment. However, some difficulty has, at the same time, been found in segregating the information presented under these two indicators. For example, the limitation with the indicator on women's participation is that it deals with two types of participation together - first, women's physical presence in meetings and while performing various other project activities; and second, women's strategic involvement through making decisions either by themselves or together with the male members about the project activities. The problem while focusing on these two kinds of participation together is that it can increase the chances of losing useful information for one or the other if there is a lack of equal and serious attention on both these aspects.

One can argue here that the first level of participation is not directly related to women's strategic involvement and thus can be ignored. However, what is important to understand is that the first level of participation is a means to achieve women's second level of participation i.e., women's strategic involvement, especially in the rural areas of Nepal, where there are a lot of social and cultural factors inhibiting women's physical presence in project activities. Hence, it is only through their first level of participation that rural Nepali women can expand their knowledge base, gain more confidence, and get exposure to the development sector so that they can mentally prepare themselves to fulfil their various strategic needs. This does not, however, mean that the water projects should not look for women's strategic involvement until they are satisfied with women's physical presence in various project activities. Rather the message is that both these levels of women's participation are necessary and thus need to be analysed separately.

Similarly, the indicator on 'women's access to and control over resources' also deals with two types of information - first, women's decision-making power related to the use and control of various project resources, which concerns water resources in this study; and second, women's access to and control over income, since this has appeared as an important indicator of women's empowerment both in the literature and this research. The confusion appears, sometimes, concerning where the activities related to women's decision-making power should fall under the indicator of "women's participation" or under the indicator of "women's access to and control over resources". The author thus feels that these two indicators - women's participation in project activities and women's access to and control over resources - should be split into three to make the analysis of women's strategic gender needs even clearer, precise and user friendly. The division is as follows: i) women's physical presence in project activities, ii) women's participation in decision-making, and iii) women's access to and control over income. These discussions suggest that the community level framework of women's strategic gender needs suggested earlier in this book needs to be expanded for its future use as follows:

1. women's physical presence in project activities,
2. women's participation in decision-making,
3. changes in the traditional gender division of labour,
4. women's access to and control over income,
5. equity in sharing of benefits, and
6. women's increased status and new development initiatives.

PART III

Gender Transformation in Water Policies, Conclusion and Policy Implications

Part III presents four chapters that deal with gender transformation in water policies, a conclusion of the discussions made in various chapters and some policy implications for consideration by the agencies engaged in the water sector at various levels- international to local- to make their policies and practices fully gender-aware for meeting women's practical and strategic gender needs, sustaining the project benefits and achieving gender equality and women's empowerment. Chapter nine presents gender transformation in international water policies while chapter ten deals with gender integration in Nepal's development plans, both formulated after 2000. Similarly, chapter eleven presents gender integration in Nepal's water sector post-2000 and chapter twelve offers conclusion and policy implications.

CHAPTER 9

Gender Transformation in International Water Policies Post-2000

The discussions presented in Part II Chapter IV revealed that the water policies of most of the international organisations, like the World Bank, Asian Development Bank (ADB), FINNIDA/ The Government of Finland, and WaterAid, which were reviewed for the research undertaken from 1997-2000, were relatively weak regarding gender sensitivity. This chapter will discuss the gender-related changes which have taken place in the water policies of these organisations over the last 20 years as well as of some others like the United Nations Children's Fund (UNICEF), which was one of the initial supporters of the community-based water supply schemes in Nepal, and has still been supporting the water, sanitation and hygiene (WASH) programme within its health portfolio. The chapter will also point out the areas where these international organisations need to pay extra attention to make their WASH policies as well as the projects implemented under those policies gender-sensitive.

The key message that guided the donors and their water policies before 2000 was the demand-driven cost-recovery approach. The basic premises of this approach were: improved water services led to higher income, payment increases the feeling of ownership towards the water systems, private sector involvement leads to effective and efficient services, improved water services led to enormous health benefits, and local, more so women's, involvement in decision-making makes the water projects sustainable. However, the findings of the research (Regmi, 2000), as summarised in Part II Chapters IV and VIII of this book, depicted that these claims made by the donors in favour of demand-driven cost-recovery approach were not fully realised by the water projects due to the failure in addressing many gender issues in the design, implementation and operation and maintenance stages of the water supplies.

In absence of the sharing of women's household chores by the male family members, women were not able to use their time saved from water hauling in productive activities, thereby increasing income; in absence of women's involvement in the design phase, the water points were located in places that were not convenient for women and girls to carry out activities like bathing and washing undergarments at the water points. In turn, women were compelled to carry water several times to their home to undertake these activities at the household itself, which not only resulted in spending too much time fetching water but also affected women's and girls' health. Similarly, because women were hardly involved in key positions of the water users and sanitation committees (WUSCs), including in the position of caretaker or maintenance worker, there were hardly two women selected to be in WUSCs consisting of 9-13 members, there were virtually no women hired in paid positions, and because women were not selected for technical training that would give them skills as well as some extra income, they could neither influence the decision-making process nor could they fully own the water systems. This situation resulted in an increase in the number of malfunctioning tap-stands and tube-wells in the project communities. Moreover, the important policy documents of the donors were found relying too much on the use of the terminologies like poor, community, consumers, beneficiaries seeming as though these gender-neutral terminologies would provide equal opportunities and benefits to women and men. The reality, however, was completely different as discussed in the earlier chapters.

The World Bank

The idea of including the World Bank's policy documents in the research was guided by the assumption that if its policies were gender-focused, the national water policies of the recipient countries like Nepal, will also be gender-specific because of the financing power of the former.

"Safely managed WASH services are an essential part of preventing and protecting human health during infectious disease outbreaks, including the current COVID-19 pandemic" (World Bank, 2020a). As the world's largest multilateral source of financing for water in developing countries, the World Bank is working closely with partners to achieve "a water-secure world for all", by sustaining water resources, delivering services and building resilience". As per a World Bank report, the World Bank's Water Global Practice (WGP) is currently funding USD 24.5 billion, accounting for about 11 per cent of its total lending, over 177 WASH projects around the globe, which is almost 2.5 times higher than the funding of

USD 10 billion coming from the other global practices. As such, the WASH sector accounts for about 60 per cent of the total water portfolio, with about one-third devoted to urban water supply and one-quarter to the rural water supply. Unlike in the past, sanitation has now been given profound attention as a result of the influence of the long-term Water and Sanitation Programme (WSP), which is particularly active in rural areas (World Bank, 2017b). Following the recommendations of its first economic mission sent to Nepal in 1963, the Bank's lending to the latter began with a telecommunications project in 1969. Since then, the World Bank has provided Nepal USD 4.75 billion in assistance (USD 3.48 billion in credits and USD 1.27 billion in grants). Apart from this, the Bank, through its International Development Association (IDA), has also been providing Nepal extra funds for crisis response and emergency needs. The Bank committed USD 1.2 billion to Nepal during the IDA17 period (17th replenishment of IDA covering FY2015-2017), which included additional financing of USD 300 million to respond to the emergency needs after the 2015 earthquake. The current portfolio comprises 22 active projects with a net commitment of USD 2.32 billion. In terms of the number of projects, the energy sector makes up the largest share (5 projects) followed by agriculture and education, with four projects in each sector (World Bank, 2018).

Gender Integration in the World Bank's Water Policies: In the hope that the World Bank's water policies formulated after the earlier research might have been more gender-sensitive over the last 20 years, some of the Bank's key documents released after 2000 were also reviewed to examine the extent to which the gender concerns were addressed in those documents. Consequently, Water Resources Sector Strategy: Strategic Directions for World Bank Engagement 2004, the highly informed progressive version of the World Bank's Water Resources Management Policy Paper released after 1993, was reviewed. This Sector Strategy 2004 was prepared based on the on-the-ground experience of the World Bank-funded projects, country consultations, comments received from the massive consultations with a range of stakeholders on the draft version of this document, and in-house consultations with the Bank's board, management and some selected staff. Apart from the inputs received to the formulation of this strategy, the massive consultations also highlighted the Bank's attention on two sets of challenges (World Bank, 2004).

First, there was a need to continue doing things like providing water and sanitation services, increasing local participation in the management of water projects, properly handling the operation and maintenance phases of the water supply schemes, etc. as before, but ensuring that the water quality has improved, water has been conserved well, groundwater and watershed have been effectively managed, and institutional reform has taken place. The second set of challenges were the ones that were either new or those where the Bank had not performed well in a timely and effective manner. The Bank's Water Sector Strategy 2004 focuses on seven such areas, of which only the first three areas that are relevant to the water supply and within the reach of the local community, including women, for its management, have been reviewed using a gender lens for this book. The other four areas such as climatic variability, lending for projects requiring the construction of huge infrastructure, a comparative advantage to fund in mega-projects, and contextualising the Bank policies were kept out of this review.

As presented in the Executive Summary of the Bank's Strategy (World Bank, 2004), those three key areas, most pertinent to the water supply, are: i) Water resources management and development are central to sustainable growth and poverty reduction and therefore of central importance to the mission of the World Bank; ii) Most developing countries need to be active in both management and development of water resources infrastructure; iii) The main management challenge is not a vision of integrated water resources management but a "pragmatic but principled" approach that respects principles of efficiency, equity and sustainability while recognising that water resources management is intensely political and that reform requires the articulation of prioritised, sequenced, practical and patient interventions.

On its analysis on the linkage between the integrated water resources development and management, and sustainable growth and poverty reduction, the Bank explains how the broad-based poverty-targeted water service interventions that include the building of large infrastructures such as dams and inter-basin transfers, as well as improvements of degraded landscapes and catchment areas can provide benefits to 'people', including the 'poor', by having more opportunities for new jobs and livelihood. Similarly, in its analysis that highlights the importance of not only building the infrastructure but also managing them, the Strategy's focus is on 'community' mobilisation. Likewise, in its discussion on the principles of efficiency, equity and sustainability in the delivery of water supply and sanitation services, the Strategy has laid heavy emphasis on the increased role of the private sector to achieve these objectives, evident by nearly 40% of the Bank-funded projects commissioning private sector involvement for their management. The reasons provided for bringing in the private sector were: cost-effectiveness, transparent business, impartial regulation, greater disclosure of information, thereby greater accountable services to the taxpayers and billions of people who still do not have access to water supply and sanitation services (World Bank, 2004).

Despite the Strategy 2004 being comprehensive in many areas, it, however, is still found to be relatively gender-weak in several areas while looking at it using a gender lens. For instance, the document is still found using gender-insensitive terminologies like 'community', 'people', 'poor' etc. to define the community as a generic group, instead of using the gender-specific terminologies to acknowledge that women and men have different roles, needs and concerns in the WASH sector, and hence the need to develop gender-specific strategies. The heavy emphasis of this document on the engagement of the private sector without paying much attention to the economic capacity of the local people, more so of women, makes it a gender-weak document. This strategic document can thus be considered as a poverty-sensitive document rather than a gender-sensitive document.

However, looking at the Bank's latest documents, it can be said that its gender thinking and analysis have gradually been changing over the years. The findings of a study of the water supply and sanitation projects conducted in 18 low-income, fragile and middle-income countries selected representing six regions from all over the world confirm this finding (World Bank, 2017b). In this document, the Bank has clearly emphasised the impact which the projects have made on women and the other disadvantaged people while talking about the disparities in the services: "the evidence shows significant disparities in the quality of drinking water, sanitation, and hygiene facilities and services between the poor and non-poor, between rural and urban areas, and across and within geographic regions of the same country, with traditionally disadvantaged groups, including women, the indigenous, and the disabled, suffering an additional burden." The same study being even more gender-responsive further reports: "the gender of the household head may play a small role in explaining differences in access to water and sanitation, but women and girls continue to bear the burden of most household water-related tasks. Such tasks are often very time-consuming. Where paths to water sources are long and through remote areas, this may put women at risk of sexual and other physical violence, which is prevalent in fragile countries". Being well-informed about the gender concerns this time, unlike previously, the

Bank's report, while analysing the inequalities in access to WASH services by various factors, further mentions that the wealthier countries, the urban areas within the countries, and the geographically convenient locations, among others, have better access to improved WASH services, while women, ethnic minorities, and religious minorities have disproportionately low access to WASH services across the globe. The gender and social inclusion specific analysis made in this study is a clear departure from the gender-weak focus observed in the earlier policy documents like Policy Paper 1993 and Water Resources Strategy 2004.

To realise a water-secure world for all, as envisioned by the WGP (World Bank, 2020a; World Bank, 2020b), the Bank's analysis of universal access to water supply and sanitation has continuously been advancing over the years with an increased focus on social inclusion. Some of its analyses made concerning universal access to water supply and sanitation are: "strong economies require healthy, skilled, and knowledgeable people"; "a lack of safe water, sanitation, and hygiene not only harms economic potential, but also harms people's dignity, safety, health, and educational achievements"; "the smart investments in clean water and sanitation, on the other hand, prevent needless deaths and transform lives: healthier children become healthier adults who can fulfil their potential and contribute more to the economy". Acknowledging further the importance of being socially inclusive in its water programmes, it writes: social inclusion in water is a process of improving the ability, opportunity and dignity of people disadvantaged based on their identity to take part in society. The activities that are to be implemented in achieving social inclusion include building evidence on female employment in water utilities and supporting participatory and inclusive approaches in water governance and decision-making (World Bank, 2019a).

Concerning its engagement with the SDGs, the Bank, committed to the idea of a water-secure world for all, has got a clear vision, analysis, and strategic action plan. Accordingly, it has emphasised a fundamental shift in how the world should understand, value and manage water, and ensure the right balance between sustainability of water resources, delivering services and building resilience. The Bank has put a great emphasis on coordination, targeting and governance to achieve a water-secure world for all (World Bank, 2019b; World Bank, 2017a). At the same time, it also has identified five priority themes namely, resilience, sustainability, inclusion, institutions and financing, aimed to be achieved through the formation of the Global Water Security & Sanitation Partnership (GWSP). The GWSP, a multi-donor trust fund, was launched in

2017 to enable the WGP to address those five priority themes across its global portfolio (World Bank, 2020a; World Bank, 2020b). In 2018, the 2030 Water Resources Group, a public-private-civil society partnership, that supports the government-accelerated reforms intending to ensure sustainable water resources management for long-term development and economic growth, also became part of the WGP family (World Bank, 2020b).

Looking at the changes that have taken place in the World Bank's analysis, concerning the role of women and poor in the WASH sector, one can remark, -based on the various policy documents released throughout 2004-2020, that the Bank's policy documents are gradually advancing towards making their WASH programmes socially inclusive and women sensitive.

Areas Demanding for Further Gender Attention: In both the Policy Paper 1993 and Water Sector Strategy 2004, the Bank's focus has been on 'poor' with less elaboration on who those poor are since it is a well-accepted phenomenon that even within the category of poor, women are further poor. So, unless and until gender-specific strategies are developed and gender-specific languages are used, not everyone even within the category of poor can equally benefit. These documents claim that when the investment is increased for the construction of dams, hydropower, irrigation and other heavy infrastructures, it will create enormous opportunities for jobs for poor people. However, history has exhibited the bitter reality that in absence of a specific mentioning of women or women-focused strategies, such opportunities and benefits are mostly exercised by men and the powerful only. This is more so in countries like Nepal where women have been forced to lag behind men due to the strong patriarchal thinking which considers men superior to women. Similarly, while highlighting the importance of building the water infrastructure, the strategic document also emphasises its management. However, here too, the Strategy does not speak much about the need for women's and poor people's involvement even though the lack of women's effective participation can jeopardise the sustainability of the water schemes since they are the traditionally well-known primary managers of the water resources. Likewise, in its discussion on the principles of efficiency, equity and sustainability, the Strategy does not mention what role the local people, more so the women, should play in fulfilling these objectives.

What is worse, the Strategy 2004, being perceived as a well-informed document of the World Bank, is full of the use of the gender-neutral looking terminologies like 'poor', 'people', 'community', 'stakeholders' as in the Policy

Paper 1993 and with minimal use of words like 'women or gender'. Despite that the water projects implemented under the policy documents that are using such seemingly gender-neutral terminologies have failed to address women's concerns and needs, the continued use of such words without being specific to the context indicates the Bank's oversight in empowering women through the water projects it funds. For instance, in the 'water supply and sanitation section', some of its gender-weak statements are: "an overriding thrust of the World Bank's work on water and sanitation is to ensure that **poor people** gain access to safe, affordable water supply and sanitation services by reducing costs and increasing accountability"; "in small towns and rural areas this means empowering **communities** to make informed choices about their participation, service levels and service delivery mechanisms"; and "realigning the rights and obligations of key **stakeholders**". Similarly, some other gender-weak statements in the Strategy are: "vesting 'communities' with ownership rights and authority to select service providers"; "building 'local' capacity to support 'community' decision making in planning, management and delivery of services"; and "establishing financial policies and instruments that provide incentives for 'communities' to contribute to capital costs and pay for all operation and maintenance costs" (World Bank, 2004). All these strategic statements lack gender-specificity. The only statement in its 'water supply and sanitation section' of Strategy 2004 where 'women' have been mentioned is: "an important element of such approaches is to make sure that women can, in forms that are practical in each cultural setting, play a meaningful role that is commensurate with their knowledge of local water services and interest in improving them".

The clubbing of women and men in gender-neutral looking terminologies implies that the benefits arising out of the Bank-funded projects will mostly be enjoyed by men since these terminologies have traditionally been used to refer to men only. The questions that can be raised then are: i) will the WASH projects funded under such gender-weak policy guidance empower women as has been claimed? ii) can such gender-unaware WASH projects fill in the prevailing social and economic gaps between the women and their fellow men in a given community? iii) why could not gender obtain prominence on the Bank's policy document despite so much focus given on this matter at the international arena, both by the IDWSSD (1981-1990) and various international women's conferences that had taken place around the same time and afterwards as well?

The other area of gender concern on the Strategy 2004 is on the emphasis on private sector involvement in the delivery of water services. Despite the reasons provided for the private sector involvement as explained earlier in Chapter IV, what the Bank is missing, like before, is the analysis on the interconnections between the rural women's ability to pay, due to the lack of access to and control over income, and the engagement of the private sector in providing water services to these women. The lack of opportunity for women to engage in productive activities as discussed earlier along with men's continued expectations of the former to pay the water tariff, on the one hand, and the engagement of the private sector operating on a demand-driven cost-recovery approach to provide the water service, on the other hand, makes women doubly disadvantaged. The document does not clarify how the private sector will guarantee the delivery of water supply services to women and poor households, including female-headed, regardless of their ability to pay for such services.

An equally important gender concern is in the Bank's approach to achieve a 'water-secure world for all'. Although the Bank has laid a strong emphasis on social inclusion in its thinking, analysis, strategies and practices proposed to achieve this goal, there is a lack of the same level of importance accorded to gender equality. It has been well agreed universally by now that unless and until women are empowered and the development projects, including the WASH projects, do not aim for gender equality along with the fulfilment of practical needs, a society with sustained human development is not possible. Because social inclusion does not necessarily mean gender equality and this alone cannot ensure the overall empowerment of women and contribute to achieving gender equality, the concept of GESI (gender equality and social inclusion) was coined. This means both the gender equality and social inclusion dimension need to be blended as a GESI approach to get the desired level of changes at all levels -social, economic and political. The gap in the Bank's strategies proposed to meet the goal 'water-secure world for all' is that it has fully endorsed the social inclusion approach but lacks the same level of recognition to gender equality approach. The question that gets raised then is whether the WASH projects supported by the Bank would even be able to address women's practical gender needs in a sustained manner when women's strategic gender needs are overlooked.

What is, hence, important is to revise using a gender lens the Water Resources Strategy 2004 which is still playing an imperative role in the Bank's funding on the WASH sector. Being the largest multilateral donor in the water sector, the stakeholders from the WASH sector expect the Bank's policies and practices to be truly gender-focused. It is only by being more consistent, clear and bold in acknowledging and addressing in its policy documents the role women along with men play in the WASH sector that the Bank can influence the national policies as well as the policies of its alliance partners to help achieve a society with greater gender equality.

The Asian Development Bank

Although its first lending to the Nepal government started in 1969, it was only since 1984 that The Asian Development Bank (ADB) emerged as a leading multilateral lending agency in Nepal's water supply and sanitation sector. The ADB has been able to influence Nepal's water policies and practices as a result of its ever-increasing loans and a long-standing relationship with the GoN, especially the ministries and the departments responsible for the drinking water and sanitation services. Some of Nepal's water policies that were influenced by the ADB include: Eighth Five-Year Plan with the mentioning of the participatory development principles and demand-driven approach, Drinking Water Rules 1998, Rural Water Supply and Sanitation National Policy 2004, Rural Water Supply and Sanitation National Strategy 2004, Rural Water Supply and Sanitation Action Plan 2004, the establishment of a Drinking Water Management Board 2005 (WaterAid, 2006) and several other national water policies, including the various phases of the Drinking Water Supply and Sanitation Sector Projects (DWSSSPs) implemented by the then Department of Water Supply and Sewerage (DWSS).

Gender Integration in ADB's Water Policies: For being a major donor in the water sector of its Developing Member Countries (DMCs), including Nepal, the ADB's water policies were reviewed using a gender lens in the research undertaken during 1997-2000 with an assumption that if its policies were gender-sensitive, it would lead to the formulation of gender-focused national water policies in Nepal. What came out from the review was that the ADB, like the other international donors, was also strongly advocating for a 'demand-driven cost-recovery approach' in the water sector during that time. The Bank's argument at that time was that the improved water supplies designed and implemented following this approach can lead to: i) rational use of water resources due to the private sector involvement, ii) increase in family income with the use of water for multiple purposes, iii) increased local participation resulting in increased ownership and sustainability of water projects, iv) water's economic value initiates its effective and efficient use, and v) equity in benefits. However, the findings of the research (Regmi, 2000), also summarised in Part II Chapter IV of this book, revealed that the reality in the community is different since the local people, more so the women and poor were not able to fully enjoy the benefits of the water supplies implemented following the demand-driven approach unlike what was claimed for.

For instance, in the Hile Drinking Water Project implemented under the ADB supported FRWSSSP, only 1-2 women were involved in WUSCs and ironically, these women did not know for months that they were selected to be in the WUSCs; no women were involved in decision-making positions of the WUSCs; only men were recruited as VMWs; more men than women were earning extra income; tap-stands were located along the road-side without consulting women resulting in more labour to be spent by women to carry water to their homes so that they could freely bathe and wash their inner-garments; the increased water collection time had impacted on women's health, among others (Regmi, 2000). To understand the gender changes which had taken place in the ADB's water policies over the years, several of the Bank's water policies formulated after 2000 have been reviewed for this book. The specific intention behind this review was to examine if women got a more pronounced role in the Bank's water policies and if gender issues, in terms of varying needs and concerns of women and men, were taken into consideration while formulating them, with the same assumption that the donor's gender-sensitive policies would lead to the formulation of gender-specific water policies at the national level as well.

Water Policy 2001 is one important policy document of the ADB. Although it was formulated 20 years ago, it still carries the same importance for the Bank. As a result of the focus made by the IDWSSD 1981-1990 and various women's international conferences held around the '80s and '90s on women's contribution in the water sector and the need to involve them in all stages of water projects, this policy also got to be more progressive in appreciating and acknowledging women's role in the water sector as opposed to the policies formulated before 2000. The Water Policy 2001 has also been informed by the Bank's experiences gained from the assessment of the projects it funded before 2000. Some such experiences directly related to women's role include: i) the local communities, more so the women who are primarily concerned with managing water, have not been thoroughly consulted during the project design and also while developing implementation and monitoring and evaluation mechanisms; ii) the poor people need to be targeted and the local communities empowered, capacitated, and involved in managing water; iii) informed participation of all stakeholders- government, civil society and others- should be sought openly and inclusively; iv) water should be treated both as a resource and as a service. The Policy further depicts the ADB's commitment to helping the DMCs either in amending their existing water policies or formulating new water policies to achieve these objectives. The Water Policy 2001 has not only been informed by these valuable learnings but also by a clear commitment towards serving the poor since one of the seven key elements of this Policy is: improving and expanding the delivery of water services (involving the private sector and emphasising equity in access to water for the poor) for which, it suggests 'facilitating the exchange of water sector information and experiences, including public and private-community-NGO partnerships, improving governance, and promoting decentralisation, among others (ADB, 2011; ADB, 2001).

The Water Policy 2001 also acknowledges that the DMCs have not made much progress in addressing gender concerns despite its relevance for the success of the water supplies. It, therefore, has expressed its commitment to promote gender integration at all levels- policies, plans, programmes and projects- by ensuring that i) a gender analysis is undertaken at the design stage, (ii) gender equity provisions are clearly stated in the objectives and scope of the activity, and (iii) monitoring data are disaggregated by gender (ADB, 2001). Following on the gender commitment expressed in its Water Policy 2001, ADB has continued to be more committed towards the GAD approach as could be reflected from the review of its subsequent important project documents: In-house Review Report 2004 (ADB, 2004) and Comprehensive Review Report 2006 (ADB, 2006). Given the rapid economic growth in the Asia and Pacific region and significant shifts in the development, aid, and financial landscape, the ADB felt a need and an opportunity to set a new strategic course and thus released its new long-term strategic framework 'Strategy 2020' covering the period 2008–2020.

The Strategy 2020, replacing the then long-term strategy framework 2001-2015, is expected to serve as ADB's corporate-wide planning document and provide it with a more relevant and innovative role in shaping the region's future. This important policy document also has given high value to gender by considering 'gender equity' as one of the five drivers of change, with four others being- private sector development and operations, good governance and capacity development, knowledge solutions and partnerships- to pursue its vision and three strategic agenda- inclusive economic growth, environmentally sustainable growth, and regional integration (ADB, 2011; ADB, 2008). Citing the experience of the last 10 years, which confirm the importance of women's empowerment and gender equity as essential to enormous social and economic gains, including poverty reduction, improved living standards, and sustainable economic growth, Strategy 2020 conveys ADB's intention to promote and support gender equity by designing gender-inclusive projects and paying careful attention to gender issues across the full range of its operations for yielding specific gender outcomes such as improved access for females to education and health services, clean water, better sanitation, and basic infrastructure (ADB, 2008).

Furthermore, in the elaboration of its first strategic approach "inclusive economic growth" to reduce poverty in Asia, the Bank has indicated that it is only through investment made on women, thereby women's empowerment, that this goal can be achieved. The Bank mentions that it will support investment in education and essential public services, such as water and sanitation so that the poor, especially women that comprise the largest group among those excluded from the benefits of the region's economic expansion, could benefit more. Gender equality and the empowerment of women being the fundamental elements in achieving inclusive growth, the Bank is committed to continually increasing investments aiming to increase women's access to various social and economic resources, such as credit, so that all get the opportunity to improve their standards of living, thereby contributing to economic growth, poverty reduction, and the mitigation of extreme inequalities (ADB, 2008).

To achieve the objectives of the Water Policy 2001 and the vision and strategic agenda of its Strategy 2020, the ADB developed an Operational Plan in 2011 (ADB, 2011). This document also well reflects ADB's commitment towards the need to address gender concerns and empower women in the water sector. Highlighting the importance of health, education and equity in the sharing of water and sanitation benefits, ADB acknowledges in this operational plan that the lack of access to safe water and adequate sanitation facilities affects the women and girls, who generally spend hours collecting water from distant sources, and more so the girls than the boys when they are in schools. In turn, this situation will constrain the improvement in general health, increased access to education, and women's and girls' empowerment. Likewise, the Bank's commitment towards women's effective role in water management can be well understood from its emphasis on community participation in planning and implementation of water development and management activities. The Bank believes that community empowerment and community participation improve governance, innovation, infrastructure quality, cost-effectiveness, and the sustainability of projects. While talking about the factors that contribute to increased community participation, the Bank has specifically mentioned 'education and awareness-raising (i.e., capacity building) of communities and individuals on water management issues, seeking to afford closer attention to mainstreaming gender considerations' among others (ADB, 2011).

To assess the impact of such gender-sensitive policies at the national and local level, a review of the project documents of the ADB funded Third Small Towns Water Supply and Sanitation Sector Project (TSTWSSSP)-Nepal, showing the progress for the period March 2015 to March 2020, was undertaken as a part of this research. The status of the integration of gender concerns in this project is as follows.

Third Small Towns Water Supply and Sanitation Sector Project (TSTWSSSP): The TSTWSSSP implemented by the Department of Water Supply and Sewerage Management (DWSSM) under the ADB funding in 20 towns of Nepal beginning March 2015 is providing water services to small towns with a population of 5,000 to 40,000 that show the potential for growth by having access to roads, power supply and telecommunications. The project work has been completed in 18 towns and is about to be completed in the remaining two towns. The project includes the upgrade or construction of water supply systems involving 1,450 kilometres of water supply pipelines; 67,500 household connections; and 20 water treatment systems with an estimated capacity of 50,000 cubic meters per day. The project will also provide about 5,000 household toilets with septic tanks, as well as the provision of septic management facilities and equipment (ADB, 2020).

Regarding the gender integration in the project, there has been remarkable progress in this aspect as compared to the FRWSSSP implemented by the DWSS under the ADB funding during the late '90s. During the time of review, it was found that the FRWSSSP documents were mostly gender-blind, there was no mentioning of women or gender in its goals, objectives and strategies, no women were found in senior decision-making positions since the number of women engineers was less than 10 in the entire DWSS- the implementing agency with more than 5,000 male engineers. Similarly, the project staff was unable to spend an adequate amount of time with community people, more so women, in the project communities during the design phase resulting in an inequitable sharing of project benefits between women and men. Moreover, the project field staff did not have an idea that a water supply and sanitation project could achieve women's empowerment, thereby the fulfilment of women's various other strategic gender needs. In fact, in some situations, despite the availability of improved water and sanitation facilities in the community, the local women had to spend even more time and labour to get their water-related works done in these facilities as compared to the time they had to spend while using traditional water sources. The organisational culture in most of the Nepali organisations was male-dominated and DWSS and its projects were no exception to this reality implying that the limited number of women staff members would either not get the opportunity to participate in the official meetings or even when they participated the chances of voicing their concerns was almost nil. Despite the impact that regular gender training and follow-up training could make in increasing staff's understanding of gender issues, gender norms, gender roles and the varying needs and concerns of women and men in the WASH sector, and thereby on their gendered mindset, there was no budget allocated for gender training and no efforts were made by the senior management to sensitise their staff on these matters as discussed in detail in Part II, Chapter VI-VIII.

In contrast to the FRWSSSP, the TSTWSSSP considers gender equity and mainstreaming along with governance and capacity developments, and partnerships as its drivers of change- the features borrowed from its donor's Strategy 2020 (ADB, 2020). From a time when the senior government officials were not even willing to talk about gender and accept that the water projects need to be thinking of addressing gender issues in the water sector (since it is a technical sector good for men only), to come to a stage when the government officials of the same department- DWSSM, approve a policy document that accepts gender equity and mainstreaming as one of the key drivers of change in the project is an incredible achievement. Further, as per the project document, the project's main focus is on gender equity and the expected outcome is inclusive, gender-focused and sustainable water supply and sanitation services in project towns, which are the big milestones of the TSTWSSSP in its contribution towards gender equality. Likewise, the design of this project is also gender-informed since it is firmly acknowledged in the project document that the project should carefully determine the design so that the poor, female-headed and minority households are not excluded from access to improved WASH services. In turn, the project document (ADB, 2020) further suggests that the project personnel should make every effort to consult with these people using people-friendly methods such as the focus group discussion, interviews and local meetings and the consultations should be held separately to maintain privacy if so desired.

The sensitivity maintained by the TSTWSSSP in addressing gender concerns while setting the project goals, objectives, strategies, outcomes and design during the implementation phase also explains the ADB's profoundness in acknowledging and addressing gender concerns in its projects. For instance, while presenting the progress made on its Output 2 'strengthened sector policy, regulatory and institutional capacity, and service delivery', the project report mentions that "the National Water Supply and Sanitation Training Centre (NWSSTC) under the DWSSM has been supporting the project management office (PMO) in providing training related to livelihood enhancement, leadership and utility management training etc. as stipulated in the GESI action plan of the project. The progress report also depicts that some of the training like WASH campaign in schools and girls' menstrual hygiene have also been satisfactorily completed" (ADB, 2020). These signs of progress on gender aspects imply that the project has well-acknowledged the challenges that poor people and women encounter while meeting their WASH needs in the community and those that the girls encounter while managing their menstruation in the schools.

To get to see women and the poor mentioned in most relevant sections of the document, space created for women and poor people's inclusion in the project, information disaggregated by gender, among others, in the TSTWSSSP for women's overall empowerment is greatly satisfying for those working in the field of GAD. The appreciation of gender roles and the analysis made considering the different needs and concerns of men and women and boys and girls reflected in the project documents certainly confirms the consistency expressed in addressing women's and poor people's concerns. Although the end-result of the project concerning the real changes it will bring in women's and girls' lives vis-à-vis men's and boys' lives by ensuring equal opportunities and benefits to all of them is yet to be seen, the gender sensitivity shown in the design and implementation phases of the project as reflected in the project documents will certainly qualify it to be called a much more gender-sensitive and socially inclusive project as compared to the Bank-funded water supply projects implemented during the late '90s.

Areas Demanding for Further Gender Attention: The presentation made in the earlier section depicted the ADB's commitment towards integrating gender concerns in its water and sanitation policies beginning early '00s till the implementation of the TSTWSSSP funded in Nepal in 2015-2020. Although the review of the ADB's water policies confirms its profoundness in progressively advancing its WASH policies towards women's empowerment, thereby gender equality, over the last 20 years, there are certain areas where it will still be useful for the Bank to pay extra attention to make their WASH policies even more gender-focused. The expectation behind the recommendation to pay extra attention to certain areas has to do with the Bank's influencing role in shaping the water policies of its DMCs in the Asia-Pacific region, including Nepal. The analogy is that if the Bank's policies are fully gender-informed, the WASH policies of its DMCs will also tend to be gender-aware and instrumental to achieve women's social, economic and political empowerment.

In the third year of the commencement of its Water Policy 2001, the 'bedrock of ADB water operations' (ADB, 2011), the Bank's Water Sector Committee led an in-house review of 41 ADB funded projects to assess how this policy had been integrated into ADB operations, take stock of achievements, and stimulate improvements in project design and implementation. In turn, this review recommended carrying out a comprehensive survey of the ADB-funded projects in 2005 covering 10 important areas, including 'mainstreaming gender and development', in its water operations (ADB, 2004). While the recommendation to include gender mainstreaming indicates the presence of a gender-aware in-house team and the Bank's commitment towards gender equality, it also, at the same time, implicitly indicates the Bank's weak gender performance in the projects it funded in the DMCs till the in-house review of 2004. One of the core reasons behind this could be that the Water Policy 2001 is more poor-focused than women or gender-focused. Further, the in-house review team also evaluated the completed checklists of the 26 recently approved projects concerning their incorporation of water policy actions directly aimed at poverty reduction, including i) developing 'pro-poor' water policies and the 'participation of the poor' in the project, ii) developing water rights in a manner that protects the 'rights of the poor' to equitable water services, iii) turning over-irrigation operation and maintenance to farmer groups, iv) targeting the 'needs of the poor' in flood management projects, and v) addressing water pollution 'problems affecting the poor' (ADB, 2004).

Given the focus on 'poor' in all of the Bank's policy actions, it can be said that it is a reflection of the inconsistent focus provided on women's role by the Water Policy 2001, which probably could be due to the lack of a clear understanding at that time that even within poor, women are further poor in most of its DMCs like Nepal. The Bank's analysis made in its various publications released after 2001 and the analysis of some other organisations makes it clear that women are the poorest of the poor (UNDP, 2014; ADB, 2008; ADB, 2006; ADB, 2004). Hence, unless and until women and girls are categorically mentioned in all stages of a WASH project, it cannot benefit them as equal to men and boys.

In general, when projects are evaluated, different types of tools and checklists are used for it just the way the Bank's in-house team did it as mentioned above. However, it is essential to consider that when checklists and tools are developed to assess the impact of WASH projects or for that matter any other project, it is necessary to use a gender lens so that they could ensure gender disaggregation in the collection of data and its analysis. Since the management of water supplies has traditionally been considered a women's domain, it is only through the gender-sensitive tools that the women's reality and the impact of the WASH projects on the beneficiaries, more so the poor, women and girls, can be captured. Equally important is to implement the WASH projects considering that women and men have different needs and concerns so that when the projects are assessed, the gender-sensitive tools could facilitate the collection of gender-disaggregated data to know the extent to which those projects benefitted women and girls as compared to men and boys. The discussion made below based on the findings of the comprehensive external review, however, confirms that these factors were paid relatively less attention in the Water Policy 2001.

The comprehensive external review that took place in 2005 focusing on several key areas of the Water Policy 2001 found that the ADB had made progress to advance integrated water resource management (IWRM) and improve water service delivery through targeted investments, capacity building of water users' associations, and improved project design that is sensitive of social and environmental concerns. However, the review team also disclosed that IWRM is neither well understood at any level nor is it effectively implemented due to various institutional and organisational constraints in the DMCs. The external review team also reported that operations and maintenance were severely hampered by the lack of resources and capacities in DMCs, causing inefficiencies and premature deterioration of water service assets. Consequently, the external review team came up with several recommendations to mitigate adverse project impacts and ensure environmental sustainability, gender equity, and pro-poor and participatory practices in both the management and delivery of water services. The recommendations and action points related to the women and poor were: i) ADB must catalyse broader inclusion of women, civil society, and poor and other marginalised groups in the decision-making processes and institutions governing the water sector; and ii) ADB should include these groups in the development of national water policies, legal systems, and establishment of various water authorities (ADB, 2006). These recommendations confirm that gender focus was lacking in the Water Policy 2001 which is why the projects that ADB funded in its DMCs were unable to well address gender concerns and create space for women and the poor for their effective participation in WASH activities.

The scarcity of water has always been an unfolding disaster in the Bank's DMCs. As an important donor and a key influencer in the region's water sector, the Bank is always concerned about addressing the shortage of water in its DMCs. In turn, to address the imbalance between the demand for and supply of water, the Bank has proposed a range of choices that include: i) increased efficiencies in water use across the range of users; ii) expanded wastewater management and reuse, including sanitation; iii) embedded integrated water resources management, including improved risk management to mitigate floods, droughts, and other water-related disasters; iv) expanded knowledge and capacity development that uses technology and innovation more directly, and v) enhanced partnerships with the private sector. Similarly, while talking about its strategy to enhance water security and ensure equitable access among a range of users, one of its recommendations, among others, is that the region will need to use available water resources more efficiently and improve demand management (ADB, 2011). Notwithstanding the crucial role that women play in various important stages of a WASH project, including increasing efficiency in water use, wastewater management, use and promotion of sanitation and hygiene practices, and operation and maintenance of water supplies, among others, the Bank overlooked the need to specify the women's role either in any of its five choices suggested as solutions or in its strategy where it talks about the efficient use of water to address the imbalance between the demand and supply of water.

Similarly, the other strategy that the Bank has proposed to strike a balance between the demand and supply of water, is the involvement of the private sector and the increased collaboration between the public and private entities (ADB, 2011). Again, what the Bank has missed out on while proposing the involvement of the private sector as its strategy is the GESI consideration. Since the engagement of the private sector is basically for profit, the Bank and the agencies alike need to come up with some strategies to ensure that the women and the other poor, vulnerable and marginalised people, including female-headed households, do not get deprived of water for drinking purposes simply because they cannot afford to pay for it due to the lack of access to and control over income. Indeed, in one of the ADB-funded projects, although the project was able to increase the coverage of clean drinking water in rural communities, this coverage could not include poor and marginalised people due to the 50% capital contribution expected of the latter by the project. Since the poor and marginalised people were unable to meet the costs, they were excluded from the benefits (WaterAid, 2006). It, therefore, needs to be well understood by the agencies, be they international or local, that simply having a separate section on gender equality or women's empowerment does not guarantee women's inclusion unless gender issues are well integrated into every aspect of the organisation.

Given the ADB's increasing commitment towards gender equality and women's empowerment through women's increased participation in WASH activities as discussed above, the discussion made around the areas requiring further gender attention should be perceived as the recommendations that help the Bank to exert adequate pressure on its DMCs due to its financing power.

United Nations Children's Fund

"United Nations Children's Fund (UNICEF) works in over 190 countries and territories to save children's lives, to defend their rights, and to help them fulfil their potential, from early childhood through adolescence. And we never give up" (https://www.unicef.org/).

In Nepal, UNICEF started its operations through its Delhi office in 1964 and a full-fledged office in 1972. In its 50 years in Nepal, UNICEF has been supporting many strides the country has taken, focusing mainly on the changing needs of children, adolescents and women (UNICEF, 2018).

Gender Integration in UNICEF's Strategic Plan 2016-2030: Being one of the initial donors in the water and sanitation sector of Nepal, and the UN agency which is still implicitly engaged in contributing to this sector through health and gender equality components, UNICEF's Strategic Plan 2016-2030 (UNICEF,

2016) was reviewed to assess the extent to which it has addressed gender issues in its WASH sector. The review depicts UNICEF's acknowledgement of the interconnectedness between WASH and gender equality as well as several other development goals like education, health, nutrition, poverty and economic growth, urban services, resilience and climate change. The strategic plan recognises that the lack of access to proper WASH services not only causes child mortality and morbidity but also contributes to under-nutrition and stunting and acts as a barrier to education for girls and to economic opportunities for the poor. Moreover, the strategic plan also admits that the challenges posed by the shortage of water supply, poor quality of drinking water, and weak operation and maintenance of the systems along with the low sanitation coverage, open defecation practices of almost 946 million people, and the destructive impacts of climate change and emergencies threaten the sustainability of the WASH systems, and thereby the lives of the vulnerable groups, including isolated communities, poor households, people with disabilities, and in particular, women and girls.

Accordingly, UNICEF has prioritised two overarching objectives in its strategic plan: i) achieve universal and equitable access to safe and affordable drinking water for all; and ii) achieve access to adequate and equitable sanitation and hygiene for all and end open defecation, paying special attention to the needs of women and girls and those in vulnerable situations. To achieve the two objectives, UNICEF intends to work in several areas including climate change, private sector mobilisation, strengthening the national systems, establishing effective sector institutions, and capacity building of the concerned stakeholders. Similarly, the other areas where UNICEF aims to seriously engage to meet its objectives are: advocating for women's and girls' right to WASH services, menstrual hygiene management for adolescent girls, emergency and disaster management, and developing a sound accountability framework to make the government more responsive to the public needs. With an acknowledgement that vulnerable and disadvantaged groups, more so women and girls and those marginalised based on ethnicity or geography, climate change and emergency-affected communities, different kinds of disabilities, and poverty, are the ones that suffer the most when WASH facilities are not in their easy access, UNICEF has committed to pay more attention in supporting and strengthening the monitoring systems so that these groups could easily be identified and proper services ensured on time. Moreover, it also has clearly expressed its intention to pay special attention to girls in poor households or children with disabilities living in isolated communities since these groups experience multiple disadvantages. Furthermore, UNICEF programmes also aim to ensure that children and adolescents, along with others, are given the opportunity to voice their concerns and take part in decision-making.

Since the scarcity of water and poor sanitation and hygienic practices disproportionately affect the women and girls as it affects their maternal and neonatal health, increases their drudgery of fetching water considerably, leads to their insecurity and indignity associated with open defecation and compels girls to miss out school, UNICEF firmly recommends the WASH strategy to be GESI sensitive. Nevertheless, UNICEF, at the same time, discloses that women continue to be under-represented in positions of authority in the sector at all levels, from community WASH committees to within ministries and international agencies, including its own organisation (UNICEF, 2016).

Areas Demanding for Further Gender Attention: The discussions presented above indicate that the GESI approach has been well reflected in UNICEF's Strategic Plan 2016-2030. However, as in the case of several other international donors, the lack of consistency in reflecting the gender dimension in all aspects of the WASH sector can be noticed in UNICEF's strategic plan as well. For instance, while highlighting the concept of community empowering as one of its programmatic approaches, it mentions that UNICEF will continue to place communities at the centre of its programming so that they can effectively engage with all concerned stakeholders, voice their concerns for meaningful participation in all stages of the WASH projects, ask for complete information- social, technical and financial- about the projects, and demand for the fulfilment of their WASH rights. Accordingly, UNICEF intends to provide all kinds of support to the communities as they need (UNICEF, 2016). What is, however, lacking in this commitment towards community empowerment is the unpacking of the word 'community' since this terminology is not gender-neutral although it appears to be. The lack of the use of gender-specific language can also be seen in UNICEF's programmatic approach 'delivering services and supplies', where it talks about three specific purposes to guide this activity for **people** most in need: i) to model evidence-based and innovative approaches and technologies on a large scale; ii) to act in emergencies when children are most vulnerable, and iii) to reach the **poorest and most marginalised** groups where no one else is able to do so.

Since the beginning of the implementation of improved water services, the service providers, governments, and donors have been heavily relying on the use of so-called gender-neutral terminologies but the result has neither been in favour of women and girls nor has it been in favour of the poor, vulnerable and marginalised. In a patriarchal society like that of Nepal, the community, in general, refers to men and the resourceful, which is why it is the men and the resourceful that have been mostly enjoying the benefits of the development projects, including those of the WASH sector. This oversight can thus question, learning from the earlier experiences in Nepal as well as other countries, whether the water supplies supported by UNICEF can ensure the project benefits reaching equally to men, women- particularly those from female-headed households, and poor. Experiences have confirmed that for women and girls to benefit at par with men, they need to be categorically mentioned in the policy documents.

In its strategic plan, UNICEF also highlights the involvement of the private sector, along with others, to strengthen the resilience of supply chains through times of crisis in the delivery of WASH services. It also admits, at the same time, in its Result Areas that the interruption of WASH services during crisis affects health, nutritional status, and the safety and dignity of children and women, and therefore, UNICEF will focus its response on WASH programmes that are culturally appropriate, secure, user/disabled-friendly, and gender-appropriate, including the management of menstrual hygiene (UNICEF, 2016). The missing element in the discussion, however, is the elaboration on the limitations around the engagement of the private sector. Since the private sector lacks the experience of working in remote communities, more so during times of crisis; fails to spend adequate time to understand the gender, ethnic, and cultural sensitivities of the community; works basically for profit, and generally has a different work style which is beyond the comprehension of a typical uneducated rural poor person; the women, girls and the poor and marginalised people, who do not generally come forward to voice their concerns, may not be able to enjoy the benefits as opposed to men, boys and the other normal people.

Since women and the poor always lack access to information, knowledge, income and other various resources, and thus, fail to meet the various requirements mandated by the private sector- be it in a normal situation or emergencies, these categories are unlikely to benefit from such WASH projects unless special attention is given on their practical difficulties and limitations. As GWA (2003) comments, 'women need to be provided with economically and socially sound subsidies taking into account the power dynamics in the family. The cash subsidies provided to men for constructing toilets are not used for this purpose since these are women's concerns and needs related to their dignity and safety; men, on the other hand, can do their business anytime anywhere'.

Government of Finland: Rural Village Water Resources Management Project

Rural Village Water Resources Management Project (RVWRMP) is a multilateral project between the Government of Nepal (GoN), the European Union (EU), and the Ministry for Foreign Affairs of Finland (MfFAoF), with technical assistance coming from FCG, Finland. This project is a continuation of the three-decade-long non-stop water sector collaboration between the GoN and MfFAoF. Since 2006, the project is being implemented in eight districts in *Sudurpashchim* (Far-Western) Province and two districts in *Karnali* Province of Nepal, with a focus on rural water resources management and livelihood promotion. The current project Phase III started in March 2016 and will end in 2022 (RVWRMP, 2020a; GoN, 2015). The MfFAoF has been supporting the GoN with various development projects, including rural water supplies and sanitation, for the last thirty years. The Rural Water Supply and Sanitation Support Programme (RWSSP) funded by the MfFAoF and implemented by a Nepali team of consultants, with technical assistance from Plancentre Ltd. of Finland, was included in the research undertaken during 1997-2000.

The key findings of the review of the then RWSSP policies and practices while looking at it from a gender perspective were: limited women were working in the project and only one woman in the senior team, women's contribution in policymaking was almost nil, and the project's goals, objectives and strategies were not gender-informed as the focus was only on making water available in the project communities, and not on women's empowerment or meeting their strategic gender needs. Similarly, the other observations that came out of the research were: the project documents were not gender-specific as they relied on the use of gender-neutral looking terminologies like 'users', 'community', 'beneficiaries', 'members' etc. like many other donors at that time overseeing the fact that there are differences between women's and men's needs and concerns in a water and sanitation project so such words unless unpacked and gender-specific strategies developed, cannot benefit women as equal as to men. In turn, these gender-insensitive project documents led to the inclusion of only one woman in an 11-member water user's committee and no woman in decision-making positions.

Likewise, the other findings were that no staff were provided formal gender training implying the lack of profoundness on the part of the project management to integrate gender in organisational policies and practices. Consequently, it led to the absence of even maternity leave (this issue was addressed in RWSSP Phase II) in the project policy documents although such leave was already established as a women's right in the GoN as well as many other international and national organisations operating in Nepal. The results of these gender-insensitive policies and practices as presented in Part II Chapters VI and VIII of this book were that the project was not able to benefit the community people to the extent that the project anticipated since the number of malfunctioning tube-wells was increasing, the project was not saving women's water hauling time in a real sense, women were not able to increase their income by participating in various economic opportunities and it also did not contribute much to meeting women's strategic gender needs, among other things.

Given that many gender-related changes have taken place in the policy documents of the international donors, national governments, and the other organisations engaged in the water sector in the last two decades, and that RVWRMP is the continuation of the RWSSP reviewed 20 years ago, as well as of RWSSP Phase I and Phase II which was just recently completed, the project completion report of RWSSP Phase II and some other project documents of RVWRMP were reviewed to assess the magnitude of gender changes taking place in these projects implemented over the years.

Gender Integration in RWSSP Phase II and RVWRMP: A review of the RWSSP Phase II Completion Report (RWSSP, 2019) shows that women's role, in general, and gender issues, in particular, were profoundly addressed in this phase as opposed to the earlier phases of this project. The credit goes to the Human Rights Based Approach (HRBA) and GESI Strategy and Action Plan prepared in 2015 for this big gender change achieved during the RWSSP Phase II (GoN, 2015). Concerning women's participation in WUSCs, the RWSSP Phase I had aimed for 33% women in WUSCs following the national target while the RWSSP Phase II had set a target of 50%, with a commitment to ensure a balance between the number of women and men in the WUSC. To assess the progress made on women's participation in WUSCs between the two phases, the project developed eight indicators and selected 402 WUSCs from

Phase I and 397 WUSCs from Phase II. As can be seen in Table 8 below, which summarises the progress made by the RWSSP on these indicators while moving from Phase I to Phase II, the project was successful in making good progress in all indicators, except the indicator 'female as chairperson in the WUSC'. The indicators related to women's participation in the WUSCs show that 29-42% of the WUSCs in Phase II had either more women or a gender-balanced composition as compared to Phase I. Similarly, on indicator concerning women's participation in key positions of the WUSCs, there was an increase of 2% in general, and from 7-23% in key positions- treasurer (7%), vice-chairperson (9%) and secretary (23%), in particular. It was only in the position of the chairperson that the change was reported to be negative, with 9% of the WUSCs reporting to have a woman as the chairperson in Phase I as opposed to only 8% in Phase II. Interestingly, although the RWSSP had 10 'all-women WUSCs', it did not have any 'all-men WUSCs', a sign indicating the acknowledgement of the role that women play in the WASH sector.

Table 8: Status of Women's Participation in WUSCs in RWSSP Phase I and Phase II, 2019

Indicators of Women's Participation in WUCs	**Phase I** (N=402)	**Phase II** (N= 397)	**Change** (%)
Gender balance in WUSC (range)	60%	78%	30%
Gender balance in WUSC (>42%)	72%	93%	29%
WUSC has more women than men	36%	51%	42%
Female in WUSC key positions	97%	99%	2%
WUSC has a female chairperson	9%	8%	(11%)
WUSC has female Vice-Chairperson	23%	25%	9%
WUSC has female Secretary	31%	38%	23%
WUSC has female Treasurer	75%	80%	7%

Source: RWSSP Phase II Completion Report 2019

An equally positive aspect of the RWSSP Phase II was the provision to ensure training on technical aspects to women so that they could earn extra income using their increased skills. For instance, out of a total of 869 Village Maintenance Workers (VMWs) in the WUSCs, 18% were women, with a progressive move from 14% in Phase I to 20% in Phase II (RWSSP, 2019). The project claims that although Phase II had aimed for 50% of the total VMWs

(525) to be women, the achievement of 20% should still be considered positively given the patriarchal mindset prevalent in the country. In terms of beneficiaries, Phase II of the RWSSP was, however, able to ensure women's proportion at 51%, with the total number of beneficiaries being 337,863 against the target of 250,000. Out of a total of 330 new schemes in Phase II, 97% had an operation and maintenance plan and 93% had collected water tariff (RWSSP, 2019). Apart from women's increased participation in various WASH activities in the project areas, the RWSSP Phase II was also able to increase the decision-making ability of the local women.

> *Sobmaya Rana, a 28-year-old Magar woman from Rishing Rural Municipality, Tanahun district, Nepal, is the WUSC Secretary of Todkedi Drinking Water Supply Scheme which lifts water from 500 meters below using electric pumps at two access points and benefits 1,228 people and two schools. Although it is Sobmaya's first experience as a WUSC member, she is effectively handling the writing of the meeting minutes, storage of all paperwork and management of the bookkeeping. There are four other women in the WUSC and two of them are also in key positions. According to Sobmaya, they have learned a lot and now feel confident in expressing their views during meetings. She also thinks that although she is not affiliated with any political party at the moment, she would consider being a candidate in the next local elections (RWSSP, 2019).*

About 92% of the 1,280 respondents, with women's representation being at 94%, of a survey undertaken to understand the impact of the water projects stated that women could influence decision-making while the scheme was being planned and implemented. It also came out from the survey that women's effective participation was not only contributing to the effectiveness of the water systems but also to providing women with the opportunity to fulfil their strategic gender needs such as tangible work experience and thereby, access to resources, confidence, enhancing leadership skills, the decision-making power on matters other than the WASH-related, social dignity and great personal satisfaction. The women who were reluctant even to tell their names in the initial meetings had, however, started to freely express themselves and influence the decision-making processes after attending training sessions and participating in several WUSC meetings and activities. Such active participation also has led women to be looking for other personal as well as economic development opportunities now that they have saved a considerable amount of time earlier spent in water hauling. Another strong finding of the study is that the functionality of the water scheme is associated with the number of women in the WUSCs; the higher the number of women in the WUSCs, the greater the likelihood of the water schemes being fully functional. However, what is also important for this success is the presence of at least one woman in the key position of the WUSCs (RWSSP, 2019).

The reasons attributed to the impressive gender changes that took place from the RWSSP implemented in the late '90s to the RWSSP Phase I and mainly Phase II implemented afterwards are the adoption of human rights and GESI strategies along with the continued organisational focus on GESI themes and increased commitment of the project staff towards GESI. These strategies led Phase II of the project to focus on women, poor, marginalised and excluded sections of the society for their equitable sharing of project resources and opportunities, including participation in WUCs, meaningful presence in key positions in the WUSCs and VMWs, and training, among others. The women WUSC members were further provided targeted training on leadership and confidence building. Any training provided to the duty bearers and the rights holders also had human rights and GESI approaches built in it. The RWSSP Phase II, learning from its experience, therefore, recommends that the guidelines on WUSC formation should spell out the need for women's and disadvantaged groups' active participation in the committee activities followed up by training to build their confidence, capacity, and skills (RWSSP, 2019), which is in line with what others have learned as well (Regmi, 2000).

While talking about the RVWRMP, the Phase III of the RWSSP, what is new is the GESI focused contextual analysis which it undertakes before implementing its WASH interventions in the project areas. For a WASH project to be successful in providing equal benefits to women, men, the poor and other marginalised people, a GESI focused analysis of the project area is a must. Only a properly done gender analysis can lead to the funding and the implementing agencies to design a project that is appropriate, relevant, GESI friendly, and has the potential for long-term sustainability. Accordingly, in 2008, the initial phase of the RVWRMP carried out a Gender and Social Discrimination Study to find out the social, cultural, religious, economic and political practices that were causing gender and social discrimination in the project areas. The findings of this study which highlighted the areas where the project had to pay more attention in its next phase and the findings of the GESI Impact Assessment of the District WASH Programme (RWSSP, 2013) which highlighted the positive aspects of GESI in the RWSSP (Western Nepal) Phase I and demanded its continuation in the upcoming phase of the project, guided the drafting of the HRBA and GESI Strategy Action Plan 2015 for the Phase II of the project (GoN, 2015).

The above-mentioned findings along with the findings coming out of the Phase II projects led to carry out a socio-economic analysis in Phase III of the RVWRMP as well, with an appreciation that social discrimination based on ethnicity, caste and gender plays a significant role in keeping people poor and marginalised. Drawing on all these experiences, RVWRMP Phase III acknowledges that women generally have an immense workload- both inside and outside the home, are the poorest of the poor, have limited options available for improvements, and hardly get to engage in decision-making be it at the household or the community level. In turn, the project focused on increasing women's and disadvantaged groups' meaningful participation in natural resource management and the equitable access of these groups to project benefits and opportunities. As in the other hilly and mountainous areas of Nepal, water is scarce in the project areas as well. The water has to be fetched from far away and because women have traditionally been given this task, they spend a large amount of their time in this activity. In turn, the project, ensuring that every drop of water has a rational use, focuses on multiple uses of water, intending to reach 1.5 million people with safe drinking water and toilets during the project period. For the sustainability of the water supply schemes and increased local ownership, the RVWRMP Phase III has put a strong emphasis on community involvement in all stages of a water supply scheme. Given women's important role in the water sector, the project has paid special attention to their participation from the beginning of the project till the end. Further, in its Step-by-Step approach, which is all about developing foundations for a sustainable future of the water supply schemes by ensuring active participation of all concerned stakeholders in project activities, it involves inclusive and gender-sensitive tools so that schemes are technically and socially acceptable by the potential beneficiaries (RVWRMP, 2020c; RVWRMP, 2020b; GoN, 2015; RVWRMP, 2015).

While looking at the project approach using a gender lens, one major strength noticed in the RVWRMP Phase III is the human rights dimension applied in project implementation, believing that the fulfilment of water rights, thereby human rights, is an entry point towards poverty reduction. Ensuring equitable access to WASH services and empowering women and disadvantaged groups in water management are the core principles of the project. An equally important strong point of this project is its emphasis on the GESI approach following the footsteps of the RWSSP and RVWRMP earlier phases, with a recognition that the integration of GESI strategies improves the project impact, performance and sustainability, and thereby gender equality. Because of women's primary role in water management and women being the principal residents of the households due to the increased male migration from the project areas, the project is concerned with ensuring women's voices are heard and they get to participate in all decision-making processes. Several awareness-raising and sensitisation activities, including capacity building, were introduced at the community level so that the local people, including the poor, marginalised and vulnerable, could actively engage in project activities.

Concerning the implementation of the WASH activities, the project, within the human rights and GESI frameworks, is also engrossed in addressing ill-practices such as *Chhaupadi*, which compels women and girls to stay in unhealthy, unhygienic, and insecure places, generally the cow-sheds, separate from the main house, during their menstrual period. The women and girls are restricted from attending public meetings, visiting the temple and prayer room, using the common places and items like water, toilet and sanitation facilities, as well as touching men, milk and curd, to name a few customs, during their menstruation. The RVWRMP Phase III has thus been engaging in campaigns against this discriminatory practice as well as in providing support to implement food production and income generation activities to strengthen the local livelihood. The project has set up a target that 80% of menstruating women will be using the toilet during their menstruation and that all project districts will be declared open defecation free or ODF so that women could carry out their defecation with dignity and a sense of complete security. Similarly, the project supports the building of toilets in schools and health posts ensuring the availability of water, soap, pad disposal facility and privacy so that women and girls could manage women's menstruation without having any impact on their school classes and professional work (RVWRMP, 2020c; RVWRMP, 2020b; GoN, 2015).

The discussions made above indicate that the WASH projects supported by the EU, MfFAoF and GoN and implemented under the technical support of several Finnish companies in close coordination with the local governments, starting from RWSSP in the '90s till to the implementation of the ongoing RVWRMP Phase III, are gradually being more gender-sensitive in all phases-design to implementation to operation and maintenance phases. Women's participation, together with men's, has been much higher than before and their ability to influence the decision-making processes, holding of key positions and leadership roles in WUSCs, employment in paid positions and involvement in various income-generating activities confirm project management's commitment towards ensuring not only meeting women's practical gender needs but also their strategic gender needs.

Areas Demanding for Further Gender Attention: Despite the impressive results that the earlier phases of the RWSSP and RVWRMP have got in making their WASH sector gender-focused, there are certain areas where the RVWRMP Phase III, learning from the experiences of the earlier phases, needs to pay extra attention to make its WASH work fully gender-sensitive. One such area concerning the lack of adequate gender efforts is the target of recruiting 50% women in the position of VMWs since the project could only have 20% women in this position. This poor result of the RWSSP Phase II, where 80% of the VMWs are men, who hardly visit the water systems unlike women who visit the systems every day, notice problems if any, and take immediate actions, challenges the project's learning that the water supply schemes managed by the WUSCs that had more women as members and some in key positions would have higher chances of being more functional. The other area where the RWSSP was found weak in its gender commitment was the modification of its FY05 Indicator 1.2 'disabled and gender-friendly WASH projects' for the reason that they found the criteria for 'gender-friendly' difficult to define (RWSSP, 2019). This change is hard to accept given several successfully managed gender-integrated works of the completed RWSSP and RVWRMP projects since defining gender friendliness in a WASH project simply means the materials, tools, resources, technology, design, location, among others, be aligned with women users' needs so that they could benefit. For instance, one of the findings of the earlier research was that in several water schemes in the Tarai, including those supported by the RWSSP, the handle of the tube-wells was unduly long for the height of the local women, resulting in difficulty in the use of the tube-wells, with resultant back pain reported by many local women.

Similarly, another gender issue that concerns the RWSSP results and learning is that 'women's true participation in the key positions of WUSCs is problematic, even though they seem to be well represented in papers- the project thus recommends providing training to increase women's capacity, confidence, skills, and decision-making ability' (RWSSP, 2019). What the project has missed out here is the emphasis on investing more time to prepare women to better understand the context of the WASH project, gender issues in the project community, the role women and men have been traditionally playing in this sector and the role they need to play in different stages of the project, and the practical and strategic benefits they can exercise after their meaningful participation in WUSCs etc. The time invested to do all this is called social preparation time. The Gender and Social Discrimination Study carried out by the RWSSP in 2008 and the subsequent contextual analysis that its succeeding phases have been carrying out are all part of social preparation. The problem encountered by the RWSSP Phase II that women's true participation in WUSC key positions is nothing new since many other development agencies have also been facing this challenge whenever they have started implementing a development project seeking women and poor people's participation in a rural community. But, those who, learning from their initial experience, put on more time in preparing women to better exhibit their roles and responsibilities, have been successful in ensuring sustained benefits. The exact duration of social preparation time, however, varies depending on the progressive stage of a community- the stronger the patriarchal thoughts, the longer the social preparation time (Regmi, 2000; RWSSP, 2019; GoN, 2015). Likewise, despite their emphasis on the declaration of the project areas as ODF and implementation of various activities to achieve it, the finding that 'menstruating women were still not using their toilets' as mentioned above, again indicates the inadequacy of social preparation time spent to persuade the women, their families and the larger community about the importance of using the toilet to ensure women's and girls' health, hygiene, security and dignity. This is another gender issue demanding extra attention during the RVWRMP implementation.

Concerning RVWRMP Phase III, GESI has been integrated into its core values. The project has also made efforts to ensure its integration with organisational policies and practices, to increase women's and ethnic group's involvement in key WUSC positions and other project activities. However, a review of the project factsheets uploaded on its website provides a different impression since the project information is not gender-disaggregated. The factsheets show that women have been clubbed under the terminologies like 'people', 'beneficiaries', 'community', 'households' despite the need to unpack such words for ensuring women's integration in all stages of the project activities. The project document reflects that the 'community' should contribute in cash and kind for the water supply schemes depending on one's economic status. The project also expects labour contribution from the 'community' during the construction and operation and maintenance phases on a 'communal basis', and 'community input' as significant and crucial to the success of schemes (RVWRMP, 2020c).

What is, however, not clear from the focus provided on 'community' is how will women and poor households, including female-headed, pay towards the construction as well as operation and maintenance of the schemes since they generally lack access to and control over resources. Since these categories of the community people are dependent on daily wage labour for their survival, they cannot afford even to contribute their labour during either the construction phase or the operation and maintenance phase. Does it mean these sections of people will not get the service? Moreover, given the fact that the WASH sector is being gradually driven by the 'cost-recovery concept' and the private sector is expected to play the important role of service provider, a serious question emerges- 'will such categories of people get to enjoy the benefits of the improved water supplies irrespective of their inability to pay towards the scheme when the private sector, which works for profit, is on board to deliver the water services?'

Likewise, the project information sheet, which describes the RVWRMP activities like home gardens, income generation, cooperatives, renewable energy, cooking stoves, improved water mills implemented for promoting the local livelihood and the WASH services meant for millions of people, is also heavily relied on the use of the word 'people' (RVWRMP, 2020a) instead of disaggregating the information by gender. Despite the reality that these activities are mostly concerned with women, and thus fall under their domain, the use of misrepresentative gender-neutral words such as "people", which has traditionally been used to indicate to men only, symbolises the gender insensitivity on the part of the project management. Experiences over time have demonstrated that unless and until the data are collected, analysed and presented using a gender lens, the development projects, including the WASH sector, would not benefit women in the same manner that they do to men.

Another area that requires the extra attention of the RVWRMP is the local governments' understanding of gender and the gender issues involved in the WASH sector. As observed in the project information sheet, the RVWRMP's mission is to work with local people and municipalities for achieving 100% access to safe drinking water supply and basic sanitation in the project area. The water supply project, which has already served around 600,000 beneficiaries (RWSSP, 2019), supports the rural municipalities of the project area to manage the water resources and to implement livelihood programmes. To achieve this, the project provides support in preparing Municipality Water Use Master Plans and Livelihoods Implementation Plans, formulating policies, and providing various training to the concerned employees. Learning from the experiences of the RWSSP Phase II, the project expects the municipalities to have an oversight on the employment of VMWs and Pump Operators, equal pay for equal work, subsidies for those who cannot afford to pay for water services, and management of schemes keeping in mind the GESI approach and overall empowerment of women and poor (RVWRMP, 2020a; GoN, 2015). To verify the extent to which the RVWRMP's gender understanding and principles were incorporated at the local level, a municipality level WASH plan of Harinas Rural Municipality (HRM, 2018) was randomly chosen for review.

To one's surprise, the only place where the word 'women' has been mentioned in the municipal level plan is while presenting the population data: "there are total 3,394 households residing in the municipality based on the survey done while preparing the WASH plan. The total population is 21,778, of which 10,708 are women and 11,070 are men" (HRM, 2018). This plan details the water supply, sanitation and hygiene situation in Harinas Rural Municipality and also presents prioritised activities for implementation. Despite the entire world appreciating women's role in the WASH sector and the donors, the EU and MfFAoF, putting profound emphasis on gender integration in the WASH sector, this plan has neither disaggregated the information collected on the WASH situation by gender nor has it acknowledged women's role anywhere in the prioritised activities. It indicates the inability of the RVWRMP and the donor to instil the importance of gender issues at the local government level by questioning the sustainability of the WASH projects implemented under such a gender-insensitive plan. Despite the learning of the RWSSP Phase II that the guidelines on WUSC formation should spell out the need for women's and disadvantaged groups' active participation in the committee activities and they should be provided with confidence building, capacity building and skill development training, it was ironic to see that the Municipal level WASH plan did not have any such provisions. This raises the question of whether the WASH projects implemented by the local governments following such a GESI weak plan can address women's practical gender needs, not to mention their strategic gender needs, required for their empowerment as well as for gender equality.

WaterAid

Established in 1981, WaterAid, as the world's largest civil society organisation focused solely on WASH, has reached over 25 million people with clean water, 25 million people with decent toilets, and 18 million people with good hygiene, and has been able to build a deep understanding of the issues that face communities living without these basic services and of the solutions needed, by working together with the country partners in some of the poorest and most marginalised communities (WaterAid, 2015). A review of its earlier strategies was carried out as part of a research conducted to look at gender issues in the management of water supply projects during 1997-2000 (Regmi, 2000), and it disclosed a different scenario. The review presented WaterAid as an organisation that considered water as a technical sector since gender roles or for that matter, women's role, was not seriously considered in its initial years of operation. The scenario now, 20 years down the road, is completely different since its Global Strategy 2015-2022 is categorically advanced in terms of its GESI focus.

Gender Integration in WaterAid's Global Strategy: Women's crucial role in the water supply and sanitation sector was well appreciated in the IDWSSD 1981-1990 and also in the various international women's conferences that took place around that time. However, WaterAid's strategies (1996) followed before 2000 did not seem to have been informed by the outcomes of these international conferences. For instance, it talked about various training to be provided to its partner organisations but the need to provide gender training was not felt. The strategy mentioned 13 key issues to be considered in the water supply and sanitation projects but women's role or gender issues were not considered to be among them. The strategy document did talk about people's willingness to pay but it did not consider the need to talk about women's ability to pay despite the global experiences that although women are willing to pay, they cannot afford to pay due to not having access to and control over income. Similarly, to address the scarcity of drinking water for billions of people in the world, the strategy presented many options like the need for more water projects to be constructed and malfunctioning water systems to be repaired and maintained. But it did not acknowledge that one of the primary reasons for the failure of the water projects, thereby the scarcity of water, is the lack of women's effective participation in their planning, implementation and operation and maintenance stages. Likewise, several criteria, including the technology involved, were developed in the strategy for assessing partners' proposals but no emphasis was given on the need for that technology to be women-friendly given that it is mostly women that do the collection of water. The document was also full of the use of gender-neutral looking terminologies like people, community, users etc. with no appreciation that the needs and concerns of men and women are different in the WASH sector, thus, the need for the use of gender-specific language and disaggregated strategies in such a policy document.

WaterAid's global strategy 'Everyone, everywhere 2030', which was initially prepared covering the period 2015-2020 and revised later in 2017 extending its life by two more years in its original time frame spanning its life for the period 2015-2022, is, however, progressive (WaterAid, 2017). Despite the view that the latest global strategy also has some areas for improvement while looking at it from a gender perspective, it is largely liberal and advanced in acknowledging women's role vis-à-vis men's in the WASH sector. While talking of the challenges related to WASH, with 844 million not having access to water supply, 2.3 billion not having access to a decent toilet and 289,000 children under five dying annually of diarrhoeal diseases caused due to poor water and sanitation, it mentions that this shortage of water and poor sanitation and unhygienic practices affects the women and the children the most. It further states that this wholly unacceptable situation not only affects sustainable development but it also particularly affects women, who carry the burden of collecting water and caring for sick children, and girls who often fail to finish their education because their schools lack decent toilets.

WaterAid's commitment towards the advancement of women can also be realised from its purpose statement: 'ending the extreme poverty and building a healthier, fairer and more productive world for everyone, particularly women and girls, through increased access to clean water, decent toilets and good hygiene (WaterAid, 2017).' While talking of the various opportunities and challenges for ensuring access to clean water, proper sanitation and good hygiene to the global population, the strategy also talks about the prevailing social and economic inequality that is obstructing the poor and marginalised people, more so women, from being able to exercise their right to have access to these services and thus the need for government and their partners to be more profound in ensuring a fairer distribution of resources. The global strategy also mentions four basic strategic aims- reduce inequality, strengthen sustainable services, integrate into sustainable development, and improve hygiene behaviour- to deliver WASH services to the needy population. The following discussion presents the extent of gender sensitivity addressed in these aims.

While talking of 'reducing inequality', the document admits that it is the poorest and the most marginalised people, particularly women and girls, that are often victimised from realising their right to safe water, proper sanitation and good hygiene resulting in the greatest impact on women and girls, not only because they are the poorest of the poor but also because they have been expected to be meeting these needs of their families since time immemorial. Accordingly, the document recognises that to address the current failure of the water and sanitation services and hygiene promotion to reach out to these people, the WASH agencies should make efforts to reduce the inequality in access as well as in resource sharing by these people. Regarding its role to address the perceived inequality, it proposes the following: i) provide evidence of the underlying causes of inequalities in access to clean water, decent toilets and good hygiene between and within countries, and influence those responsible for addressing these inequalities; ii) work with organisations that promote the rights of women and the poorest and most marginalised people to water, sanitation and hygiene; and iii) demonstrate gender-sensitive and inclusive designs and approaches that meet the diverse needs of marginalised people (WaterAid, 2017). These action points demonstrate WaterAid's understanding of the gender issues in the WASH sector as it has firmly presented that it is the women, girls, and the poor and marginalised people that are the most vulnerable in terms of their access to resources and that various gender-sensitive strategies need to be adopted to ensure that the constraints that are making this group vulnerable in their access to WASH services are well addressed.

Regarding 'strengthening sustainable services', WaterAid's another strategic aim, the document states that the weak service delivery mechanism and limited capabilities of the service providers are hindering the delivery of sustainable water, sanitation and hygiene services to the people in need of the WASH services. It further elaborates that the specific reasons for the lack of sustainable, affordable and accessible delivery of WASH services to the people are: poor governance, lack of technical expertise, limited managerial skills and capacity, inadequate resources, weak financial management, lack of appropriate technology, lack of enabling environment, and limited scope for innovation. This implies that there is a need for strengthening the systems as well as planning to address the issues that are constraining the sustainability of the WASH services. What WaterAid thus proposes to address this situation are i) work with partners to develop robust governance, financial, institutional, environmental and technical capacity and systems to reach those who may otherwise miss out, with a particular focus on women and children; ii) work in a programmatic way at community, district, town and city level to invest in its partners to deliver sustainable services, demonstrating effective solutions and encouraging innovation; iii) use evidence generated from its work to influence and inform national strategies and to support the strengthening of planning, implementation and monitoring systems (WaterAid, 2017). The focus that the document has put on women and girls as the ones mostly affected by the unsustainable, unaffordable and inaccessible WASH services and the action points suggested to change this scenario also confirm WaterAid's pronounced understanding of the gender issues in the sustainability of WASH services.

Similarly, in the section on 'integrate into sustainable development', the other strategic aim of WaterAid, the document draws upon government's attention to integrating WASH with poverty eradication work, mainly child and maternal health, women's empowerment, education, nutrition, food security, housing and urban planning, water resource and waste management since these sectors cannot assure sustainable development without reliable access to and proper planning of clean water, decent toilets and good hygiene. The action points proposed for its consideration to achieve the integration into sustainable development, therefore, are: i) strengthen its contextual analysis in the countries where it works to identify new partners and opportunities for influencing and accelerating change; ii) champion the role of water, sanitation and hygiene and their integration within other sector plans; and iii) work with governments, civil society and the private sector from local to international level to promote sustainable development and clean water, decent toilets and good hygiene (WaterAid, 2017). Here also, women's empowerment has been fairly acknowledged through well-integrated and effective WASH services.

About the fulfilment of its final strategic aim 'improve hygiene behaviour', WaterAid's basic idea is to maximise the benefits of access to safe water and sanitation by understanding and improving hygiene practices and improving people's ability to practice good hygiene. While discussing the factors such as open defecation, inadequate disposal of human waste, unhygienic handling of food and water, poorly-designed toilets or a lack of clean water or soap that are contributing to the spread of common diseases and affecting poor and marginalised people, especially the opportunities of health and dignity for women and girls, WaterAid proposes three action points: i) work with a range of women's organisations, health, education, academic and marketing partners to support and deliver effective behaviour change and hygiene campaigns; ii) work with partners in governments, public institutions and civil society to promote good hygiene in their work and to ensure suitable water and sanitation facilities; and iii) champion the development, implementation and monitoring of national hygiene policies, strategies and systems (WaterAid, 2017). In this strategic aim and the action points suggested to achieve the same, WaterAid's understanding of, commitment to and focus on women and girls is highly commendable.

Overall, WaterAid has well-integrated gender in its strategic aims and the action points proposed to fulfil them even though there are areas where it needs to work further to be a fully gender-focused organisation as discussed below.

Areas Demanding for Further Gender Attention: The discussions mentioned above have firmly conveyed WaterAid's commitment towards addressing gender issues, and thereby, women's empowerment. Nevertheless, there are still certain areas where WaterAid should pay special attention and make extra efforts to make itself a truly gender-sensitive organisation. For instance, although WaterAid has well addressed the gender concerns while talking about 'strengthening sustainable services'- one of its strategic aims, what it lacked was the emphasis on the need to support the government and its local partners, including service providers, with appropriate training and capacity building on GESI sensitive policies, procedures and approaches. Unless and until its local partners and the government develop a better understanding of gender issues in the WASH sector, including a perspective on how gender-sensitive programming can lead to women's empowerment and gender equality, neither the implementing partners can design a gender-responsive project ensuring sustained benefits nor will the government policies be gender-focused. Only through a concerted effort of all the concerned stakeholders to make the water policies and organisational practices gender-specific, the women, poor and marginalised people can have sustained access to WASH services and consequently, overall equitable development.

The other area where WaterAid has to pay extra attention in making their WASH policies and practices gender-informed is in ensuring the integration of the GAD approach in all areas of the strategic document. For instance, although WaterAid has acknowledged the need to integrate WASH with various sectors, including women's empowerment, in the contextual analysis of its strategic aim 'integrate into sustainable development', what it has missed out is to put the same emphasis on integrating women and gender issues in its action points. Given that women play a vital role in the WASH sector, the emphasis should also have been on undertaking a gender-disaggregated contextual analysis and the selection of partners that have got enough GESI experience.

Similarly, in its another action point to work with the government, civil society and the private sector, emphasis should have been laid on building their capacity on GESI for a better understanding of gender issues in the WASH sector. In turn, this emphasis would help its implementing partners and the other concerned stakeholders to develop a similar understanding of gender issues in the WASH sector, of the importance of women's and poor people's active participation in WUSC activities, of women's and poor people's limitations in paying the water tariff for not having access to and control over income and resources, and of the role that these people can play in sustaining the WASH benefits so that appropriate strategies and action points could be developed to address these challenges. The need to have a proper gender analysis and increased understanding of GESI on the part of the implementing agencies, service providers and the government, among others, is even more important while involving the private sector in the delivery of WASH services. Since the private sector works mainly for profit, the lack of understanding of gender and social issues, such as women's and poor people's limited capacity to contribute the cost during the construction phase and pay water tariff during the operation and maintenance phase on its part may lead it to stop the delivery of water services to the needy people. This situation can be even more alarming for female-headed households. However, the increased understanding of GESI of the implementing agencies, government and service providers can help to build up the capacity of the latter on this matter.

Likewise, in its other strategic aim 'promoting hygiene behaviour', one of the action points it has proposed is 'to work with partners in governments, public institutions and civil society'. What might be useful to add here is the need for providing capacity building and training on GESI to the partners in government, public institutions and civil society for sensitising them on the gender and social issues in the prevailing unhygienic practices and how the lack of this informed understanding is depriving the community, more so the women and girls, from benefitting the improved hygiene services.

To deliver the four strategic aims and change normal for everyone, everywhere, WaterAid intends to focus on five key areas – influencing, sustainability, capacity development, partnerships, and disaster resilience- as its mode of operation (WaterAid, 2017). However, no gender dimension has been integrated into any of these five key areas although a clearer understanding of gender issues in the WASH sector at all levels is required for: influencing the WASH projects to be owned and managed by the local people, more so women and the poor; providing sustained benefits to the people in need, including women, girls and female-headed households; designing appropriate GESI focused training and capacity building for all actors at all levels to develop GESI sensitive project designs; selecting partners that are GESI aware, committed and prepared to ensure gender equality in sharing WASH benefits; and responding properly to the needs of women, men, poor and marginalised people during the time of disaster.

The strategic document also has a section on 'assessing performance' which describes the steps that WaterAid will follow to have its performance assessed in the delivery of WASH services. At the international level, it aims to review the relevance and effectiveness of its strategic approaches in influencing: i) change in its commitment to safe water and sanitation as a fundamental human right at the international, regional and national level; ii) collective effort of development partners, government, the private sector and civil society to deliver sustainable services; and iii) resource allocation for investments in water supply, sanitation and hygiene services that prioritise the needs of the poorest and most marginalised people. At the country level, the assessment will include a comparative analysis of its own business and strategic plans and national country measures against the context-specific strategies. Finally, at the operational level, the assessment includes the progress made against the agreed plans and budgets (WaterAid, 2017). Like in the case of the five areas proposed as its mode of operation, WaterAid's procedures suggested for assessing its performance at all levels are gender-weak since they do not acknowledge the gender issues involved around these procedures. What it means is no one can raise questions or call for accountability if the performance review team completes the assessment without having any idea regarding how the WaterAid funded projects benefited women, in general, and female-headed households, in particular. This is so because the review procedures do not speak about the need for gender-disaggregated analysis. When women or gender is not mentioned in the assessment procedures, the field staff, given their limited understanding of the GAD/ GESI approaches, on the one hand, and the limited time given to complete the fieldwork, on the other hand, may not be self-motivated and self-reflective enough to make the analysis gender-focused by going beyond the suggested procedural guidelines.

Likewise, a review of WaterAid's vision, mission and values conducted within the GAD framework also compels one to ask whether WaterAid has been able to integrate gender adequately in its overall organisational thinking. Its mission states that it aims to transform the lives of the poorest and the most marginalised people but it fails to acknowledge that even among the people in this category, women are further poor and marginalised, thus, they need to be specifically mentioned. The vision, mission and values are fundamentally the faces of any organisation as they reflect the precedence assigned by the organisation to the gender aspects. In the case of WaterAid, this impression has not, however, come out well because of the use of gender-neutral looking terminologies like the 'poorest' and 'most marginalised' in its mission statement. Consequently, it has led to inconsistency in the importance WaterAid has given to the gender dimensions in its strategy, including its 'approach' to the delivery of WASH services as well as its 'key aspects' which are leadership, active communities, equality, sustainability, and integration.

While talking about developing leadership, it could have mentioned the need to invest in developing women leaders. Similarly, while talking of active communities, developing approaches to ensure a fairer distribution of resources to all poor and marginalised, sustenance of WASH services etc., WaterAid could have specified the need to consult with women, girls and female-headed households since this group plays a crucial role in the WASH sector for its success. Because it is mostly women and female-headed households who will have limited or no access to resources, the strategy should have been more realistic while talking about equity and equality. Many WASH projects implemented so far have clearly shown that women have always been unequally benefitted as compared to their fellow men mainly because they are not categorically mentioned and the important information is not gender-disaggregated, which, in turn, eliminates the chances of developing GESI specific strategies.

Experiences, as discussed earlier, have proven that there is no guarantee that even when the project benefits are meant to be going to the poorest and the marginalised section, they will automatically be obtained by women, girls and the other poor sections as well. Even though donors, national governments and non-governmental agencies working in the WASH sector have been talking about ensuring gender equity and gender equality in their projects, the field experiences do not verify that this has been achieved. For instance, the information presented earlier shows that it is hardly 2-3 women that get to be seen in the WUSCs, women's presence in the decision-making positions is less and it is mostly men who are hired in the paid positions of caretakers and maintenance workers, among others. The issue related to inconsistent use of gender-specific language and the lack of integration of gender in all organisational policies and practices becomes pertinent in WaterAid even when its publication 'A Guide to Support Planning, Monitoring, Evaluation and Learning: Integrating Adaptive Programming with Theory of Change' (WaterAid, 2019a) is reviewed. Despite its focus on the need to carry out a GESI analysis along with the political economy analysis and sector strengthening building block analysis to ensure a proper context analysis for its WASH projects, it is surprising to see that women friendliness or gender sensitivity neither appears to be a part of the organisational culture nor of its highly valued 'adaptive programming: why, what and how' as could be perceived from the reading of its introductory chapter.

The review of WaterAid's Global Strategy was followed by a review of WaterAid Nepal's Five-Year Strategy (2017-2021) since two of the water projects included in the research undertaken earlier were funded by WaterAid Nepal through its local partner NGO- NEWAH. WaterAid Nepal has identified four key objectives for its operation in Nepal for the next five years: i) enable marginalised communities and individuals, and people in vulnerable situations to take action for their rights to water and sanitation; ii) promote greater accountability and effectiveness for delivering WASH services; iii) influence and demonstrate WASH as foundational to all aspects of development, with a focus on health and education; and iv) apply new research, holistic approaches and innovative technology to WASH. To support these four objectives, WaterAid Nepal has designed four interconnected flagship programmes: i) reaching the unreached; ii) recovery and resilient WASH; iii) hygiene; and iv) sector effectiveness (WaterAid, 2017a).

To understand whether it has been successful in meeting its strategic objectives through the effective implementation of its flagship programmes, WaterAid Nepal has developed a couple of indicators: i) healthier and more dignified living of the marginalised groups and individuals, and people in vulnerable situations as a result of their sustainable access to safe water, sanitation and hygiene; ii) government policies and mechanisms in place to help exercise the right for everyone in Nepal for equitable access to safe water and sanitation; iii) demonstrated leadership in the WASH sector; and iv) WaterAid Nepal is well-known as a champion for the rights to water and sanitation of marginalised groups and individuals in Nepal. WaterAid Nepal expects that the desired change of people, including marginalised and vulnerable populations, of having equitable access to sustainable and safe water and sanitation services, practising good hygiene behaviours, and using the right technology can be achieved when communities become aware of their rights, take self-action on the WASH matters and manage the WASH projects themselves, and the government demonstrates accountable behaviour in delivering WASH services, among others. Accordingly, WaterAid Nepal implements, promotes and supports activities that help to realise this state in the WASH sector (WaterAid, 2017a).

A brief highlight of WaterAid Nepal's strategic plan as presented above depicts that it has a strong focus on social inclusion with clear emphasis provided on marginalised and vulnerable populations. The strategic plan is comprehensive in providing a good analysis of the social discrimination caused by caste and gender and how such discriminations can affect women's and girls' access to sustainable WASH services and living a healthy and dignified life. However, when looked at the strategic plan using a gender lens, the following areas have been found missing in the strategy.

Although WaterAid Nepal's programme areas have got lowest ranking HDI, severe water and sanitation issues and intense social discrimination caused due to gender and caste system, its objectives, flagship programmes, theory of change, indicators of success, assumptions regarding how the change will occur, and what the changes look like, do not have a categorical focus on women. The entire strategic plan is full of the use of gender-neutral looking terminologies like 'people', 'marginalised', 'communities' etc., with no efforts made to understand whether a given context is demanding for the use of gender-free terminologies or gender-specific terminologies.

In the Challenges and Opportunities section of the strategic plan, WaterAid Nepal admits that women and girls spend 2-3 hours collecting water every day and are therefore unable to ensure active involvement in development. Despite its acknowledgement of the dangerous conditions that the people have to walk through to collect water from unsafe sources in remote areas, its emphasis is still on the word 'people', instead of 'women and girls'. It is an irony to note: i) why the organisations like WaterAid Nepal are reluctant to ensure special mention of 'women and girls' when they have already acknowledged that it is these categories, more than men and boys, who suffer the most from the lack of access to proper WASH services? ii) what is inaccurate about documenting that it is mostly and often, women and girls, not people in general, who have to walk long distances in dangerous conditions to collect water from unsafe sources, therefore, the need to develop gender-specific objectives and corresponding strategies to address the gender-specific challenges? iii) what prevents these organisations from integrating the gender focus in their objectives, strategies, and actions when they have already appreciated that women and girls play a crucial role in the water sector and that access to proper sanitation is the need for their security and dignity? The only plausible answer to these questions is the lack of a comprehensive gender analysis caused due to the erroneous preconceived notion that the mentioning of 'poor and marginalised people' will automatically include women, girls and female-headed households. This assumption, as mentioned above, indicates the oversight in the agency's understanding that even within the poor and marginalised categories, women, including female-headed households, and girls, are further poor and marginalised.

The inconsistent importance given by WaterAid Nepal to integrate gender in its policies and practices is another area of concern. For instance, while talking about design approaches, systems and methods in its WASH services, the strategic plan mentions that if a toilet is constructed that cannot be used by someone with a physical disability, or without private space for women and girls to safely manage their periods, then it is not possible to say that everyone everywhere is being reached. Similarly, in its Discussion Paper focused on the integration of disability in its water and sanitation programmes (WaterAid, 2008), it firmly states that it has included a GESI approach in its WASH projects to ascertain everyone's active participation regardless of their social and economic status. The same paper also clearly acknowledges the extra challenges encountered by women and girls who are differently-abled as opposed to their differently-abled fellow men. Given that women and girls, irrespective of their disability, are often expected to undertake the household chores, including collecting water and firewood, washing, cleaning, cooking, taking care of livestock- all demanding intensive labour, they get further excluded if they are unable to perform these activities as expected by the family. The paper also stresses the extra workload that a normal woman has to bear if there is any member who is differently-abled in the family. This situation gets further compounded if a disabled girl is unable to get married and is compelled to stay back home since this in general goes against the prevailing social norms in Nepal. This paper has well analysed the situation of a girl and a woman, as compared to a man and a boy, in a gender-sensitive and socially inclusive manner. Likewise, a review of a report prepared by New ERA for WaterAid Nepal, which attempts to monitor the equity and inclusion in the WASH sector, also provides a clear impression that both the policies and practices of WaterAid Nepal and its partner organisations, as opposed to several other organisations engaged in the WASH sector in Nepal, are GESI sensitive and aim towards women's empowerment (New ERA, 2009).

However, the lack of its gender focus in many areas as discussed earlier and, in the report, 'Promoting WASH-related rights through SuWASH Project', which provides information on the progress made on community empowerment, among others, conveys a different impression of WaterAid Nepal's commitment towards gender. While reporting the progress of its WASH work, WaterAid Nepal asserts that 1,117 people are oriented on the right to water and sanitation, 15 persons from marginalised communities hold key positions in 16 WUSCs (not even at the rate of one per WUSC though), and 59 out of 117 members are elected from marginalised communities in 16 WUSCs (WaterAid, 2018a). One does not, however, get an idea from these data whether women benefited at all from this project and whether the project was successful in addressing women's practical and strategic gender needs. As a result, it amplifies the question of whether WaterAid Nepal considers gender as a standalone component or whether its staff need to improve their understanding of gender as an integral part of all organisational activity and that gender sensitivity needs to be consistently acknowledged and respected altogether in organisational matters.

The implication of the inconsistent appreciation of gender in the WASH projects is that the staff, more so the field staff, may not necessarily ensure gender dynamics in their fieldwork as the tendency on their part would be to simply follow the guidelines as they are without paying serious attention to whether that particular activity is gender-informed or not. Because the integration of gender issues can be challenging and time-consuming in the beginning, the staff will simply follow what is there in the documents without showing concern that they need to ensure gender sensitivity in all their activities irrespective of its mentioning in every activity in the document. The end result of a WASH project that does not seek women's consistent involvement in its various stages, does not properly analyse women's role and disaggregate the analysis by gender, and does not appreciate the gender differences in its policies and important documents is that it may not be able to sustain the WASH benefits for the community, more so for the women and girls, in the long run (RWSSP, 2019; WaterAid, 2015; ADB, 2011; Regmi, 2000).

Interestingly, despite its WASH documents being relatively gender-insensitive, WaterAid Nepal's engagement in Menstrual Hygiene Management (MHM), an important gender issue, is a bold and timely step when looked at from a gender perspective. The women and girls, especially in the rural areas of Nepal, encounter many social, economic, emotional, and psychological challenges to manage their menstruation. The situation of the women and girls coming from the western parts of Nepal is worse off as they are compelled to stay in the cattle sheds and makeshift huts, during their menstrual period called *Chhaupadi*. In one of its publications 'Menstruation Matters', WaterAid (2017b) reports that managing menstrual hygiene is crucial since it can otherwise adversely impact adolescent girls' physical, emotional and psychological well-being along with their education, employment, livelihoods and active participation in the national economy. In turn, access to basic facilities such as clean materials to absorb or collect menstrual blood, a private place to change these materials, soap and water for washing the body, access to safe and convenient facilities to dispose of used materials along with timely information is critically important for MHM. The unavailability of these facilities along with the taboos and stigma associated with menstruation is not only a violation of women's and girls' human rights but is also a threat to women's health, safety and dignity. To correct such a wrong course, WaterAid Nepal facilitated 63 MHM training sessions, 900 school level MHM orientation sessions covering 98 schools and 1,160 adolescent girls and 870 adolescent boys in Kavrepalanchowk and Lalitpur districts during the period September 2015- March 2018 (WaterAid, 2018).

As a result of the above-mentioned activities along with the advocacy efforts of WaterAid Nepal and its alliance and implementing partners, the GoN introduced a new law in 2017 criminalising the *Chhaupadi* system, with a three-month jail sentence and/or a fine of Rs. 3,000 or both to anyone forcing a woman to practice this inhumane act. Although the GoN has initiated several policy measures on MHM, there are still areas for policy improvements such as harmonising MHM across the various government plans and policies, translation of MHM related policies into actions, formulation of policy on disabled women-friendly menstrual hygiene as well as disposal of used materials. Some other areas requiring policy improvements are the integration of MHM as a cross-cutting theme across all development plans and policies, better coordination among the governmental and non-governmental agencies working on MHM, and packaging the awareness and sensitisation programmes taking into account women's and girls' human rights, health, and their social, economic and political development (WaterAid, 2017b). Only through the realisation of these actions, the creation of a society with sustainable human development is possible.

Given the important role that WaterAid has been playing in Nepal in addressing the pertinent inhumane practice like *Chhaupadi* and the overall MHM practices, more so of school-going girls, it is of utmost importance for it to use a gender lens while designing and implementing its WASH programmes, collecting data for explaining the project results and documenting them since there is a direct connection between MHM and the availability of WASH facilities. Simply because the WASH projects have been targeted towards the poor and marginalised, it does not necessarily mean the project benefits are being enjoyed by women and girls as well. At least, the data presented above concerning SuWASH project and the analysis made of its country strategy does not convey that WaterAid Nepal is following a GESI approach in the true spirit of the term. Because women and girls form a majority even within the poor and marginalised categories, there is a need for a gender-disaggregated analysis throughout. As of now, WaterAid Nepal's strategy is found to be focusing more on social inclusion, with a stronger emphasis on the poor, marginalised, and vulnerable population. Although the integration of the social inclusion approach is timely and essential from a human rights perspective, it may not necessarily ensure that the WASH project benefits will also reach women and girls unless their status within the poor and the marginalised population is well-analysed and subsequently appropriate gender-specific strategies are developed.

The discussions made above reveal that while WaterAid's Global Strategy 2015-2022, is gender-informed to a greater extent, WaterAid Nepal's Country Strategy 2017-2021 is less gender-sensitive and more socially inclusive. Even though there are areas such as goals, objectives, approaches and desired changes, among others, in the global strategy where gender focus needs to be better ensured, WaterAid has disaggregated the information by gender in several other areas such as challenges, strategies and proposed actions, mentioned the importance of women's and girls' role in the WASH sector, and explained the future of a WASH project if gender issues are ignored. WaterAid Nepal's Strategy needs to follow this direction along with the integration of gender in many other aspects of the document.

CHAPTER 10

Gender Integration in Nepal's Development Plans

Evolution of Gender in Development Plans

Nepal, formerly the only Hindu Kingdom in the world, became a secular republic following the 10-year long civil war (1996-2006) and witnessed the fall of the centuries-old monarchy in 2008. Nevertheless, religion still holds an important position in Nepali society, with Hinduism being the major religion followed by 81.3% of the population. There are 125 distinct castes/ ethnicities in Nepal (GoN, 2011a). The Nepali caste system is the major way of social stratification, which is again rooted in Hindu religion, and based on the classical Hindu Chaturvarnashram model entailing four broad social classes, namely- Brahmin, Kshatriya, Vaishya and Sudra. Though heavily criticised and constitutionally prohibited, caste endogamy is still informally the norm of the land. According to the 2011 Census, there are 123 languages spoken as mother tongues in Nepal, with Nepali as the mother tongue of 44.6% of the population and the official language of the government.

The Gross Domestic Product (GDP) in Nepal was worth USD 21.14 billion in 2016, ranking it 96th in the world by purchasing power parity (DeSilver, 2018). Agriculture, which accounts for 33% of the country's GDP, is the principal economy of the country, providing a livelihood to 66% of the population (GoN, 2017). With 57% of the working-age population of 15-49 years, the country experiences about one-fourth of the population (25.16%) falling below the poverty line as per the Nepal Living Standards Survey (NLSS) of the Central Bureau of Statistics (CBS) (GoN, 2010/11). Remittance plays a major role in the Nepalese economy, with its contribution of 25.4% (NPR 879.3

billion/ USD 7.8 billion) to the national GDP of NPR 3.4 trillion (USD 29.8 billion) (IMF, 2019).

The literacy rate (for the population aged 5 years and above), though relatively low, has increased from 54.1% in 2001 to 65.9% in 2011, with male literacy rate at 75.1% and female literacy rate at 57.4% (GoN, 2011a).

After emerging as a federal republic in 2008, Nepal adopted a new constitution beginning September 2015. The new constitution has made a provision of one federal government, seven provincial governments and 753 local governments for administrative purposes. Nepal has been lagging in terms of economic development due to factors resulting mainly from political instability, public protests, civil war and underdeveloped transportation infrastructure. Nepal's economy went further down creating a big setback on much-needed economic reforms of the country after it experienced the massive earthquakes in April and May 2015 since they not only affected eight million lives (including deaths of nearly 9,000 people and injury of nearly 22,000 people) but also damaged infrastructure and homes resulting in a loss of USD seven billion (ILO, 2017).

Nepalese women make up more than half the population of the country and they will continue to be in majority due to the increasing male migration in the coming decades as well. For Nepal to prosper, the country must invest in women either more than or on equal terms as men so that the country could immensely benefit from everyone's active participation and meaningful contribution to its development. The increasing number of female-headed households which has almost doubled in the past 15 years, from 16% in 2001 to 31% in 2016 as a result of mostly male migration confirms this reality of the country (GoN, New ERA and ICF International, 2016). Within the certainty of the need to invest more in women's empowerment, the following section unveils the history of GoN's commitment towards women's development as reflected in its long-term development plans implemented over the last 60 years.

First (1956–61), Second (1962-65), Third (1965–70) and Fourth (1970–75) Five-Year Development Plans: Acknowledging the importance of long-term plans for systematic development since they prioritise the activities that need more focus, attention and investment based on the country's need, the GoN initiated the five-year development plan approach beginning 1956. The initial five-year development plans mainly concentrated on infrastructure (primarily road construction) to ease the facilitation of the movement of goods and services from one place to another, and to increase the size of the market (Skerry et.al.,1991). The government's policy on women in development, though initiated during this period, was based on the 'welfare approach' focusing on the reproductive role of women as mothers, wives and homemakers.

Fifth Five-Year Development Plan (1975-1980): This plan for the first time addressed poverty. Although this plan did not incorporate any specific Women in Development (WID) policy, the GoN ratified ILO's Equal Remuneration-1951 during this period (Regmi and Fawcett, 2001). However, due to the lack of political will, the weak justice system, and the male-dominated patriarchal structure, which solely confined women to household chores and hardly provided the opportunity to engage in income-generating activities, laws like 'equal pay' were as good as meaningless. Nevertheless, a gradual shift occurred during the mid- and late 1970s with Nepal's exposure to international events like International Women's Year and First World Conference on Women in 1975 and the initiation of the first-ever comprehensive study on the Status of Women in Nepal in 1981. Following the welfare approach as mentioned earlier, the state level WID activities were confined to education and training till the 1980s.

Sixth Five-Year Development Plan (1980-1985): This plan clearly mentioned the WID policy for the first time and adopted an 'efficiency approach' to WID recognising the productive role of women in Nepal's planned development (Bhadra et.al., 2007; Regmi et.al., 2001). It contained provisions that aimed to enhance women's participation in the development process. The plan also stressed women's involvement in all programmes and projects, recognised legal hurdles to their economic empowerment, and detailed special programmes to meet their needs (Baral, 2017; ADB, 1999). The Sixth Plan, therefore, can be considered a milestone in GoN's appreciation of women's role in the country's development since this is the first time it released a clearly written policy on WID.

Seventh Five-Year Development Plan (1985–90): The Seventh Plan, expanded on the Sixth Plan, adopted an '(equal) participatory approach' along with the efficient approach to WID (Bhadra et.al., 2007). A specific chapter on women was incorporated into this plan. The plan spelt out policy statements to the effect that quotas were to be instituted for women in state-run literacy and training programmes in diverse fields, including health, engineering and agriculture. It also highlighted entailing legal reforms to remove provisions hindering women's participation in national development (ADB, 1999). The

Seventh Plan for the first time indicated increasing women's involvement in the field of forestry, including conservation, growth and development apart from education, training and routine income-generating activities.

Eighth Five-Year Development Plan (1990-1995): The Eighth Plan further expanded on previous plans and adopted an 'equity approach' along with a realisation of the need to mainstreaming women in development (Bhadra et.al., 2007). The government committed to equal and meaningful participation of women in the development process and acknowledged the need for increasing women's representation at decision-making levels in the government, semi-government and non-governmental sectors. It also spelt out developing a monitoring system to record gender discrimination at work and move towards an empowerment approach. This approach further included mandatory representation of women in the formulation of policies and programmes at all levels and envisaged the establishment of an appropriate organisational structure realised later as Ministry of Women, Children and Social Welfare (MoWCSW) in 1995 (ADB, 1999), and the institution of gender-focal points in many of the government ministries, including health, finance, labour and industry. It also spelt out strategies, such as introducing new technologies to lighten the burden of women from collecting firewood, fodder, water etc. (ADB, 1999; JICA, 1999). The sectoral programmes of the Eighth Plan were informed by the WID policy but it also at the same time was gradually gearing towards the GAD approach (Regmi et.al., 2001).

During the Eighth Plan period, the Government formulated and presented an Action Plan in the United Nation's Fourth World Conference on Women (Beijing, 4-15 September 1995) with a major focus on the integration of women rather than on sectoral representation; reform of discriminatory laws relating to property rights; GBV; incorporation of women's needs and concerns in national poverty reduction programmes; reduction of maternal mortality; women's access to technical schools and short-term training through scholarship and quotas for female students; and NGOs to actively engage in delivering services to women (ADB, 1999; JICA, 1999).

Ninth Five-Year Development Plan (1997-2002): A paradigm shift from WID to GAD was witnessed in the Ninth Plan and subsequent development policies. This plan stipulated GAD programmes by mainstreaming gender equality, reducing gender inequality, and empowering women in different sectors. As per the National Plan of Action for Gender Equality and Women's

Empowerment, which was formulated to implement the Beijing Platform for Action, the GoN changed the traditional approach of addressing women's problems through the WID approach to gender equality and women's empowerment approach (Bhadra, 2007). This plan, therefore, was perceived to be a progressive long-term plan which expressed a clear commitment of the GoN to increase women's participation in all fields- technical, entrepreneurial, social and political. The other positive aspect of the Ninth Plan was its acknowledgement of Violence Against Women (VAW) as a development issue.

Tenth Five-Year Development Plan (2002-2007): The Tenth Plan provided continuation to the GAD approach initiated in the Ninth Plan, with a strong focus on gender mainstreaming, gender equality and women's empowerment. It also identified the empowerment of women as one of the focused areas of development and recognised gender equality as a key indicator in poverty analysis. It also emphasised women's participation in all cycles of local level poverty alleviation and income-generating projects. Sensitisation on gender equality in all sectors and at all levels and revision of discriminatory laws against women based on equality and international commitments were stressed in this plan (Bhadra et.al., 2007). It was during the Tenth Plan period that The National Women's Commission (NWC) was established in 2002, with an aim to support and advise the concerned ministry of the government on effective implementation of the international human rights instruments and monitor the progress made on it as well. Apart from its watchdog role to ensure that the government is complying with all international human rights commitments, the NWC, at the same time, was also mandated to develop policies and plans aimed at advancing women. The Tenth Plan objectives were aligned with the Millennium Development Goals (MDGs).

Eleventh Three-Year Development Plan (2007-2010): Taking into account the then post-conflict situation, the GoN decided to follow a three-year planning cycle beginning with the Eleventh Plan. Moreover, due to the uncertainty of the appropriateness and effectiveness of the five-year plans due to the changing context of the country as a result of almost a decade-long conflict, the Eleventh Plan was considered to be an 'interim plan'. Nevertheless, the Eleventh Three-Year Interim Plan (2007-2010) also provided continuation to the GAD approach and focused on attaining the MDGs following participatory and inclusive development processes. Accordingly, the plan prioritised the projects that sought more employment opportunities for women and minority groups and focused on the formulation of appropriate policies, types of machinery, and institutional structures. The plan also prioritised health, education and drinking water sectors, with a strong commitment to increasing the investment for them. A policy of affirmative action was also introduced during this plan period to fulfil the commitment made in the Beijing Conference (GoN, 2014). Although the Eleventh Plan was perceived to be an ambitious but practical plan, its progress had been mixed due to the political instability and a lack of adequate infrastructure development.

Twelfth Three-Year Development Plan (2010-2013): Given its experience with the Eleventh Three-Year Interim Plan, the GoN decided to continue the same three-year cycle for the Twelfth Development Plan as well. The difference, however, was that the Twelfth Plan, unlike the Eleventh Plan, was a confirmed three-year plan, not an interim plan. The GAD approach was again reiterated in the Twelfth Plan and its objectives like sustainable economic growth, poverty reduction, creating employment opportunities, reducing economic inequalities, achieving regional balances, and eliminating social exclusions were fully aligned with the MDGs. Like the Eleventh Plan, the Twelfth Plan's focus was also on the attainment of gender equality, women's empowerment and elimination of VAW, including women's trafficking, and establishment and strengthening of appropriate mechanisms for the same. In this plan period, the government extended the women's development programme to all the then 3,570 VDCs so that the rural women from all over the country could have easy access to various women development activities. The other positive aspects of the Twelfth Plan were: emphasis on the collection of gender-disaggregated data, implementation of gender-sensitive monitoring and evaluation framework, assessment of inequalities among various social and ethnic groups, and one-third representation of women in all government offices, among others (GoN, 2013).

Thirteenth Three-Year Development Plan (2013-2016): The Thirteenth Plan was characterised by a rights-based approach and inclusive development that was started in the Tenth Plan period and was continued in the Eleventh and Twelfth Plans as well. Some strong aspects of this plan were: i) emphasis to upgrade Nepal from LDC to a developing country by 2022; ii) reduction in economic and human poverty and raising people's standard of living; iii) advancing women's social, economic and political empowerment regardless of their caste, ethnicity, religion, and social background; iv) elimination of all forms of gender-based violence, discrimination and exclusion; v) prioritisation of basic education, health, drinking water, and sanitation services; vi) mobilisation of the private sector in development activities; and vi) close attention in addressing the shortcomings of the Twelfth Plan, including weak implementation of gender-sensitive monitoring and evaluation, and various other policy measures (GoN, 2013). The massive earthquakes that hit Nepal in April and May 2015, along with the political transition, border blockade and power outage in the country, however, deterred the effective implementation of the various planned objectives, including the target of attaining six per cent economic growth annually and reducing the poverty level to 18% (GoN, 2016).

Fourteenth Three-Year Development Plan (2016-2019): After the completion of the MDG targets in 2015, the United Nations introduced Sustainable Development Goals (SDGs) to be achieved globally by 2030. Accordingly, the Fourteenth Plan (2016-2019) was fully aligned with SDGs. Expanding on previous periodic plans in areas such as the implementation of participatory and inclusive development approaches, the Fourteenth Plan aimed to facilitate socio-economic transformation by reducing and attaining a high economic growth rate, productive employment and equitable distribution of resources. Some other specific features of the Fourteenth Plan include: i) economic growth rate targeted at 6.5%, 7.2% and 7.9% in FY16/17, FY17/18 and FY18/19 respectively, with an annual average of 7.2% for the plan period; ii) increase in domestic production by transforming the agriculture sector and expanding tourism, industry and small and medium enterprises; iii) considerable investment on infrastructure development related to energy, road, air travel and information and communications; iv) strengthening of social security and social protection systems; v) reforms in the economic and social sectors, ensuring sound and accountable public finance, delivery of quality public services in a transparent manner and promoting good governance by protecting and promoting human rights; and vi) attainment of gender empowerment index (GEI) at 0.58% (GoN, 2017; TKP, 2017; Shakya, undated). To achieve these objectives, the Fourteenth Plan considered gender equality, inclusive society, environmental protection and capacity development as cross-cutting issues.

With the progress made on its targets, the results of the Fourteenth Plan were mixed. Although it failed to meet most of its targets at 100% level, the plan also, at the same time, reached closer to 100% in most of them. Progress made on some of the key targets of the Fourteenth Plan was: 6.9% of average annual economic growth rate against the target of 7.2, and 4.2% and 8.0% of annual growth rate in the agriculture and non-agriculture sector as against the target of 4.7% and 8.4% respectively. Similarly, the plan had targeted to reduce the level of poverty from 21.6% to 17% which, however, stayed at 18.4% by the end of the plan period. The plan also had aimed to achieve the life expectancy level at 72 years and the GEI at 0.58% but these figures remained only at 69.7 years and 0.56% levels. While the lack of political will and commitment, on the one hand, and the vested partisan politics, on the other hand, were some major reasons for the failure to attain the desired goals, the fact that the Fourteenth Plan started at a difficult juncture of the post-earthquake and border blockade period, these also made the fulfilment of the targets difficult.

Fifteenth Five-Year Development Plan (2019-2024): The then GoN, after following the three-year plan cycle for almost 12 years, decided to move back to the five-year cycle in the Fifteenth Plan on the ground that it had got a two-thirds majority in the parliament so is stable and can thus deliver its commitments to the people of Nepal. This plan has been drafted keeping in mind the long-term vision of 'Prosperous Nepal-Happy Nepali'. To achieve this vision, the Fifteenth Plan has embarked on the following objectives: i) development of modern infrastructure; increase in productive and dignified employment opportunities; high, sustainable, and inclusive economic growth; poverty reduction and; creating a base for long-term prosperity; ii) ensuring quality health and education; creating a healthy and balanced environment; providing social justice and accountable public service; strengthening federal structure; and ensuring a dignified and decent living for the people of Nepal; iii) protecting the national sovereignty, independence and national interest through socio-economic transformation and creating an independent national economy (GoN, 2020).

Accordingly, the plan aims to achieve an average of 9.4% annual economic growth rate during the plan period. The per capita income (PCI) target has been set at USD 1,595 which is an increase of almost 52% in the current PCI of USD 1,047. Similarly, while the average growth rate for the agriculture sector has been set at 5.6% per annum, it is set at 17.1% for the industrial sector and 9.9% for the service sector (THT, 2020). Likewise, the Fifteenth Plan intends to reduce the percentage of the population living below the poverty line by 40% bringing the number down from 18.4% at present to 11% at the end of the plan period. Regarding GAD indicators, the plan, with a clear focus on gender equality, has specified a target of 0.963 for gender development indicator, with the current figure being 0.925; 13% for women victimised physically, mentally and sexually, with the current figure being 26.3%; and 100% for registration of cases of women victimised under GBV/ VAW, which, at present, is 86.7% (GoN, 2020).

In the backdrop of the continuation of some of the challenges encountered by the Fourteenth Plan, confusion seen in ensuring effective coordination between the three tiers of the government under the federal structure and the recent collapse of the government (made up of Communist Party Nepal- United Marxist Leninist/ CPN-UML and Communist Party Nepal- Maoist Centre/ CPN-MC Prachanda) despite having two-thirds majority in the parliament due to the intra-party conflicts, some serious doubts could be raised regarding the attainment of the Fifteenth Plan targets, including those related to gender equality and women's empowerment. Moreover, whether the new coalition government, formed under the leadership of the Nepali Congress Party, will have profound focus on the fulfilment of the Fifteenth Plan targets is also unclear, since its priority will be more in safeguarding the coalition government at least until the upcoming elections than anything else.

Status of Women's Empowerment

The discussion made earlier depicts that Nepal's long-term development plans have been evolving to be gender-sensitive. However, the sensitivity expressed in papers may not mean much unless and until they are translated into action and women in general and the entire Nepalese society, in particular, feel the difference. Looking at the various indicators that explain women's empowerment as presented in the long-term development plans as well as in the Constitution of Nepal 2015, it can be said that the country has come a long way since the release of the first five-year development plan in 1956 and the signing of the Comprehensive Peace Agreement in 2006. Consequently, Nepal's Constitution 2015 has been a huge improvement not only over the previous constitutions but also over all the long-term plans and policies that the country has released as of now. For instance, Article 38 deals with the rights of women, which include, equal lineage rights without gender-based discrimination; right to safe motherhood and reproductive health; right to be free from all forms of violence or exploitation; right to obtain special opportunity in education, health, employment and social security, based on positive discrimination; and equal right to property and family matters (GoN, 2015).

The discussions presented earlier in various chapters have depicted the plight of Nepalese women and girls in their day-to-day life. The plight extends from harmful effects of early marriage to physical and sexual violence, to fewer jobs and schooling opportunities, to discriminatory societal traditions- all of which interfere in almost every aspect of women's life. A Study on the Social, Economic and Political Situation of Women in Nepal led by NWC also confirms that Nepalese women have lower access to education, property ownership and inheritance, social security, health care and freedom, and decision-making processes, among others (NWC, 2014). Consequently, the firm commitment expressed in the Constitution of Nepal 2015 towards women's rights, equality and empowerment is a big achievement in the country. The analysis made below presents the changes felt by Nepalese women over the years concerning their overall social, economic and political empowerment vis-à-vis Nepalese men.

A major indicator of women's empowerment and gender equality is **property ownership**, which provides women more power over household decisions, and even decreases the risks of domestic violence (Habitat, 2016). The reality, however, indicates that Nepali women have lesser ownership of productive assets, as the patrilineal system of land inheritance is predominantly owned and controlled by men (IOM, 2016; Acharya and Bennett, 1981). Though the number of female-headed households in the country has increased by about 11 per cent from 14.87% in 2001 to 25.73% in 2011, the poorest of the poor in Nepal are still mostly women (CBS, 2011; Acharya, 1997). The NDHS 2016 report cites that although 79% of women know how much property their household owns and 89% know under whose name the property is registered, only 8% of women own a house and 11% own land alone or both. The proportion of men owning a house and land alone or both is 19% and 21% respectively (GoN, New ERA and ICF International, 2016). Discriminatory provisions on the National Civil Code (Act) of 1963 (also known as Muluki Ain 2020 B.S.), the major law of the State comprising of civil, criminal, and procedural law, certainly became an influencing factor to dissuade women's property ownership, as it entitled daughters to an equal share of the property only if they remained unmarried, and further stated that the property should be returned if they got married.

However, recent developments, including the promulgation of the Gender Justice Act 2015 (also perceived as Gender Equality Act 2015) (GoN, 2015), have extended property rights to women, irrespective of their marital status, after a span of almost four decades of continuous battle. Similarly, the new National Civil Code (Act) 2017 (2074 B.S.) is also much progressive than the earlier one in terms of ensuring rights to women as equal as to men (GoN, 2017) although the effectiveness of its implementation in terms of meeting all of the objectives that it has committed to is yet to be seen. Nevertheless, it is ironic that even though women constitute more than half of Nepal's population (51.5 %) and that about 75% of them are engaged in agriculture as their primary occupation, they do not have ownership of the land that they are cultivating (IOM, 2016). The reasons identified as barriers to women's land ownership are patriarchy and conservative social structure.

Another important indicator of women's empowerment is **control over their own body and reproductive rights (fertility)** because a woman who can make decisions regarding her reproductive health can help change her life and transform her society. However, looking at the age at marriage of Nepalese women, one can be disappointed that they have been found to be marrying at a much earlier age until recently. Even though early marriage results in distressing effects and is a serious violation of women's reproductive health rights, the UNICEF data indicates that Nepal still has the third-highest child marriage rate in Asia with 37% of girls marrying before the age of 18 and 10% by the age of 15, irrespective of the fact that the minimum age of marriage under Nepali law is 20 years (HRW, 2016). The NDHS report also shows that the median age at first marriage of Nepalese women is 17.9 years and of men aged 25-49 years is 21.7 years (GoN, New ERA, and ICF International, 2016). Regarding the consequences of such an early marriage, girls dropping out of school and having babies early, affecting their health and also their children's as well as their career and professional development, are the major ones.

The other important indicator of women's empowerment related to reproductive health rights is the **use of a family planning method and the extent of their involvement in making decisions** about its use. As per the NDHS report 2016, 53% of currently married women use a method of family planning, with 43% using a modern method and 10% using a traditional method. Interestingly, there was no increase in the proportion of women using modern methods between 2006-2016 (GoN, New ERA and ICF International, 2016). Regarding women's involvement in making decisions regarding the use of family planning methods, the same report presents that 66% of the women who are the current users of family planning methods made the decision jointly with their husband, 19% made the decision mainly themselves, and 15% reported that their husband mainly made the decision. The lack of increase in the proportion of women using modern family planning methods even in 10 years despite the increase in the number of literate and educated women in the country and only 19% of women deciding on the use of family planning method themselves indicates that there is a long way to go for Nepalese women towards their genuine empowerment.

An equally important indicator of women's empowerment is their **ability to decide the number of children** they would like to have and the appropriate age for it. According to the NDHS report 2016, the total fertility rate in Nepal is 2.3 children per woman and the median age at first birth among women aged 25-49 is 20.4 years. Although the total fertility rate has drastically declined over the last 20 years, from 4.6 in 1996 to 2.3 children in 2016, the median age of women while delivering a birth has only slightly changed- from 19.8 years to 20.4 years - during the same period (GoN, New ERA and ICF International, 2016). Again, like the low level of change observed in the use of family planning method and weak engagement in making decisions about it, the very small change seen in Nepalese women's median age of marriage even in 20 years' time span indicates that they, as well as the other concerned stakeholders working in the area of women's rights, have to work further in empowering women in this front.

Similarly, the other strong indicator of women's empowerment is their **ability to decide on their pregnancy** for various justifiable reasons. Following on the women's reproductive health rights enshrined in Nepal's Constitution 2015, the GoN released The Right to Safe Motherhood and Reproductive Health Act in 2018 (GoN, 2018). Although there was a delay in bringing an Act like this into implementation, the GoN, with continued pressure of the women's rights activists and agencies, human rights organisations and supporters of women's rights working in various walks of life, had legalised abortion in Nepal long back in September 2002 (GoN, 2002). As a result of legalised abortion, among other factors, Nepal has experienced a sharp decline in its maternal mortality- from 580 maternal deaths per 100,000 live births in 1995 to 239 for the period 2009-2016 (GoN, 2016; WHO, 2014). Nevertheless, many women in Nepal continue to face barriers to obtaining safe and legal procedures for abortion due to a lack of adequate knowledge about it on time. The NDHS 2016 report indicates that 59% of the women aged 15-49 years have no idea that abortion is legal and 52% have no idea about a place where the abortion service is available. The other challenges being faced by the Nepalese women and girls regarding their timely access to safe abortion service are the absence of service in the approved health service institutions during their visit, lack of transportation to the approved health facilities, patriarchal norms that hinder women's decision-making autonomy, the often-prohibitive cost of the procedure, and fear of abortion-related stigma, among others (Shrestha, Regmi and Dangal, 2018; Thapa et.al., 2014). This situation again indicates that there is a need for individuals and agencies working in the area of women's rights and empowerment to continue their struggle in this area of women's empowerment in the days to come as well.

Literacy level, the other vital indicator of women's social status and empowerment, is also not yet at a satisfactory level though this has increased over the years. In 1991, the proportion of literate Nepali women, 15 years or older, was only 17%, while this proportion has increased to almost 60% in 2016 (GoN, 2016; GoN, 2011). Although women's literacy has increased by almost 253% in the last 25 years, the literacy rates of men and women in Nepal differ by nearly 20% even now (60% for women vs. 80% for men), which indicates that women have been discriminated and they have a long way to fill in this gap.

Among the various reasons for women's low level of literacy, *Chhaupadi*, an inhuman practice that requires banishing women and girls out of their homes to unhygienic cowsheds or outbuildings during menstruation is a major one. This flawed and obsolete practice is limiting Nepalese girls' access to education for a large portion of the academic year. As per the Nepal Multiple Indicator Cluster Survey 2010, although only 19 per cent of Nepali women, in general, practised *Chhaupadi*, the figure was nearly 50 per cent in the mid and far-western regions of the country (GoN, 2010). Such ill-practices that compel young girls and women to be out of home for 4-7 days every month not only puts them at physical and mental risks but also keeps the girls away from schools and all other opportunities, thereby forcing them to lag behind boys and men in schools, colleges, workplace and elsewhere. The National (Preliminary) Report on Sustainable Development Goals (SDG), 2016-2030 (GoN, 2015), also acknowledges that although Nepal has made substantial progress in ensuring equal access to education, with gender parity in primary and secondary level school enrolment, discrimination remains. Consequently, the proposed target of SDG 5 'achieving gender equality and empowering all women and girls' includes eliminating gender disparity in all levels of education.

Gender-Based Violence (GBV), an inhumane form of discrimination, is both a cause and a consequence of inequalities between women and men (Equinet, 2018). GBV can be referred to as any form of discrimination, marginalisation, inequality and criminal activities based on the sex of a person. This means the victims could include women, children, men and any other gender. Nevertheless, in general, it is women who are more affected by GBV, which is why GBV often relates to Violence Against Women (VAW) and these two terms -GBV and VAW- are interchangeably used in Nepal (Regmi et.al., 2013). The United Nations, acknowledged long back that VAW is a serious form of GBV and in many instances, it is referred to as GBV (UN, 1993). In Nepal, VAW is common and present in various forms, such as domestic violence, marital rape, dowry-related violence, child marriage, witchcraft accusations, *Chhaupadi*, trafficking of women, female infanticide and the marginalisation of girls and women across castes and cultural groups (UNFPA, 2016). A survey carried out by the GoN in 2012 showed that almost half of the surveyed women (48%) experienced one or the other form of GBV at some point in their lifetime, and over a quarter (28%) experienced GBV in the past 12 months (GoN, 2012). The National (Preliminary) Report on SDG, 2016-2030 (GoN, 2015), also acknowledges that although Nepal has made substantial progress in various aspects of gender equality, VAW still exists. Accordingly, the proposed target of SDG 5 includes eliminating wage discrimination for similar work, physical and sexual violence, and all harmful practices as one of its key objectives.

The NDHS 2016 Report depicts that the figure of Nepalese women facing spousal violence is 26%. The perpetrators of GBV are in general often intimate partners, with over 85 per cent of perpetrators of physical and sexual violence being current and /or former husbands (GoN, New ERA, and ICF International, 2016). Although the proportion of women being victimised by spousal violence has decreased by two per cent in five years from 2011-2016, the absolute number of women being the victims of spousal violence has increased during this period since two per cent of the 2016 population is higher than the two per cent of the 2011 population, given the fact that the country had experienced an increase of more than two per cent population growth during this period. Such a situation implies that GBV is a major impediment to women's empowerment in Nepal. Regmi et.al. (2013) write that despite the increase in efforts made by both the governmental and non-governmental partners to eliminate GBV, the problem persists and continues obstructing women from exercising their rights and participating in development processes encompassing their professional, public and private lives.

Regarding the factors contributing to GBV, education seems to have played an important role since physical and sexual violence is declining with an increase in the level of education in Nepal. For instance, while 34% of the women with no education experienced physical violence, the figure was only 8% among women with a School Leaving Certificate (SLC) or higher education. Similarly, sexual violence also seems to be declining with the level of educational attainment as indicated by 17% of women with no education to only 7% of women with SLC and higher education experiencing sexual violence (UNFPA, 2017) and 9% of women with no education or primary education to only 4% of women with SLC and higher education experiencing the same (GoN, New ERA and ICF International, 2016).

Despite the serious impact of GBV on girls' and women's education and professional career and development, ending VAW has been difficult, if not impossible, to attain for social, economic and political reasons. Even now many legal provisions place women in a subordinated position to men, which in turn compel women to be: economically dependent on men, following harmful socio-cultural practices, and accepting a lower social position as compared to men irrespective of the many hours that they spend inside and outside their households and the meaningful contribution they make in the wellbeing of their families, society and the nation. The fact that 29% of the surveyed women in NDHS 2016 as against 23% in 2006, and 23% men in 2016 as against 21% in 2006 (GoN, New ERA and ICF International, 2016) agreed even in this modern era that wife-beating is justified under specific circumstances, it confirms that empowerment of women is going to be a continuous struggle for all concerned stakeholders in Nepal. Implementation of a human rights and victim-centric approach as it creates a favourable environment for victims to seek justice may, therefore, be the need to address the slow progress in addressing the GBV in Nepal (Regmi et.al., 2013).

Economic empowerment, another key indicator of women's empowerment, is also not in the favour of Nepalese women. The figures from the latest NDHS 2016 report elucidate that while 97% of men between the age of 15-49 years were employed in the past 12 months, it is only 68% for women in the same age group and the same period. What is worse off is that the proportion of employed women has shown a downward trend with figures decreasing from 83% in 2006 and 77% in 2011 to 68% in 2016. Moreover, the same source reports that women are almost three times less likely to be paid compared to men- 52% for men versus 16% for women (GoN, New ERA and ICF International, 2016). While men are employed in highly paid and skilled jobs, women's employment is not only limited to low paid and unskilled jobs but also to the informal and private sector jobs, with their wages being lower than those of their male counterparts for the same type of job (UNFPA, 2017). Regarding control over income, another important indicator of women's empowerment, the NDHS report 2016 presents that only 52% of women can decide independently regarding the use of their earnings (GoN, New ERA, and ICF International, 2016). It is an irony that almost half the surveyed women (48%) cannot make independent decisions even about their own earnings, thereby implying that the existing patriarchal beliefs and practices have deprived them of operating on a level playing field with their male counterparts despite the forward strides that the Nepalese women have made in the economic spheres over the years.

An equally important prerequisite for gender equality and women's empowerment is women's **meaningful participation in politics**. Although the history of Nepalese women's participation in politics has been long, it has always been in a limited role and capacity. Since the senior leadership in all political parties is made up of men, they have never been welcoming towards the idea to increase the number of women in senior roles, be it at the parliament or the local levels. Such a narrow mindset of the male political leaders has restricted women's meaningful participation in the parliament, in the council of ministers and the local level governments as well. But, the positive side of such a narrow perspective is that it has provided an impetus for Nepalese women to continue their struggle for their strategic positions and role in politics. As a result of such continued women's rights movements, the Constitution of Nepal 2015 has come out to be much more progressive than any other previous constitutions regarding women's rights. One among such rights includes the quota system for women's seats in the parliament. As of today, Nepal's Constitution 2015 mandates at least one-third representation of women from each political party representing in the federal parliament.

Accordingly, the parliament, instituted in 2017 after the promulgation of the new progressive Constitution 2015, received almost 30% representation of women. Although this proportion of women's representation in the parliament is no different than in 2016, 2015 and 2014, the fact that Nepal's parliament got 30% of women's representation for four consecutive years despite the patriarchal mentality that exists everywhere, should be perceived as a remarkable achievement in ensuring women's empowerment in the country. However, at the same time, this feat is to be taken with a pinch of salt because figures show that this representation is less than what it was in 2013- 33.2% (Code for Nepal,

2018). Given the enactment of a progressive Constitution in 2015, the people involved in women's rights movements had expected that women's representation will be much higher in 2017 than what it had been in the past. But, sadly, because of the poor commitment and the lack of willingness of the male political leaders, no political parties allocated more than the minimum quota asserted in the constitution for women to be in the parliament. To improve this situation, the National (Preliminary) Report on SDG, 2016-2030 (GoN, 2015), specifies the need to eliminate all forms of discrimination against women as a way out.

The situation of women's representation at the local level is also not so different from that of their representation at the parliament. Taking into account the women's population of 51.5% (GoN, 2011), the Nepal Election Commission mandated the political parties that at least 40.4% of the nominee seats be reserved for women in the local level election that took place in May, June and September 2017. The Election Commission had also made it mandatory that one of the two key positions- Mayor and Deputy Mayor at the municipality level- and Chairperson and Deputy Chairperson at the rural municipality level -has to be a woman. However, because a majority of the senior leaders in almost all political parties are men, they decided to not let their women cadres, but only men cadres, contest in the position of Mayor of municipalities, sub-metropolitan cities and metropolitan cities, and Chairperson of rural municipalities in this election. Since these are politically important and powerful positions and that the male political leaders were not hopeful that women candidates would be elected, they mostly nominated men to contest for these positions.

Consequently, out of a total of 35,041 representatives elected from 753 local governments (6 metropolitan cities, 11 sub-metropolitan cities, 276 municipalities and 460 rural municipalities), women won only in 14,352 (40.96%) seats holding mainly the second position, with 91% being elected in the position of Deputy Mayor, the second position, and only 2% being elected in the position of Mayor and Chairperson, the first position. Similarly, at the ward committee level with four-member seats and one ward chair, the parties had to have at least two women ward members, including one from the Dalit community. Out of the 13,484 non-quota ward member positions, only 2% went to women and out of a total of 6,742 ward chairperson seats, only 1% went to women (Paswan, 2018; Asia Foundation et.al., 2018) implying that women's leadership is still not well accepted within the political parties, thereby the general population as well.

Although there exist tremendous opportunities for Nepalese women's increased and meaningful participation in the country's new political structure, bagging this opportunity in reality for women in general, and women from socially marginalised, discriminated and excluded, including minority ethnic groups, in particular, has not been as easy as it was envisioned. Although factors such as the lack of awareness about the legal provisions and information regarding their rights and electoral procedures, among others, have been pointed out as key barriers for Nepalese women to rise into positions of leadership (UNDP, 2017), the patriarchal mindset causing the inadequate representation of women in decision-making levels within the political parties also needs to be perceived as the root cause for it. As Hewitt (2017) writes: all things considered, what has been observed in the context of Nepal is that although women's rights have made long, forward strides, it is equally, if not more, important to address the socially entrenched barriers to women's productive, meaningful participation and decision-making in all realms- sociocultural, economic, and political. Patriarchal expectations, constraints on women's and men's roles, and gender inequalities in education, literacy level, economic opportunities and ownership, life skills, including confidence and experience, have been some of the major deterrents, which have limited women's potential to influence decision-making in Nepal.

Taking into consideration the social, economic, legal and political changes that have taken place in the lives of Nepalese women over the last 20 years, as discussed in this chapter, the next chapter will look at the space created for them by the GoN as well as the other key actors in Nepal's water sector. The anticipation is that the progress of women which has taken place on various fronts- social, economic, legal and political- will have a bearing on their meaningful participation in the water sector as well.

❍❍❍

CHAPTER 11

Gender Integration in Nepal's Water Sector Post 2000

Gender Changes in Government's Water Policies

The discussions made in the preceding chapter reveal that many policy changes and legislative frameworks have taken place concerning women's rights and gender equality in Nepal since 2000. Against this backdrop, one expects that Nepal's water sector has also evolved through various gender-sensitive changes over the same time. Consequently, this chapter reviews the gender sensitivity in Nepal's water policies and legislative frameworks to get an idea of the extent to which the drinking water and sanitation projects implemented under these legal instruments will be able to meet women's practical and strategic gender needs. This review is essential in that many studies conducted after 2000, like those conducted prior to 2000, also disclose that unless and until drinking water policies integrate gender perspectives, the drinking water projects implemented within those policy frameworks will not yield sustainable results for its users (RWSSP, 2019; Wallace, 2003; van Wijk and Garcia, 2002; Regmi and Fawcett, 2001).

In Nepal, 88% of the total population has access to the basic level of drinking water services, up from 72% in 2001 and 98% has access to basic sanitation facilities, such as access to toilets, up from 30% in 2001 (GoN, 2019). The review of the progress made on water-related MDG targets also depicts that Nepal has made significant progress in the proportion of the population using an improved drinking-water source from 46% in 1990 to 83.65% in 2014. The proportion of the population using an improved sanitation facility also rose from 6% in 1990 to 60.1% in 2014 (GoN, 2015). Some other reports also confirm that 85% of the population have access to the basic level of drinking water supply, while

62% have got access to the basic level of sanitation facilities (Budhathoki, 2019; UNICEF, 2018; GLASS, 2014).

Although one can gather from the reports mentioned above that Nepal has made extensive progress both in water supply and sanitation over the last 20 years, the services have been severely questioned due to the disparity in access, inequality in services, quality of water and services, and the functionality and sustainability of the systems. UNICEF reports that only 25% of the water supply is reported to be fully functioning and almost 40% require major repairs in Nepal (UNICEF, 2018). The National (Preliminary) Report on SDGs also acknowledges that while at least 15 per cent of Nepal's households are yet to be covered by such services, about half of all water supply schemes are not functional implying that strong efforts are needed to achieve the universal coverage, maintenance, and monitoring of water supply services in the country (GoN, 2015). Similarly, the National Water Supply and Sanitation Sector Policy (NWSSSP) 2014 reports that though with the substantial investment in the rural water supply sub-sector, a good coverage has been achieved in the past decades, the functionality of the completed schemes has been a major issue since about half of the schemes are reported to be non-functioning and need immediate rehabilitation (GoN, 2014). NEWAH (2020) reports, despite the progress, 558 million people in the region still practise open defecation and about 177,000 children die of diarrhoea each year. While it is encouraging that water supply coverage in Nepal has risen from 46% in 1990 to 88% in 2018, only 25% of the available systems are estimated to be fully functional. Ironically, the figures mentioned above indicate that there has been no improvement even in 20 years in the quality of the water supply schemes since the proportion of less functional or non-functional schemes was around 48% in the hills and 66% in the Tarai in the early 2000s too (NEWAH, 2003).

The 7.9 and 6.9 Richter scale tremors that occurred one after another in a two-week period of April-May 2015 not only devastated central Nepal further but also heavily damaged the WASH infrastructure. The findings from the Post-Disaster Needs Assessment indicates that, in 14 severely affected districts, out of a total of 11,288 water supply systems, 1,570 sustained major damages and 3,663 partial damages, and approximately 220,000 toilets endured partial or total destruction. Similarly, in 17 moderately affected districts, out of 16,433 water supply systems, 747 sustained major damages and 1,761 partial damages, and approximately 168,000 toilets endured partial or total destruction (NPC,

2015). Within this backdrop, the Fifteenth Plan (2019-2024) aims to achieve 99% coverage for basic level drinking water service and 100% for basic level sanitation service by the end of the plan period (GoN, 2019).

Regarding the role played by women in Nepal's water sector, although their role is not yet fully appreciated by the government as well as the donors and agencies working in the water sector, it can be gladly stipulated that Nepal has come a long way since the 1980s when women's rights were nearly non-existent. The role and continued efforts of the national and international NGOs and the UN organisations cannot be ignored while speaking about the advancement of Nepalese women's involvement and participation in water-related matters. For instance, organisations like Helvetas, UNICEF, Nepal Red Cross Society etc. were some of the pioneers in ensuring women's formal involvement in the water supply programmes in Nepal back in the '80s. Later on, these entities, along with many other donors like the ADB, the World Bank, WaterAid (INGO), Government of Finland as well as international conferences and conventions on women that took place in Mexico, Beijing, Copenhagen etc., have been influential to assert the principles of gender equality, including in the water sector, and to pressurise the governments, including the GoN, to reform the water laws using a gender lens (Regmi, 2000).

Currently, the GoN has been implementing WASH programmes through the Ministry of Water Supply and Sanitation, with support from development partners like UNICEF, UN-Habitat, ADB, the World Bank, the Government of Finland, and INGOs like WaterAid. The WASH programme contributes to the achievement of SDG 6- "Ensure availability and sustainable management of water and sanitation for all" (GoN, 2015). The recently released Fifteenth Plan (2019-2024) and the Sector Development Plan 2016-2030 further guide the government efforts in the WASH sector for the coming five years and 15 years respectively, with an aim of not only ensuring safe and adequate water, and proper sanitation facilities but also sustaining these services over a longer period. Both these important documents have been prepared in alignment with the SDGs. Following its commitments expressed in various international and regional conventions and becoming a signatory to the legislations and declarations approved by these forums, Nepal has also developed, and over the years, strengthened national legislative frameworks and policies on water. A lot has already been discussed that no water and sanitation projects, be it in Nepal or elsewhere, will succeed without women's effective participation in their management. Accordingly, the following section will discuss and analyse the GoN's current water policies from a gender lens to conclude whether the water supplies implemented under these policies will yield sustained practical and strategic benefits to the people of Nepal, especially women.

Water Resources Act 1992: The Water Resources Act (WRA), formulated in 1992, is still the umbrella Act governing water resource management in Nepal. This Act gives priority to the right to water for drinking purposes followed by irrigation, agricultural use and animal husbandry, hydropower, industrial and mining, navigation, recreation and other uses (GoN, 1992). The WRA 1992 has gone through a couple of amendments in the last 28 years but those amendments have only been on routine matters related to the political changes, not on the content. The WRA 1992 is as gender-weak as it was 28 years ago despite several amendments. Hence, to avoid the repetition of what has already been discussed in Part II, this section briefly summarises the two major gender weaknesses of the WRA 1992 as follows:

1. The WRA 1992 still relies heavily on the use of so-called gender-neutral terminologies like 'users', 'consumers', 'beneficiaries', 'community' etc. be it in the formation of water users' association and tariff fixation committee or the formation of water conflict resolution committee, among others, without appreciating the fact that women's needs and concerns in the water sector are different from those of men. As a result, the water projects designed under such gender-insensitive policy will only partially benefit in addressing women's needs and concerns as exemplified in greater detail in Part II of this book.
2. The WRA 1992 has put heavy emphasis on the payments to be made by the users for getting the water service without considering that women, in general, and female-headed households, in particular, will have difficulty in paying for water services as they have no or limited access to control over income implying that they may remain outside the purview of improved water services just like what was observed 22 years ago (Regmi and Fawcet, 2001; Regmi, 2000).

Water Resource Regulations 1993: The Water Resources Regulations (WRR) 1993, the primary Regulation governing water resource management in the country, sets out the procedure to form and register consumer's association, comprising of at least seven members, to use the water resources on an institutionalised basis. Like the WRA 1992, the WRR 1993 also has gone through an amendment in 2013. However, the amended version is no different from what it was nearly 27 years ago since this version is still influenced by the use of gender-neutral terminologies like 'consumers', 'users', 'members', 'beneficiaries', 'community', 'people', 'representatives', 'local residents', 'group', in the entire document (GoN, 1993) without showing any appreciation that the needs and interests of women and men are, at times, different. There is no appreciation in the amended version of WRR 1993 that unless and until women are categorically mentioned, the chances of women's representation in any of the committees, associations, groups etc. are minimal in a patriarchal society like Nepal and so are the chances of women benefitting as equal as to men through various components such as training, technical knowledge, employment, exposure visits etc. of the water projects built under such gender-weak policy as depicted in Part II. The amended version of WRR 1993 ignores the fact that when women don't get to be involved in important committees like -Water User's Committees, Tariff Fixation Committees, Water Conflict Resolution Committees -despite their primary role in the water sector, the decisions made by such committees may not be in women's favour as what happened in water projects designed and implemented 27 years ago. It's an irony that the author cannot add anything new to the gender analysis of the WRR 1993 done 22 years ago as has been presented in Part II Chapter V.

Drinking Water Rules 1998: Despite the knowledge that the country has made tremendous progress in formulating policies gearing towards ensuring gender equality and women's empowerment as enshrined in the Constitution of Nepal 2015, the gender-insensitive Drinking Water Rules (DWR) 1998, formulated 23 years ago (GoN, 1998), still prevails in the same spirit. Since there is nothing new that the author can add to the gender analysis of the DWR 1998 made earlier, the author would like to close the discussion on this topic by saying that the water projects that get implemented under such policies, which have created limited space or none, for women to engage in various important activities and committees and have failed to develop mechanisms for poor men and women, including female-headed households, to enjoy the benefits of the water supplies regardless of their inability to pay for the services, will in the long run fail to sustain the benefits.

Rural Water Supply and Sanitation National Policy (RWSSNP) 2004 and Rural Water Supply and Sanitation National Strategy (RWSSNS) 2004: The RWSSNP 2004 and RWSSNS 2004 have put profound emphasis on the application of participatory approach and social inclusion, local ownership of the systems, and meaningful engagement of women, backward people and disadvantaged ethnic groups in all aspects of water supply projects for effective delivery of the water services. Equally, an important focus has been provided on matters such as gender equality, social justice, decentralisation, transparency, accountability, and use of local knowledge, skills and technology as applicable in these policies. While aiming for "safe, accessible and adequate water supply and sanitation facility" for all individuals, especially backward people and ethnic groups, these policies also intend to utilise women's, men's, and children's time and labour saved from water hauling, in other productive works (HMG, 2004). In fact, these are the first GoN's water policies that have mentioned women, backward people and ethnic groups. An equally important feature of these policies is their provision to consider local consumers', especially women's and disadvantaged households', willingness as well as capacity to pay for water services before fixing the amount of contribution be it during the construction phase or the operation and maintenance phase. The other gender-sensitive feature of these policies is the consideration of gender, caste and ethnicity while formulating and implementing local level plans and provision for the selection of women in the position of health workers and married women in the position of VMW in each water supply and sanitation scheme.

Having a separate section 'Enhancing Participation by Gender, Caste and Disadvantaged Groups' in the national policy confirms a better understanding of the planners and policy-makers about women's vis-à-vis men's, and other excluded people's roles, needs and concerns in the water sector. The focus on gender equity in the water and sanitation services, proportional representation of other ethnic and disadvantaged groups and 30% participation in case of women in local water users and sanitation committees, and implementation of adult education and income generation activities for empowerment of women etc. also indicates the GoN's commitment towards gender equality. Likewise, to ensure the increased participation of women and people from disadvantaged groups, the RWSSNP 2004 and RWSSNS 2004 suggest a simplified procedure for registering water supply and sanitation committees.

Nevertheless, there are some areas where the RWSSNP 2004 and RWSSNS 2004 can further be improved in their integration of gender concerns. The policy has failed to unpack the traditionally gender-neutral looking terminologies such as 'population', 'leaders', 'community', 'consumers', 'users', 'customers' and 'groups' repeating the same mistakes as of the various earlier policies like- WRA 1992, WRR 1993 and DWR 1998. The blanket use of such terminologies in the entire policy document without understanding the context in which it is being used points out the need for an increased understanding of gender needs and concerns on the part of planners and policy-makers. For instance, if water hauling and its management are done mainly by women and girls, their involvement needs to be categorically mentioned while selecting the water source, technology, location of the water points, amount of contribution in cash/ kind, among others, since the women not only know better than men in these aspects but also get harshly affected if the decisions made by men turn out to be wrong. If women and girls are not specifically mentioned in the policy document and the project implementation procedures, the field staff may not necessarily spend extra time to ensure women's and girls' presence in meetings, discussions and water users committees. The ultimate result of the lack of clarification on women's role vis-à-vis men's is that the water supply schemes will fail to meet women's practical as well as strategic gender needs.

National Water Plan 2005: The National Water Plan (NWP) 2005, meant to cover a period of 25 years (2002-2027), was prepared to operationalise the output objectives of the Water Resource Strategy approved by the GoN in January 2002, and plan short-term, medium-term and long-term action plans for Water Resource Sector, including programme and project activities, investments and institutional aspects. Although the major focus of the NWP is on environmental concerns and sustainable development, it simultaneously aims to achieve economic development, poverty alleviation, food security, public health, and decent standards of living for all people. Accordingly, it introduces the Integrated Water Resources Management (IWRM) approach, and specifies the need to view water from a holistic perspective, both in its natural state and in balancing its competing demands on areas, including domestic, agriculture, hydropower, industrial, cultural and environmental, along with a profound emphasis on the design and implementation of water projects following demand-driven approach (HMG, 2005).

The gender focus on the NWP is that it firmly highlights the importance of equity enhancing policies, social inclusion and women's participation in water management committees, riverbank protection, irrigation development, and conservation of critical areas. What is, however, missing in the NWP is the elaboration on women's limited access to and control over resources and the need for a special consideration/ provision to include women and poor households, including female-headed ones while designing and implementing a water project following demand-driven principles. There are many instances where women have failed to benefit from the water projects which were solely based on the users' ability to contribute during the construction phase and pay during the operation and maintenance phase as has been discussed in detail in Part II.

Water Supply Management Board Act 2006: In 2006, the government formulated the Water Supply Management Board (WSMB) Act, with objectives to acquire, build, expand, reform and rehabilitate the service system, or cause to do so; to formulate and implement, or cause to be implemented, policies on the use of the service; to prevent the misuse of potable water and the pollution of potable water; and to carry out, or cause to be carried out, study, research and survey on the source, distribution of potable water, and sanitation; among others (GoN, 2006).

Despite the WSMB Act being powerful in terms of managing the water supply mainly in the Kathmandu Valley, it is relatively weak in integrating gender in many aspects of water supply management. Like the earlier policies -WRA 1992, WRR 1993 and DWR 1998-, the WSMB Act is also heavily influenced by the use of gender-deceiving terminologies like users, committee, communities, members etc. without appreciating that the use of such terminologies may not necessarily create space for women like what happened in the past. Section 10 talks about the formation of an Executive Committee but women's representation is not made mandatory in this committee. In another clause, it is mentioned that a representative from among the NGOs working in the water sector will be selected to be in the Executive Committee and priority will be given to a woman while selecting a member from this category. The oversight of this clause is that it cannot guarantee that a woman will be selected through this process since there may not be women in the leadership positions in such NGOs. The policy-makers seem to have failed to realise while drafting the Act that when a woman's presence is not made mandatory, women hardly get selected to be in such committees as what has been the reality in many such committees formed earlier. Consequently, the committees fail to analyse the water issues from a gender perspective and make decisions that may not necessarily be women-friendly. One such decision can be related to the responsibility of making payment for water services. If there are women involved in the committee that decides the amount of water to be paid by users, the former ensures that the users are first divided into two categories of men and women and their ability to pay is assessed before fixing the amount of payment so that the chances of poor women, that fail to pay the contribution expected by the water projects, being out of the project benefits, unlike what happened in the past, can be prevented.

Urban Water Supply and Sanitation Sector Policy 2009: Since the RWSSNP 2004 was only partially relevant to the urban context, and failed to tackle the complex operational issue of urban water supply and sanitation service delivery, the need for a policy covering the urban sector was felt resulting in the formulation of Urban Water Supply and Sanitation Sector Policy (UWSSSP) in 2009. This policy seeks to make available all urban populations with a basic, safe, accessible and adequate water supply and sanitation services for improved quality of life and health status. It ensures the participation of users, especially women and vulnerable groups, in voicing their concerns and in decision-making at all practical levels. Although the UWSSSP emphasises on demand-driven cost-recovery approach while implementing a water supply scheme considering fresh and usable water as a finite and precious resource, it simultaneously acknowledges that poor and marginalised groups may not be adequately served due to the emphasis on cost-recovery. The UWSSSP thus stresses the need to take sufficient safeguards like financial incentives as required to protect such a population. The UWSSSP also mentions instituting statutory and proportional representation and enhancing decision-making roles of poor and marginalised groups, especially women's, by adopting effective capacity building measures at both programme and project levels. Women's participation is emphasised in various aspects of planning, implementation, management, operation and maintenance of water supply and sanitation. It also recognises the equally important role that men play in realising the benefits of water supply and sanitation services and aims to encourage them through education and awareness programmes for effectively managing the water supply and sanitation at household levels. Overall, this policy is more progressive in integrating gender issues as compared to many other water policies formulated earlier.

Nonetheless, there are areas where the policy can be made even more gender-focused. For instance, despite the traditionally acknowledged important role of women in the water sector, the policy, at times, has overlooked to specify the role of women and relied on the use of so-called gender-neutral terminologies like users, groups, poor and marginalised, consumers, members etc. as in the other previous policies. This policy fails to appreciate that even among the urban users, consumers, poor and marginalised groups, squatters and slum dwellers, women's, and more so female-headed households', needs, concerns and realities are different both for biological as well as socio-economic reasons. This oversight in the UWSSSP implies that women, particularly from female-headed households, may not be able to fully address their practical and strategic needs from the improved water supply projects implemented under such gender-weak provisions.

National Sanitation and Hygiene Master Plan 2011: The National Sanitation and Hygiene Master Plan (NSHMP) 2011 attempts to maintain uniformity and standards in the hygiene and sanitation sector, and aims to mobilise action to accelerate the pace at the local and national levels to meet the national targets. Though the Master Plan mainly focuses on the institutionalisation of ODF areas with universal access to a toilet in both the urban and rural areas as the bottom line for all sanitation interventions, one of its major shifts has been on its coverage of sanitation in broader terms. Moving beyond equating sanitation with just toilet coverage, the Master Plan also focuses on sustained hygiene habits and it, at the same time, aims to teach children and adults about proper sanitation practices and seeks to approach this cause by emphasising it in schools through the School Sanitation and Hygiene Education programmes. Moreover, it also aims to include easy accessibility of toilets by people of different ages and genders and supports the ultra-poor and other disadvantaged groups to build toilets and adopt proper sanitation and hygiene habits. It is more progressive in the view that it also ensures user-friendly facilities for physically challenged individuals, by including features such as wheelchairs, handrails, ramps, etc. The Master Plan also iterates the requirement for one-third of women to represent in the coordination committees related to hygiene and sanitation. It further stresses that in addition to having water services, the schools and public institutions should have facilities to maintain menstrual hygiene management. Overall, the NSHMP is a gender-sensitive document.

National Water Supply and Sanitation Sector Policy 2014: The National Water Supply and Sanitation Sector Policy (NWSSSP) 2014 is the revision and unification of the two separate policy documents, discussed above, namely- RWSSSP 2004 and UWSSSP 2009. The policy focuses on women and poor and marginalised groups on enhancing their capacity to voice concerns and to make them participate in decision-making processes. Given women's crucial role in the water and sanitation sector, the policy puts special emphasis on their participation in planning, implementation, and operation and maintenance phases of the water supply and sanitation projects and strives to ensure their access to those services along with the access of other disadvantaged groups, including slum dwellers, squatters, and the differently-abled. The NWSSSP underlines the implementation of effective community education programmes to eradicate social discrimination against menstruating women, postpartum mothers and *Dalits* from using household and public water and sanitation facilities. Acknowledging that sanitation facilities in public places and schools are unfavourable to girl students, women, and physically challenged individuals, the policy aims to take all measures to safeguard equal accessibility of all to water supply and sanitation services (GoN, 2014).

Despite the NWSSSP 2014 being advanced in defining women's concerns and acknowledging the need for their active participation in all stages of a drinking water and sanitation project, this policy has still failed to fully integrate gender concerns into it. For instance, in the technical approach on rural water supply and sanitation sector section, the policy talks about more than half the schemes being non-functional. It does not, however, acknowledge that if women were trained as operation and maintenance workers, the number of malfunctioning schemes would not have been so high since the women, who visit the water sources more than men, would notice the problem immediately and take prompt actions to resolve it. Similarly, in the same section, the policy mentions the inadequacy of water, the use of unreliable sources while designing schemes and water disputes between the users. Here too, the policy fails to appreciate that because women visit the water source to collect water almost every day, they are more informed than men on matters related to adequacy and reliability of the water sources and are also better placed to discuss with fellow women if there are any problems/ disputes in the schemes and how to resolve them.

Likewise, in the same section, the policy highlights the importance of the cost-recovery approach to increase efficiency and effectiveness in the water services and the involvement of the private sector for the same. Here also, the policy dodges the acknowledgement of the financial limitations of women and poor households, including female-headed ones, to meet the cash and in-kind project requirements to get the water services. The danger is that if the women and poor people are not allowed to use the improved water services simply because they cannot afford to pay for it, they might have to revert to the unhygienic traditional water sources. GWA (2003) notes because women and men have different income patterns and mobility, the concerned agencies should charge them fair, reasonable and flexible rates depending on their socioeconomic backgrounds while providing the water services.

Constitution of Nepal 2015: The Constitution of Nepal 2015, the fundamental law of the land, has stipulated that each citizen shall have the right to access clean water and sanitation (Article 35). The constitution also states in Article 51 that the State shall pursue a policy of prioritising national investment in water resources based on public participation and make a multi-purpose development of water resources. The same Article also expands on developing a sustainable and dependable irrigation system by controlling water-induced disasters and ensuring the management of the river systems (GoN, 2015). This Constitution has been perceived to be the most progressive constitution regarding women's rights. The Preamble, as well as Clause 18 of the Constitution, commit that there will be no discrimination towards women based on sex, gender, among others, in their demand for the fulfilment of the right to equality, including the right to equal wage and right to inherit parental property. Given the emphasis laid by the Constitution on women's right to equality in all aspects as stipulated in this umbrella policy document, it can be expected that Nepalese women will be able to exercise their rights as equal as to those of men, in the water sector as well.

Sustainable Development Goals 2016-2030: The SDGs, which extends from 2016-2030, are the continuation of the MDGs, the outcome of the Millennium Declaration made by the United Nations (UN) in 2000, that ran through 2015. The SDGs are the declaration made to give continuity to the progress made on the MDGs and also to initiate new agenda which were not covered by the MDGs earlier. Accordingly, the UN Conference on Sustainable Development held in Rio de Janeiro in June 2012 and United Nations General Assembly (UNGA) held in September 2014 prepared a solid foundation for SDGs and finally agreed to it in the UNGA held in September 2015 (GoN, 2015). As many other UN member countries, Nepal is also a signatory to the SDG, the global initiative. The learning and the achievements Nepal made from the implementation of MDGs laid a favourable environment for it to adopt and implement the SDGs for 2016-2030. While the implementation of the MDGs has significantly improved Nepal's social and environmental indicators, other issues such as human rights, access to justice, inequalities, social inclusion, infrastructure and sustainable development, which were not explicitly addressed in the MDGs, have now become the focus of the SDGs.

With the SDG's focus on water, SDG 6 is about ensuring the availability and sustainable management of water and sanitation for all. At the time the SDG was about to start, the basic water supply coverage in Nepal was 83.6%, while sanitation had reached 70.3% of the population. Two-thirds of the Nepali population were using latrines and 30% of urban households were connected to sewerage systems. The SDG 6 has got six targets and 15 indicators related to water supply and sanitation although no targets have been set for some indicators as yet. The proposed targets for 2030 include 95 per cent of households having access to piped water supplies and improved unshared sanitation facilities, 99% of households having access to basic water supply and sanitation coverage, 90% of the population having access to safe drinking water, 98% of the population using latrines and all urban households being connected to a sewerage system, 100% of urban households having sewerage connection, and 99% of local authority declaring ODF (GoN, 2015).

While looking at the SDG 6 targets, it is only the target 6.2 that specifically mentions the need to pay special attention to the needs of women and girls as well as the vulnerable population while ensuring access to adequate and equitable sanitation and hygiene for all and ending open defecation. The mentioning of women and girls only in this target, however, makes little sense since this target, as many other gender-blind targets and their indicators, does not have gender-disaggregated indicators. In most rural areas, it is women who mostly collect the water for drinking, cleaning, washing, feeding the cattle etc. spending hours every day; it is women who mostly maintain the water supply and sanitation systems spending hours from time to time; it is women who need the toilets close by the household more than men for reasons that include privacy and dignity; it is women who are insecure and vulnerable while going far from home for defecation, and it is women who are expected to pay the water tariff as drinking water and sanitation is said to fall in their domain of responsibilities. Considering all these important roles that women play and the different needs and concerns they have in the WASH sector, the planners and policy-makers should have developed indicators that would explain the extent to which the WASH projects paid attention to address the women's and girls' necessities in their lives. The SDGs, on the other hand, have completely overlooked it. This is an irony that despite the SDG 5 having a clear emphasis on gender equality and women's empowerment, the SDG 6 targets and indicators, which are all about drinking water and sanitation, traditionally perceived to be women's spectrum, remain gender-unspecific.

Nepal Water Supply, Sanitation and Hygiene Sector Development Plan (2016 – 2030- *DRAFT*): The Nepal WASH Sector Development Plan (SDP-DRAFT) developed by the Ministry of Water Supply and Sanitation intends to improve public health and living standards of individuals through "safe, sufficient, accessible, acceptable, and affordable water, sanitation and hygiene services for all". The WASH SDP realises that though there has been some progress made in the WASH sector over the past decade, it was not as expected due to the difficulties concerning structural and operational challenges. The WASH SDP recognises the necessity for WASH services to move towards GESI oriented approach going beyond technical solutions. It stresses the need to consider existing power relations between men, women and social groups to ensure their meaningful engagement in decision-making processes to protect every individual right to sustainable and affordable WASH services. It further states that in terms of water supply system planning, while women encounter additional challenges about safety, overwork and low decision-making status, the physically challenged people face difficulties associated with access. The WASH SDP thus suggests the planning and the implementation of the WASH projects to be done within this reality. The WASH SDP also recommends the WASH sector project estimate to allocate some funds to develop the technical capacity of women, poor and excluded (WPE) groups to develop them as VMW, WSST, Sub-engineers and Engineers (WHO, 2018/19). The SDP, which is still in the process of being finalised, is the most progressive document in terms of its commitment to women's empowerment and gender equality. It is hoped that such a gender-progressive policy gets approved and implemented soon.

Drinking Water and Sanitation Management Act, 2018 (Draft): The Drinking Water and Sanitation Management Act (DWSMA) 2018, which is at present in the draft stage, has been prepared to ensure the regular access of the Nepali citizens to clean, reliable and safe drinking water; build a clean and hygienic environment in both the rural and urban areas by processing the human excreta through proper sewerage management; and improve the living standard of the poor, backward and all others by ensuring their easy access to drinking water and sanitation services (GoN, 2018). However, as in several Acts and policies like WRA 1998, WRA 1999, DWR 1998 etc. discussed above, the DWSMA 2018 also uses the gender-neutral looking terminology like 'consumers', 'users', throughout the document showing no appreciation that there are differences between the water and sanitation-related needs and concerns of the women and men. Despite some other Acts and policies like RWSSSNP 2004, RWSSSNS 2004, NWP 2005, UWSSSP 2009, NWSSSP 2014, Constitution of Nepal 2015 and the SDP 2016-2030 being progressively gender-sensitive, it is strange to see that the DWSMA 2018, even being the latest Act, is gender-unaware. Chapter 4 Clause 15 of this Act mentions the duty of the license holder to make the water and sanitation services available to all the people without any discrimination based on their caste, ethnicity and other factors. But it overlooks the need to mention the role of women or gender concerns despite identifying that women generally constitute more than half the population in all communities, with even more proportion in areas that are sending their male members for overseas employment. Similarly, in Chapter 4 Clause 22, which has a provision for the sale of water for household, institutional and commercial use, fails to acknowledge that the commercial use of water can affect the household use of drinking water. Once there is less water available for drinking purposes, it will result in extra burden, poor health and loss of income-earning opportunities on the part of women since they will then have to walk long distances in search of alternative sources of water, compromise with their water necessities and go back to unhygienic sources of water risking their health.

Similarly, Chapter 4 Clause 23 talks about the termination of the water service by the service providers on various conditions, including the condition when users are unable to make the timely payment of the water tariff. While talking about this condition, the Act does not seem to be acknowledging even till 2018 that it is women and the poor who can fall in this category for not having access to and control over income. Although Clause 28 has acknowledged the purchasing power of the consumers, among others, while fixing the tariff, it fails to appreciate that even among the consumers, there are women consumers, including those from female-headed households who, as compared to their male counterparts, will have difficulty to pay the water tariff due to their limited or zero income. It is encouraging to note that Clause 29 talks about the possibility of providing subsidies to those living below the poverty line or are ultra-poor if these categories have difficulty in paying the tariff fixed by the service providers. But following similar precedents, the Act is again silent about women despite the bitter reality that women are further poor even in these categories of poor and ultra-poor. Chapter 9 Clause 45 has a provision that allows the GoN to either exempt or lessen the amount of tariff for squatters and the absolute poor living below the poverty line if these categories of people have difficulty in paying it.

However, this provision also fails to appreciate the unquestionable reality that women hold a big proportion even among the squatters, for being the permanent residents of the households. The gender insensitivity can be seen in Chapter 9 Clause 52 as well which has got a provision for the formation of a Coordination Committee to provide advice to the government in the formulation as well as planning and implementation of water and sanitation policies and ensure inter-agency coordination. But similarly, in this seven-member committee led by the minister for drinking water, there is no mentioning of women's representation despite the reality that drinking water and sanitation is women's domain and they know much more than their menfolk on this matter.

Fifteenth Five-Year Development Plan 2019-2024: The Fifteenth Plan aims to expand the coverage of the basic level of drinking water service from 88% in 2019 to 99% of the population by the end of the plan period in 2024. The plan aspires to cover nearly 40% of the population by improved water supply during the same period. While envisioning a clean, safe and accessible drinking water and sanitation service to the people of Nepal, the plan also aims to improve the quality of the service. The main objectives of the plan about the drinking water and sanitation service are i) to improve public health by ensuring the availability of adequate, safe and easily accessible drinking water and sanitation service; ii) to ensure access to the basic level of sanitation service to all citizens and ascertain environmental cleanliness through effective management of human waste and sewerage; iii) to ensure climate change favourable and disaster management friendly drinking water and sanitation service; and iv) to build the capacity of the federal, provincial and local level governments while ascertaining their role in the sustainable delivery of drinking water and sanitation service. To achieve the vision, goal and objectives, the plan has proposed eight long-term strategies and 28 working policies (GoN, 2019).

While reviewing the vision, goal, objectives, strategies and key activities prepared concerning the Fifteenth Plan's focus on drinking water and sanitation using a gender lens, one is compelled to note that the plan is completely gender-insensitive. Despite the Constitution of Nepal 2015 that came earlier than the Fifteenth Plan being progressive in addressing women's concerns and acknowledging their role and contribution to Nepal's development in general and the drinking water sector in particular, the Fifteenth Plan did not feel the need to be gender-specific in any aspect of the drinking water and sanitation service to be provided by the government to its people. The plan is full of the so-called gender-neutral terminologies like users, communities, beneficiaries etc. in the illusion that the use of such terminologies can benefit both women and men equally. While talking about the improvement in public health, one of its WASH objectives, the Fifteenth Plan fails to acknowledge that it is mostly women who do most of the water-related activities, including fetching water from the source to managing it at the household, and if the source is far, or the design is faulty, or the handle of the tube-well is short/ long, or the location of the tap-stands/ tube-wells is inappropriate, it is women who suffer the most, and therefore, there is a need to pay special attention to women's health while talking about public health. Similarly, the plan has got an objective which intends to make the sanitation service available for all citizens. Again, the use of the term 'all citizens' implies that the planners/ policy-makers have failed to recognise that sanitation-related needs and concerns of women and girls have to do with their biology, dignity and security which, however, are different for men so one single strategy cannot address the concerns of the both.

Additionally, the Fifteenth Plan, in another one of its objectives, proposes to build the capacity of all levels of government for sustained delivery of WASH service. What is, however, missing here is the need to build the capacity of local women since it is they who primarily take care of most of the WASH-related activities in the rural areas. If it is a drinking water project, it is women who visit the water points every day to fetch water so they know better about the source and what needs to be done to keep the project going. If it is a toilet, the need and functionality are many times higher for women than it is for men given that the latter, in the absence of a toilet, can openly do their business, while the same will not be possible for women for reasons related to their dignity and security. In turn, women will do everything possible to ensure the regular up-keeping of the toilet.

A review of the strategies and the working policies of the Fifteenth Plan also suggests that the plan has emphasised the participation of those who have been so far excluded from the WASH which is noteworthy. But again, like what has been stated above, the plan lacks the categorical mentioning of women and the poor. The experiences have shown that women in general, and-female headed households in particular, along with the other poor and minorities, are mostly deprived of such facilities since they cannot come in front to voice their concerns. As a result, it is either men or influential women from so-called higher caste/ ethnicity or class who try to present themselves as the representative of the poor women and female-headed households and divert the design of the project to benefit mostly themselves, their relatives and friends, at the cost of the wellbeing of women and poor. Another equally concerning strategy and the working policy of the Fifteenth Plan is the one related to the financial contribution and cost-recovery aspects which expect the implementation of the drinking water and sanitation project based on the capacity of the local community to meet these financial requirements. With such requirements imposed, likely, the women, poor and the other marginalised sections of the community will not be able to benefit much from such services since they will face a difficult time meeting these financial requirements.

To conclude the discussions made above, what can be said is although it is understandable why the initial Acts, policies and plans concerning the WASH sector formulated back in the late '90s and early '00s lacked gender focus, it is hard to comprehend why even the latest policies, which were introduced after the enactment of several progressive legislations and policies, have remained to be gender-weak. The only plausible answer to this inconsistent focus on gender would be the lack of political will and commitment on the part of planners and policy-makers who are mostly men. Another equally important possibility is the lack of understanding of the gender issues in the WASH sector among these male policy-makers and planners. The next chapter thus provides some recommendations for consideration by all concerned to make their policies and practices, be they WASH-related or development-related in general, gender-focused.

Gender Changes in NGO Water Policies

In the research undertaken 20 years ago to explore gender issues in the management of water projects in Nepal, Nepal Water for Health (NEWAH), a non-governmental organisation (NGO) engaged in implementing water supply and sanitation schemes, was selected to be a part of it. The reasons for selecting NEWAH were: i) it was the largest NGO implementing water supply and sanitation schemes; ii) it used to work closely with the GoN and follow its policies and plans, which meant if the national water policies were gender-aware, NEWAH's policies and practices would also be gender-specific; and iii) it was an implementing partner of WaterAid, which meant if the WaterAid's WASH policies were gender-informed, NEWAH's water policies and practices would also be gender-focused. For a cross-reference of the gender situation in NGOs, other than the NEWAH which was involved in both the earlier research and the current one, another big NGO 'Gurkha Welfare Trust (GWT)/ Nepal' was also selected to be a part of the latest research so that a firm opinion could be made regarding the gender consideration in the WASH projects implemented by the NGO sector.

Nepal Water for Health (NEWAH): As discussed in Part II of this book, although NEWAH and its water supply schemes were found to be more gender-aware than the donor and government-funded projects, it still had a long way to go in achieving gender equality in its drinking water and sanitation projects and the organisational policies and practices. At the time of the earlier research, NEWAH had a leadership which was committed towards gender integration in the organisation, it was piloting gender and poverty (GAP) approach in some of its water supply schemes, it had organised some gender training for its staff, and it was also in the process of reviewing its organisational policies to make them gender-specific. Consequently, NEWAH has been included in the second phase of the research as well to examine the extent to which gender integration has advanced in its policies and practices over the last two decades. Accordingly, some of NEWAH's important documents were reviewed and some concerned senior staff interviewed to get an understanding of the gender sensitivity ensured in their WASH policies and practices. The NEWAH documents reviewed for this purpose are Commitment to Community (NEWAH, 2003), Long-Term Sustainability Study (2006), Stories from the Field: A Collection of WASH Case Studies (NEWAH, 2011), Annual Report July 2015 to June 2016 (NEWAH, 2015/2016), Five-Year Strategic Plan 2017-2021 (NEWAH, 2017) and Web-based articles like 'Need: Why NEWAH is involved in water supply, sanitation and hygiene sector (NEWAH, 2020)?'

Over the past two decades, NEWAH integrated the GAP, GESI, and community-led total sanitation (CLTS) approaches to ensure the delivery of water and sanitation services to the poor and marginalised communities in a more efficient, equitable and sustainable manner. Since its establishment in 1992, NEWAH has been actively engaged in the WASH sector, with a commitment to support the underprivileged and socially excluded people who are in the greatest need of WASH services. By working actively to secure these services most sustainably and inclusively in partnership with different development partners, bilateral agencies, NGOs, CBOs and others, NEWAH, with the professional support of over 250 staff, and through its central office located in Kathmandu and three regional offices located in the- Eastern Regional Office, Biratnagar, Central Regional Office, Bharatpur, and Western Regional office, Pokhara- had, by 2017, assisted over 2,000 communities of 51 districts serving over 1.9 million people to access WASH services. Similarly, NEWAH was also successful in achieving universal WASH coverage in five VDCs as well as declaring 89 VDCs/ Municipalities as ODF areas. Its annual funding received through various donors amounted to around USD 2.5 million (NEWAH, 2017; NEWAH, 2016).

NEWAH's journey to being a GAP sensitive organisation, as per its guiding principle that it will remain to be a committed national NGO for appropriate, innovative and poverty sensitive programmes by promoting gender equity and transparency, began in the early 2000s. Since then, it has been making various efforts to ensure gender reforms in its organisational policies and WASH projects. The effort to mainstream the GAP approach based on the findings of its pilot project implemented in five districts is a case in point. As a result of these efforts, NEWAH was progressively introducing several gender-related changes in the organisation intending to address women's practical as well as strategic gender needs as discussed below.

Being fully informed of the important role women have been exhibiting in the WASH sector, NEWAH has profoundly engaged with the community to increase women's participation in the local WSUCs. Accordingly, NEWAH was able to achieve an increase of 11% in the number of female WSUC members in its water projects (NEWAH, 2003). Similarly, taking into account the feedback it got from the community women regarding the latter's difficulty in bathing and washing their undergarments when the tap-stands are located along the walking trail or the roadside (Regmi, 2000), NEWAH added a structure adjacent to the water points to install clothes hangers in its hills and Tarai projects so that women could have some privacy. Learning from the local women's positive experience of this added structure, NEWAH decided to mainstream this technology in all of its projects (NEWAH, 2003). Likewise, during the same period, NEWAH also learned, as a result of its GAP pilot projects, that even under subsidised schemes the poorest households, including female-headed households and physically disabled people, still have difficulty in meeting the cost of the superstructure. Consequently, NEWAH decided to develop different strategies to ensure the participation of these vulnerable groups as beneficiaries in its WASH projects.

Through its continued efforts to address the women's practical gender needs related to water and sanitation, NEWAH, by bringing the water supply schemes and toilets near their households has undeniably benefited hundreds of thousands of households, including female-headed, elderly women, women from ethnic minorities, poor women, disabled women, young girls, and Dalit women, among others. NEWAH has always been flexible in its application of the GAP, GESI and CLTS approaches taking into account their relevance in the local context and the importance of multiple uses of water sources. This flexibility has enabled NEWAH to ensure pro-poor and gender-equitable programming in its projects so that the poorest people, including women from various strata, could be easily identified, supported and benefited. It considers various factors during the implementation phase so that the poor people, especially women, could actively participate throughout the project activities. In fact, NEWAH's progressive learning from the application of various gender-sensitive strategies has not only benefited the poor people, including women from various strata, but also contributed to improving the understanding of community women and men regarding gender relations between and towards each other.

"Kaushi Maya Bhul, a 60-year-old Dalit woman from Doti district, Latamandu VDC, Umali, Ward 1, had never thought that she would ever be owning a personal latrine after almost six decades of her going to riverside, jungles and fields for defecation, and have a comfortable, less embarrassing and happy life at this old age." Similarly, "Bishwa Maksi, a blind woman, from Surkhet district, Salkund VDC, Koiralachula, Ward 3, had never expected that she would have access both to a water tap and a toilet nearby her home as opposed to a situation when she had to go to a river to carry out her morning activities and fetch the water on her way back home every day. Although she, in general, would have someone to support her while performing these activities, she, at times, would fall and badly bruise herself when she had no one to support her to carry out these daily activities." Likewise, "the kitchen gardening, that NEWAH supported, under its WASH projects to the people of Doti district, Pachnali VDC, Dekurali, Ward 9, had not only been a major source of livelihood for Dhana Bhatta and her family of eight members but was also an indicator of the sustainability of the water and sanitation facilities installed in the community since the increased income from the sale of vegetables could also be spent on the repair and maintenance of those facilities as needed. Looking at Dhana's enthusiasm, daily intake of the self-grown fresh vegetables by her family, and the good income of about USD 100 that she is making from the sale of these vegetables every two months, many villagers, who had not shown any interest initially, had later started growing vegetables in their garden" (NEWAH, 2011).

The case of a 65-year-old Deela Ramjali of Surkhet district, Kunathari VDC, Aaldanda village, Ward 1, is also insightful. Being the eldest member of a 24-members' family, Deela was always worried regarding the adequacy of water for her family. Before NEWAH implemented a WASH project in her community, Deela and her family members had to spend several hours fetching water from a distant source which would take an hour per trip. But, after the implementation of the NEWAH WASH project, many families in the community, including Deela's, have got their toilet, drinking water nearby home, a dishwashing slab, a dish drying rack, and ropes for drying clothes. In fact, for Deela and her family, the NEWAH WASH project was a real blessing since it had not only saved their many hours from water hauling every day and reduced the risk of going far to riverside or jungle for defecation but had also created an opportunity to use the saved time in some productive activities like kitchen gardening allowing the family to consume the fresh vegetables grown in their own farm and make some earnings from its sale as well (NEWAH, 2011).

The case of Gauri Tamang, a young girl, the resident of Chitwan district, Piple VDC, Mainatar, Ward 6 is also worth mentioning here. Gauri had to walk an hour one way to fetch water from Sirukhola river and she usually had to travel five times a day. Accordingly, she had to wake up early every morning every day to fetch the water from the river. On top of the five hours that she had to put on fetching water every day, she also had to prepare food, feed cattle, clean the house and take care of the other daily household chores. This all compelled her to stop even from going to school. The frustrating remark from Gauri was "my life would be ruined carrying the bucket like this for hours every day!" However, the same Gauri was the happiest person after NEWAH implemented a WASH project in her community since the water tap installed nearby her home had saved her several hours spent every day on water hauling and allowed her to enrol at Grade 8 in the local school after missing it for two years and to use some of these hours to do things of her own choice (NEWAH, 2016).

The changes mentioned above have been experienced not only by Gauri but also by many other women in NEWAH supported communities. As per NEWAH's end-line survey carried out with 470 WASH beneficiaries, mostly women, during December 2015 and January to February 2016, NEWAH was successful in reducing the water hauling time from an average of 23.07 minutes to 7.98 minutes and the wait time from an average of 3.56 minutes to 0.4 minutes, with an increase in the volume of collected water from 112.59 litters to 145.48 litters at the same time (NEWAH, 2016).

Apart from addressing the practical gender needs of women by bringing the water and sanitation services near their households, NEWAH has also been continuing its efforts to address women's strategic gender needs that include an increase in women's status, income, and meaningful participation in meetings; change in perceptions of men towards women; change in the gender division of labour etc. For instance, as its commitment to increase the income of the local community, including women, by providing support to use the time saved from water hauling in productive activities, NEWAH added saving and credit programmes as an integral component of its WASH projects. As it was a timely intervention complemented by providing training and orientations on gender-awareness, three of its seven saving and credit initiatives, which started informally initially, had later upgraded themselves into saving and credit cooperatives, implying that the local women and the poor households had started to have increased access to credit and income and make the best use of their time saved from water hauling in some productive activities.

> *Similarly, through its GAP sensitive strategies, NEWAH was able to transform the mindset of the predominantly conservative Muslim community in Jigariya village of the central region of Nepal. This Muslim community, which was not, in general, endorsing of their women members engaging in public activities, backed two of its women– to get elected to the positions of the vice-chairperson and treasurer respectively in the local WSUC after being impressed by NEWAH's GESI, GAP and CLTS approaches. After receiving gender training along with some other training, these two women members soon stood out to be confident and knowledgeable to spread the importance of sanitation and hygiene and motivate their fellow women to build household latrines and improve hygienic behaviour. Moreover, these women, along with some others in the community, were also able to be in paid jobs, actively participate in household and community decision-making, voice their concerns in public meetings, and gain respect as equal as to their fellow men, as a result of the social work that provided several benefits to the local community (NEWAH, 2003).*

Another example comes from Surkhet district, Salkot VDC, Ward 8, where Gaura Majhi, a female, led, as the Chairperson of the local WSUC, the construction of a water supply and sanitation scheme supported by AusAid and managed by NEWAH and WaterAid Nepal. Apart from their active involvement in the construction of the scheme, Gaura Majhi and the other women committee members were also actively engaged in promoting hygiene and sanitation education and motivating the local residents to build their personal toilet along with declaring their community, resided by 132 households, as ODF community (NEWAH, 2011).

Likewise, realising the importance of women's presence in decision-making positions, NEWAH made a policy of having 50% women in WSUCs. Correspondingly, its field staff made extra efforts to ensure that the local WSUCs strictly follow this policy. This affirmative action, along with the extra efforts of the field staff, definitely resulted in some impressive changes in its project communities. For instance, NEWAH's Long-Term Sustainability Study (LTSS) shows that women's representation in WSUCs was on average 46%, almost close to the policy, in its projects implemented in 2004/05. The study further revealed that while 14% of the women members of the WSUCs held the position of chairperson, vice-chairperson, treasurer and secretary in the hills, the figure was 22% in the Tarai (NEWAH, 2006). Although 14-22% representation may not necessarily create much space for women to influence the decisions in the WSUC meetings where men were always in a majority, the fact that there used to be hardly any woman in these positions in such committees formed before 2000, this proportion of women being in decision-making positions could be considered as good progress towards achieving gender equality in the WASH sector.

An equally important outcome of NEWAH's work on GESI was its success in changing men's perception of women's work in many of its project communities. A case in hand is Chandra Bahadur of Surkhet district, Dasharathpur VDC, Tirtire village, Ward 1.

> *As an integral part of NEWAH's WASH projects, the local community, including Chandra Bahadur, was provided training on Gender and Health/ Hygiene Education. The impact of the training was that Chandra Bahadur, who had two daughters and was always longing for a son, changed his mind and declared that he will not long for a son anymore. He will rather focus on providing good education to his two daughters and will do his level best to provide them with all the opportunities that are generally provided by parents like him to their sons so that his daughters could stand on their own feet. NEWAH's gender and health training helped Chandra Bahadur and many other local men to not only internalise the importance of women's role and contribution in the family, thereby the nation, but also to share the household chores that traditionally always fell on the part of women. To illustrate, Chandra Bahadur, who never attended any household chores in the past, had started to actively participate in activities such as cleaning the house and the front yard, washing dishes, cooking, and looking after the girls etc. after he received the gender training. Many other men in the community have also started to follow the footsteps of Chandra Bahadur which implies that they are gradually moving towards building a gender-transformative society through NEWAH supported WASH projects (NEWAH, 2011).*

With a conviction that a truly gender-sensitive WASH project should also be aiming for creating space for women to be more actively participating in the various household as well as community decisions although traditionally this opportunity has always remained with men, NEWAH implemented various activities to empower and encourage the community women to voice their concerns and engage themselves in the decision-making of water and sanitation projects, thereby other household and community matters. To elucidate is the case of Balkumari Maski, a female resident of Surkhet district, Salkot VDC, Ward 3.

NEWAH, following the principle of empowering women by providing them with the opportunity to be in the decision-making and paid positions, selected Balkumari, along with two other men from the adjacent community, to attend the maintenance worker's training. As a result of the training, the pressure to prove that even a woman can do it (or else the other women would not get such opportunities in the future), and her hard work, determination and commitment, Balkumari was able to effectively take care of two intakes, eight distribution tanks and 15 water taps, and ensure regular flow of water for 45 households in her vicinity. Regular operation of the water systems, participation in various meetings and providing information to visitors along with motivating her fellow women were the activities that kept Balkumari busy. She was happy that she has got the name, fame and money; has been perceived as a role model by other women in the community, and is also consulted by men whenever the latter encountered any problems although this was not the case in the past. Looking at Balkumari's performance as an effective maintenance worker and the satisfaction expressed by her community towards her performance, the other two male maintenance workers stopped visiting this community since they understood that they were no longer needed as Balkumari was fully capable and efficient in taking care of the water system in the community (NEWAH, 2011).

Unlike its exciting experience with Balkumari as a female maintenance worker, NEWAH's earlier experience with the maintenance of its gravity flow schemes and tube-wells was not positive since only 30% of the gravity flow schemes and tube-wells that it had supported till 2006 were found to be functioning to the design capacity while the remaining 70% either needed further attention or were completely dysfunctional. Similarly, NEWAH's other experience in the maintenance of the water points was that while 57% of the gravity flow schemes in the hills and 28% of the tube-wells in the Tarai implemented after 1995 were found to be functioning to the design capacity, only 32% of the gravity flow schemes in the hills and 19% of the tube-wells in the Tarai implemented before 1995 were found to be functioning to the design capacity (NEWAH, 2006).

Even though NEWAH has not carried out any study to examine the linkage between the placement of female maintenance workers and the functioning of the water points to the design capacity, the fact that there were more malfunctioning water points before 1995, when NEWAH did not have women's meaningful involvement either in the WSUC senior positions or as the maintenance workers, and more functioning water points after 1995, when NEWAH did have women's meaningful engagement in most project activities, including the holding of WSUC senior positions and caretaker positions, it can be said that there is a strong linkage between women's effective participation and the higher number of functioning water points. The increased involvement of community women in the position of caretaker/ maintenance worker (21% as against 79% for men out of a total of 4,093 caretakers) and the senior WSUC positions (48% as against 52% for men) in NEWAH's recent projects being implemented from March 2019 to July 2020, with a funding of USD 2.7 million, also points out the same direction (based on personal communications with the NEWAH Director, June 2020). Although the higher figures for men may reveal that there are still more men than women in the position of maintenance workers and WSUC positions, they also convey at the same time that NEWAH's latest water schemes have got much higher chances of functioning to the design capacity due to women's increased representation in these positions. This finding can also be validated from the emphasis put on by the IDWSSD 1981-90 and various women's international conferences that took place around the same time that unless and until women are effectively engaged in WASH activities, no such projects can ensure sustained benefits to the target population (RWSSP, 2019; van Wijk and Garcia, 2002; Regmi, 2000).

Moreover, the reasons like lack of users' interest, drying up of sources, missing/ damaging of some basic parts like nuts, bolts, pins, among others, provided for the higher number of malfunctioning water points in the NEWAH projects also support that the lack of women's active engagement in the operation and maintenance of the water points is the major reason for the non-functioning of water points. If women, for being the primary users of water, were actively engaged in all stages of water supply schemes, including the operation and maintenance stage, they could have immediately noticed the problem as they visit the source every day and thus could take immediate measures to address it then and there. But, this could not happen in the projects that NEWAH implemented before 1995 since women's profound involvement in its projects started only in the late '90s. Equally important evidence to confirm that the lack of women's serious involvement, including in the operation and maintenance stage, was the reason for the higher number of malfunctioning water points before 1995 is that the lately implemented NEWAH schemes with higher women's participation have got impressive functionality record of 90%. The basis of this impressive record was the three rounds of 'hello monitoring' and one round of Project Information and Management System (PIMS) monitoring of the projects implemented in Nepal's five districts- Sindhuli, Chitwan, Baglung, Nuwakot, and Dhading during the period 2010-2013 (NEWAH, 2016).

Being confident of the results coming out of its WASH projects in addressing women's practical gender needs as well as some of their strategic gender needs, and using the learning coming out of its five pilot projects that were implemented following the GAP approach, NEWAH also got enough confidence to profoundly engage in and influence several national water and sanitation policy processes and international campaign initiatives. NEWAH, as a member of the National Sanitation Sector Committee, was able to influence the committee to incorporate some GAP elements like participatory well-being ranking to identify poor households and develop targeted subsidies for the poorest households in the government's RWSSNP 2004. Similarly, NEWAH also contributed to the drafting of the National Sanitation and Hygiene Master Plan 2011, Implementation Directive, and Total Sanitation Directive using the learning arising out of its GAP approach. Further, as a result of the consultancy service which it provided to the Asian Development Bank during the implementation of the latter's Nepal Community Based Water Supply and Sanitation Project Preparation Technical Assistance (PPTA) on Socioeconomic and Household Income and Expenditure Survey, the Bank expressed its willingness to incorporate the GAP sensitive strategies in its forthcoming loan to the GoN for developing the water and sanitation sector (NEWAH, 2003).

Realising that the incorporation of the GAP sensitive approach is essential not only while implementing water supply and sanitation projects in the communities but also in its policies and staff's existing knowledge, NEWAH's Administration and Human Resource Policy included a provision to consider gender during hiring, transfer and promotion. During the screening of applications, women candidates that meet the minimum criteria are selected for the next step and those who make up to the interview stage are given 20% extra marks as per their gender and social inclusion consideration (based on personal communications with the NEWAH Director).

Despite some good progress that NEWAH was making towards achieving gender equality through women's empowerment in various stages of its WASH projects, there, however, are some areas where NEWAH can do better. One of such areas is the capacity building of the community women on GAD since NEWAH has neither mentioned this need nor has it allocated any funds for gender-related activities in its Commitment to Community Report 2003 (NEWAH, 2003). It is needless to say that capacity building of the organisation staff, partner organisations and community people, including women, should be seen as a continuous process, not a one-off event, and appropriate funds must be allocated for it. The real commitment towards mainstreaming gender gets reflected only when the organisation puts aside some funds for such activities. The absence of the capacity building activities and the corresponding funds for it will lead to the deprivation of the staff, both new and old, partner organisations and the community women and men, from systematic learning of the GAP, GESI and other contemporary GAD experiences, without which the projects can neither sustain the benefits nor can it help to create a society with gender equality.

Similarly, the other area needing further attention to be a gender-sensitive organisation is the language used in the organisational documents since the use of gender-sensitive language in the regular organisational conversation and the important policy documents is a strong indicator of gender transformation. However, in the case of NEWAH, the use of gender-sensitive language in its organisational policy documents, annual reports, project reports etc. is not consistent even until now. To illuminate, in its report 'Stories from the Field: A Collection of WASH Case Studies', NEWAH has presented its progress made against the various outputs. One of its progress statements is 'NEWAH's project selection process gives clear priority to the areas of greatest need so that projects serve poor, marginalised and vulnerable people' and the corresponding output statement is 'NEWAH is established as a people-centred, cost-effective, efficient and sustainable organisation'. While reviewing these statements using a gender lens, one can say that they are not gender-specific.

Although NEWAH has acknowledged in this document and some others that these categories will have difficulty in benefiting from the project services unless different strategies are adopted, it, at times, has been unsuccessful to disaggregate its strategies, objectives, outputs, activities and results by gender. The lack of categorical mentioning of women in the policy documents may bypass them in various important phases of the WASH projects, including the delivery of services to meet women's practical gender needs and interventions to meet women's strategic gender needs. It is, thus, essential that the staff, especially senior staff, know better, through proper GAD and GESI training, the difference in the impact of their work on women and poor households, including female-headed, when the gender-neutral and gender-specific languages are used. It is equally important to understand that gender needs to be treated as a cross-cutting issue, not as a standalone component where the organisation, by having a separate section on women or gender, assumes that it has done its job of being gender-sensitive. For women and the poor to benefit from the organisational activities, gender and poverty should be integrated everywhere- culture, behaviour, thinking, policies, reports and publications, practices, general conversation, to name a few.

The same argument holds when looked at NEWAH's other policy documents like 'Strategic Plan of NEWAH 2017-2021'. Although NEWAH has categorically mentioned GESI, as its commitment and major focus to achieve the WASH goals, in the executive summary as well as some other sections of this document, the fact that it is still indiscriminately using the gender-neutral looking terminologies (though they are not) like communities, people, poor, marginalised throughout this important document that it compels one to question whether the senior staff at NEWAH have been able to understand well the huge distinction that exists between the needs and concerns of women and men concerning water and sanitation. The lack of gender sensitivity observed in NEWAH's mission, vision, objectives and strategic focuses as presented in its five-year strategic plan also dilutes some of NEWAH's good women's empowerment related works done so far. None of these four important organisational identities have mentioned a single word about women. For instance, three of the very well elaborated strategic focuses of NEWAH- Service Delivery Excellence, Sustainable Funding, Securing the Future- and the objectives and indicators developed to achieve those strategic focuses are gender-blank. NEWAH has developed three objectives- Operations, Effective Project Management, and Target Based Management- and seven indicators to achieve the first strategic focus 'Service Delivery Excellence', but none of these are either GESI or GAP informed. Similarly, it has developed three objectives- Donor Relation, Brand Image and Pro-active Approach to Project Selection- along with five indicators to achieve another strategic focus 'Sustainable Funding'. Again, none of the objectives and their indicators are gender-informed. Finally, it has got another three objectives- Human Resources, Sector Diversification and New Business Model Innovation, and Government Relation, Networking and Lobbying- and four indicators to achieve those objectives under its third strategic focus 'Securing the Future'. However, like with the other two strategic focuses, none of these objectives and indicators is gender-specific.

Although in the same document, NEWAH has mentioned the poor, excluded and marginalised groups in the rural areas across the country as the groups getting its support under section 'Uniqueness of its Service', it has overlooked the reality that even within these vulnerable categories, women and female-headed households are further poor, excluded and marginalised. This means there is no guarantee that women and female-headed households will benefit equally as men from the WASH projects implemented under such gender-weak policy statements. The experiences presented earlier have made it clear that women will not benefit in the same manner that men do when they are not specifically mentioned in the policy and programme implementation documents. Despite its gender-related works initiated beginning late '90s and early '00, it is an irony to note that NEWAH's five-year strategic plan (2017-2021) prepared 20 years down the road is still gender-weak as opposed to the other documents like Commitment to Community, Stories from the Field, Long-Term Sustainability Study, among others, prepared in between. This document, although prepared only in 2017, indicates NEWAH's mixed understanding of gender issues in the water sector, thereby the danger of their water project benefits being enjoyed more by men than women as before.

For instance, although NEWAH has introduced both the savings and credit activities and kitchen gardening as a means to make earnings from the time saved from water hauling, what one can draw from the experiences presented in one of its reports 'Stories from the Field: A Collection of WASH Case Studies' (NEWAH, 2011) is that while women are engaged more in kitchen gardening, which is labour intensive and family centred, men, are engaged more in savings and credit activities, a far less labour intensive activity and the one granting greater status and higher control over bigger income at the same time. This implies that such segregation of women's and men's involvement will further reinforce the traditional gender norms that women should be targeted for activities that earn less income but demand more time and labour, and men should be targeted for activities that provide more status and income but require less time and labour.

Being surprised with the sudden fall of NEWAH on its gender commitment, its Director was contacted for clarifications. What came out from the communication with the NEWAH Director is that the organisation had to go through unexpectedly difficult times beginning in 2014 due to some conflicts within its board and senior management. As reported, this internal conflict challenged not only the organisational growth and gender commitment but also the donor relation, funding as well as the survival of the organisation itself. The situation became worse for NEWAH when the outgoing board member and some staff members expelled on disciplinary action filed false cases of fraud and fund misappropriation against the NEWAH management resulting in the withdrawal of some donor funding and the delay in renewing/ approving project agreements by the concerned government agency. The impact of this led to the loss of donor projects and the discontinuation of staff contracts, including that of the Director himself, in August 2017.

However, with due perseverance and commitment of the remaining members of the Board and some senior staff, on the one hand, and the clearance it got from the concerned donor and government agencies after their scrutiny of the allegations and financial audits of the organisation, on the other hand, NEWAH was able to revive from these challenges in October 2017. The Director also disclosed that those people are still trying to create problems for the organisation as they are not happy that NEWAH got clearance on the charges that they had managed to file against it. Because the identity of the outgoing board member and the staff members were not disclosed, the author couldn't solicit their opinion on this matter. As NEWAH had to divert its energy, resources and time, among other things, to face those problems, it affected in many areas, including its gender efforts resulting in the proportion of female staff being only at 25%, with the senior management team at 0%, the general members at 25%, and the board at 28%. Nevertheless, the Director committed that they will gradually bring the organisation back on track to be a successful and effective non-governmental WASH organisation, with gender fully integrated both in policies and practices.

Gurkha Welfare Trust/ Nepal: Established in 1969, Gurkha Welfare Trust/ Nepal (GWT/N) aims to ensure a dignified life for Gurkha veterans, their widows and their wider communities in Nepal by providing them with financial, medical and community aid. While its headquarters based in the UK is engaged in providing advice and support to the retired Gurkhas and their families living in the UK, the 21 Area Welfare Centres spread across traditional Gurkha recruiting areas in Nepal to operate various activities such as distribution of financial aid to retired soldiers affected by disasters such as landslides and floods, buying land for ex-Gurkhas to become subsistence farmers and provide enough food to support their families, paying welfare pension to the retired Gurkha soldiers, and implementing community-level activities such as building schools, water projects and medical aid. In recognition of the country's debt of honour to the retired Gurkha soldiers, eight of the greatest wartime Field Marshalls raised £1m through a public appeal to establish the GWT/N back in the late '60s (Source: https://www.gwt.org.uk/about-us/mission-history/).

As of January 2021, the GWT/N, supported by its own headquarters and DfID, is one of the large NGOs engaged in implementing WASH programmes initially in the mid-western region and currently, in all seven provinces of Nepal. A number of its publications available online and those sent by the concerned GWT/N officials such as Simple Drip Irrigation (SDI) Programme Impact Evaluation Report (2016), Mid-Term Review Report (2017), Functionality Status Report (2017), and Annual Review Report (2020) were reviewed to get an idea about the extent to which GWT/N's Rural Water and Sanitation Programme (RWSP) has integrated gender concerns in its WASH activities, the focus of this book. What comes out from this review is that GWT/N's RWSP which started in 2012, follows and adapts GoN's WASH Policy and DfID's inclusion strategy, among others. The review also depicts that GWT/N's RWSP considers GESI as a crosscutting approach and has been able to meet the GESI targets as per its Project Logical Framework 2020.

Indeed, the increase of women's involvement in Community/Village Maintenance Workers (C/VMW) and Village Hygiene Promoter (VHP) positions and WUSCs, including their decision-making positions, during the period 2012/13-2019/20, as shown by the figures presented in Table 9, confirms that GWT/N's RWSP has well-integrated gender in its project activities to ensure their sustainability.

Table 9: Women's Participation in GWT/N's RWSP in 2012/13 and 2019/20

Project Components/Topics	2012/13	2019/20
Increase of female C/VMW	0%	19%
Increase of female VHP	91%	100%
Increase in Women's participation in WUSCs	38%	56%
Increase of Women in key decision-making positions	35%	63%

Source: GWT/N RSWP's Monitoring Data and Logical Framework for 2012/13 and 2019/20, Published Date: August 8, 2020

Realising that along with social empowerment, the economic empowerment of women, together with that of men, is equally important, GWT/N's RWSP has developed a mechanism by which the operation and maintenance funds are invested in women's savings and credit groups to increase women's access to income and promote the local livelihood. In appreciation of women's and other excluded groups' inability to meet the project capital costs, the GWT/N's RWSP makes considerable efforts in discussing with the local communities how poor women and other marginalised and excluded households could participate in the project activities, a strong indicator towards increasing local ownership and sustainability of the RWSP supported water taps and toilets. The focus on the recruitment of women and people from excluded categories in the training of C/VMWs, CHWs and WUSCs is another example of RWSP's commitment towards engendering and achieving social inclusion in its WASH projects.

The prioritised groups in GWT/N's RWSP are women, children, adolescents, older people, people with disabilities, excluded and marginalised, and those living in areas affected by natural disasters. Because of women's important role in the WASH activities, GWT/N's RWSP encourages the community women to actively participate in WUSCs as well as in decision-making positions. The organisation has also introduced several women-focused activities in its programme areas such as the construction of toilets keeping women, among others, at the centre, making provision for incinerator for disposal of sanitary pads, engaging women in productive activities for their economic empowerment, selection of women in the position C/VMW ensuring equal wage like men, training and advocacy for management of menstrual hygiene, general sanitation and personal hygiene, and capacity building on various social and economic activities, including improvements in interpersonal communication, so that they could voice their concerns not only in the communities where they live but also outside the communities while dealing with government agencies and any other stakeholders (Source: personal communication with GWT/N's M&E officer, dated January 2021).

Indeed, a review of some of GWT/N's case studies reveals its profound commitment towards women's inclusion in its WASH activities.

> *Kalpana, a 42 years-old housewife from rural Nepal living in one of the GWT/N's programme communities, reports that she, along with the other women in the community, had to walk over difficult terrain for hours to fetch water. With two young sons and a husband working long hours as a teacher, Kalpana's days were always filled with arduous hours of household chores, farm activities, caring for children and the family, and as if these were not enough for her, she also had to fetch water from a river located at a far distance from her home. Her life, however, changed once GWT/N's RWSP implemented a water project in her community. To get the water project, Kalpana, together with some other local women, not only visited the GWT/N's project office to put their request for a water project but also decided to be in the WUSC to oversee the implementation of the project. Since the scarcity of the water was affecting more women than men and there were only a few men present in the village as most men had gone for overseas employment, the responsibility of up-keeping the household and the family remained with women.*
>
> *Consequently, Kalpana and her colleagues from the community got involved in the water project from day one of forming a women's group to attending various training to acquire skills required for smooth and effective operation and maintenance of the water project, including water purification, personal hygiene and sanitation, and implementing various WUSC activities. In fact, Kalpana and her fellow women were able to complete the implementation of the water project 10-15 days earlier than the schedule. Kalpana, contented with the success achieved in having water in front of her house, is fully confident that she now can visit any government offices for things that she needs in her community. The local women are currently engaged in various community development as well as economic activities using the time saved from water hauling.*
>
> ***(Source: https://www.gwt.org.uk/news/how-were-empowering-women-in-nepal/).***

Another example of gender equality that the GWT/N's RWSP has tried to achieve in its WASH activities comes from the story of Deepa Sayangtang, a 40 years-old woman, who lives with her parents and a daughter in a small village in the Chitwan district of Nepal. Water was a very scarce commodity in her village since she, along with the other women in the community, had to not only walk for long distances to collect the water but also had to spend a significant amount of money as the water at times had to be pumped up using electricity. Moreover, during the dry season (March-May), even this water would not be available and the community people had to dig a separate well for it. The water availability was much higher during the monsoon period (June–August), but the water during this time would contain mud, earthworms, frogs and insects making it very difficult to purify it. When GWT/N's RWSP team reached Deepa's village to implement a water project, she enthusiastically participated in all its activities and also offered her name to be in the WUSC. Although the active participation in the WUSC meant more and extra work for her since she already had many other responsibilities on her plate like attending regular household chores, including collecting water, taking care of her daughter and parents, and putting labour on the farm, among others, she still wanted to engage in the implementation of the water project as it not only meant ensuring access to water for her and her community but also an opportunity to learn new skills. Considering her active participation, interest and positive attitude, she was chosen both by the community and the project staff to take the role of a VMW, a matter of great pride for her.

Deepa Syangtang is now trained in plumbing, masonry, and maintenance of the water system. She is confident that with all the added skills, knowledge and experience, she now can encounter the challenges she has in her life. She is also happy that her new role and active engagement in community activities can be insightful for her growing daughter who will witness the role played by her mother both in the family and the community. With new skills and the increased confidence, Deepa thinks that no work should be gender-biased. Given the opportunity, she adds that women can fulfil all the responsibilities that used to be in the men's domain in the past. She is confident that the GWT/N's RWSP, with everyone's active participation, will be completed on time and all in the community will soon have access to clean drinking water along with marked improvement in their sanitation and health status. Deepa is also pleased that her active engagement in the WASH project has motivated many other women to participate not only in GWT/N's RWSP activities but also in several other community development activities.

(Source: https://www.gwt.org.uk/news/international-womens-day-empowering-women-like-deepa/).

Ensuring menstruating women's access to water and toilets is another major focus of GWT/N's RWSP. A thorough review of its Menstrual Hygiene Management (MHM) in Schools and Communities Guideline (2019) confirms that all menstruating women and girls have access to safe and affordable drinking water as well as adequate and equitable sanitation and hygiene facilities. The RWSP has programmed various interventions to ensure: availability of water inside the toilets for all women, including menstruating women; availability of water for all hygiene-related practices, including washing of under-garments; awareness-raising of female WUSC members on MHM and its linkage with WASH activities; displaying of MHM awareness materials in every water scheme; and inclusion of menstruating women in all WASH-related activities from the design to the project completion. GWT/N's RWSP targets both the schools and communities with MHM sensitive interventions while implementing its WASH activities.

Despite its MHM Guideline being sensitive to menstruating women, increased participation of women in various WASH activities, and the case studies presented above confirming the implementation of gender-responsive water projects by the GWT/N's RWSP, its publication 'Steps for New Schemes (GWT, 2020)' is relatively less gender-sensitive. This document entails nine steps and detailed procedures within each of those nine steps to be followed concerning the implementation of RWSP activities. It also highlights the need to follow GESI criteria while forming a WUSC. Nevertheless, the shortcomings of this document while reviewing it using a gender lens are:

- it treats its beneficiary population as a homogenous group by putting them under 'community' instead of defining 'who' in the community is the focus of the water projects, identifying women's and men's specific needs and concerns as they are mostly different from each other, and developing gender-specific strategies accordingly;
- it does not specify the number of women to be selected/ elected in a WUSC which invites the danger of being happy with women's tokenistic involvement rather than their strategic engagement in the WUSC matters;
- the document also does not categorically mention the need for women's presence in decision-making positions of the WUSC;
- the document talks about the selection of VHPs and VMWs but it does not clarify if women will be selected in these positions since history has shown that when women's selection is not specified such positions are generally taken by men;

- the document mentions that the GWT/N's RWSP team will assess the ability and willingness of the community to pay for water and sanitation services but it does not clarify if women's ability to pay is also assessed since it is specifically women who are in general expected by men to pay the water tariff for the reason that it is women who mostly handle the water-related activities.

Similarly, a review of GWT/N's RWSP Manual for Pre-Construction Training to Water and Sanitation Management Committee (WSMC) (GWT/N, 2016) following a gender perspective indicates that this document is also relatively gender-weak. This manual details out 15 session plans for the training of WSMC members. However, it's only the 12th session plan that deals with gender equality. The discussion on gender issues in the water and sanitation in only one session plan implies that gender has been treated as a standalone component instead of treating it as a crosscutting component integrating with all session plans. This raises the question of whether the training participants can understand the importance of integrating gender in every water and sanitation activity since its absence can otherwise lead to the failure of the GWT/N supported projects from being sustainable and meeting both the practical and strategic needs of women as has been confirmed by the failure of such water projects implemented by various agencies in Nepal and elsewhere in the past.

What can thus be said from the discussions presented above is that although some of its documents like MHM Guideline, case studies, mid-term review and evaluation reports, data derived through monitoring reports and logical framework, and information obtained through personal communication tend to be gender-sensitive, the commitment towards gender sensitivity is not well integrated throughout GWT/N's RWSP policies and practices or consistently reflected in its publications. One of the reasons for this inconsistent focus on gender integration could be the gender-imbalanced team of the RWSP where only 20% of the staff are women as opposed to 80% of men. The lack of women's presence in the senior management team of GWT/N's RWSP is another area of concern despite its emphasis on women's inclusion as VMW, VHW, CHW, WUSC members and decision-makers. Hence, because of its large budget, the huge scope of work and the tremendous role it can play in influencing the national water policies as well as the other stakeholders in the WASH sector, it will be essential for GWT/N's RWSP to pay some extra attention in ensuring consistency in integrating gender in its policies and practices so that all its staff, stakeholders and project beneficiaries could have a common understanding about the importance and the impact of gender-sensitive development projects, including those of the WASH sector, in safeguarding women's rights and dignity and meeting their practical and strategic gender needs in a sustained manner.

CHAPTER 12

Conclusion and Policy Implications

This chapter presents some conclusions and policy implications based on the discussions made in the preceding chapters regarding the integration of gender in the water and sanitation sector policies and practices at international, national, institutional and project levels. It is hoped that the propositions presented in this chapter will contribute to make the WASH sector sustainable and gear towards gender equality and women's empowerment. The conclusions and the policy implications have been drawn taking into account the findings of the field research undertaken during the late '90s as presented in Part II and the one conducted in 2020 to examine the changes taking place in integrating gender in the policies and practices of various actors over the last 20 years. Even though the policy implications presented in this chapter have been drawn from the research undertaken in the water sector, these implications will also be useful for other sectors which are willing to turn out to be more gender-focused for ensuring sustained sectoral benefits to the entire project beneficiaries, including women, girls and female-headed households.

Gender Integration in Water Policies Prior to 2000

The drinking water sector in the pre-2000 era was considered to be a technical sector, thereby falling under men's domain. It was mostly boys who were sent to study civil engineering while girls were mostly sent to study arts and social sciences resulting in the presence of more men as overseers and civil engineers in the water sector. The woman's role as a technician was almost nil or limited. In turn, the involvement of the community women was not perceived to be important in any stages of the water supply projects- designing, planning, implementing, and monitoring and evaluation- due to the presence of a large number of men with technical skills. Despite the reality that women were the primary managers of water resources given their traditional role of fetching water and taking care of almost all water-related activities, their meaningful involvement in the water systems was not given a priority. As a result of women's absence in the important phases of water supplies, the water systems could not be effective as expected in providing sustained benefits to the community. In no time, more than half the systems were not functioning to their design capacity. While the weak operation and maintenance was the major reason behind the increasing number of malfunctioning water points, the faulty design, early drying up of sources, use of water sources that were under a conflict of interest, improper location of the water points, among others, were the other reasons for the failure of the water supplies to ensure continued benefits. The lack of women's meaningful involvement in all the important stages of the water projects despite their pivotal role in this sector was reported as the major reason for these challenges. In short, the lack of ownership of the water systems by the primary actor i.e., women, was the major reason for the ineffectiveness of the water systems designed and implemented prior to 2000.

Realising the seriousness of the scarcity of water, for it is a finite resource, and weak management of the installed water systems, on the other hand, the IDWSSD (1981-1990) stressed the need for women's meaningful participation in all phases of the water projects. The various international women's conferences held around that time also highlighted women's strategic involvement in all development projects, including the WASH sector, not only for the success of the projects but also for women's empowerment to meet both their practical and strategic gender needs. Beginning with the Dublin Conference in 1992, water started to be perceived as an economic good which gave birth to the demand-driven cost-recovery concept, and consequently to the idea of commoditising water and involving the private sector for effective and efficient delivery of water services.

A review of the water policies of some international donors like the World Bank, the ADB, RWSSP funded by the Government of Finland/ FINNIDA and WaterAid made in the late 1990s showed that their policies were fully driven by the outcomes of the Dublin conference, including the principle of water to be perceived as an economic good, and these policies lacked gender perspectives. None of the donor policies had provisions for looking into gender roles, needs and concerns in the water supplies they supported, with women's roles hardly mentioned in the policy documents. The focus was more on 'community' assuming that all the communities are homogenous and everyone- women, men, girls, boys- living in them had the same needs and concerns related to water and sanitation. In turn, the water and sanitation projects were designed and implemented under the notion that they would automatically and equally benefit all. The dominant thinking was that one single strategy would work for both women and girls and men and boys i.e., the agencies followed the 'same size fits all' approach before 2000!

Similarly, a review of the national water policies, policies of the FRWSSSP funded by the ADB, the RWSSP funded by the Government of Finland/ FINNIDA and the policy of NEWAH, an NGO- funded primarily by WaterAid during those years, showed that the lack of gender perspective observed in the donor water policies was prevalent on the recipient side as well. In other words, the water policies, be it of the GoN or the agencies and projects funded by the donors, were gender-weak, with only some space inconsistently given to the women. The situation was slightly different in the case of NEWAH as it had more progressive policies and practices when looked at from a gender lens. Interestingly, even the slight gender sensitivity shown by NEWAH in its organisational policies and practices resulted in the presence of relatively more women staff, including in the senior management, more women in the WSUCs, more women in decision-making positions, more women's involvement in various stages of the water projects, including in the position of caretakers, as compared to the government project and the bilateral project.

The overall status of the water projects implemented under gender-weak policies was that they were not able to satisfactorily address women's practical and strategic issues although the presence of women in various meetings had increased when compared to earlier times. With some exception to NEWAH, in all water projects, women's roles were mainly perceived as mothers, wives, and sisters within the larger definition of housewives. This notion of women's 'housewife role' resulted in their involvement solely in voluntary, unpaid and manual works like attending meetings as silent participants, labour contribution, and cooking and feeding during the construction phase. Under the 'gendered role' women's participation in decision-making in PMCs and WSUCs was limited and wherever their number was high owing to a requirement of the project, a male advisory committee was created in the name of helping the women members. The hidden agenda was, however, that the men wanted to make all decisions. Women were hardly allowed to participate in skills development and technical training, operation and maintenance of the water points, paid jobs, income-earning opportunities etc. as these were reserved mostly for men.

Despite the improved water services being near their homes, women were not able to save much time since the use of water in the households had tremendously increased with its proximity to home and it was the women again who were expected to fetch the additional water and not the men- an instance that points out the pronounced absence of the projects' focus on changing the traditional gender division of labour between women and men. The water supplies implemented at that time failed to understand that without women's participation, the water projects cannot be effective and without men sharing women's work, women cannot participate in project activities. Likewise, despite many positive effects of women's higher income such as effective operation and maintenance of the water systems, a better livelihood of the family, increase in the nutritional status of the children, improvement in children's education, including that of daughters etc., the project results showed that they failed to increase women's access to and control over income, and thereby over their bargaining power and decision-making ability. The normal tendency in all projects was to provide technical training to men, not to women, since such training would generate income. Similarly, men, and not women, were generally hired in paid jobs. The lack of gender focus also led the projects to bypass the poor and female-headed households since they could not meet the cost of water services which compelled these people to continue using the unhygienic traditional sources inviting several consequences to their health.

The selected drinking water and sanitation projects also failed to enhance the confidence, self-esteem and status of the community women which could have helped them not only to increase their participation in water projects and initiate new development projects but also to deal with other social issues like domestic violence, a common phenomenon in many rural areas of Nepal, which could have helped to develop a more gender-egalitarian society.

One serious implication of such unequal treatment was that, in many instances, it had further widened the gap between the women and men, and the ones having access to improved water supplies and those not having this access resulting in the lack of ownership of the project on the part of many people, thereby their lack of interest in protecting the water systems. Moreover, this unfair and unjust action also diminished the likelihood of achieving a society with gender equality and balanced power relationships between women and men, a strong indicator of sustainable human development. The main reason that came out for this situation was the patriarchal thinking about women that i) women are good only for household chores and supporting roles, not for outside home activities that require paperwork, decision-making, visiting offices etc. ii) boys are more important than girls since the boys inherit the parental property and take care of the parents during the latter's old age while girls, once married off, are of no help for their parents; iii) there is no need to invest on girls' education as parents cannot benefit out of it in the long run and even in cases where some parents decide to send their daughters to school, the quality of such schools and colleges would be lower than those of the boys. Consequently, it created a wide gap between the knowledge, ability (mainly technical) and administrative and management skills, especially related to doing paper works and dealing with other people, on the part of women. The biased view of men towards women had also led to the lack of a women-friendly organisational culture; the lack of women staff in general, and at the policy and technical positions in particular; and the lack of provision for adequate human and capital resources for gender-related activities etc., in all selected agencies. In turn, the institutional policies, objectives, and strategies as well as the project implementation guidelines were biased against women which altogether led to bypassing the latter in most of the project activities.

Gender Integration in Water Policies Post-2000

To see the gender changes that had taken place in the post-2000 policies, the water policies of the international actors like the World Bank, the ADB, UNICEF, Government of Finland, and WaterAid that play a key role in Nepal's water sector, were reviewed as presented in chapter nine. The conclusions derived from this review are as follows.

The WASH policies formulated after 2000 are relatively more women-focused than they were earlier. While the World Bank and WaterAid Nepal have put more emphasis on social inclusion, the ADB has emphasised more on gender equality and women's empowerment. Although social inclusion is getting more prominence and is the need of many countries like Nepal, it is also important for the concerned donors to understand that social inclusion alone cannot ensure gender equality which is why the idea of GESI was coined. Accordingly, UNICEF's strategic plan 2016-2030, WaterAid's strategic plan 2015-2022 and RWSSP Phase II and RVWRMPs supported by the Government of Finland/ FINNIDA have been fully informed by GESI. In the case of RWSSP Phase II and RVWRMP, the use of a human rights approach along with GESI has helped the implementing agencies to plan, design, and implement WASH projects, with gender well-integrated in them.

Both the ADB and UNICEF have ensured a firm interconnection between WASH and gender equality and paid special attention to the needs of women and girls, including the need for training and advocacy skills, to ensure their right to WASH services and involvement in decision-making of the water systems as a whole. A case in point of the ADB's commitment towards gender equality is the TSTWSSSP implemented under its financial support since this project has ensured the inclusion of women, including female-headed households, in every phase of the project. The TSTWSSSP, UNICEF and WaterAid all have strongly emphasised the collection of gender-disaggregated information to monitor the progress made by women and men, and formulation of MHM strategies, including the management of *Chhaupadi*, so that girls could effectively manage their menstruation and continue their education without any disruption and women could live a life with dignity and security.

Interestingly, the consistent use of the so-called gender-free terminologies like users, beneficiaries, people, community by all the donors etc. even in the policies formulated after 2000 implies that they have not yet fully appreciated the varying needs and concerns of women and men in each of these categories. The donors' tendency of considering women and girls and men and boys as homogenous groups has constrained the formulation of gender-specific strategies and actions and yet again increased the chances of the project benefits being utilised more by men and boys than women and girls. The other major change in all donors' post-2000 policies is the expanded role of the private sector to deliver efficient and effective water services to the project beneficiaries. However, it is not evident in those policies how the private sector would benefit the poor, marginalised, and women and female-headed households, who are unable to meet the project's financial requirements.

Despite the donor policies formulated post-2000 being relatively more gender-sensitive than the earlier policies, the experiences of some projects like TSTWSSSP, RWSSP Phase II and RVWRMP reflect that women's participation is still much lower than men's in many aspects like decision-making, holding key positions, and in paid technical works like repair and maintenance of the water systems, among others. The lack of adequate time spent to prepare and counsel women given the patriarchal culture they are surrounded by and the lack of follow up training and guidance to help them retain what they learnt from the training are the reasons for women's weaker participation when compared to men. Moreover, in the case of the RWSSP and RVWRMP, their claim that they have closely worked with the local governments to ensure the same level of gender sensitivity in the municipal level plans has not been true since the review of a local level plan chosen randomly indicates how gender-blind it is, implying the bleak possibility of women benefiting equally to men once the WASH projects supported by them are fully taken over by the local governments. Similarly, there are still several areas in WaterAid's strategic plan like goal, objectives, strategies, approach, desired change, context analysis, partner selection, mode of operation, partners' capacity building in the recipient countries, and procedures for assessing its performance at all levels- international, country and local levels- where WaterAid lacks gender focus despite the other areas in the plan being well informed by gender.

Regarding gender integration in Nepal's legislation, development plans and water policies, it is gradually advancing over the years and the latest Constitution of Nepal 2015 is a classic example of it. Each new long-term plan is more progressive than the preceding plan in acknowledging, respecting and advancing women's role, gender equality and women's empowerment, and so is the Constitution of Nepal 2015 which has many progressive provisions on women's right to property, reproductive health, education, employment, equality, security and dignity, and participation in politics. However, the discussions made earlier have highlighted that indicators related to women's situation in these areas are not yet satisfactory. In the water sector too, the tendency of perceiving it as a technical sector, appropriate only for men, persists. Accordingly, gender perspectives are not yet well integrated and consistently reflected in national water policies whose emphasis is still on meeting the construction targets and spending budgets as these are valued more than the work with women and the poor. Wherever women's involvement has been acknowledged in water policies, strategies and guidelines, the reason given for it is to increase the effectiveness and efficiency of the water supplies, not to achieve gender equality and women's empowerment.

Although Nepal's development plans have been progressively integrating gender, the water legislations and policies have failed to show the same level of commitment. While some water policies are fully GESI informed, promoting women's meaningful participation as well as social inclusion to include women and men from different marginalised and excluded categories, some others, despite going through several amendments and some even being the latest, are still gender-blind. This inconsistency in ensuring gender sensitivity even in the latest policies simply indicates that the planners and policy-makers in the water sector, who are mostly men, are still not fully convinced that women can play a meaningful role in the planning, design, implementation and operation and maintenance of water supplies. Although women were responsible for collecting and managing water for daily consumption, household use and farming, the laws have failed to recognise women's contribution and promote their participation in water-related matters. The consequence of the WASH projects implemented under such gender-insensitive policies and plans is that they will most likely fail to meet women's practical and strategic gender needs if they are not revised from a gender perspective or some new gender-aware policies and plans are not soon introduced.

Unlike the government water policies, the NGO sector water policies and practices relatively were more gender-informed both before and after 2000. Both NEWAH and GWT/N have made profound efforts to increase women's involvement in WSUCs, decision-making, VMW/ caretaker positions, and several other organisational activities during the post-2000 period resulting in the availability of more functioning water points to the design capacity as opposed to the prior 2000 period. These agencies have tried out various approaches like GAP, GESI, human rights and CLTS to ensure better integration of gender needs and concerns in their policies and practices. They also have introduced various income-generating activities so that women could earn income from the use of their time saved from water hauling. As a result of various leadership and confidence-building training, they provided to the local men and women, the latter were found to be handling several responsibilities, including managing some sophisticated water systems in case of GWT/N projects. Learning from their gender-sensitive WASH practices, NEWAH and GWT/N have also been able to influence the national policies.

The drawback with the NGOs, however, was the lack of consistency in those gender efforts- in using gender-specific language in their policy documents, in making even their latest policy documents like strategic plan and manuals gender-focused, and in integrating gender across all organisational activities in a systematic manner. Despite all the wonderful gender efforts that these NGOs made in various fronts of their WASH projects, the inconsistent focus on gender across their various documents, the imbalance between the number of women and men staff, the small number of women in the executive board and the senior management even in 2020, among others, rather question if they will be able to retain the gender efforts made in the other fronts, sustain the WASH project benefits both for women and men, and achieve gender equality and women's empowerment.

Policy Implications

Engendering the water sector is not only to increase the WASH projects' effectiveness and efficiency but also to achieve gender equity and women's empowerment, thereby gender equality. Hence, based on the discussions and analysis made in the earlier chapters, this section provides some policy implications for consideration by all agencies- international, to national to local- if they are willing, committed and concerned in sustaining the benefits of their WASH projects and achieving gender equality. Although a detailed list of the areas for each level- international to local- where agencies need to be gender-sensitive and gender-focused in the WASH sector (as well as any other development sector) to be able to meet both the practical and strategic gender needs of women and men has been presented at the end of this section (Table 10), some key directions are provided below as well:

Increased understanding of gender: As has been discussed in the preceding chapters, a better understanding of 'gender' on the part of all individuals- be them women or men, and agencies- be them international, national or local, is a must if they genuinely want to mainstream gender in their organisational policies and practices. Gender, which is about the interrelations between women and men, should mainly be understood as reversing what and how things were done earlier by women and men; as ensuring a consistent focus on women together with men; as considering gender relations in every part and parcel of the organisational matters; and as guaranteeing spontaneous attention towards women, just the way the organisations traditionally tend to think about men and put them in the centre of every organisational activity. Only with this understanding, things start to be 'gender-normal' in the organisations.

Gender is not a stand-alone component: Gender should be treated as a cross-cutting approach and integrated within each activity in the organisation instead of treating it as a stand-alone component if the latter is genuinely willing to empower women towards achieving gender equality. What is required for this is to solidify the understanding of women's role, contribution, rights, empowerment and the overall benefits of their equality with men's, for sustained human development. This understanding will ensure that women will get well integrated both in the organisational policies despite there being a separate section on women and practices despite those being traditionally in favour of men.

Critical strength of women: Strenuous efforts need to be made by all concerned to increase the number of women in the organisation and in the committees within the organisation since unless and until there is a critical mass of women in general and in senior positions in particular, no substantive results can be attained in the process of integrating gender in organisational matters. The challenge, however, is that unless and until there is a change in the patriarchal mindset of the senior male staff, there will be no efforts made to hire more women. Given the limited results coming out of the 33% representation of women in Nepal's parliament and some other government bodies, the critical number of women should be higher at 40-50% for meaningful results. One crucial aspect to be considered by organisations while doing activities like meetings, planning, designing, feasibility studies, committee formation, training, field visits, implementation, monitoring and evaluation etc. is that they should ensure women's meaningful representation in those activities so that they could get sustained gender-sensitive results.

Women and the poor need to be categorically mentioned: Women and the poor, excluded and marginalised groups of people need to be categorically mentioned in all policy documents, be it about their participation in organisational/ project activities, attending meetings and training, holding key positions or being recruited in paid jobs. History has provided tonnes of evidence that the mentioning of community, users, people, considering that these are homogenous groups, has never been in the favour of women and poor people. The agencies need to know the distinction between the use of gender-neutral and gender-specific language in a given context and how it can impact positively or negatively on meeting women's practical and strategic gender needs.

Special provisions for women and the marginalised groups: The agencies engaged in the development sector, including the water sector, should clearly state in their policy documents how everyone in the community, including the women and the poor and marginalised sections, regardless of their financial ability to meet the cost of services, can benefit from the projects. If required, the agencies should also mention some special provisions like providing subsidies to these people so that the women and the poor, including female-headed households, do not get deprived of the water services, mainly the very essential services like drinking water.

Gender division of labour: Gender sensitisation activities for the local women and men and gender training to all agency staff should be regularly conducted so that they could understand the importance of each other's roles in every aspect of the development/ water sector, start engaging in activities that could help change the traditional gender division of labour, and collectively involve in meeting women's and men's practical and strategic gender needs. Unless and until agencies make efforts to change the traditional gender division of labour and create an environment where women and men start sharing each other's works without gendering them, women's real empowerment is not possible.

Gender-specific organisational identities: The agencies involved in the water sector at any levels- international, national, institutional, and local- should have gender-specific organisational identities- vision, mission, goals, objectives, and strategies- that allow space for formulating gender-sensitive policies and creating a conducive operational environment- to lead to sustained practical and strategic benefits for both women and men. Since these identities are the face of any organisation and they guide the formulation of policies and organisational practices, they need to specify how the organisation aims to improve the lives of women along with those of men. The use of gender-neutral language in such cases does not benefit and empower women.

Higher representation of women in WSUCs: The organisational policy should categorically mention 50% representation of women in WSUCs as well as in other project activities, including paid positions. Only through the considerable presence of women in organisational activities, the effectiveness and efficiency can be guaranteed in the water systems and gender equality and women's empowerment be achieved. Given the strong patriarchal norms, beliefs, and practices in rural communities that hardly allow women to be active in outside home activities, the limited number of women like 1-2 currently at most WSUCs cannot guarantee any change in the existing gender roles and relations. The critical mass of women to bring any changes at the WSUC activities should constitute a 50% representation of women.

More women in key positions of the WSUCs: The other crucial issue to be considered is that the concerned agencies should always make efforts to increase women's representation in the key positions of the WSUCs since experiences have shown that the higher the number of women in key positions of the WSUCs, the greater the transparency in the management of funds. Also reported are the experiences that the high number of women in the WSUCs always leads to regular and timely collection of maintenance funds. Yet another equally meaningful outcome of more women's involvement in decision-making positions is the design, planning and implementation of gender-sensitive projects, which result in the continued benefits both for women and men in the project communities.

Capacity building of women members of the WSUC: The female members, together with the male members of the local WSUCs, should be provided with training in GAD, GESI, literacy and numeracy, leadership, technical components, income generation and skills development, among others, to build up their confidence and efficiency in managing project activities. Given women's confinement mostly in the household activities since time immemorial, it will be unfair to expect that the women, once selected to be in the WSUCs and the other committees, can start functioning as effectively as men. By providing confidence-building training to women and increasing their access to and control over income introducing various productive activities can rather boost up women's confidence. The increased income can also be a good support to the family, including in the paying of water tariff, since women, by taking care of almost all water-related activities, are also expected to meet this responsibility.

Training on GAD/ GESI: There should be a provision in all organisations to build the capacity of the agency staff at all levels in GAD/ GESI aspects. Since one-off training does not lead to required changes, the initial training should always be followed by refresher training. To ensure that gender gets onto the agency's agenda, it is essential to have a gender-focal person and/ or a gender unit to keep pushing gender integration in organisational activities till gender becomes an integral part of the organisational culture.

Allocation of budget for GAD/ GESI activities: Another important area where the concerned agencies should always be profound and committed is the allocation of budget for GAD/ GESI activities so that gender always gets onto the organisational agenda without which gender mainstreaming or integration is not possible in any organisation.

Gender disaggregation of information: Equally important area where all development agencies, including those engaged in the water sector, should pay attention is in the disaggregation of the information/ data by sex so that the progress could be monitored to know the proportion of women vs. men benefitting from the project and take corrective measures on time as relevant.

Social preparation time: The concerned agencies should allocate adequate time on social preparation to understand the gender dynamics, local socio-cultural practices, gender roles and relations, women's and men's participation in outside home activities and community meetings, decision-making practices, sources of income etc. so that appropriate strategies could be developed to create a conducive environment for women's, together with men's, increased meaningful participation, in project activities.

Table 10 presents a detailed list of the GESI indicators to be considered at international to local levels while formulating policies as well as planning, designing, implementing, and monitoring and evaluating WASH projects. The application of these indicators in the WASH sector as well as any other development sector can ensure them to be truly gender-sensitive, meet the practical and strategic gender needs of women together with men, sustain the project benefits both for women and men, and achieve women's equality and empowerment.

Table 10: Indicators and their Variables to ensure GESI Sensitivity at Various Levels in the Water and Sanitation Projects (will also be useful for other sectors)

Level	Indicators	Variables
International	Policies & Strategies	❖ Use of GESI specific terminologies ❖ GESI sensitive goals, objectives, strategies ❖ Clarity on gender roles in the sector ❖ Emphasis on women's empowerment ❖ GAD/ Gender equality/ GESI as one of the objectives of the WASH sector
National	Legislation & Acts	❖ Use of GESI specific terminologies
	National Plans & Policies	❖ Use of GESI specific terminologies ❖ GESI sensitive goals, objectives, strategies ❖ Clarity on gender roles in the WASH projects ❖ Emphasis on women's empowerment ❖ Focus on GAD/ gender equality/ GESI ❖ Composition of policymaking bodies ❖ Presence of GESI unit/person ❖ Provision of GESI orientation/ training ❖ Provision of budget for GAD/ GESI activities ❖ GAD/GESI based M&E framework

Institutional	Policy Formulation	❖ Composition of policymaking bodies ❖ Sex of participants attending meetings with policy-makers ❖ Women's participation in policy meetings ❖ GESI training received by policy-makers ❖ Agencies/partners influencing policy formulation ❖ Sex of persons involved in consultative processes
	Goal, Objectives & Strategies	❖ Use of GESI specific terminologies ❖ GESI focus on goal, objectives, strategies ❖ Focus on women's practical gender needs ❖ Emphasis on women's effective involvement ❖ Focus on improvement in women's status ❖ Emphasis on changing traditional gender division of labour ❖ Clarity on Women's access to & control over resources ❖ Focus on women's decision-making power ❖ Emphasis on gender equity and equality
	Personnel Policy	❖ GESI sensitivity in personnel Policy ❖ GESI specific recruitment policy ❖ Sexual harassment policy ❖ GESI sensitive vacancy announcements ❖ Gender-balanced interview panel ❖ GESI knowledge as a recruitment criterion ❖ GESI sensitive working environment ❖ GESI-friendly facilities
	Organisational Structure	❖ Flat vs. vertical structure ❖ Number of women & men staff ❖ Number of women & men staff in senior positions ❖ Number of women & men staff in technical positions ❖ Division of job between women & men staff ❖ Efforts made for a GESI balanced staffing structure ❖ Number of women & men members in the AGM (in the case of NGO) ❖ Number of women & men on the board (in the case of NGO)

	Organisational Culture	❖ Participatory vs. authoritarian approach ❖ Staff involved in extra agency work ❖ Roles played by staff involved in extra agency work ❖ Consultations while undertaking agency activities ❖ Formal/ casual relationships among the agency staff ❖ The value attached to one's hierarchy ❖ Power & authority held by women and men staff ❖ GESI-friendly environment ❖ Separate toilets for women staff or others as relevant ❖ Space allocated for baby care to women staff
	Gender Training	❖ Staff's understanding of GESI issues in the sector ❖ Agency's understanding of women's triple roles ❖ Provision for GESI training to agency staff ❖ Number of women and men staff trained in GESI ❖ Provision for follow-up GESI training ❖ Budget for GESI training & other GAD activities ❖ Presence of a GESI person/unit for GAD/ GESI activities
	Capital & Human Resources	❖ Budget for GESI activities ❖ Budget for field staff for GESI sensitive works ❖ Budget for GESI preparation time (social preparation) ❖ Budget for GESI sensitive M&E ❖ Budget for GESI person/ Unit or both
	Role of Change Agents	❖ Staff willing to see GESI related changes ❖ Power & authority of the change agents ❖ GESI activities performed by change agents earlier

	Sharing of Power	❖ Nature of job held by women and men staff ❖ Level of positions held by women & men staff ❖ Level of income of women and men staff ❖ Level of participation in decision-making by women and men staff ❖ Peer group support for GESI changes
	External Relationships	❖ Relationships with government agencies ❖ Relationships with other similar agencies ❖ Degree of autonomy from donors ❖ External influence on policy matters
Project	Pre-Construction Stage	❖ Presence of women in the need identification team ❖ Team's understanding of GESI issues in the sector ❖ Women's role in materialising the project ❖ Women's role in negotiating the project ❖ GESI sensitivity in data collection forms ❖ GESI knowledge criterion to select NGOs ❖ Presence of women in the feasibility study team ❖ GESI integration in baseline survey & analysis ❖ Team's understanding of GESI issues ❖ Time provided to collect GESI focused information ❖ Disaggregation of information by GESI/ gender ❖ Composition of users' committee ❖ Women's role in the selection of technology ❖ Women's role in selecting water point locations ❖ Selection of women as caretakers / maintenance workers ❖ GESI integration in training provided to NGO and local community ❖ Types of people providing & receiving training ❖ GESI sensitivity in contract agreements ❖ Social mobilisation time provided for preparing women

	Construction Stage	❖ Composition of the construction committee ❖ Women's involvement in financial management ❖ Women's role in the management of materials ❖ Division of labour between women & men ❖ Types of labour hired for paid work ❖ GESI sensitivity while collecting contribution for the construction ❖ Wage rates paid to women & men labourers ❖ Appropriateness of meeting time for local women
	Post-Construction Stage	❖ Provision of women & men caretakers ❖ O&M training to women & men caretakers ❖ Provision of payment to men & women caretakers ❖ Availability of spare parts and tools for repair works ❖ GESI sensitivity while fixing tariff ❖ Provision for monitoring project outcomes ❖ Disaggregation of data by GESI
Community	Women's Physical Presence in Project Activities	❖ Number of women attending planning meetings ❖ Number of women present while forming WUC ❖ Number of women in the WUC and their positions ❖ Number of women in various other sub-committees ❖ Women's involvement in the selection of caretakers ❖ Number of women caretakers vs. men caretakers ❖ Types of training received by men & women ❖ Number of women & men receiving training ❖ Women's cash and kind contribution to project work

	Women's Participation in Decision Making	• Women's involvement in the negotiation of a water project • Women's participation in project activities • Women's role in making decisions in meetings • Women's roles in the selection of WUC members • Women's roles in the selection of the location of tap-stands or tube-wells or water sources and technology • Women's roles in carrying out WUC activities • Women's roles in the monitoring of project activities • Women's role in household decision-making • Women's role in agricultural matter decisions • Women's role in household expenditure decisions • Women's role in capital expenditure decisions • Women's decision-making power in the community
	Change in the Traditional Gender Division of Labour	• Types of work done by women and men in the household • Type of person collecting water • Change in the use of water before and after the project • Saving in women's and men's water hauling time, if any • Use of time saved from water hauling

	Change in Women's Access to & Control Over Income	• Gender role in income-generating activities • Increase in women's income and bargaining power • Women and men in paid positions • Women and men receiving technical training • Wages given to women and men
	Equity in Sharing of Benefits	• Types of benefits received by women and men • Number of women and men beneficiaries • Time spent collecting water before and after the project • Types of people receiving benefits • Payment of water tariffs by women and men • Provision for subsidies to poor men and women • Provision for remuneration to women and men caretakers • Condition of water points or water sources • Performance of women caretakers vs. men caretakers
	Change in Women's Status & New Development Initiatives	• Increase in the self-esteem of women and their number • Increase in the confidence of women and their number • Improvement in the skills of women and their number • The number of women who emerged as leaders • New development initiatives taken by women and men

Bibliography

Acharya, Meena. 1994. The Statistical Profile on Nepalese Women: An Update in the Policy Context. Institute for Integrated Development Studies, Kathmandu, Nepal.

Acharya, Meena. 1997. Gender Equality and Empowerment of Women. A status report submitted to United Nations Population Fund (UNFPA), Kathmandu, Nepal.

Acharya, Meena and Bennett, Lynn. 1981. The Rural Women of Nepal: An Aggregate Analysis and Summary of 8 Village Studies; The Status of Women in Nepal Volume II Part 9. Centre for Economic Development and Administration, Tribhuvan University, Kathmandu, Nepal.

ActionAid. 2004. Policy Briefs. April/May.

ADB (Asian Development Bank). 1990. Women and Water: Domestic Shallow Well Water Supplies: The Family Hand-Pump Scenario. In proceedings of a regional seminar, Manila, 29 August-1 September, 1989.

ADB (Asian Development Bank). 1998. The Bank's Policy on Water Working Paper. August, Manila, Philippines.

ADB (Asian Development Bank). 1999. Country Briefing Paper Women in Nepal. Asian Development Bank Programs Department West Division 1 December 1999. Manila, The Philippines.

ADB (Asian Development Bank). 2001. Water for All: The Water Policy of the Asian Development Bank. Asian Development Bank, October 2001. Manila, Philippines.

ADB (Asian Development Bank). 2004. INTERIM REVIEW OF THE ADB'S WATER POLICY IMPLEMENTATION Report of the In-House Study by ADB's Water Sector Committee. Asian Development Bank, February 2004. Manila, Philippines.

ADB (Asian Development Bank). 2006. Comprehensive Review of ADB's Water Policy Implementation FINAL REPORT AND RECOMMENDATION. Prepared by an independent expert review panel for the Asian Development Bank (ADB), April 2006.

ADB (Asian Development Bank). 2008. STRATEGY2020: The Long-Term Strategic Framework of the Asian Development Bank 2008-2020. Asian Development Bank. Manila, Philippines.

ADB (Asian Development Bank). 2011. Water Operational Plan 2011-2020. Asian Development Bank, October 2011. Manila, Philippines.

ADB (Asian Development Bank). 2020. Nepal: The Third Small Towns Water Supply and Sanitation Sector Project- Project Data Sheet. Ministry of Water Supply and Sanitation, Department of Water Supply, Sanitation and Sewerage Management, Government of Nepal, Kathmandu, Nepal. https://www.adb.org/projects/35173-013/main#project-pds https://dwssm.gov.np/en/projects/small-town-water-supply-sanitation-sector-project/

Ahmad, Tameez and Raza, Haider. 1999. Pakora in Pakistan: Moving Towards Democratic Management. In Community Water Management, Participatory Learning and Action (PLA) Notes, International Institute for Environment and Development (IIED), June, London.

Albuquerque, C. D. 2014. *Realizing the human rights to water and sanitation - A handbook by the UN Special Rapporteur Catarina de Albuquerque.* UN Special Rapporteur on the human right to safe drinking water and sanitation, Portugal. Geneva: OHCHR.

Asia Foundation et.al. 2018. Nepal's Locally Elected Women Representatives Exploratory Study of Needs and Capacity. The Australian Government and The Asia Foundation Partnership on Subnational Governance in Nepal. https://asiafoundation.org/wp-content/uploads/2018/07/Nepals-Locally-Elected-Women-RepresentativesExploratory-Study-of-Needs-and-Capacity-Assessment.pdf

AusAID (Australian Agency for International Development). 2000. *Health and Population: Water Supply and Sanitation.* Australia: AusAID Guide to Gender and Development -- Supplement Feb 2000.

Retrieved from: http://www.oecd.org/social/gender-development/1896488.pdf.

Aziz, Nahida and Halvorson, Sarah. 1999. Women's Involvement: A Switch in Thinking, Hoto, Pakistan. In Community Water Management, Participatory Learning and Action (PLA) Notes, International Institute for Environment and Development (IIED), June, London.

Baden, Sally. 1993. Practical Strategies for Involving Women as well as Men in Water and Sanitation Activities. Report prepared for Gender Office, Swedish International Development Office. SIDA Bureau. Briefings on Development and Gender (BRIDGE) Report No. 11.

Baidya, Bal Gopal. 2000. Women in Governance: A Case Study of Nepal. February 2000, Kathmandu.

Bajracharya, R. M., Sharma, P. M. and Sharma, S. 1997. A Study on the Social and Legal Aspects of Water Users and Sanitation Committees. Facilitating Capacity Building and Participation Activities Project TA No. 5692-NEP. Asian Development Bank and His Majesty's Government of Nepal, Ministry of Housing and Physical Planning, Department of Water Supply and Sewerage, Kathmandu, Nepal (Draft Report).

Baral, Balkrishna. 2017. Gender development perspective: A contemporary review in global and Nepalese context. The Geographical Journal of Nepal Vol. 10: 141-152, 2017 Central Department of Geography, Tribhuvan University, Kathmandu, Nepal.

Berg, Bruce L. 1989. Qualitative Research Methods for the Social Sciences. Indiana University of Pennsylvania, USA.

Berger, M., et al. 1984. Bridging the Gender Gap in Agricultural Extension. International Centre for Research on Women, Washington.

Bhadra, Chandra. 2004. NEPAL: Review of the Implementation of the Beijing Platform for Action and the Outcome Documents of the Twenty-Third Special Session of the General Assembly. Paper prepared for Mainstreaming Gender Equity Programme, Ministry of Women, Children & Social Welfare, May 2004. Singhdurbar, Kathmandu, Nepal.

Bhadra, Chandra and Thapa, Mani. 2007. FINAL REPORT NEPAL: Country Gender Profile. Japan International Cooperation Agency (JICA), March 2007, Kathmandu, Nepal.

Bilgi, Meena. 1998. Entering Women's World through Men's Eyes: using PRAP to sensitise men towards women's issues. In The Myth of Community: Gender Issues in Participatory Development edited by Irene Guijt and Meera Kaul Shah. Intermediate Technology Publications, London.

Bilqis, Amin Hoque., et al. 1991. Maintaining Village Water Pumps by Women Volunteers in Bangladesh. In Health Policy and Planning, Vol. 6, No. 2.

Biswas, Asit. K. 1988. *United nations water conference action plan- Implementation over the last decade (p. 148-159).* International Journal of Water Resources Development. Butterworth & Co (Publishers) Ltd. DOI: 10.1080/07900628808722385.

Boesveld, Mary. 1994. Working with Women and Men on Water and Sanitation: An African Field Guide. Occasional Paper Series, No. 25, IRC International Water and Sanitation Centre, The Hague, The Netherlands.

Bogdan, Robert. 1972. Participant Observation in Organisational Settings. Syracuse, N. Y.: Syracuse University Press.

BRAC (Bangladesh Rural Action Committee). 1997. BRAC Technical Manual: A Learning Approach to Gender and Organisational Change. BRAC Gender Resource Centre, BRAC, Dhaka.

Budhathoki, Chitra B. 2019. Water Supply, Sanitation and Hygiene Situation in Nepal: A Review. Journal of Health Promotion, Vol. 7, June 2019, pp. 65-76 ISSN: 2631-2441.

Carloni, A. S. 1987. Women in Development: AID's Experience 1973-1985. Vol. 1 Synthesis Paper. AID Programme Evaluation Report, No. 18.

CBS (Central Bureau of Statistics). 2011. Statistical Pocket Book Nepal. His Majesty's Government, National Planning Commission Secretariat, CBS, Kathmandu.

Chambers, Robert. 1994a. The Origins and Practice of Participatory Rural Appraisal. World Development, Vol. 22, No. 7, pp. 953-969.

Chambers, Robert. 1994b. Participatory Rural Appraisal (PRA): Challenges, Potentials and Paradigm. World Development, Vol. 22, No. 10, pp. 1437-1454.

Chapman, J. 2016. *Women Disproportionately Affected by Global Water Crises: Global Water Scarcity.* California: Pacific Council on International Policy.

Chibuye, Gwen I. 1996. Gender Perspectives of the Water Sector. Water Sector News, No. 4, pp. 5-6.

Chigudu, Hope. 1997. Establishing a Feminist Culture: The experience of Zimbabwe Women's Resource Centre and Network. Gender and Development, Vol. 5, No. 1, February, Oxfam, UK and Ireland.

Choguill C; Franceys R; and Cotton A. 1993. "Planning for Water and Sanitation", Centre for Development Planning Studies, Loughborough University.

Cleaver, Frances. 1997. Making the Reality of 'Lowers' Count More. In Project Appraisal, No. 12, Part 2, June.

Cleaver, Frances and Elson, Diane. 1995. Women and Water Resources: Continued Marginalisation and New Policies. International Institute of Environment and Development (IIED), Gatekeeper Series No. 49.

Cleaver, Frances and Jobes, Katja. 1996. Donor Policies and Gender in the Water and Sanitation Sector. Natural Resources Forum, Vol. 20, No. 2, pp. 111-116.

CMS (Consolidated Management Services Nepal (P.) Ltd.). 1996. Study in Gender Issues Related to Water and Energy Sectors in the Far-Western Development Region of Nepal. His Majesty's Government, Ministry of Water Resources, Water and Energy Commission Secretariat (WECS), Kathmandu.

Code for Nepal. 2018. https://codefornepal.org/2018/03/women-nepal-2018/

(This work is licensed under a Creative Commons Attribution- ShareAlike 3.0 License! Code for Nepal is a registered 501(c)(3) non-profit organization. EIN: 47-3620037).

Collins, S.M., Miller, J.D., Mbullo, P., Boateng, G.O., Wekesa, P., Onono, M., & Young, S.L. 2017. *You Take the Cash Meant for Beans and You Buy Water": The Multi-Faceted Consequences Of Water Insecurity For Pregnant And Postpartum Kenyan Women Of Mixed HIV Status.* Maryland: FASEB Journal Vol. 31, April 1, 2017.

Curtis, Val. 1986. Women and the Transport of Water. Intermediate Technology Publications.

Dabbs, James M., Jr. 1982. Making Things Visible. In Varieties of Qualitative Research, ed. John Van Maanen. Beverly Hills, California: Sage.

DAC (Development Assistance Committee) Sourcebook. 1998. Concepts and Approaches Linked to Gender Equality. Organisation for Economic Co-operation and Development (OECD)/OCDE, Paris.

Davis, Jan., Gerry Garvey and Michael Wood. 1993. Developing and Managing Community Water Supplies. Oxfam Development Guidelines No. 8, Oxfam, UK and Ireland.

Denzin, Norman K. 1978. The Research Act. McGraw-Hill, New York.

Desilver, Drew. 2018. Remittances from abroad are major economic assets for some developing countries. FACTANK, News in the Numbers, Pew Research Centre, Analysis of World Bank and CIA World Factbook Data accessed on January 25, 2018, and published on January 29, 2018.

DfID (Department for International Development). 1998. Guidance Manual for Water Supply and Sanitation Programmes. A manual prepared by Water and Environmental Health at London and Loughborough and published by Water Engineering and Development Centre (WEDC), Loughborough University, UK.

Dixit, Ajaya and Crippen, John N. 1993. Issues in Maintenance Management of Community Water Supply Schemes in Nepal. In Water Nepal, Vol. 3, No. 2-3, October, published by Nepal Water Conservation Foundation, Kathmandu.

Drop in the Bucket. 2016. *Want To Know More About The World Water Crisis?* Drop in the Bucket.

Elson, Diane. 1991. Structural Adjustment: Its Effect on Women. In Changing Perceptions: Writings on Gender and Development, ed. by Tina Wallace and Candida March. Oxfam, Oxford.

Equinet. 2018. Equinet Highlights 2018. Equinet Secretariat, Brussels, Belgium.

Evans, Phil. 1992. Paying the Piper: An Overview of Community Financing of Water and Sanitation. IRC International Water and Sanitation Centre, Occasional Paper No. 18, April, IRC, The Hague.

FEMCONSULT (Consultants on Gender and Development). 1998. Men, Women and Water Participatory Approaches in Water Management. Newsletter, No. 1, ISSN 0925 - 3912

FINNIDA (Finnish International Development Agency). 1993. Looking at Gender, Water Supply and Sanitation. FINNIDA, Helsinki.

FINNIDA (Finnish International Development Agency). 1994. Looking at Gender, Water Supply and Sanitation. FINNIDA, Helsinki.

FINNIDA (Finnish International Development Agency). 1998. Finland's Experiences Sustainable Water Management. Ministry of the Environment, Ministry of Agriculture and Forestry, Ministry for Foreign Affairs, Finish Environment Institute, FINNIDA, Helsinki.

Fong, Monica S.; Wakeman, Wendy; and Bhusan, Anjana. 1996. Toolkit on Gender in Water and Sanitation. Gender Toolkit Series No. 2, The World Bank, Washington, DC.

Fowler, Alan. 1997. Striking a Balance: A Guide to Enhancing the Effectiveness of Non-Governmental Organisations in International Development. Earthscan, Earthscan Publications Ltd, London.

Frischmuth, Christiane. 1997. Gender is not a sensitive issue: institutionalising a gender-oriented participatory approach in Siavonga, Zambia. Gatekeeper Series no. 72, International Institute for Environment and Development (IIED), UK.

Garn, Mike. 1998. Managing Water as an Economic Good: The Transition from Supply-Oriented to Demand-Responsive Services, World Bank, Washington, DC.

GLASS (Global Analysis and Assessment of Sanitation and Drinking Water). 2014. Nepal Country Highlights. WHO, Geneva. http://www.who.int/water_sanitation_health/glaas/2014/nepal-10-nov.pdf.

GLASS (Global Analysis and Assessment of Sanitation and Drinking Water). 2014. Sanitation, drinking-water and hygiene status overview. UN Water and WHO, Geneva. phttps://www.who.int/water_sanitation_health/glaas/2014/nepal-10-nov.pdf

Goetz, Anne Marie. 1992. Gender Administration. IDS Bulletin, Vol. 23, No. 4.

Goetz, Anne Marie. 1995. Institutionalising Women's Interests and Gender Sensitive Accountability in Development, IDS Bulletin 26/3 (July), 1-10.

Goetz, Anne Marie. 1997a. Introduction: Getting Institutions Right for Women in Development. In Getting Institutions Right for Women in Development ed. by Anne Marie Goetz. Zed Books, London and New York.

Goetz, Anne Marie. 1997b. Managing Organisational Change: The 'Gendered' Organisation of Space and Time. In Gender and Development: Organisational Structure. An Oxfam Journal, Volume 5, No. 1, February, Oxfam, Oxford, UK.

Goetz, Anne Marie. 1998. Mainstreaming Gender Equity to National Development Planning. In Missionaries and Mandarins Feminist Engagement with Development Institutions ed. by Carol Miller and Shahra Razavi. Intermediate Technology Publications in association with the UN Research Institute for Social Development.

GoN (Government of Nepal), 1992. Water Resources Act B.S. 2049. Government of Nepal, Ministry of Law, Justice and Federal Affairs, Singhdurbar, Kathmandu, Nepal.

GoN (Government of Nepal). 1993. Water Resources Regulations B.S. 2050 including amendments till 2075 Mangsir (November/ December 2018). Government of Nepal, Ministry of Law, Justice and Federal Affairs, Singhdurbar, Kathmandu, Nepal.

GoN (Government of Nepal). 1998. Drinking Water Rules B.S. 2055. Government of Nepal, Ministry of Housing and Physical Planning, Department of Water Supply and Sewerage (DWSS), Singhdurbar, Kathmandu, Nepal.

GoN (Government of Nepal). 2006. Water Supply Management Board Act B.S. 2063. Government of Nepal, Nepal Law Commission, November 24, 2006 (B.S. 2063 Mangsir 8). Kathmandu, Nepal.

GoN (Government of Nepal). 2009. National Urban Water Supply and Sanitation Sector Policy B.S. 2066. Government of Nepal, Ministry of Physical Planning and Works, April 2009, Singhdurbar, Kathmandu, Nepal.

GoN (Government of Nepal). 2010. Multiple Indicator Cluster Survey Final Report 2010. Government of Nepal, National Planning Commission, Central Bureau of Statistics, and UNICEF, Kathmandu, Nepal

GoN (Government of Nepal). 2010/11. Nepal Living Standard Survey 2010-11. Government of Nepal, National Planning Commission Secretariat, Central Bureau of Statistics, Singhdurbar, Kathmandu, Nepal.

GoN (Government of Nepal). 2011. Nepal in Figures. National Planning Commission Secretariat, Central Bureau of Statistics, Kathmandu, Nepal.

GoN (Government of Nepal). 2011. National Sanitation and Hygiene Master Plan. Government of Nepal, National Planning Commission, Steering Committee for National Sanitation Action, Singhdurbar, Kathmandu, Nepal.

GoN (Government of Nepal). 2012. A Study on Gender-Based Violence Conducted in Selected Rural Districts of Nepal. Government of Nepal, Office of the Prime Minister and Council of Ministers, November 2012, Singhdurbar, Kathmandu, Nepal.

GoN (Government of Nepal), New ERA and ICF International. 2012. Nepal Demographic and Health Survey 2011. Government of Nepal, Ministry of Health and Population, Population Division; New ERA; and ICF International. Kathmandu, Nepal.

GoN (Government of Nepal). 2013. An approach paper to the Thirteenth Plan (2013-2016). National Planning Commission (NPC), Singhadurbar, July 2013, Kathmandu, Nepal.

GoN (Government of Nepal). 2014. National Review on the implementation of the Beijing Declaration and Platform for Action (1995) and the Outcomes of the Twenty-Third Special Session of the General Assembly (2000). Ministry of Women, Children and Social Welfare, Singhdurbar, Kathmandu, Nepal. https://

scholar.google.com/scholar_lookup?hl=en&publication_year=2014&author=Government+of+Nepal&title=National+review+on+the+implementation+of+the+Beijing+Declaration+and+Platform+for+Action+%281995%29+and+the+outcomes+of+the+Twenty-Third+Special+Session+of+the+General+Assembly+%282000%29

GoN (Government of Nepal). 2014. National Water Supply and Sanitation Policy 2014 (DRAFT- Unofficial Translation). Government of Nepal, Ministry of Urban Development, 31 December 2014. Singhdurbar, Kathmandu, Nepal.

GoN (Government of Nepal). 2015. Nepal Earthquake 2015: Post Disaster Needs Assessment. Government of Nepal, National Planning Commission, Vol. A: Key Findings. Singhdurbar, Kathmandu, Nepal.

GoN (Government of Nepal). 2015. HRBA and GESI Strategy and Action Plan: Human Rights Based Approach and Gender Equality and Social Inclusion in Water and Sanitation Sector. Rural Water Supply and Sanitation Project in Western Nepal Phase II and Rural Village Water Resources Management Project Phase II. Government of Nepal, Ministry of Federal Affairs and Local Development, Department of Local Infrastructure Development and Agricultural Roads (DoLIDAR), June 2015.

GoN (Government of Nepal). 2015. Gender Justice/ Equality Act B.S. 2072 (Bill amending some Nepal Acts related to achieving Gender Equality and controlling Gender Based Violence). Government of Nepal, Ministry of Law, Justice and Parliamentary Affairs, Singhdurbar, Kathmandu, Nepal.

GoN (Government of Nepal). 2015. Constitution of Nepal 2015. Ministry of Law, Justice and Parliamentary Affairs, Singhdurbar, Kathmandu, Nepal. Also in the unofficial translation of the Constitution of Nepal <http://extwprlegs1.fao.org/docs/pdf/nep155698b.pdf>.

GoN (Government of Nepal). 2015. Sustainable Development Goals, 2016-2030, National (Preliminary) Report. Government of Nepal, National Planning Commission, Singhdurbar, Kathmandu, Nepal.

GoN (Government of Nepal). 2016. Fourteenth Three-Year Development Plan 2016-2019. Government of Nepal, National Planning Commission, Singhdurbar, Kathmandu, Nepal.

GoN (Government of Nepal). 2017. The National Civil (Code) Act, 2017 (B.S. 2074). Nepal Law Commission, Kathmandu, Nepal.

GoN (Government of Nepal). 2018. The Right to Safe Motherhood and Reproductive Health Act B.S. 2075. Ministry of Health, B.S. 2075/6/2 (18 September 2018), Kathmandu, Nepal.

GoN (Government of Nepal). 2018. Drinking Water and Sanitation Management Act (Draft Version) https://mail.google.com/mail/u/0/#label/Water+supply%2C+sanitation+and+hygiene +reports?projector=1

GoN (Government of Nepal). 2019. Fifteenth Five-Year Development Plan 2019-2024. Government of Nepal. National Planning Commission. Singhdurbar, Kathmandu, Nepal.

GoN (Government of Nepal). 2017. Open Data Nepal, Ministry of Agriculture, Land Management and Cooperatives, Singhdurbar, Kathmandu, Nepal http://opendatanepal.com/organization/about/ministry-of-agricultural-development.

GoN (Government of Nepal), New ERA and ICF International. 2016. Nepal Demographic and Health Survey 2016. Government of Nepal, Ministry of Health and Population, Population Division; New ERA; and ICF International. Kathmandu, Nepal.

Green, Cathy and Baden, Sally. 1994a. Water Resources Management: A Macro Level Analysis from a Gender Perspective. An issue paper prepared for the Gender Office, Swedish International Development Authority (SIDA). Briefings on Development and Gender (BRIDGE), Report No. 21, Institute of Development Studies (IDS), UK.

Green, Cathy and Baden, Sally. 1994b. Gender Issues in Water and Sanitation Projects in Senegal. Institute of Development Studies, Sussex.

GWA (Gender and Water Alliance). 2003. Tapping into Sustainability: issues and trends in gender mainstreaming in water and sanitation. A Background Document for the Gender and Water Session 3rd World Water Forum, Kyoto, Japan, 2003. IRC, The Netherlands.

GWA (Gender and Water Alliance). 2003. The Gender and Water Development Report 2003: Gender Perspectives on Policies in the Water Sector. Gender and Water Alliance Secretariat, IRC International Water and Sanitation Centre, Delft, The Netherlands.

GWT/N (Gurkha Welfare Trust/Nepal) <https://www.gwt.org.uk/news/how-were-empowering-women-in-nepal/>.

GWT/N (Gurkha Welfare Trust/Nepal) <https://www.gwt.org.uk/news/international-womens-day-empowering-women-like-deepa/>.

GWT/N (Gurkha Welfare Trust/Nepal). 2016. Manual for Pre-Construction Training to Water and Sanitation Management Committee. GWT, Pokhara, Nepal.

GWT/N (Gurkha Welfare Trust/Nepal. 2019. RWSP Guideline for Menstrual Hygiene Management (MHM) in Schools and Community, GWT, Pokhara, Nepal.

GWT/N (Gurkha Welfare Trust/Nepal). 2020. ANNEX L TO GWT (N)/G3/315 RWSP Summary of Implementation Steps for New Schemes. August 8, 2020. GWT, Pokhara, Nepal.

GWT/N (Gurkha Welfare Trust/ Nepal). 2020. Annual Review Report. October 2020.

Habitat for Humanity Nepal. 2016. Annual Report FY 2016 Looking Back. Lalitpur, Nepal.

Hadjipateras, Angela. 1996. Community Participation in Gender Impact Assessment: Lessons from recent ACORD research. ACORD (RAPP), London, UK.

Hadjipateras, Angela. 1997. Implementing a Gender Policy in ACORD: Strategies, Constraints and Challenges. In Gender and Development Organisational Culture. An Oxfam Journal, Vol. 5, No. 1 (February).

Hadjipateras, Angela. 1998. Putting Gender Policy into Practice: Lessons from ACORD. In BRIDGE (Development and Gender in Brief), Issue 5.

Hamerschlag, Kari and Reerink, Annemarie. 1998. Best Practices: For Gender Integration in Organisations and Programmes from the InterAction Community Findings from a Survey of Member Agencies. InterAction, American Council for Voluntary International Action, Commission on the Advancement of Women, Washington, DC.

Hannan-Andersson, C. 1990. The Challenge of Measuring Gender Issues in Water and Sanitation. Paper presented at the Workshop on Goals and indicators for Monitoring and Evaluation for Water Supply and Sanitation, Geneva, 25-29, June, 1990.

Hannan-Andersson, C. 1995. Gender Perspectives on Water Resources Management: Domestic Water Supply and Environmental Sanitation. Paper prepared for a panel presentation at the UNICEF/INSTRAW Workshop on Women, Water and Environmental Sanitation held at the UN Fourth World Conference on Women and Development, Beijing, September 1995. Stockholm, Sweden, Swedish International Development Co-operation Agency, Department for Policy and Legal Issues, Gender Group.

Hewitt, Sarah. 2017. Money, Power and Muscles: Women in Nepalese Politics. May 8, 2017, Australian Institute of International Affairs, Australia.

Hill, Philippa. 1998. Femconsult Newsletter: Men, Women and Water Participatory Approaches in Water Management. No. 1, pp. 2-14.

HMG/Nepal (His Majesty's Government of Nepal). 1991. Village Development Committee Act 1991, Municipality Act 1991 and District Development Committee Act 1991 along with Local Level Election Procedure Act 1991. His Majesty's Government, Ministry of Law, Justice and Parliament, Legal Book Management Committee, pp. 1-36 and 91-130.

HMG/Nepal (His Majesty's Government of Nepal). 1995. Guidelines for the Incorporation of Gender Issues in the Water and Energy Sectors. Water and Energy Commission Secretariat, October, Report No. 6/4/271095/1/1, Seq. No. 478, Kathmandu, Nepal.

HMG/Nepal (His Majesty's Government of Nepal). 1996a. ADB Project Document: Fourth Rural Water Supply and Sanitation Sector Project. Ministry of Housing and Physical Planning, Department of Water Supply and Sewerage. Panipokhari, Kathmandu.

HMG/Nepal (His Majesty's Government of Nepal). 1996b. Nepal Gazette. Part 46. Additional Series 66, March, Kathmandu.

HMG/Nepal (His Majesty's Government of Nepal). 1998a. Ninth Plan (1997 - 2002). National Planning Commission Secretariat, Singhdurbar, Kathmandu, Nepal.

HMG/Nepal (His Majesty's Government of Nepal). 1998b. National Water Supply Sector Policy (Policies and Strategies). Ministry of Housing and Physical and Planning, Singhdurbar, Kathmandu, Nepal.

HMG/Nepal (His Majesty's Government of Nepal). 1998c. Nepal Gazette. Part 48 (Asadh 29, 2055), Extra Issue 26, Kathmandu.

HMG/Nepal (His Majesty's Government of Nepal). 1999. Water Resources Regulation 1998 and Water Resources Act 1992. Environment Sanitation Project, Ministry of Housing and Physical Planning, Department of Water Supply and Sewerage, Kathmandu.

HMG (His Majesty's Government of Nepal). 2002. Tenth Five-Year Development Plan (2002-2007). National Planning Commission, Singhdurbar, Kathmandu.

HMG (His Majesty's Government of Nepal). 2002. National Safe Abortion Policy. His Majesty's Government of Nepal, Ministry of Health, Kathmandu, Nepal http://www.mohp.gov.np/images/pdf/policy/National%20abortion%20Policy.pdf.

HMG (His Majesty's Government of Nepal). 2004. Rural Water Supply and Sanitation National Policy B.S. 2060 and Rural Water Supply and Sanitation National Strategy B.S. 2060. His Majesty's Government of Nepal, Ministry of Physical Planning and Works, Singhdurbar, Kathmandu, Nepal, January 12, 2004.

HMG (His Majesty's Government of Nepal). 2005. National Water Plan B.S. 2062. His Majesty's Government, Water and Energy Commission, Water and Energy Commission Secretariat, Singhdurbar, Kathmandu, Nepal.

Howard, G and Bartram, J. 2003. *Domestic Water Quantity, Service, Level and Health.* World Health Organization (WHO). Retrieved from: https://www.who.int/water_sanitation_health/diseases/WSH0302.pdf.

HRM (Harinas Rural Municipality). 2018. Rural Municipality Level Water, Sanitation and Hygiene Plan. Harinas Rural Municipality, Rural Municipality WASH Coordination Committee, Gandaki Province, Nepal, August 2018.

HRW (Human Rights Watch). 2016. Child Marriage in Nepal: Our Time to Sing and Play. Human Rights Watch, New York, USA.

Huber, C. 2017. *Carrying Water can be a Pain in the Neck.* Africa: World Vision. April 2017.

Hutton, G., & Haller, L. 2004. *Evaluation of the Costs and Benefits of Water and Sanitation Improvements at the Global Level.* Geneva: World Health Organization (WHO).

ICESCR (International Covenant on Economic, Social and Cultural Rights). 1966. December 16 *entered into force 1976, January 3.* New York: United Nations., 1966. Retrieved from https://www.ohchr.org/Documents/ProfessionalInterest/cescr.pdf.

ICIMOD and FAO. 1998. Capacity Building in Participatory Upland Watershed Planning, Monitoring and Evaluation A Resource Kit. (eds.) Anupam Bhatia, Chandra K. Sen, Gopa Pandey and Judith Amtzis. International Centre for Integrated Mountain Development (ICIMOD) and Participatory Watershed Management Training in Asia (PWMTA), Food and Agriculture Organisation (FAO), Netherlands/UNDP/FAO, GCP/RAS/161/NET-RAS/93/062, Kathmandu, Nepal.

IDRC (International Development Research Centre). 1985. Women's Issues in Water and Sanitation Attempts to Address an Age-Old Challenge. International Development Research Centre (IDRC) Proceedings Series No. 236e, pp. 11-17, Canada.

IDS (Institute of Development Studies). 1995. New Thinking on Gender and the Environment. In IDS Policy Briefing Issue, no. 5, University of Sussex, Brighton, UK.

IFRC (International Federation of Red Cross) and RCS (Red Crescent Societies). 2006. *4th World Water Forum Ministerial Declaration-* Mexico City. Retrieved from https://www.ifrc.org/docs/idrl/I278EN.pdf.

IIED (International Institute for Environment and Development). 1998. Participatory Monitoring and Evaluation. PLA (Participatory Learning and Actions) Notes, February, London, UK.

IISD (International Institute for Sustainable Development). 2003. *Summary of The 3rd World Water Forum & Ministerial Conference: 16-23 March 2003.* World Water Council 3rd World Water Forum. Retrieved from https://enb.iisd.org/crs/3wwf/sdvol82num8.html.

IISD (International Institute for Sustainable Development). 2009a. *5th World Water Forum 16-22 March 2009 - Istanbul, Turkey.* Retrieved from http://enb.iisd.org/crs/WATER/WORLDWATER5/.

IISD (International Institute for Sustainable Development). 2009b. *World Water Forum Bulletin. Summary of the 5th World Forum - 16-22 MARCH 2009.* Retrieved from http://enb.iisd.org/crs/water/worldwater5/html/ymbvol82num23e.html.

ILO (International Labour Organization). 2017. Nepal Labour Market Update. ILO Country Office for Nepal, Kathmandu, Nepal, January 2017.

IMF (International Monetary Fund). 2019. "World Economic Outlook Database." IMF, October, 2019.

INSTRAW (International Research and Training Institute for the Advancement of Women) News. 1997. Special Issue, No. 26, First Semester.

INSTRAW (International Research and Training Institute for the Advancement of Women) and UNICEF. 1988. Women and Water Supply and Sanitation: A National Training Seminar held at Kadugli, Sudan, January 16 - 21, 1988. Santo Domingo, UN International Research and Training Institute for the Advancement of Women.

IOM (Institute of Medicine). 2009. *Global Issues in Water, Sanitation, and Health.* Institute of Medicine (USA). Forum on Microbial Threats. Washington DC: National Academies Press (US).

IOM (International Organization for Migration). 2016. Barriers to Women's Land and Property Access and Ownership in Nepal. IOM 65 Years, Kathmandu, Nepal.

IRC (International Water and Sanitation Centre). 1991. Women, Water, Sanitation: Annual Abstract Journal, No. 1, May, IRC, The Hague.

IRC (International Water and Sanitation Centre). 1992. Women, Water, Sanitation: Annual Abstract Journal, No. 2 (September 1992), IRC, The Hague.

IRC (International Water and Sanitation Centre). 1994. Working with Women and Men on Water and Sanitation, An African Field Guide. Occasional Paper Series 25, IRC, The Hague.

IWA (International Water Association). 2014. *An avoidable crisis: WASH human resource capacity gaps in 15 developing economies.*

Jahan, Rounag. 1995. The Elusive Agenda: Mainstreaming Women in Development. Bangladesh and United States: University Press Limited and Zed Books.

Jansz S, and Wilbur J. 2013. *Women and WASH: Water, sanitation and hygiene for women's rights and gender equality.* WaterAid Briefing.

Jazairy, An; Alamgir, Mohiuddin; and Panuccio, Theresa. 1992. The State of World Rural Poverty: An Enquiry into Its Causes and Consequences. Published for the International Fund for Agricultural Development (IFAD), Rome.

JICA (Japan International Cooperation Agency). 1999. Country WID Profile (Nepal). Japan International Cooperation Agency Planning Department December 1999 https://www.jica.go.jp/english/our_work/thematic_issues/gender/background/pdf/e99nep.pdf.

Joekes, Susan. 1991. Women in Nepal. Bridge Report 1, Institute of Development Studies (IDS), Sussex, Brighton.

Joosten, Lis. 1998. Women do make a difference. Waterlines. 1998. Vol. 17, No. 1, Quarterly (July).

Joshi, D. 1999. The Non-existence of Functional Women Civil Engineers - A Case Study in the Drinking Water Sector in Uttar Pradesh, India.

JVS (Jalsrot Vikas Sanstha). 2002. Nepal Water Vision 2025. Anamnagar, Kathmandu.

Kabeer, Naila. 1994a. Reversed Realities: Gender Hierarchies in Development Thought, Verso, London.

Kabeer, Naila. 1994b. Gender-aware Policy and Planning: A Social Relations Perspective. In Gender Planning in Development Agencies (in March et.al 1999). Oxfam (UK and Ireland).

Kamminga, E. M. 1991. Economic Benefits from Improved Rural Water Supply: A Review with a focus on Women. Occasional Paper No. 17, IRC International Water and Sanitation Centre, The Hague.

Kardam, N. 1989. Women and Development Agencies in R. Gallin and A. Ferguson (eds.), Women and International Development Annual, Westview Press, Boulder: 133-154.

KBC (Kenya Broadcasting Corporation- English Service). 2017. *Water and Food Shortage In West Pokot Resulting From Drought.* West Pokot: KBC English Service National News, January 16.

Kilsby, D. 2012. *Now we feel like respected adults: positive change in gender roles and relations in a Timor Leste WASH program.* Deakin, Australia: IWDA/ WaterAid. Retrieved from: https://www.iwda.org.au/assets/files/Now-We-Feel-Like-Respected-Adults.pdf.

Lenton, Roberto; Right, Albert M.; Lewis, Kristen. 2005. Health, dignity and development: what will it take? UN Millennium Project, Task Force on Water and Sanitation 2005. EARTHSCAN, London and Sterling, VA, and UN Millennium Project.

Lerner, B. W., & Lerner, K. L. 2011. *Food: In context.* Detroit: Gale, Cengage Learning.

Levy, Caren. 1998. Institutionalisation of Gender through Participatory Practice. In The Myth of Community: Gender Issues in Participatory Development edited by Irene Guijt and Meera Kaul Shah. Intermediate Technology Publications, London.

Longwe, Sara Hlupekile. 1991. Gender Awareness: The Missing Element in the Third World Development Project. In Changing Perceptions ed. by Tina Wallace and Candida March. Oxfam, Oxford.

Longwe, Sara Hlupekile. 1995. A Development Agency as a Patriarchal Cooking Pot: The Evaporation of Policies for Women's Advancement. A paper presented at a seminar on Women's Rights and Development: Vision and Strategy for the 21st Century, organised by One World Action, Wolfson College, Oxford, 24 May 1995.

Macdonald, Mandy. 1994. Gender Planning in Development Agencies. A report of a workshop held at The Cherwell Centre, Oxford, England in May 1993. Eurostep, Oxfam, UK and Ireland.

Macdonald, Mandy; Sprenger, Ellen; and Dubel, Ireen. 1997. Gender and Organisational Change Bridging the Gap between Policy and Practice. Royal Tropical Institute - The Netherlands.

Malik, A., Yasar, A., Tabinda, A., & Abubakar, M. 2012. Water-borne diseases, cost of illness and willingness to pay for diseases interventions in rural communities of developing countries. *Iranian journal of public health*, *41*(6), 39-49.

March, Candida; Smyth, Ines; and Mukhopadhyay, Maitree. 1999. A Guide to Gender Analysis Frameworks. Oxfam, Oxford, UK.

Mathew, B. 1991. The Planner Manager Guide to Third World Water Projects. In T. Wallace 1991 (edited with Candida March) Changing Perceptions: Writings on Gender and Development, Oxfam, Oxford.

Maxine Molyneux. 1985. Mobilization without Emancipation? Women's Interests, the State, and Revolution in Nicaragua. Feminist Studies, Vol. 11, No. 2 (Summer, 1985), pp. 227-254.

May, Nicky. 1997. Challenging Assumptions Gender Issues in Urban Regeneration. Joseph Rowntree Foundation, UK.

Mayoux, Linda C. 1991. The Poverty of Income Generation: A Critique of Women's Handicraft Schemes in India. In Changing Perceptions: Writings on Gender and Development ed. by Tina Wallace and Candida March. Oxfam, Oxford.

Mekonnan, M. and Hoekstra, A. 2016. Four billion people facing water scarcity. In Science Advances, Vol. 2, No. 2, http://advances.sciencemag.org/content//2/2/e1500323.

Mills, J. E., & Cumming, O. 2016. *The Impact of Water, Sanitation and Hygiene on Key Health and Social Outcomes: Review of Evidence*. UNICEF, UK AID, & London School of Hygiene and Tropical Medicine. DOI: 10.13140/RG.2.2.36572.49280.

Ministry of Health (MOH). 1997.Nepal Family Health Survey 1996. Family Health Division, Ministry of Health, Kathmandu, Nepal.

Mlama, P. (1994) in van Wijk-Sijbesma (1998) & Mlama, Penina. 1994. Reinforcing Existing Communication Skills: the use of Dance in Tanzania. In Riano, Pilar (ed). Women in Grassroots Communication. Thousand Oaks, USA, Sage Publications, pp. 51-64.

Mommen, B., Humphries-Waa, K., & Gwavuya, S. 2017. *Does women's participation in water committees affect management and water system performance in rural Vanuatu?* Vanuatu: Practical Action Publishing. Retrieved from: https://www.developmentbookshelf.com/doi/pdf/10.3362/1756-3488.16-00026.

Morgan, T. 1992. Training Female Sanitation Volunteers. Waterlines, Vol. 11, No. 2, Intermediate Technology Publications.

Moser, Caroline O. N. 1989. Gender Planning in the Third World: Meeting Practical and Strategic Gender Needs. World Development, vol. 17, No. 11, pp. 1799-1825, Great Britain.

Moser, Caroline O. N. 1993. Gender Planning and Development: Theory Practice and Training. Routledge, London and New York.

Mosse, Julia Cleves. 1993. Half the World Half a Chance: An Introduction to Gender and Development. Oxfam, Oxford.

Mullen, R. 2004. *Safer Water*. Emory University: Woodruff Health Sciences Center.

Murthy, S. L. 2013. *The Human Right(s) to Water and Sanitation: History, Meaning, and the Controversy Over-Privatization*. Berkeley: Berkeley Journal of International Law (Volume 31).

Mustanoja, U. M. 1998. Gender Analysis and Integrated Gender Plan. Rural Water Supply and Sanitation Project (RWSSP), Plancentre Ltd., Ministry for Foreign Affairs, Department for International Development Co-operation, Lumbini Zone, Nepal.

Nepal, Ganga Datta. 2017. Study of Functionality status of Rural Water Supply and Sanitation Project. Research Study Report. Gurkha Welfare Trust/ Nepal. August 2017.

NEST (Nucleus for Empowerment through Skill Transfer). 2016. A Case Study of Impact of Simple Drip Irrigation (SDI) Programme in Rural Community of Nepal 2004/05-2015/16. Gurkha Welfare Trust/ Nepal- Rural Water and Sanitation Programme (GWT/N-RWSP). December 2016.

NEWAH (Nepal Water for Health). 1997. NEWAH Brochure and Leaflets. Thapathali, Kathmandu.

NEWAH (Nepal Water for Health). 1998. Strategic Plan 1998-2002. Thapathali, Kathmandu.

NEWAH (Nepal Water for Health). 1998/99. Project Summary for 1998/99 by Region. Thapathali, Kathmandu.

NEWAH (Nepal Water for Health). 2003. Commitment to Community. Nepal Water for Health. Kathmandu, Nepal.

NEWAH (Nepal Water for Health). 2006. Long Term Sustainability Study (LTSS) Findings. Nepal Water for Health, March 2006. Lohasal, Kathmandu, Nepal https://www.newah.org.np/sites/default/files/Long%20Term%20Sustainability%20Study%20Findings%202005.pdf.

NEWAH (Nepal Water for Health). 2011. Stories from the Field: A Collection of WASH Case Studies. Nepal Water for Health, December 2011. Lohasal, Kathmandu.

NEWAH (Nepal Water for Health). 2016. Annual Report July 2015 to June 2016. Nepal Water for Health. Kathmandu, Nepal https://www.newah.org.np/sites/default/files/Newah-Annual-Report-Final_22-Feb-2018.pdf

NEWAH (Nepal Water for Health). 2017. Strategic Plan of Nepal Water for Health 2017-2021. Nepal Water for Health, Lohasal, Kathmandu, Nepal.

NEWAH (Nepal Water for Health). 2020. Why NEWAH is working in Water, Sanitation and Hygiene Sector: The Need. Nepal Water for Health. Lohasal, Kathmandu, Nepal https://www.newah.org.np/node/11.

New ERA. 1990. A Socio-economic Analysis of Drinking Water and Sanitation Situation in Nepal. A report submitted to the World Bank and Department of Water Supply and Sewerage, Kathmandu.

New ERA. 1991. Evaluation Report on Women Involvement and Sanitation in Community Water Supply and Sanitation. A report submitted to UNICEF, Kathmandu.

New ERA et. al. 1994. A Study on Knowledge, Attitude and Practices Relating to Water and Sanitation (Volume I: Quantitative Analysis). A report submitted to the Environmental Sanitation Section, DWSS, Ministry of Housing and Physical Planning, Kathmandu.

New ERA. 1997. Health Impact Study of Rural Water Supply and Sanitation Project in the Lumbini Zone Western Development Region, Nepal. Kathmandu, Nepal.

New ERA. 2009. Monitoring Equity and Inclusion in Water, Sanitation and Hygiene Sector. A report submitted by New ERA to WaterAid Nepal. Kathmandu, Nepal.

Nguyen, T.V. 2018. *Women and Water Management: A case study from the rural communities in Vietnam.* American Journal of Qualitative Research. Vietnam: An Giang University.

Nichols, Paul. 1991. Social Survey Methods: A Field Guide for Development Workers. Development Guidelines, No. 6, Oxfam, Oxford, UK.

NMIP (National Management Information Project) & DWSS (Department of Water Supply and Sewerage. 2011. *Nationwide Coverage and Functionality Status of Water Supply and Sanitation in Nepal.* Nepal: NMIP & DWSS.

NPR (National Public Radio). 2016. *Millions of Women Take A Long Walk With A 40-Pound Water Can.* United States: National Public Radio (NPR). Retrieved from: https://www.npr.org/sections/goatsandsoda/2016/07/07/484793736/millions-of-women-take-a-long-walk-with-a-40-pound-water-can.

NSAC (Nepal South Asia Centre). 1998. Nepal Human Development Report, Kathmandu, Nepal.

NWC (National Women's Commission Nepal). 2014. A Study on the Status of Social, Economic and Political Situation of Women in Nepal (*Nepalma Mahilako Samajik, Arthik Tatha Rajnitik Awastha: Ek Adhyayan, B.S. 2070*). National Women's Commission and Shanti Malika, Kathmandu, Nepal.

Oxfam. 1997. Gender and Development Organisational Culture. An Oxfam Journal, Volume 5, No. 1, February, UK and Ireland.

Pant, N.D., Poudyal, N., & Bhattacharya, S.K. 2016. *Bacteriological quality of bottled drinking water versus municipal tap water in Dharan municipality, Nepal.* Journal of Health, Population and Nutrition, Volume 35, June 7.

Paswan, Bhola. 2017. Data Reveals Local Elections a Disaster for Gender Equality. In The Record. October 24, 2017 **<https://www.recordnepal.com/wire/features/data-reveals-local-electionsa-disaster-for-gender-equality/>.**

Penny, Anne. 1991. The Forward Looking Strategies. In Changing Perceptions: Writings on Gender and Development ed. by Tina Wallace and Candida March. Oxfam, Oxford.

Poluha, E., G. Engstrand, A. Idemalm, J. Melchert and J. Narrowee. 1990. Concern and Responsibility: An Evaluation of the Dodota Water Supply Project in Ethiopia. In

SIDA Swedish International Development Agency Evaluation Report: Rural Water Supply, Ethiopia.

Population Reports. 1998. Series M, No. 14, Special Topics.

Pratt, Brian and Loizis, Peter. 1992. Choosing Research Methods: Data Collection for Development Workers. Development Guidelines, No. 7, Oxfam, Oxford, UK.

Price, G. et al. 2014. *Attitudes to Water in South Asia.* India: Chatham House- The Royal Institute of International Affairs.

PROWWESS (Promotion of the Role of Women in Water and Environmental Sanitation Services)/ UNDP (United Nations Development Programme). 1988. People, Pumps and Agencies: The South Coast Hand-Pump Project, Technical Series: Involving Women in Water and Sanitation: Lessons, Strategies, Tools. PROWWESS/UNDP, New York. (Deepa Narayan Parker).

Prüss-Ustün, A., Bartram, J., Clasen, T., Colford, J. M., Cumming, O., Curtis, V., Bonjour, S., Dangour, A. D., De France, J., Fewtrell, L., Freeman, M. C., Gordon, B., Hunter, P. R., Johnston, R. B., Mathers, C., Mäusezahl, D., Medlicott, K., Neira, M., Stocks, M., Wolf, J., Cairncross, S. 2014. Burden of disease from inadequate water, sanitation and hygiene in low- and middle-income settings: a retrospective analysis of data from 145 countries. *Tropical Medicine & International Health: TM & IH, 19*(8), 894-905.

Pugansoa, Ben and Amuah, Donald. 1991. Resources for Women: A Case Study of the Oxfam Sheanut Loan Scheme in Ghana. In Changing Perceptions: Writings on Gender and Development ed. by Tina Wallace and Candida March. Oxfam, Oxford.

Rao, Aruna and Stuart, Rieky. 1997. Rethinking Organisations: A Feminist Perspective. In Gender and Development: Organisational Structure. An Oxfam Journal, Volume 5, No. 1, February, Oxfam, Oxford, UK.

Ray, I. 2007. *Women, Water, and Development.* Berkeley: Annual Review of Environment and Resources- Vol. 32. pp. 421-449.

Regmi, Shibesh C. 1995. *Drutgami Tatha Sahabhagitatmak Gramin Lekhajokha: Ek Nirdeshika* (Rapid/Participatory Rural Appraisal: A Field Manual - Nepali Version). Winrock International, His Majesty's Government, Ministry of Agriculture, Kathmandu, Nepal.

Regmi, Shibesh C. and Fawcett, Ben. 1999. Integrating Gender Needs into Drinking Water Projects in Nepal. In Gender and Development: Women, Land and Agriculture, An Oxfam Journal, Vol. 7, No. 3, November.

Regmi, Shibesh Chandra. 2000. Gender Issues in the Management of Water Projects in Nepal. A Ph.D. thesis submitted to the Institute of Irrigation and Development Studies, Faculty of Engineering and Applied Sciences, University of Southampton, Southampton, UK.

Regmi, Shibesh Chandra and Fawcett, Ben. 2000. Water Supplies, Gender Relations and Sustainability: some lessons from Nepal (main-author). In Men, Masculinities and Gender Relations in Development, UK, June 2000.

Regmi, Shibesh Chandra. & Fawcett, Ben. 2001. Men's roles, gender relations, and sustainability in water supplies: some lessons from Nepal. In Men's Involvement in

Gender and Development Policy and Practice: Beyond Rhetoric (edited by Caroline Sweetman). Oxfam Working Papers, pg. 52-55, Oxfam GB, UK.

Regmi, Shibesh C.; and Fawcett, Ben. 2001. Gender implications of the move from supply-driven to demand-driven approaches in the drinking water sector: a developing country perspective. Paper presented at the First South Asia Forum on Water, November 2001, Kathmandu, Nepal.

Regmi, Shibesh C.; Adhikari, Mona S.; and Shrestha, Ankeeta. 2013. Ten-Year Strategic Plan 2014-2024 & First-Year Action Plan. Submitted to Ministry of Women, Children and Social Welfare (MoWCSW) under the consultancy with Enabling State Programme (ESP) of Department for International Development (DfID). Kathmandu, Nepal.

Rowlands, Jo. 1997. Questioning Empowerment: Working with Women in Honduras. An Oxfam Publication, Oxfam, UK and Ireland.

RVWRMP (Rural Village Water Resources Management Project). 2015. Step by Step Approach. Rural Village Water Resources Management Project, Ministry for Foreign Affairs of Finland <https://www.rwsspwn.org.np/ws-step-by-step>.

RVWRMP (Rural Village Water Resources Management Project). 2020a. Improving Livelihoods in Sudurpashchim and Karnali Provinces in Nepal. GoN, EU, Ministry for Foreign Affairs of Finland. https://www.rvwrmp.org.np/who-we-are; https://www.rvwrmp.org.np/; https://www.rvwrmp.org.np/where-we-work.

RVWRMP (Rural Village Water Resources Management Project). 2020b. Improving Livelihoods in Sudurpashchim and Karnali Provinces in Nepal. GoN, EU, Ministry for Foreign Affairs of Finland https://www.rvwrmp.org.np/gender-equality-and-social-inclusio.

RVWRMP (Rural Village Water Resources Management Project). 2020c. Improving Livelihoods in Sudurpashchim and Karnali Provinces in Nepal. GoN, EU, Ministry for Foreign Affairs of Finland <https://www.rvwrmp.org.np/wash>.

RWSSP (Rural Water Supply and Sanitation Project). 1989. Rural Water Supply and Sanitation Project in the Western Development Region Phase I 1990 - 1993. The Kingdom of Nepal and The Republic of Finland, FINNIDA, June.

RWSSP (Rural Water Supply and Sanitation Project). 1996a. Rural Water Supply and Sanitation Project in the Lumbini Zone Project Document Phase II 1996 - 1999. The Kingdom of Nepal and The Republic of Finland, FINNIDA, June.

RWSSP (Rural Water Supply and Sanitation Project). 1996b. Rural Water Supply and Sanitation Project Lumbini Zone, Nepal Completion Report of the First Phase January 1990 - July 1996. HMG/MHPP/DWSS and The Government of Finland, Ministry of Foreign Affairs, Department for International Development Co-operation, December. Plancentre Ltd., Butwal, Nepal.

RWSSP (Rural Water Supply and Sanitation Project). 1997/98. Work Plan. Butwal, Nepal.

RWSSP (Rural Water Supply and Sanitation Project). 2019. Rural Water Supply and Sanitation Project in Western Nepal Phase II Project Completion Report 09/2013-10/2019. Government of Nepal and Ministry of Foreign Affairs of Finland with Technical Support of FCG.

Samath, Feizal. 1998. Politics - Sri Lanka: Women Promised Quotas in Parliament. In World News Service from Inter Press Service, Colombo, March 25.

Sarin, Madhu. 1998. Community Forest Management: Whose Participation...? In The Myth of Community Gender Issues in Participatory Development edited by Irene Guijt and Meera Kaul Shah. Intermediate Technology Publications, London, UK.

Schulz, A. (2012). *6th World Water Forum Adopts Marseille Declaration.* The International Institute for Sustainable Development. IISD. 2012.

Seed, Jan. 1991. Gender Training. GADU Newspack, July, No. 14, pp. 1-8.

Shakya, Pushpa Lal. Undated. Development (Periodic) Plan Formulation in Nepal http://dms.nasc.org.np/sites/default/files/documents/Plan%20Formulation.pdf

Shrestha, D.R.; Regmi, Shibesh C.; and Dangal, G. 2018. Abortion: Still Unfinished Agenda in Nepal. Nepal Health Research Council, Vol. 16, No. 1, Issue 38 January- March 2018, pp. 97-102, Kathmandu, Nepal.

Shtrii Shakti. 1995. Women Development Democracy A Study of the Socio-Economic Changes in the Status of Women in Nepal (1981-1993). Kathmandu, Nepal.

SIDA Swedish International Development Agency. 1990. Dodota Water Supply Project. In Development Journal, Issue 3, Ethiopia.

Simpson-Hebert, Mayling. 1989. Theme Paper - Women and Water. In Proceedings of a Regional Seminar on Women and Water - The Family Hand-Pump, 29 August - 1 September 1989, Asian Development Bank, United Nations Development Programme, Manila, the Philippines.

Singh, Sabitri. 1995. Statistical Profile on Women of Nepal. Shtrii Shakti, Kathmandu, Nepal.

Srinivas, H. *The First Water Decade- International Decade for Clean Drinking Water, 1981-1990.* Global Development Research Centre.

Swieringa, Joop and Wierdsma, Andre. 1992. Becoming a Learning Organisation: Beyond the Learning Curve. Reading, MA: Addison Wesley.

Tadle, Ma. Arlene M. 1990. Evaluation of Water Supply Projects: An Economic Framework. Economics and Development Resource Centre Report Series, Report No. 51, June, Asian Development Bank (ADB), Manila, Philippines.

Thapa, S.; Sharma, S.K.; and Khatiwada, N. 2014. Women's knowledge of abortion law and availability of services in Nepal, Journal of Biosocial Science, 46(2): 266–277.

The Guardian. 2016. *Arsenic in Bangladesh: how to protect 20 million from the world's largest poisoning.* The Guardian US Edition, October 18. Retrieved from: https://www.theguardian.com/global-development-professionals-network/2016/oct/18/arsenic-contamination-poisoning-bangladesh-solutions.

The Water Project. 2016. *Facts About Water: Statistics of the Water Crisis- Updated on 8/31/2016.* Retrieved from: https://thewaterproject.org/water-scarcity/water_stats.

Thompson, K., O'dell, K., Syed, S., & Kemp, H. 2017. *Thirsty for change: The untapped potential of women in urban water management.* Deloitte: Deloitte Insights.

Thresiamma, Mathew. 1998. New Skills, New Lives: Kerala's Women Masons. Waterlines, Vol. 17, No. 1, pp. 22-24.

THT (The Himalayan Times). 2020. National Planning Commission endorses 15th periodic plan. March 3, 2020. Kathmandu, Nepal (https://thehimalayantimes.com/business/national-planning-commission-endorses-15th-periodic-plan/.

Tillet, Will and Burr, Peter. 2017. Mid-Term Review. Gurkha, Welfare Scheme: Rural Water and Sanitation Programme (Phase V). Gurkha Welfare Trust/ Nepal.

Tiwari, Dirgha N. 1998. Users' Willingness to Pay and Alternative Implementation Strategies for Improving Water Supply and Sanitation Facilities in Rural Nepal. Rural Water Supply and Sanitation Project, Lumbini Zone, Western Nepal.

TKP (The Kathmandu Post). 2017. Planning Commission endorses 14th 3-yr plan. The Kathmandu Post, January 10, 2017. Kathmandu, Nepal https://kathmandupost.com/money/2017/01/10/planning-commission-endorses-14th-3-yr-plan.

UN (United Nations). 1993. United Nations Juridical Yearbook. Codification Division, Office of Legal Affairs, United Nations.

UNCED (United Nations Conference on the Environment and Development). 1992. The Global Partnership for Environment and Development: A Guide to Agenda 21. United Nations, Switzerland, Geneva.

UN CESCR (United Nations Committee on Economic, Social and Cultural Rights). 2002. *General Comment No. 15: The Right to Water (Arts. 11 and 12 of the* International Covenant on Economic, Social and Cultural Rights, 2002*).* UN Economic and Social Council. January 20. Retrieved from: http://www.refworld.org/docid/4538838d11.html.

UNDP (United Nations Development Programme). 1998. Gender Reference Guide: Mainstreaming Gender Equity. Kathmandu, Nepal.

UNDP (United Nations Development Programme). 2006. Human Development Report 2006: *Beyond scarcity power, poverty and the global water crisis.* New York.

UNDP (United Nations Development Programme). 2011. Human Development Report 2011. *Sustainability and Equity: A Better Future for All.* New York: UNDP. Retrieved from: http://hdr.undp.org/sites/default/files/reports/271/hdr_2011_en_complete.pdf.

UNDP (United Nations Development Programme). 2014. Nepal Human Development Report (NHDR), Kathmandu, Nepal.

UNDP (United Nations Development Programme). 2017. Annual Report 2017. UNDP, UN Building, Kathmandu, Nepal.

UNDP (United Nations Development Programme)/ PROWWESS (Promotion of the Role of Women in Water and Environmental Sanitation Services). 1990. Global Consultation on Safe Water and Sanitation for the 1990s: Background Paper. United Nations Development Programme (UNDP), New Delhi, India, pp. x-25.

UNESCO (United Nations Educational, Scientific and Cultural Organization). 2012. World Water Assessment Programme (WWAP). *The United Nations World Water Development Report 4: Managing Water under Uncertainty and Risk.* Paris.

UNESCO (United Nations Educational, Scientific and Cultural Organization). 2016. *International Day for the Elimination of Violence Against Women- Event.* © UNESCO-2017.

UNFPA (United Nations Populations Fund). 2016. Fact Sheet: Gender-based Violence in Nepal. UNFPA, Lalitpur, Nepal: http://nepal.unfpa.org/en/publications/fact-sheet-gender-based-violence-nepal.

UNFPA (United Nations Population Fund). 2017. Population Situation Analysis of Nepal: With Respect to Sustainable Development. UNFPA, November 2017, Lalitpur, Nepal.

UNGA (United Nations General Assembly). 2010. *General Assembly Resolution 64/292 (*A/RES/64/292)*- The human right to water and sanitation. August 3.* New York.

UNGA (United Nations General Assembly). 2010a. *General Assembly 108th Plenary Meeting- A/64/PV.108.* New York: United Nations General Assembly. July 28. Retrieved from: http://www.un.org/en/ga/search/view_doc.asp?symbol=A/64/PV.108.

UNGA (United Nations General Assembly). 2010b. *General Assembly Adopts Resolution Recognizing Access to Clean Water, Sanitation as Human Right, by Recorded Vote of 122 in Favour, None against, 41 Abstentions.* New York: United Nations. July 28. Retrieved from: https://www.un.org/press/en/2010/ga10967.doc.htm.

UNHRC (United Nations Human Rights Council (UNHRC). 2010. *Resolution 15/9 (A/HRC/RES/15/9)- Human rights and access to safe drinking water and sanitation.* October 6. Geneva.

UNICEF (United Nations Children's Fund). 1997. Statistics of South Asian Children and Women. United Nations Children's Fund Regional Office for South Asia, Kathmandu, Nepal.

UNICEF (United Nations Children's Fund). 2010. *Raising Clean Hands: Advancing Learning, Health and Participation through WASH in Schools.* Joint Call to Action for WASH in Schools. Retrieved from: https://www.unicef.org/esaro/raising_clean_hands.pdf.

UNICEF (United Nations Children's Fund). 2012. *WASH for School Children*. Nepal: UNICEF Regional Office for South Asia. Retrieved from: https://www.unicef.org/wash/schools/files/UNICEF_WASH_for_School_Children_South_Asia_Report.pdf.

UNICEF (United Nations Children's Fund). 2016. Strategy for Water, Sanitation and Hygiene 2016-2030. UNICEF. August 2016. New York, USA, https://www.unicef.org/wash/files/UNICEF_Strategy_for_WASH_2016_2030.PDF.

UNICEF (United Nations Children's Fund). 2016. *Collecting water is often a colossal waste of time for women and girls*. New York/ Stockholm: UNICEF. August 29. Retrieved from: https://www.unicef.org/press-releases/unicef-collecting-water-often-colossal-waste-time-women-and-girls.

UNICEF (United Nations Children's Fund). 2018. UNICEF in Nepal: A Five-Decade Partnership <https://www.unicef.org/nepal/about-us>.

UNICEF (United Nations Children's Fund). 2018. Water and Sanitation (WASH): work to provide safe drinking water and eliminate open defecation. UNICEF Nepal, UN Complex, Lalitpur, Nepal **<https://www.unicef.org/nepal/water-and-sanitation-wash>.**

UNICEF (United Nations Children's Fund). Undated. https://www.unicef.org/.

UNICEF (United Nations Children's Fund) & WHO (World Health Organization). 2012. Progress on Drinking Water and Sanitation 2012 Update. UNICEF and WHO.

UNICEF (United Nations Children's Fund) & WHO (World Health Organization). 2015. *Progress on sanitation and drinking water – 2015 update and MDG assessment.* United States of America: UNICEF & WHO.

UNICEF (United Nations Children's Fund) and WHO (World Health Organization). 2019. Progress on household drinking water, sanitation and hygiene 2000-2017. Special focus on inequalities. New York.

United Nations. 1948. Universal Declaration of Human Rights (217 [III] A). UN General Assembly, Paris: UN.

United Nations. 1977. *Mar del Plata Action Plan.* United Nations Water Conference, Mar del Plata, Argentina: 14-25 March 1977.

United Nations. 1980. *World Conference of the United Nations Decade for Women: Equality, Development and Peace.* Copenhagen (14 to 30 July 1980). New York: UN.

United Nations. 1995. *The Fourth World Conference on Women- Beijing Declaration and Platform for Action.* UN. Retrieved from: https://www.un.org/womenwatch/daw/beijing/pdf/BDPfA%20E.pdf.

United Nations. 2003. *Water for people, water for life: The United Nations World Water Development Report.* World Water Assessment Program. Paris: UNESCO.

United Nations. 2003. *Water-related Diseases Responsible for 80 % of All Illnesses, Deaths in Developing World', says Secretary-General in Environment Day Message.* May 16. Retrieved from: https://www.un.org/press/en/2003/sgsm8707.doc.htm.

United Nations. 2003. *General Comment No. 15: The Right to Water (Arts. 11 and 12 of the* International Covenant on Economic, Social and Cultural Rights, 2002*).* UN Economic and Social Council. January 20. Retrieved from: http://www.refworld.org/docid/4538838d11.html.

United Nations. 2005. Women2000 and Beyond: Women and Water. United Nations Entity for Gender Equality and the Empowerment of Women (UN Women), UN Women Headquarters.

United Nations. 2010. Resolution A/RES/64/292. United Nations General Assembly. July.

United Nations. 2015. The Millennium Development Goals Report: Summary. United Nations, New York 2015 and 2015 Time for Global Action for People and Planet.

United Nations Department of Economic and Social Affairs and UN (United Nations) Water. 2014. *UN Water Factsheet on Gender and Water.* UNDESA and UN Water. Retrieved from: https://www.un.org/waterforlifedecade/gender.shtml.

UN (United Nations) News. 2010a. UN expert welcomes declaration that clean water and sanitation is a human right. July 7. Retrieved from: http://www.un.org/apps/news/story.asp?NewsID=35487#.WYuPK9Pys00.

UN (United Nations) News. 2010b. *Right to water and sanitation is legally binding, affirms key UN body. October 1.* Retrieved from: http://www.un.org/apps/news/story.asp?NewsID=36308#.WaXBx5OGM00.

UN (United Nations) Water. 2007. *Coping with Water Scarcity: Challenge of the Twenty-first Century.* Retrieved from: http://www.fao.org/3/a-aq444e.pdf.

UN (United Nations) Water. 2016. *Water Scarcity Facts and Figures- February 2016.* Retrieved from: http://www.unwater.org/water-facts/scarcity/.

UN (United Nations) Water. 2018. Water Facts: Water Scarcity. United Nations- September 2018.

UN (United Nations) Water & WHO (World Health Organization). 2013. *UN-Water Global Analysis and Assessment of Sanitation and Drinking-Water: The challenge of extending and sustaining service- GLASS 2013 Report.* UN Water & WHO.

UN (United Nations) Water & WHO (World Health Organization). 2014. *Investing In Water And Sanitation: Increasing Access, Reducing Inequalities: UN-Water Global Analysis and Assessment of Sanitation and Drinking-water (GLAAS).* Geneva: UN Water & WHO.

UN (United Nations) Women. 2012. *Gender perspectives on water and food security.* Remarks Laxmi Puri- 2012 World Water Week in Stockholm, Sweden, 31 August 2012. UN Women.

UN (United Nations) Women. 2016. *Facts and figures: Humanitarian action.* © UN Women-2017. Retrieved from: http://www.unwomen.org/en/what-we-do/humanitarian-action/facts-and-figures#notes.

US (United States) Geological Survey, & Perlman, H. 2016. *The World's Water.* US Geological Survey. Retrieved from: https://water.usgs.gov/edu/earthwherewater.html.

Van der Laan, Anita. 1998. Case Study: A Participatory Water Supply Scheme on a Tea Estate in Central Sri Lanka. The Hague, The Netherlands.

van Wijk-Sijbesma, C. 1985. Participation of Women in Water Supply and Sanitation: Roles and Realities. International Reference Centre (IRC) for Community Water Supply and Sanitation Technical Paper, No. 22, IRC, The Hague.

van Wijk-Sijbesma, C. 1998. Gender in Water Resources Management, Water Supply and Sanitation Roles and Realities Revisited. International Water and Sanitation Centre (IRC), Technical Paper Series 33-E, The Hague.

Van Wijk, C. and Garcia, M. 2002. Having it both ways: Local participatory learning informing global policy and programme management. In The Gender and Water Development Report 2003: Gender Perspectives on Policies in the Water Sector. Gender and Water Alliance (GWA) Secretariat, IRC International Water and Sanitation Centre, Delft, The Netherlands.

Vikman, H. 1998. Objectives and Strategies of Finnish Development Cooperation in the Water Supply and Sanitation Sector. In Toward Viable Water Services: Seminar on Water Supply and Sanitation Sector Policies and Strategies, Hanoi and Haiphong, Vietnam, 10-12 November 1997 ed. Hukka, Jarmo J. and Vikman, Hannu, 1998. Ministry for Foreign Affairs of Finland, Department for International Development Co-operation, Helsinki.

Wadehra, Renu. 1991. Breaking the Mould: Women Masons in India. In Changing Perceptions: Writings on Gender and Development ed. by Tina Wallace and Candida March. Oxfam, Oxford.

Wakeman, W. 1995. Gender Issues Sourcebook for Water and Sanitation Projects. UNDP-World Bank Water and Sanitation Programme/PROWWESS, Working Group on Gender Issues, Water Supply and Sanitation Collaborative Council (WSSCC), January, World Bank, Washington, DC.

Wakeman, Wendy.; Davis, Susan; van Wijk, Christine; and Naithani, Alka. 1996. Sourcebook for Gender Issues at the Policy Level in the Water and Sanitation Sector. International Bank for Reconstruction and Development/The World Bank, Washington, DC.

Wallace, Tina. 1991. Case Studies of Ways of Working with Gender. In Changing Perceptions ed., by Tina Wallace and Candida March. Oxfam, Oxford.

Wallace, Tina. 2003. Water: A Gender Issue Findings from Research in India and Nepal. University of Southampton, School of Engineering and Applied Sciences, Institute of Irrigation and Development Studies, July 2003. Southampton, UK.

WASH (Water and Sanitation for Health Project). 1990a. Final Evaluation of the CARE/ Bolivia Child Survival and Rural Sanitation Project. WASH Field Report No. 312, August, WASH, Arlington.

WASH (Water and Sanitation for Health Project). 1990b. Technical Assistance and Planning for Health and Hygiene Education and Women's Involvement in the Tunisia Rural Potable Water Institutions Projects. WASH Field Report No. 307, May, WASH, Arlington.

WaterAid. 1996. Strategic Framework. January.

WaterAid. 2006. Water for All? Review of Asian Development Bank's Water Policy Implementation in Nepal's Context- Main Report. WaterAid Nepal. March 2006. Lalitpur, Nepal.

WaterAid. 2008. Creating user-friendly water and sanitation services for the disabled: the experience of WaterAid Nepal and its partners. Discussion Paper, March 2008. Lalitpur, Nepal.

WaterAid. 2016. *Girl Strong. WaterAid US.* New York, USA.

WaterAid. 2017. Everyone, everywhere 2030: Global Strategy 2015-2022 file:///Users/user/Downloads/our-global-strategy-2015---2022.pdf

WaterAid. 2017a. Nepal Country Strategy 2017-2021. WaterAid Nepal. Lalitpur, Nepal.

WaterAid. 2017b. Menstruation Matters! WaterAid Nepal. Lalitpur, Nepal.

WaterAid. 2018. Resilient WASH services in Kavre and Lalitpur districts of Nepal. September 2015-March 2018, WaterAid Nepal. Lalitpur, Nepal.

WaterAid. 2018a. Promoting WASH-related rights through SuWASH Project. WaterAid Nepal. Lalitpur, Nepal.

WaterAid. 2019. Beneath the Surface: The State of World's Water 2019. WaterAid, March 2019.

WaterAid. 2019a. A Guide to Support Planning, Monitoring, Evaluation and Learning: Integrating Adaptive Programming with Theory of Change. WaterAid, East Melbourne, Australia. December 2019.

Water for People. 2016. *Women + Girls- The Facts.* Water for People. Retrieved from: https://www.waterforpeople.org/stories/girls.

Water.org. 2018. *Key Water + Sanitation Facts for use in 2018. ©Water.org – 2018.* Retrieved from: https://water.org/.../79/2018_water__sanitation_facts_for_use_-_from_Water.org.pdf.

WATSAN (Water and Sanitation) News. 1996. More Women Train in Latrine Construction. Vol. 2, no. 3 and 4.

WECS (Water and Energy Commission Secretariat). 1995. Gender Issues Related to Water Resources and Energy Development in Mid-Western Development Region of Nepal: Final Report. His Majesty's Government of Nepal, Ministry of Water Resources, WECS and Canadian International Water and Energy Consultants, Kathmandu.

WHO (World Health Organization). 2014. *Preventing Diarrhoea Through Better Water, Sanitation and Hygiene: Exposures and Impacts in Low- and Middle-Income Countries.* France.

WHO (World Health Organization). 2015. *Water Sanitation Hygiene: Key facts from JMP 2015 report* phttps://www.who.int/water_sanitation_health/monitoring/jmp-2015-key-facts/en/.

WHO (World Health Organization). 2016. *Climate change and human health: Water services for health.*

WHO (World Health Organization). 2017a. *Diarrhoeal Disease Fact Sheets- May 2017.* Retrieved from http://www.who.int/mediacentre/factsheets/fs330/en/.

WHO (World Health Organization). 2017b. *Don't pollute my future! The Impact of the Environment On Children's Health.* Switzerland.

WHO (World Health Organization). 2018a. *Drinking-Water Fact Sheets- February 2018a.* Retrieved from http://www.who.int/mediacentre/factsheets/fs391/en/.

WHO (World Health Organization). 2018b. *Sanitation Fact Sheets- February 2018b.* Retrieved from http://www.who.int/mediacentre/factsheets/fs392/en/.

WHO (World Health Organization). 2018/19. Nepal Sanitation Policy and Planning Framework Case Study for Discussion. In Sanitation policy and planning framework case studies for discussion. WHO **https://www.who.int/water_sanitation_health/monitoring/investments/glaas-2019-sanitation-policy-case-studies/en/**

WHO (World Health Organization). 2019. Sanitation- Key Facts. 14 June 2019.

WHO (World Health Organization) and The World Bank. 2014. Trends in Maternal Mortality: 1990 to 2013. Geneva.

WHO (World Health Organization) and UNICEF (United Nations Children's Fund). 2006. *Meeting The MDG Drinking Water and Sanitation, The Urban and Rural Challenge of The Decade.* Geneva, Switzerland.

WHO (World Health Organization) & UNICEF (United Nations Children's Fund). 2010. Progress on Sanitation and Drinking Water. Joint Monitoring Programme, WHO & UNICEF 2010 Update https://www.who.int/water_sanitation_health/publications/9789241563956/en/.

WHO (World Health Organization) & UNICEF (United Nations Children's Fund). 2015. *Key Facts from Joint Monitoring Program 2015 report.* Geneva.

WHO (World Health Organization) & UNICEF (United Nations Children's Fund). 2017. WHO-UNICEF Joint Monitoring Programme <https://washdata.org/data/household>.

WHO (World Health Organization) & UNICEF (United Nations Children's Fund). 2017a. *Progress on drinking water, sanitation and hygiene: 2017 update and SDG baselines.* Geneva: World Health Organization (WHO) and the United Nations Children's Fund (UNICEF).

WHO (World Health Organization) & UNICEF (United Nations Children's Fund). 2017b. *Safely Managed Drinking Water.* The United States of America.

WMO (World Meteorological Organization). 1992. International Conference on Water and the Environment: Development Issues for the 21st century, 26-31 January 1992. Dublin, Ireland: The Dublin Statement and Report of the Conference. Geneva, Switzerland.

World Bank. 1992. Sanitation and Clean Water. Chapter 5 in World Development Report 1992: Development and the Environment, IBRD, Washington, DC.

World Bank. 1993. Water Resources Management. The World Bank. Washington, DC: USA http://documents.worldbank.org/curated/en/940261468325788815/pdf/multi-page.pdf.

World Bank. 1996. World Bank-UNDP Water and Sanitation Programme. Annual Report 1995-96. Internet.

World Bank. 2004. Water Resources Sector Strategy: Strategic Directions for World Bank Engagement. International Bank for Reconstruction and Development/The World Bank. Washington, DC, USA.

World Bank. 2017a. 3 Ways of Thinking and Working Differently to Ensure Water and Sanitation for All. Infographic August 28, 2017. The World Bank, Washington DC, USA https://www.worldbank.org/en/news/infographic/2017/08/28/wash-poverty-diagnostic-infographic-3-ways.

World Bank. 2017b. Reducing Inequalities in Water Supply, Sanitation, and Hygiene in the Era of the Sustainable Development Goals: Synthesis Report of the WASH Poverty Diagnostic Initiative. WASH Synthesis Report. World Bank, Washington, DC.

World Bank. 2018. World Bank Signals Strong Support for Nepal's Transition to Federalism. Press Release, March 21, 2018 https://www.worldbank.org/en/news/press-release/2018/03/21/world-bank-signals-strong-support-nepal-transition-federalism.

World Bank. 2019a. A Water-Secure World for All. World Bank, Washington, DC, USA http://pubdocs.worldbank.org/en/962901566309738776/WaterBrochure2019-complete-web.pdf.

World Bank. 2019b. Water Supply, Sanitation, and Hygiene (WASH) Poverty Diagnostic Initiative. The World Bank, February 7, 2019. Washington, DC, USA https://www.worldbank.org/en/topic/water/publication/wash-poverty-diagnostic.

World Bank. 2020a. The Water Overview. Understanding Poverty/ Topics/ Water, Updated: April 9, 2020. The World Bank, IBRD, IDA https://www.worldbank.org/en/topic/water/overview.

World Bank. 2020b. The Water Overview. Understanding Poverty/ Topics/ Water, Updated: April 9, 2020. The World Bank, IBRD, IDA https://www.worldbank.org/en/topic/water/overview#2.

World Bank and United Nations Development Programme (UNDP). 1996. World Bank-UNDP Water and Sanitation Programme. Annual Report 1995-96. Internet.

WSSCC (Water Supply and Sanitation Collaborative Council). 2016. Strategic Plan 2017-2020. Geneva, Switzerland https://www.wsscc.org/wp-content/uploads/2017/03/Strategic-Plan-2017-2020.pdf.

WWC (World Water Council). 2015. 7th World Water Forum Ten Major Outcomes. World Water Council Report. World Water Council, 7th World Water Forum https://www.worldwatercouncil.org/fileadmin/world_water_council/documents/publications/forum_documents/7th%20World%20Water%20Forum%20Outcomes%20Layout%20hyperlinks.pdf.

WWF (World Water Forum). 2012. *6th World Water Forum: Time for Solution - 2012. Marseille, France.* Worldwaterforum.org, *12-17 March.* Retrieved from: http://6.worldwaterforum.org/fileadmin/user_upload/pdf/publications_elem/Highlights_web_BD_en.pdf.

Yerian, S., Hennink, M., Greene, L.E., Kiptugen, D., Buri, J., & Freeman, M.C. 2014. *The Role of Women in Water Management and Conflict Resolution in Marsabit, Kenya.* Environmental Management. New York: Springer US.

Index

A

Abubakar, M., 4, 319

Acharya, Meena, 307

ACORD, ix, 99, 111, 118, 120, 123, 314

ActionAid, 68, 307

ADB (Asian Development Bank), ix, 53, 183, 192, 276, 307, 308, 324, 329

- DMCs (Developing Member Countries), ix, 192
- Strategy 2020, 194, 195, 197
- TSTWSSSP (Third Small Towns Water Supply and Sanitation Sector Project), xiii, 196, 197, 198, 199, 293
- Water Policy 2001, 193, 194, 195, 199, 201

Ahmad, Tameez, 308

Alamgir, Mohiuddin, 318

Albuquerque, C. D., 308

Argentina, 12, 327

AusAID (Australian Agency for International Development), ix, 308

Aziz, Nahida, 308

B

Baden, Sally, 308, 314

Baidya, Bal Gopal, xx, 308

Bajracharya, R. M., 308

Balkumari, 273, 274

Baral, Balkrishna, 308

bargaining power, 34, 40, 64, 145, 148, 162, 163, 165, 291, 306

Bartram, J., 316, 322

Beijing Conference, 236

Beijing Declaration and Platform for Action, 312, 327

Bennett, Lynn, 307

Berg, Bruce L., 308

Berger, M., 308

Bhadra, Chandra, 2004, 308

Bhattacharya, S.K. 321

Bhusan, Anjana, 311

Bilgi, Meena, 309

Bilqis, Amin Hoque, 309

Biswas, Asit. K., 309

Boateng, G.O., 310

Boesveld, Mary, 309

Bogdan, Robert, 309

BRAC (Bangladesh Rural Advancement Committee), ix, 99

BRIDGE (Development and Gender in Brief), 314

Budhathoki, Chitra B., 309

Burr, Peter, 325

C

capacity-building, 122

Carloni, A. S., 309

CBS (Central Bureau of Statistics), ix, 231, 309, 312

Chambers, Robert, 309

Chapman, J., 309

Chhaupadi, 212, 229, 230, 243, 244, 293
Chibuye, Gwen I., 309
Chigudu, Hope. 309
Choguill, C., 309
Cleaver, Frances, 309, 310
CLTS (Community Led Total Sanitation), ix
CMS (Consolidated Management Services), 310
Code for Nepal, 246, 310
Collins, S.M., 310
Conscientisation, 28
Constitution of Nepal, 239, 240, 246, 253, 260, 263, 264, 294, 313
Construction Phase, 145
PME (participatory monitoring and evaluation), 57, 149
women's involvement, 21, 51, 77, 84, 88, 118, 137, 139, 141, 147, 152, 154, 184, 233, 234, 241, 251, 281, 290, 294, 295, 299
users' association, 88
Cotton, A., 309
Country Gender Profile, 309
Crippen, John N., 310
culture, 36, 37, 52,64, 105, 107, 109, 111, 114, 115, 116, 117, 118, 119, 120, 123, 127, 131, 161, 162, 197, 225, 293
Cumming, O., 319, 322
Curtis, Val, 310
CWSS (Community Water Supply and Sanitation Schemes), 84

D

Dabbs, James M., Jr., 310
DAC (Development Assistance Committee), ix, 310
Davis, Jan, 310
Davis, Susan, 329
DDC (District Development Committee), ix, 54, 93, 315
Deela Ramjali, 270
Deepa Sayangtang, 283
Denzin, Norman K., 310
Desilver, Drew, 310
Detailed Survey, 132, 135, 136, 137, 138
DFID (Department for International Development), ix 54, 310, 320, 323, 328
Dixit, Ajaya, 310
Donald, Amuah, 322
Dublin and Rio Principles, 67
Dublin Conference, 12, 16, 96, 97, 289

E

Elson, Diane, 310
Empowerment Framework, 35, 36
Engstrand, G., 321
Equinet, 243, 311
Evans, Phil, 311
Evolution of Gender, xvi, 1, 3, 231,

F

FAO (Food and Agriculture Organisation), x, 316
Fawcett, Ben, 322, 323
female WUSC members, 285
FEMCONSULT (Consultants on Gender and Development), 311
FHV (female health volunteers), x, 63
financing power, 68, 95, 96, 184, 202
FINNIDA (Finnish International Development Agency), x, 53, 54, 311,

Fong, Monica S., 311

Fowler, Alan. 311

Franceys, R., 309

Frischmuth, Christiane, 311

FRWSSSP (Fourth Rural Water Supply and Sanitation Sector Project), x, 53, 56, 315

fundamental rights, 13

G

GAD (Gender and Development), xvi, x, xix, 12, 15, 24, 199, 308, 309, 310, 311, 314, 319, 320, 321, 322, 323,

GAD frameworks, x, 24, 25, 29, 31, 32, 62

Gajedi Drinking Water Project, 58, 169

GAP (gender and poverty) x, 267, 278,

Garcia, M., 328

Garn, Mike, 311

Garvey, Gerry, 310

Gaura Majhi, 271, 272

Gauri Tamang, 270

GBV (Gender-Based Violence), 236, 243, 312, 326

Gender Analysis Matrix, x, 25, 29

Gender Analysis Frameworks 1, 319

gender and health training, 273

gender disaggregation, 200, 299

gender discrimination, 90, 120, 234

gender division of labour, 25, 27, 34, 39, 40, 46, 49, 64, 103, 111, 133, 144, 146, 151, 157, 158, 159, 161, 162, 177, 180, 271, 291, 298, 301, 305

gender dynamics, 120, 228, 300

Gender Justice/ Equality Act, 313

Gender planning and development, 320

Gender Transformation, xvi, 181, 183, 277

gender-aware, xvi, 74, 80, 91, 99, 102, 105, 112, 128, 181, 199, 266, 267, 271, 295, 318

gender-balanced, 100, 208, 301

Gender-deceiving terminologies, 256

gender-egalitarian society, 291

gender-free terminologies, 226, 293

gender-progressive, 262

Gender-transformative, 110, 273

gender-weak, 90, 149, 187, 188, 190, 233, 252, 253, 258, 266, 279, 286, 290,

GESI (Gender Equality and Social Inclusion) 191

GESI informed, 294

GLAAS (Global Analysis and Assessment of Sanitation and Drinking-water), 328

Goetz, Anne Marie, 311, 312

GoN (Government of Nepal), 312, 313, 314

Drinking Water and Sanitation Management Act, x, 262, 313

Fifteenth Five-Year Development Plan, 238, 264, 313

Fourteenth Three-Year Development Plan, 237, 313

Ministry of Agriculture, Land Management and Cooperatives, 314

Ministry of Federal Affairs and Local Development, 313

Ministry of Health and Population, xi, 312, 314

Ministry of Women, Children &

Social Welfare (MoWCSW), 308
Nepal in Figures, 312
Nepal Law Commission, 312, 313
Nepal Living Standard Survey, xii, 312
National Sanitation and Hygiene Master Plan, xii, 258, 276, 312,
National Urban Water Supply and Sanitation Sector Policy, 312
The National Civil (Code) Act, 131
The Right to Safe Motherhood and Reproductive Health Act, 242, 313
Thirteenth Plan, 236, 312
Water Resources Act, Xiv, 87, 97, 252, 312, 315,
Water Resources Regulations, xiv, 97, 252, 312
Water Supply Management Board Act, 256, 312

Green, Cathy, 314
GSS (Gramin Sewa Sangh), x, 59
GWA (Gender and Water Alliance), 314
Gwavuya, S., 319
GWT/N (Gurkha Welfare Trust/Nepal), 314

H

Habitat for Humanity Nepal, 314
Hadjipateras, Angela, 314
Halvorson, Sarah, 308
Hamerschlag, Kari, 315
Hannan-Andersson, C., 315
Harvard Analytical Framework, 25, 26, 27, 35
Helvetas, 84, 85, 97, 251
Hewitt, Sarah, 315
Hill, Philippa, 315
His Majesty's Government of Nepal (HMG), 308, 315, 316, 330
Department of Water Supply and Sewerage (DWSS), 53, 81, 192, 312
District Development Committee Act, ix, 54, 93, 315
Fourth Rural Water Supply and Sanitation Sector Project, x, 53, 56, 315
LDD (Local Development Department), xi 81
Locally Elected Women Representatives, 308
Local Level Election Procedure Act, 315
Ministry of Housing and Physical Planning (MHPP), 53, 82
Ministry of Law, Justice and Federal Affairs, 312
Ministry of Physical Planning and Works, 312, 316
MLD (Ministry of Local Development), xi, 54
Municipality Act, 315
Nepal Gazette, 315
National Safe Abortion Policy, 316
National Water Plan, xii, 255, 316
National Water Supply and Sanitation Policy, 313
National Water Supply Sector Policy, xii, 90, 97, 315
Rural Water Supply and Sanitation National Policy, xiii, 192, 253, 316

Rural Water Supply and Sanitation National Strategy, xiii, 192, 253, 316
Tenth Five-Year Development Plan, 235, 316
Village Development Committee Act, 315

Hoekstra, A., 319
HRBA (Human Rights Based Approach), x, 207, 313
HRM (Harinas Rural Municipality), 316
HRW (Human Rights Watch), xi, 316
Huber, C., 316
Human Development Report, 4, 51, 325
Humphries-Waa, K., 319
Hutton, G., 316
Haller, L., 316

I

ICESCR (International Covenant on Economic, Social and Cultural Rights), 316
ICF International, 232, 240, 241, 242, 244, 245, 246, 312, 314
ICIMOD (International Centre for Integrated Mountain Development), xi, 316
IDRC (International Development Research Centre), xi, 316
IDS (Institute of Development Studies), xi, 30, 33, 314, 316, 337
IDWSSD (International Drinking Water Supply and Sanitation Decade), xi, 12
IFRC (International Federation of Red Cross), xi, 316
IISD (International Institute for Sustainable Development), xi, 317, 324
ILO (International Labour Organization), 317
IMF (International Monetary Fund), 317
Improved Rural Water Supply, 318
improved water services, 67, 68, 69, 70, 71, 72, 75, 76, 79, 154, 159, 169, 170, 183, 205, 252, 259, 291
INSTRAW (International Research and Training Institute for the Advancement of Women), xi, 317
International Covenant on Economic, Social and Cultural Rights, xi, 10, 316, 325, 327
International Institute for Environment and Development (IIED), xi, 308, 311, 317
International Journal of Water Resources Development, 309
International Women's Decade 13
International Women's Year, 233
IOM (Institute of Medicine), 317
IOM (International Organization for Migration), 317
IRC (International Water and Sanitation Centre), 317
IWA (International Water Association), 317

J

Jahan, Rounag, 317
Jazairy, An, 318
JICA (Japan International Cooperation Agency), 318
Jobes, Katja, 310
Joekes, Susan, 318
Joosten, Lis, 318
JVS (Jalsrot Vikas Sanstha), 318

K

Kabeer, Naila, 318
- Gender-aware Policy and Planning, 318
- Social Relations Perspective, 318
- Gender Planning in Development, 318, 319

Kamminga, E. M., 318
Kardam, N., 318
Kaushi Maya Bhul, 269
KBC (Kenya Broadcasting Corporation) 318
Kemp, H., 324
Khatiwada, N., 324
Kilsby, D., 318

L

Lenton, Roberto, 318
Lerner, B. W., 318
Lerner, K. L., 318
Levy, Caren, 318
Lewis, Kristen, 318
Local Level Election Procedure Act, 315
Locally Elected Women Representatives, 308
Loizis, Peter, 322
Longwe, Sara Hlupekile, 318, 319

M

Macdonald, Mandy, 319
Magaragadhi Drinking Water Project, 57
Mainstreaming gender, 91, 98, 127, 196, 199, 234, 277, 308, 312, 325
Malik, A., 319
Mar del Plata, 12, 13, 327
March, Candida, 319
Mathew, B., 319
Maxine Molyneux, 27, 319
May, Nicky, 319
Mayoux, Linda C., 319
Mbullo, P., 310
Mekonnan, M., 319
Menstrual Hygiene Management (MHM), 229, 284, 314,
Mexico, 13, 17, 251, 316
Miller, J.D., 310
Mills, J. E., 319
Ministry for Foreign Affairs of Finland, 206, 323, 328
Mlama, Penina, 319
Mommen, B., 319
Morgan, T., 319
Moser Framework, 25, 26, 29, 34
Moser, Caroline O. N., 320
- Gender planning and development, 320

Mosse, Julia Cleves, 320
MPS (Mahila Punaruthan Samuha), 60
Mukhopadhyay, Maitree, 319
Mullen, R., 320
Murthy, S. L., 320
Mustanoja, U. M., 320

N

Naithani, Alka, 329
Narrowee, J., 321
National Safe Abortion Policy, 316
National Sanitation and Hygiene Master Plan, xii, 258, 276, 312,
National Urban Water Supply and Sanitation Sector Policy, 312
National Water Plan, xii, 255, 316

National Water Supply and Sanitation Policy, 313

National Water Supply Sector Policy, xii, 90, 97, 315

NDHS (Nepal Demographic and Health Survey), 312, 314

Nepal Earthquake, 313

Nepal Family Health Survey, 319

Nepal Gazette, 315

Nepal Human Development Report, 51, 321, 325

Nepal Law Commission, 312, 313

Nepal Living Standard Survey, xii, 312

Nepal Water Vision, 81, 82, 318

Nepal, Ganga Datta, 320

NEST (Nucleus for Empowerment through Skill Transfer), 320

New ERA, xx, 82, 83, 84, 85, 86, 147, 159, 228, 232, 240, 241, 242, 244, 241, 242, 243, 244, 245, 246, 312, 314, 321

NEWAH (Nepal Water for Health), xii, 52, 53, 266, 267, 320

NEWAH Director, 128, 275, 276, 279

NGOs (Non-Governmental Organisations), 311

INGO, xi, 53 130, 134, 251, 317

Nguyen, T.V., 321

Nichols, Paul, 321

NMIP (National Management Information Project), xii, 321

NPR (National Public Radio), xii, 321

NRCS (Nepal Red-Cross Society), 97

NSAC (Nepal South Asia Centre), xii, 48 321

NWC (National Women's Commission), Xii, 235, 321

NWSC (Nepal Water Supply Corporation) Act, xii, 87

O

O'dell, K., 324

Onono, M., 310

Organisational Culture, 36, 37, 64, 98, 111, 114, 115, 116, 117, 119, 127, 131, 161, 162, 197, 225, 292, 299, 302, 314, 321

organisational policies and practices, 21, 98, 207, 214, 225, 267, 290, 296

Organisational Structure, 37, 64, 98, 110, 130, 234, 301, 311, 322

Oxfam, 96, 121, 127, 143, 309, 310, 311, 314, 318, 319, 320, 321, 322, 323, 328, 329

P

Pant, N.D., 321

Panuccio, Theresa, 318

participatory vs. top-down, 120

Paswan, Bhola, 321

patriarchal, 26, 48, 51, 76, 92, 105, 116, 133, 149, 177, 189, 205, 209, 214, 233, 242, 246, 248, 253, 291, 293, 297, 319

Penny, Anne, 321

Perlman, H., 328

PLA (Participatory Learning and Action), 308, 317

PME (participatory monitoring and evaluation), 57, 149

policy formulating mechanisms, 98, 101, 130, 131

Poluha, E., 321

poor and marginalised, 15, 67, 71, 72, 79, 202, 205, 211, 218, 219, 220, 221, 223, 224, 227, 230, 257, 258, 267, 297

Population Reports, 3, 14, 322

positioning of tap-stands/ tube-wells, 168

Poudyal, N., 321
PRA (Participatory Rural Appraisal), XII, 60, 309, 322
practical and strategic gender needs, xvi, xix, 1, 21, 26, 27, 28, 29, 34, 35, 37, 43, 68, 121, 144, 151, 158, 167, 181, 228, 249, 287, 289, 295, 296, 297, 298, 300
Pratt, Brian, 322
Pre-construction Phase, 133
Magaragadhi project, 58, 140, 148, 153
Motipur project, 58, 153
Selection of Technology and Location, 138
Training to NGO/PMC/WUC, 143
Signing of Agreements, 144
profound involvement, 275
provision for gender training, 37, 130
provision for human and capital resources, 37
PROWWESS (Promotion of the Role of Women in Water and Environmental Sanitation Services), 322, 325
Prüss-Ustün, 322
Pugansoa, Ben, 322

R

Rao, Aruna, 322
RAP (Rapid Assessment Procedures), 132
Ray, I., 322
Raza, Haider, 308
Razavi, Shahra, 312
Recruitment Policy, 98, 105, 301
Reerink, Annemarie, 315
Regmi, Shibesh C., 322, 323, 324
reproduction, 159
Right, Albert M., 318
Rowlands, Jo, 323
RWSP (Rural Water and Sanitation Programme), 281, 320, 325
RWSSFB (Rural Water Supply and Sanitation Fund Board), xiii, 86
RWSSP (Rural Water Supply and Sanitation Project), xiii, 53, 54, 313, 320, 321, 323
RVWRMP (Rural Village Water Resources Management Project), 206, 313, 323
maternity leave, 107, 108, 109, 110, 119, 207
HRBA (Human Rights Based Approach), x, 207, 313
Chhaupadi, 212, 229, 230, 243, 244, 293
HRM (Harinas Rural Municipality), 316

S

safety and dignity, 205, 229
Samath, Feizal, 324
'same size fits all', 290
Sarin, Madhu, 324
Schulz, A., 324
SDGs (Sustainable Development Goals) xiii, 7, 237, 243, 260, 313, 313
Seed, Jan, 324
Shakya, Pushpa Lal, 324
Sharma, S., 308
Sharma, S.K., 324
Shtrii Shakti, 47, 48, 49, 50, 73, 74, 135, 159, 164, 324
SIDA (Swedish International Development Agency), xiii, 322, 324

Simpson-Hebert, Mayling, 324
Singh, Sabitri, 324
social analysis, 138
social discrimination, 210, 211, 214, 226, 259
social preparation time, 156, 214, 300
social relationships, 31
Srinivas, H., 324
status of women in Nepal, 49, 233, 307, 324
Strategic Plan, 100, 112, 119, 122, 202, 203, 204, 205, 233, 226, 227, 267, 278, 279, 292, 294, 295, 320, 323, 332,
Stuart, Rieky, 322
sustainability, 57, 188, 189, 201, 212, 223, 224
Syed, S., 324

T

Tabinda, A., 319
Tadle, Ma. Arlene M., 324
tap-stands/ tube-wells, 265
Thapa, Mani, 309
Thapa, S., 324
The Guardian, 8, 324
The Water Project, 4, 19, 21, 32, 38, 40, 85, 91, 95, 133, 154, 156, 168, 169, 177, 178, 179, 183, 190, 197, 209, 217, 225, 252, 253, 256, 257, 283, 284, 285, 289, 290, 291, 324
Thompson, K., 324
Thresiamma, Mathew, 324
THT (The Himalayan Times), 325
Tillet, Will, 325
Tiwari, Dirgha N., 325
TKP (The Kathmandu Post), 325
training on technical aspects, 154, 208
    Training to NGO/PMC/WUC, 143
TSTWSSSP (Third Small Towns Water Supply and Sanitation Sector Project), xiii, 196, 197, 198, 199, 293

U

UDHR (Universal Declaration of Human Rights), xii, 11, 327
UN (United Nations), 325, 327, 328
UNCED (United Nations Conference on the Environment and Development), 325
UNDP (United Nations Development Programme), 322, 323, 324, 325, 332
UNESCO (United Nations Educational, Scientific and Cultural Organization), 325
UNFPA (United Nations Populations Fund), 326
UNGA (United Nations General Assembly), xiii, 7, 260, 326, 327
UNHRC (United Nations Human Rights Council, xiii, 10, 326
unhygienic traditional sources, 69, 71, 74, 291
UNICEF (United Nations Children's Fund), xiii, 183, 202, 326, 327, 330, 331
    Strategic Plan 2016-2030, 202, 204, 292
UN CESCR (United Nations Committee on Economic, Social and Cultural Rights), 325
UN (United Nations) News, 327
UN (United Nations) Water, 327, 328

UN (United Nations) Women, 328

US (United States) Geological Survey, 328

V

Van der Laan, Anita, 328

van Wijk-Sijbesma, C., 328

Van Wijk, C., 328

VAW (Violence Against Women), xiv, 235, 244, 325

VDC (Village Development Committee) xiv, 45, 50

Vikman, H., 328

Village Development Committee Act, 315

Village Economy, 46

W

Wadehra, Renu, 328

Wakeman, W., 329

Wallace, Tina, 329

WASH (Water and Sanitation for Health Project), 329

WASH (Water, Sanitation and Hygiene), xiii, xiv, 4, 18, 183, 219, 220, 225, 262, 316, 317, 319, 320, 321, 322, 326, 327, 330, 331

Water Policies, xvi, xix, 37, 43, 64, 66, 74, 79, 80, 87, 181, 183, 184, 185, 192, 193, 194, 199, 201, 221, 249, 252, 254, 257, 266, 286, 288, 289, 290, 292, 294, 295

Water.org., 330

WATERAID, xx, 3, 5, 19, 20, 52, 53, 54, 67, 78, 101, 122, 124, 142, 183, 192, 202, 217, 218, 219, 220, 221, 222, 223, 224, 225, 226, 227, 228, 229, 230, 251, 266, 272, 289, 290, 292, 293, 294, 317, 318, 321, 329

- disabled girl, 227
- Global Strategy, 217, 218, 225, 230, 329

WATSAN (Water and Sanitation) News, 330

WDO (Women Development Officer), xvi

WECS (Water and Energy Commission Secretariat), 330

Wekesa, P., 310

WHO (World Health Organization), 316, 327, 328, 330, 331

WID (women in development), xiv, 15, 24, 33, 233, 234, 309, 311, 317

Wierdsma, Andre, 324

Wilbur J., 317

willingness to pay, 70, 79, 138, 148, 217, 319, 325

WISP (Women Involvement and Sanitation Programme), xiv, 84

WMO (World Meteorological Organization), 331

Women in Nepal, 49, 83, 233, 240, 242, 243, 251, 297, 307, 315, 318, 321, 324

Wood, Michael, 310

World Bank, xx, 46, 48, 49, 67, 68, 70, 71, 75, 76, 77, 78, 86, 96, 129, 159, 183, 184, 185, 186, 187, 188, 189, 190, 251, 289, 292, 310, 311, 321, 329, 330, 331, 332

- 3 Ways of Thinking, 331

World Conference on Women, 16, 233, 234, 315, 327

WSSCC (Water Supply and Sanitation Collaborative Council), xiv, 16, 329, 332

WSST (water supply and sanitation technicians), 109

WUCs (Water User's Committees), 253
WUSCs (Water Users and Sanitation Committees), 184, 254, 308
WWC (World Water Council), xiv, 317, 322
WWF (World Water Forum), xiv, 7, 16, 17, 314, 316, 317, 324, 332

Y

Yasar, A., 319
Yerian, S., 332
Young, S.L., 310